The Rough (**W9-CRO-706**

First-Time Asia

written and researched by

Lesley Reader and Lucy Ridout

ROUGH
GUIDES

NEW YORK • LONDON • DELHI

www.roughguides.com

Contents

◀◀ Woman panning for gold, Mekong River, Laos ◀ Swayambunath stupa, Kathmandu, Nepal

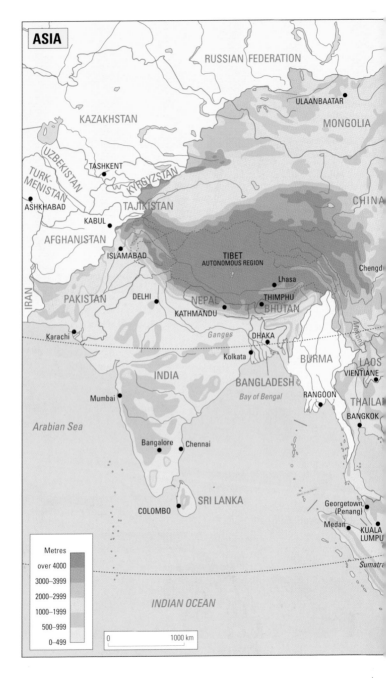

ASIA

RUSSIAN FEDERATION

ULAANBAATAR

KAZAKHSTAN

MONGOLIA

UZBEKISTAN

TASHKENT

KYRGYZSTAN

TURK-
MENISTAN

CHINA

TAJIKISTAN

ASHKHABAD

KABUL

AFGHANISTAN

ISLAMABAD

TIBET
AUTONOMOUS REGION

Chengdu

Lhasa

IRAN

PAKISTAN

DELHI

NEPAL

THIMPHU

BHUTAN

KATHMANDU

Ganges

DHAKA

Karachi

Kolkata

BURMA

LAOS

Mekong

VIENTIANE

INDIA

BANGLADESH

THAILAND

Mumbai

Bay of Bengal

RANGOON

BANGKOK

Arabian Sea

Bangalore

Chennai

SRI LANKA

COLOMBO

Georgetown
(Penang)

Medan

KUALA
LUMPUR

Metres	
over 4000	
3000–3999	
2000–2999	
1000–1999	
500–999	
0–499	

Sumatra

INDIAN OCEAN

0   1000 km

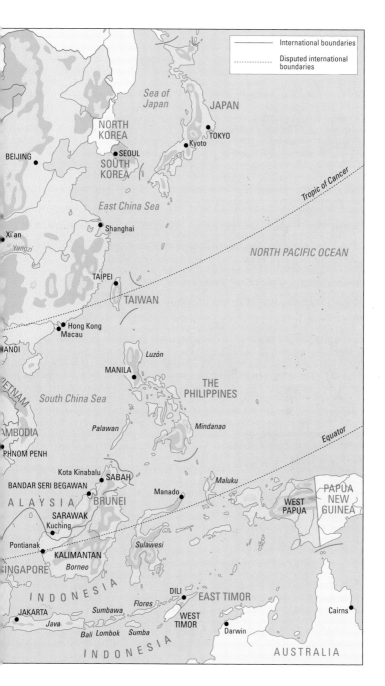

| International boundaries |
| Disputed international boundaries |

Sea of Japan

JAPAN

NORTH KOREA

TOKYO

Kyoto

BEIJING

SEOUL

SOUTH KOREA

Tropic of Cancer

East China Sea

Xi'an

Shanghai

Yangzi

NORTH PACIFIC OCEAN

TAIPEI

TAIWAN

Hong Kong
Macau

HANOI

Luzón

MANILA

THE PHILIPPINES

VIETNAM

South China Sea

CAMBODIA

Palawan

Mindanao

Equator

PHNOM PENH

Kota Kinabalu

SABAH

Maluku

BANDAR SERI BEGAWAN

Manado

PAPUA NEW GUINEA

MALAYSIA

BRUNEI

WEST PAPUA

SARAWAK

Kuching

Pontianak

Sulawesi

KALIMANTAN

SINGAPORE

Borneo

INDONESIA

DILI

EAST TIMOR

Flores

Cairns

JAKARTA

Sumbawa

WEST TIMOR

Java

Bali Lombok Sumba

Darwin

INDONESIA

AUSTRALIA

Introduction to

First-Time
Asia

Every year, millions of visitors set off on their own Asian adventure. Some want to see for themselves a few of the world's greatest monuments – to stroll along the Great Wall of China or stand beside India's Taj Mahal. Others are drawn by the scenery: the soaring Himalayas and the chance of viewing Everest at close quarters; the kaleidoscopic coral reefs of Southeast Asia, where you can swim among sharks, manta rays and turtles; and the steamy jungles of Malaysia and Indonesia, with the prospect of spotting orang-utans, elephants and even tigers. Few people would say no to a week or two on the dazzling white-sand beaches of the Philippines or pass up the chance to watch the sun rise over the Khyber Pass.

 But perhaps the greatest draw is the sheer vitality of everyday life in Asia, much of it played out on the streets. You can watch Thai boxing in Bangkok and trance dances in Bali, learn yoga in Varanasi, drink rice whisky in Vientiane, eat dim sum in Shanghai and satay in Penang, buy silver in Hanoi and bargain for mangosteens in Manila.

Nearly all these things are affordable, even for low-budget travellers, because most of Asia is still enticingly inexpensive: Western money goes much further here than it does in Africa or South America. This has put Asia firmly at the heart of the backpackers' trail, and many cities and islands already boast a lively travellers' scene, attracting young adventurers from all over the world. Few travellers leave Asia without experiencing at least one of its fabled hot spots: the beaches of Goa, perhaps, the guesthouses

Akihabara district, Tokyo

of Kathmandu, or one of Thailand's notorious full-moon parties.

On the other hand, Asian travel can also be a shocking and sobering experience. It's hard to forget your first sight of a shantytown slum or your first encounter with an amputee begging for coins. Many first-timers are distressed by the dirt, the squalor, and the lingering smell of garbage and drains in some Asian cities. They get unnerved by the ever-present crowds and stressed out by never being able to mingle unnoticed among them. On top of which there's the oppressive heat to cope with, not to mention the unfamiliar food and often unfathomable local customs. There's no such thing as a hassle-free trip and, on reflection, few travellers would want that. It's often the dramas and surprises that make the best experiences, and we all learn from our mistakes.

The Buddha

The man who became the Buddha was born Prince Gautama Siddhartha in Lumbini, in present-day Nepal, in the sixth or seventh century BC. For the first 29 years of his life the prince was closeted within the palace walls, but on his first foray into the real world he saw that suffering was an intrinsic part of human life. Keen to find

▲ Reclining Buddha, Wat Pho, Bangkok

out why, Gautama took up a life of contemplation, wandering through the countryside as a Hindu ascetic. Eventually concluding that the way to avoid suffering was to follow a "Middle Way" between asceticism and indulgence, he meditated under the now famous bodhi tree at Bodh Gaya in India until he became "an enlightened one", or Buddha. For the rest of his life the Buddha travelled the region spreading his doctrine until he finally achieved Nirvana, the blissful state of nothingness which knows no suffering. Buddhism is now one of the major world religions and is followed, in various forms, by millions of people across Asia, from Mongolia to Sri Lanka and from Thailand to Japan.

Not just beaches and temples

▲ Woodcarving lesson, Bali, Indonesia

A good way to add another dimension to a trip, and to widen your perspective, is to stay somewhere for a few days and take a beginners' class in a craft, performing art or another aspect of the local culture that interests you. You can learn woodcarving in Bali, for example, or take taekwondo lessons in Seoul. Other popular activities include Thai cookery workshops, batik painting classes in Indonesia and yoga and meditation courses in India and Nepal. Not only will you gain a skill but it's a great opportunity to become involved with local life and local people in a way that isn't always otherwise possible. Such sessions are designed for travellers and are generally cheap, accessible and scheduled flexibly to suit the clients. See p.189 for more ideas; most guidebooks also include information on this type of activity.

If you wish to get involved at a deeper level, you could also consider doing voluntary work while you're in Asia, so that your time and skills, whatever they are, benefit some of the most needy people on the continent and you gain valuable insight into lives that are probably far removed from your own. Some travellers prefer to sign up with a volunteer-placement organization before leaving home, where opportunities can range from a week on a turtle-conservation project in Malaysia to a month helping out in a Sri Lankan orphanage; others prefer to contact local charities direct on arrival after examining all the options and deciding where they'd be of most use. There's advice on how to find out more about volunteering on p.161.

Preparing for the big adventure

We've both made plenty of mistakes during our many years of travels in Asia, and this book is a distillation of what we've learnt. *First-Time Asia* is full of the advice we give to friends heading out to Asia for the first time, and it's the book we both could have done with before setting off on our own first trips. Since then we've returned again and again, backpacking

▼ Vietnamese water puppets

across India, China and Southeast Asia; living and working in the Himalayas, Thailand and Japan; and researching and writing guidebooks to Indonesia, Thailand and Tibet. And we still choose to go back to Asia for our holidays, attracted by the chaos and drama of daily lives that, even now, seem extraordinary to us, from the food, the landscapes and the climate, to the generosity and friendship of the people and the sheer buzz we get from hanging out in cultures that are so entirely different from our own.

This book is intended to prepare you for your big adventure, whether it's a fortnight in Malaysia or twelve months across the continent. It is not a guidebook: it's a book to read before you go, a planning handbook to help you make decisions about what type of trip you'd like to make. And, because we can't pretend to have explored every single corner of Asia ourselves, we've also included tips, advice and stories from lots of other travellers. The first question you'll need to address of course is which parts of Asia you most want to visit or, much more difficult, which places to leave out? The opening section of the book, Where To Go, looks at your options. We focus on the 21 most accessible and most visited countries of Asia, giving you an opinionated taste of what these destinations have in store for first-timers. Each country profile includes a round-up of the major highlights and tourist activities, as well as a selection of personal recommendations and lesser-known gems, plus suggestions on related books and films and contact details for tourist offices and embassies. The most remote parts of the continent, north and west of Pakistan, rarely feature on first-timers' itineraries, so we haven't included them in this book. Burma (Myanmar) is also omitted in the hope that

▼ Ritual bathing in the Ganges, Varanasi, India

travellers will uphold the boycott on tourism requested by Aung San Suu Kyi, the democratically elected leader of the country.

The middle section of *First-Time Asia*, The Big Adventure, deals with the nuts and bolts. This is where you'll find chapters on how to choose the right ticket and which guidebooks and websites to consult, plus advice on how long you can afford to stay away and what gear to pack. The second half of this section looks at life on the road in Asia, advising you how to stay safe and healthy while you're away, grounding you in local cultural dos and don'ts, and giving you an idea of what to expect in terms of hotels and bus services. And, finally, the Directory section at the back of the book is stuffed full of useful addresses, websites and phone numbers for further information on everything from discount flight agents and travel book-shops to mosquito-net suppliers and conservation projects.

Even after you've digested *First-Time Asia*, we can't guarantee that you'll avoid every problem on the road, but hopefully you'll at least feel well prepared – and inspired. When you come back from your trip, be sure to send in your own anecdotes for inclusion in the next edition. We can promise you'll have plenty of great stories to tell.

26

things not to miss

It's not possible to see everything that Asia has to offer on your first trip – and we don't suggest you try. What follows is a selective and subjective taste of Asia's highlights: awesome monuments, outstanding beaches, spectacular hikes and unforgettable journeys. They're arranged in five colour-coded categories, so you can browse through to find the very best things to see, do, buy and experience. All highlights have a page reference to take you straight into the guide, where you can find out more.

01 The Gili Islands, Indonesia Page **67** • Pure white-sand beaches ring these three tiny islands, each with its own character, offering as much peace and quiet or frenetic partying as visitors require.

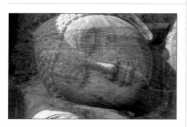

02 **Food** Page **191** • Divine, delicious, quirky, spicy, exuberant and downright weird – there's something to suit every palate in the vast culinary variety of Asia.

03 **Taking the slow boat down the Mekong River, Laos** Page **80** • Not the most comfortable way to travel, but the scenery makes it all worthwhile.

04 **Giant Buddhas, Sri Lanka** Page **128** • These huge enigmatic statues, some carved out of granite cliff faces, can be found at various locations around the island.

06 **Rajasthan, India** Page **55** • Desert, camels, ancient buildings and brilliantly coloured textiles make this one of the most exotic Indian destinations.

05 **Bhutanese masked dances** Page **25** • Time your visit to Bhutan to catch one of the colourful temple festivals and view one of these picturesque and ancient religious dances.

07 **Gunung Bromo, Indonesia** Page **66** • The stark, awesome volcanic scenery is easily accessible, with pre-dawn treks a speciality.

08 **Walking the Great Wall, China** Page **45** • Precipitous drops, magnificent views and an awesome link with fifth-century China.

09 **Banaue rice terraces, Philippines** Page **112** • Sculpted from steep-sided valleys over 2000 years ago, and now a World Heritage sight.

11 **Orang-utans** Pages **66** and **86** • A chance to meet the ancestors at sanctuaries in Indonesia and Malaysia.

10 **The beaches** Azure waters, soft white sand and a fringe of palm trees – you'll find some of the world's most beautiful beaches in East Timor Page **50**, Malaysia Page **84**, the Philippines Page **109**, Sri Lanka Page **131** and Thailand Page **140**.

12 Riding the Karakoram Highway, Pakistan Page
105 • One of the world's most dramatic roads linking Pakistan and China.

13 The Reunification Express, Vietnam Page
147 • A slow, scenic train ride from north to south, with plenty of possible stopoffs en route.

14 The Terracotta Army, China Page 45 • Nothing
compares to seeing these extraordinary figurines close up: there are over seven thousand of them, each one life-sized and with its own personality.

15 Diving and snorkelling
Page 184 • Enter a whole new world in the tropical waters of East Timor, Indonesia, Malaysia, the Philippines and Thailand.

16 Kyoto, Japan Page 74 • Japan's cultural capital is stacked with elegant temples,
serene Zen gardens and characterful neighbourhoods.

17 **The Himalayas, Nepal** Page **97** • Seen from any angle the scale and majesty of the highest mountains on the globe are simply breathtaking.

18 **Staying in a longhouse, Malaysia** Page **84** • Communal living, Sarawak style.

20 **Trekking** Page **179** • Mountain trails, jungle hikes and hill-tribe treks… there are plenty of reasons to pull on your boots and get walking.

19 **Bali, Indonesia** Page **64** • Intriguing culture, stunning rice-paddy scenery and fabulous shopping.

21 **The Gobi Desert, Mongolia** Page **93** • Featuring plains, scrub, mountains, rocks, oases and sand dunes – all on a vast scale.

| ACTIVITIES | CONSUME | EVENTS | NATURE | SIGHTS

22 Taj Mahal, India Page **55** • The must-see sight in India is familiar the world over, yet never fails to impress.

23 Angkor temples, Cambodia Page **36** • Exquisitely carved deities, giant sculpted heads, and two hundred majestic temple ruins to explore.

24 Potala Palace, Tibet Page **45** • Towering brilliant-white over the city of Lhasa, the ancient palace of the Dalai Lamas lures Tibetans and Westerners.

25 Full-moon party on Ko Pha Ngan, Thailand Page **143** • The world's biggest beach party: 30,000 clubbers get sandy.

26 Hong Kong skyline Page **45** • Nothing symbolizes the thrusting Tiger economies of modern Asia better than the skyscrapers of Hong Kong Island – at their dramatic best at night.

First-Time Asia

Where to go

Bangladesh

Capital: Dhaka
Population: 140 million
Language: Bangla
Currency: Taka (Tk)
Religion: Eighty-three percent Muslim, sixteen percent Hindu; the remainder are Buddhists and Christians

Climate: Tropical, with the monsoon from July to October
Best time to go: October to February, which avoids the monsoon and the humid build-up in the months before
Minimum daily budget: $10/£5

With its reputation as a nation of over-population, poverty, political instability and devastating floods (the alluvial plains, which comprise ninety percent of the country's area, are less than 10m above sea level), Bangladesh is not on many Asian itineraries. However, the country contains extensive rivers and lush forests to explore, as well as the longest beach in the world and excellent wildlife. Bangladesh also has some fine archeological sites, including Buddhist, Hindu and Muslim monuments, remnants of empires which flourished until the seventeenth century when the Raj – British colonial rule – was established. Some grand public buildings and *rajbaris*, palaces built by rich Hindu landowners, are the remaining evidence of the Raj era. All of this adds up to a fascinating destination which the more adventurous may wish to consider.

As tourists are still rather rare here, visitors should expect more attention than usual. Bangladesh is mostly Muslim, and both men and women should dress exceptionally modestly. Women should cover arms and legs, even ankles – a *salwaar kameez*, the baggy trousers and long tunic worn by local women, is a good investment, as is a scarf for the head. Men should stay covered up also, avoiding shorts and vests. Be aware that travel can be extremely slow because of frequent ferry crossings on both road and rail routes.

Main attractions

● **Dhaka** Almost everyone passes through the Bangladeshi capital at some point. A seething melting pot of over ten million people, which some estimates suggest will have risen to 21 million by 2015, it's an incredible city with a fascinating juxtaposition of the old and the startlingly new. Among the more recent constructions, Jatyo Sangsad, the National Assembly building designed by American architect Louis Kahn, and the National Martyrs' Memorial, commemorating those who died in the independence struggle, are the most imposing. The most famous ancient monuments include the Mogul Lalbagh Fort, the grand nineteenth-century Nawab's Palace and the Rose Garden, a dignified palace from the Raj

Metres

1000

500

0

BANGLADESH

0   100 km

era. Also here is Chowk Bazaar, a maze of twisting alleyways little changed since the nineteenth century. The city abounds in striking, attractive mosques and the modern incarnation of Bengal's rich artistic heritage is reflected in the friendly art galleries in the Dhanmondi area.

Mean temperatures (°C) and rainfall (mm)

Average daily temperatures (maximum and minimum °C) and monthly rainfall (mm)

	Jan	Feb	Mar	Apr	May	June	July	Aug	Sept	Oct	Nov	Dec
Dhaka												
max °C	25	28	33	35	34	32	31	31	31	31	29	26
min °C	12	13	16	23	25	26	26	26	26	24	18	13
rainfall mm	18	31	58	103	194	321	437	305	254	169	28	2

- **Cox's Bazaar** Bangladesh's best-known tourist destination and only seaside resort is an excellent spot for relaxation, with plenty of accommodation and restaurants. Cox's Bazaar is within a few kilometres of the stunning Inani Beach, widely claimed, at 120km long, to be the longest beach in the world. Also within easy reach are other equally attractive beaches and some quiet, offshore islands including St Martin's, Bangladesh's only coral island.

- **River travel** This affords a great opportunity to see all of Bangladeshi life as you sail past. The most useful and popular way to do this is the Rocket service from Dhaka to Khulna, on which vintage paddle steamers make the thirty-hour trip.

- **The Sunderbans** This tidal forest covers a massive area, stretching along the coastline for nearly 300km. The mangrove forest floor is dissected by rivers, their channels constantly changing as the tides ebb and flow. The area is inhabited by a variety of wildlife; it's the last reserve of the Royal Bengal tiger in Bangladesh (the 350 animals thought to live here constitute a tenth of the world's remaining population), and also home to crocodiles, monkeys, gibbons, turtles, deer, wild boar, lizards and the Ganges river dolphin. The best method of transport is by boat. Take a tour and watch the Mowali people collect wild honey from deep in the forest using ancient methods (Ⓦwww.guidetours.com).

- **Sylhet** Set among rolling hillsides, this tea-growing area consists of lush forests and terraced estates. The centre of the tea-growing district, the town of Srimangal, is an excellent place to arrange a visit to a tea estate to see the processing of the leaves. Several tribal peoples, including the Khasi, Pangou and Manipur, live in the area, and it's possible to visit their villages. The region is also known for its basketware, including furniture, small household goods and bags.

- **Paharapur** Dating from the eighth century, these are the atmospheric remains of the largest Buddhist monastery south of the Himalayas – the most imposing archeological remains in Bangladesh. The centrepiece is a mighty temple, decorated with thousands of terracotta plaques located in a huge quadrangle enclosed by a three-metre-thick wall containing nearly two hundred monks' cells.

Also recommended

- **Chittagong Hill Tracts** Atypical of Bangladesh, the hill tracts, whose steep jungle-covered peaks rise to 800m, are inhabited by more than a dozen tribal groups, all of whom are Buddhists of

Tibeto-Burmese descent. Unfortunately, most of the area is off limits to tourists with the exception of the towns of Kaptai and Rangamati. The latter, set on a peninsula overlooking the man-made Kaptai Lake, was a favoured hill station of the British; today it's an excellent centre for swimming, boating and exploring the islands of the lake. Note: check the current security situation here before heading off; see p.396.

● **Cycling** Much of the country being flat, Bangladesh is an interesting option for cyclists, and the bicycle is as ubiquitous here as in the rest of the Indian subcontinent. Cycling around is a great way of getting really close to local people as well as seeing the country at a restful pace.

● **Madhupur Forest** One of the country's few stretches of deciduous forest, this is home to primates, civets and birds, and contains villages of the Mandi tribespeople, originally a nomadic Christian/animist group from eastern India.

● **Bagerhat Area** To the north of the Sunderbans, Bagerhat is awash with historical Hindu and Muslim monuments, including the famous fifteenth-century Shait Gumbad mosque (its name means "60 domes", though it actually has 77), one of the country's most imposing. The largest surviving brick mosque in Bangladesh, it stands impressively on the bank of a vast pool in an attractive rural setting.

Festivals

September/October *Ramadan*. Month-long fast during daylight hours, but at sunset when fast ends and the delicious *iftar* meals are laid out each evening it is more than worthwhile.
October *Durga Puja*. The biggest Bangladeshi festival, celebrated with special exuberance in Dhaka. Every temple is adorned with a ten-armed statue of the goddess Durga astride a tiger, which on the tenth day are carried to the river and cast upon the waters.

Routes in and out

Zia International Airport in Dhaka has good worldwide connections;

△ Rickshaws, Dhaka

Chittagong and Sylhet also have international airports. There are several overland routes between Bangladesh and India that can be used by foreigners; between Haridaspur to the northeast of Kolkata and Benapole in western Bangladesh; between Dawki in Assam and Tamabil in the Sylhet region; between Burimari in West Bengal and Patgram; between Agartala in Tripura and Akhaura, due east of Dhaka; between Balurghat in West Bengal and Hili; and between Lalgola in West Bengal and Godagari just north of Rajshahi. There is no overland crossing between Bangladesh and Burma to the east.

Bangladesh online

Bangladeshi Art of the Ricksha – ⓦwww.asianart.com/articles /ricksha Written by an anthropologist, this is a serious examination of rickshaw art in Bangladesh. Although it was set up some years ago, the pictures are wonderful and the site is enticing enough to make readers head straight off to book their flights.
Kazi Nazrul Islam ⓦwww.nazrul .org Dedicated to the life and works of Bangladesh's national poet, with loads of links and a forum discussing the great man's work.
Virtual Bangladesh – ⓦwww .virtualbangladesh.com Pretty much everything there is to know about Bangladesh – history, geography, culture, language and literature – plus discussion forums and links to other Bangladesh-related sites.

Books

David Bornstein *The Price of a Dream*. The story of the Grameen Bank, founded in Bangladesh in 1976. One of the most successful development organizations in the world, it has offered tiny loans to more than two million village women since its foundation. Not all the stories are rosy but it's real-life Bangladesh.
Amitav Ghosh *The Glass Palace*. Located in the Sunderbans, which straddles India and Bangladesh, this tale (though set in India and told by an Indian author) gives a brilliant depiction of the area through the story of the search for the rare Irawaddy dolphin.
Tasalima Nasarina *Shame*. In 1992 Hindu extremists destroyed a mosque in Ayodhya, India. This book recounts in raw and unpolished style the retaliation against a Hindu family in Bangladesh. It caused an outrage in the country when it was originally published and a fatwa was pronounced against the author.
Rabindranath Tagore *Selected Short Stories*. This great Bengali writer of stories, poetry and plays, revered on the Indian subcontinent and little-known outside, won the Nobel Prize for Literature in 1913. He lived on a houseboat in East Bengal while writing these stories and beautifully describes the lives he witnessed.

Films

The Alienation (*Duratta*; Morshedul Islam, 2004). This film follows the friendship between privileged Putul, street boy Antu and his sister Morium.
The Clay Bird (*Matir Moina*; Targeque and Catharine Masud, 2003). Depicting the years leading up to the birth of Bangladesh in 1971 through the story of Anu, the film explores the themes of religious tolerance, cultural diversity and the complexity of Islam.
The Eclipse (Shaheen and Shameen Akhtar, 1995). Documentary exploring in horrifying detail the punishments for women who love outside their religion or engage in extra-marital affairs.

My Architect: A Son's Journey
(Nathaniel Kahn, 2003). Documentary
by the son of Louis Kahn (who died
when his son was 12 years old). Kahn's
exotic personal life is explored but the
climax of the film is Nathaniel arriving in
Bangladesh by boat.

Bangladeshi tourist offices

Ⓦwww.bdonline.com/tourism
No overseas tourist office.

Bangladeshi embassies and consulates

Ⓦwww.betelco.com/bd/bdsemb
/bdsemb.html

Australia 35 Endeavour St, PO Box 5,
Red Hill, ACT 2603, Ⓣ02/6295 3328,
Ⓕ02/6295 3351.
Canada 275 Bank St, Suite 302,
Ottawa, Ontario, KP2 2L6 Ⓣ613/236-
0138/9, Ⓕ613/567-3213.
New Zealand Contact the embassy in
Australia.
UK and Ireland 28 Queen's Gate, SW7
5JA Ⓣ020 7584 0081. Assistant High
Commissions: Birmingham Ⓣ0121/643
2386; Edinburgh Ⓣ0131/443 4627;
Manchester Ⓣ0161/236 4853.
US 2201 Wisconsin Ave NW, Suite 300-
325, Washington DC 20007 Ⓣ202/342-
8372. Consulates: Los Angeles
Ⓣ310/441-9399; New York Ⓣ212/599-
6767, Ⓕ212/682-9211.

Bhutan

Capital Thimphu **Population** 800,000 **Language** Dzongkha **Currency** Nu **Religion** The state religion is Mahayana Buddhism but there's also a sizeable minority of Hindus **Climate** Monsoonal	**Best time to go** Autumn (Oct & Nov) and spring (Feb to mid-April) **Minimum daily budget** All-inclusive tours – the only way to visit the country – cost at least \$200/£115 per person per day in the high season (March–May & Sept–Nov) and \$160/£92 per person per day at all other times.

With Tibet to the north, Sikkim and Nepal to the west and the far north-eastern states of India to the east, the Himalayan Kingdom of Bhutan is geographically remote and maintains an air of mystery and exclusivity – only around five thousand tourists a year are allowed to visit, all on organized tours.

Bhutan's allure is in its distinctive culture, which has remained largely isolated from Western influence; most of the people are subsistence farmers leading a devoutly Buddhist life in villages with distinctive architecture. The huge, ancient *dzong*s – each a combination of fortress, monastery and administrative centre – are a feature of every major valley, and the landscape is dotted with evocative temples and *chorten*s, akin to Nepalese stupas. National costume is worn everywhere, and Bhutan's intricate hand-woven textiles, their designs passed on from mother to daughter, are gaining renown across the world.

Travel in Bhutan, though time-consuming, is indubitably picturesque. Most visitors spend just a few days in the west of the country, exploring the valleys of Paro, Thimphu and Punakha. Across in central Bhutan, however, Trongsa

and Bumthang are drawing more and more visitors, while the eastern towns of Trashigang and Trashi Yangtse are equally fascinating, but only feature on the itineraries of those with the time (and money) to make the long trip across the country worthwhile (it's three days by road from Thimphu to Trashigang).

Main attractions

● **Thimphu** The town is one of the smallest and most relaxed capitals in Asia, with plenty for visitors to see, including Trashi Chhoe Dzong, centre of government in the kingdom and a massive, imposing presence in the Thimphu valley; several impressive temples; and the Memorial Chorten, dedicated to the memory of the third king of Bhutan. The weekly market is fabulously colourful.

● **Paro Valley** Broad and flat-bottomed, the valley contains the vast Paro Dzong near the airport, as well as Bhutan's National Museum, housed in the Ta Dzong – Paro Dzong's own watchtower, standing guard way up on

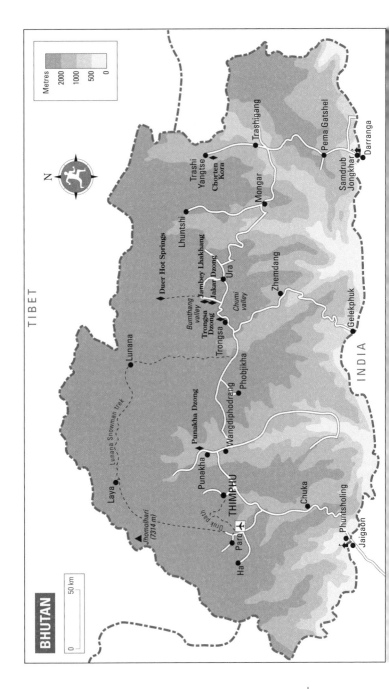

BHUTAN

Metres
2000
1000
500
0

0   50 km

N

TIBET

INDIA

Darranga
Pema Gatshel
Trashigang
Samdrub Jongkhar
Mongar
Chorten Kora
Trashi Yangtse
Lhuntshi
Duer Hot Springs
Jambey Lhakhang
Jakar Dzong
Ura
Zhemdang
Gelekphuk
Bumthang valley
Trongsa Dzong
Chumi valley
Trongsa
Phobjikha
Lunana
Wangdiphodrang
Punakha Dzong
Lunana Snowman trek
Punakha
THIMPHU
Chuka
Laya
Jhomolhari (7314 m)
Druk path
Paro
Phuntsholing
Ha
Jaigaon

Mean temperatures (°C) and rainfall (mm)

Average daily temperatures (maximum and minimum °C) and monthly rainfall (mm)

Thimphu	Jan	Feb	Mar	Apr	May	June	July	Aug	Sept	Oct	Nov	Dec
max °C	17	14	19	23	23	26	25	24	24	22	19	17
min °C	-1	-3	5	7	11	14	17	17	15	9	0	-2
rainfall mm	40	20	10	30	10	95	105	130	55	0	0	0

the hillside. At the valley's northern end, the ruined Drukyel Dzong is a popular excursion destination and there are numerous temples, large and small, grand and humble, dotted around. The ubiquitous image of Bhutan is the temple of Takshang, or Tiger's Nest, built high up into a sheer cliff on the side of the valley – a terrific two-hour hike. It's a wonder that anything could ever have been built in such an apparently impossible location; legend tells how angels laid down their hair on the cliffside to provide the temple's foundations.

- **Punakha** Lower and warmer than Thimphu, the traditional winter capital of Bhutan has a *dzong* sitting impressively at the confluence of two differently coloured rivers, with the hills rising all around. The *dzong* is a quite remarkable demonstration of the sheer brilliance and vibrancy of Bhutan's traditional woodcarving, sculpture and temple painting, having been largely rebuilt after a major fire in 1998.

- **Trongsa Dzong** The largest *dzong*, Trongsa is also one of the most dramatically situated, visible from many miles away. The watchtower above the *dzong* offers brilliant views of the area, and the tiny hotels and restaurants of the town, mostly run by Tibetan refugees who have lived in Bhutan for decades, provide a relaxed welcome.

- **Bumthang Valley** For many visitors to Bhutan, the Bumthang valley, right in the centre of the country, turns out to be their favourite spot. The local *dzong*, Jakar, is perched dramatically on a spur overlooking the valley, and there are innumerable temples along the broad valley bottom, the most famous being Kurjey and Jambey. Possible excursions from Bumthang include the weaving workshops of the Chumi valley to the west, and a trip to the beautiful, high-altitude village of Ura, with its impressive new temple.

- **Mongar, Trashigang, Trashi Yangtse** Accommodation in these eastern towns is sparse and the distances you need to travel to get to them can be tiring, but towering hills, rivers thundering through the valley bottoms, lovely temples, fabulous weaving produced on simple looms in people's houses, and the ancient Chorten Kora await those who make the trip.

- **Trekking** Bhutan is sparsely populated, the countryside attractive and uncluttered; consequently, trekkers have a wide choice of routes, from the moderately difficult five-day Druk Path between the Paro and Thimphu valleys through to the 24-day Lunana Snowman Trek. On the latter, from Paro to rejoin the road at Nikachu, west of Trongsa, trekkers make their arduous way across 4500-metre-high passes via the remote village of Laya, where the people have distinctive language, costume and customs. Make certain that you allow time to acclimatize to the altitude before you trek and as you climb higher; failure to do so can be very dangerous (see p.366).

Also recommended

- **The valley of Phobjikha** High up in the centre of the country, this is the winter home of rare black-necked cranes, who fly there every year from Siberia. The venerated monastery, Gangtey Gompa, is also located here, gloriously situated on a spur overlooking the valley.

- **Local alcoholic brews** Bhutanese people love to drink, and there are a huge variety of brews on offer, including several varieties of beer brewed by village women from locally farmed grain, and, for the bravest souls, the highly potent, distilled *ara*.

- **Bhutanese food** It isn't the most inspiring cuisine in the world, but all visitors should try the unique, delicious red rice, *aima datsi* (chilli curry, as combustible as it sounds) and *suja* (butter tea).

- **Archery** Bhutan's national sport. The tiny targets are set apparently impossible distances away from the archers, many of whom still use traditional bamboo bows. Try to catch part of a contest – the entire thing often lasts for days – and enjoy the yelling, singing and dancing and the attempts to deflect the opposition arrows by dodging in front of the target while the arrow is on its way.

Festivals

February *Punakha Dromche*. Celebrating an ancient defeat of the Tibetans by the Bhutanese, this festival features masked dances, ceremonies, a re-enactment of the event plus all the fun of a local market and fair.

March/April *Paro Tshechu*. Every temple celebrates an annual festival, commemorating the arrival of the Tibetan Guru Rimpoche in the eighth century and the victory of the Buddhism that he brought over evil spirits. Paros is a vast, orchestrated affair with thousands of spectators, masked dances and the unfurling of a massive religious hanging, the *thongdrel*.
October/November *Jambey Lhakhang Drup*. A much smaller and more intimate temple festival in the picturesque Bumthang valley, featuring a dramatic night-time fire blessing.

Routes in and out

Most visitors fly into and out of Paro on Druk Air, the national airline (indeed the only airline permitted to land in Bhutan). An alternative is to enter by road, from Jaigaon in West Bengal (India), at Phuntsholing on the southern border, from where it's a six-hour drive to Thimphu. At Samdrup Jongkhar, in the far east of the country, it's possible to exit Bhutan by road for Darranga in the Indian state of Assam, though it's not permitted to enter Bhutan this way. The border between Bhutan and Tibet is closed.

Bhutan online

Bhutan Fortress of the Gods Ⓦwww .bhutan.at Originally set up to accompany an exhibition of Bhutanese objects that toured Europe from 1997 to 2000 this is a great site showing some wonderful objects but also getting way below the surface in explaining the country, its religion, history and everyday life.
Bhutan News Online – Ⓦwww .bhutannewsonline.com Hosted and managed by expatriate Bhutanese

△ Paro Dzong

living in Europe and North America, this site has tons of up-to-the-minute news plus plenty of background information.

Bhutanese Refugees – Ⓦwww .geocities.com/bhutaneserefugees All is not perfect in this apparent paradise: since the 1980s over 100,000 Bhutanese people of Nepalese origin, many of whose families have been in Bhutan for generations, have left the country and become refugees in Nepal. This site explains their point of view.

Bootan – Ⓦwww.bootan.com Colourful and informative general site including vital tourist information plus news, plenty of pictures and some in-depth articles.

Kuensel – Ⓦwww.kuenselonline.com The weekly Bhutanese English-language newspaper gives a fascinating insight into the country. The juxtaposition of village stories with world events is wonderfully eccentric but gives an illuminating view of the current preoccupations of this remote land.

Books

Russ & Blyth Carpenter *The Blessings of Bhutan*. A compilation of short articles about every imaginable aspect of the country by a couple who have visited it and obviously grown to love it, over a number of years.

Barbara Crossette *So Close to Heaven: The Vanishing Buddhist Kingdoms of the Himalayas*. The author visits Kashmir, Nepal and Sikkim as well but by far the largest portion of the book is devoted to Bhutan. Her politics rankle with some readers but it's still a worthwhile read and perspective.

Gyurme Dorje *Bhutan*. The most exhaustive, insightful guide book to this little-visited country; it's strongest on the text and less powerful on pictures.

Christian Schichlgruber & Francoise Pommaret *Bhutan Mountain Fortress of the Gods*. Fabulous images and insightful text make this one of the best overall books on the country.

Jamie Zeppa *Beyond the Sky and the Earth: a Journey into Bhutan*. This enthralling read tells of the author's years as a teacher in the remote Himalayan kingdom, and is an intriguing introduction to the country, as well as a very open account of the highs and lows of life in an unfamiliar culture.

Films

The Cup (Khyentse Norbu, 2000). The first film by the only Bhutanese film director to receive Western notice. This is a small, delightful movie, about Tibetan monks in a small Himalayan monastery and the impact on their lives of the World Cup.
The Other Final (Johan Kramer and Matthijs de Jongh, 2003). In 2002, as Brazil and Germany played the World Cup final, the two countries ranked at the bottom of world football – Bhutan at 202nd and Montserrat at 203rd – played

in Thimphu. Following the preparation, the teams and the game itself, this documentary is a fun perspective.
Travellers and Magicians (Khyentse Norbu, 2004). The first feature film shot in Bhutan to make it into the West. It tells the interwoven stories of two Bhutanese men seeking to change their lives.

Bhutanese tourist offices

ⓦ**www.tourism.gov.bt** Contact the Department of Tourism, P.O. Box 126, Thimphu, Bhutan ⓣ975-2-323251, ⓕ975-2-323695.

Bhutanese embassies and consulates

For visa information contact specialist travel agents or use the tourism contact given above.

Brunei

Capital Bandar Seri Begawan	**Religion** Islam
Population 372,000	**Climate** Tropical
Language Malay	**Best time to go** February–August
Currency Brunei dollar (B$)	**Minimum daily budget** $50/£26

Occupying a tiny sliver of land on the northwest coast of Borneo, the Sultanate of Brunei is one of the least popular tourist destinations in Asia. This is mainly due to its size – there just aren't many attractions in the 5765 square kilometres – though it's also an expensive country to visit, with one of the highest standards of living in the region. The country's wealth comes from oil, which was first discovered here in 1903 and generates so much income that all Bruneians enjoy free health care and education, and subsidized cars, houses and pilgrimages to Mecca. The Sultan of Brunei, who rules the country, is widely acknowledged to be the richest non-American in the world.

Despite Brunei's dearth of tourist attractions, you may find yourself in

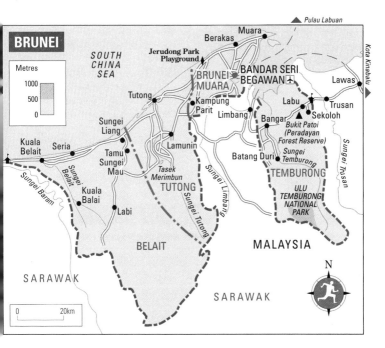

transit here, as Royal Brunei Airlines often has good deals on its long-haul flights, some of which have connections that leave you with half a day or more to play with. Alternatively, if you're exploring the east Malaysian states of Sarawak and Sabah, which lie either side of Brunei, you can easily stop in Brunei en route between the two.

As nearly seventy percent of Brunei is covered in almost impenetrable rainforest, the country's most accessible sights are all in and around the capital, Bandar Seri Begawan (often simply called "Bandar"). Accommodation will be your biggest expense if you stay here – rooms are much costlier than in neighbouring Malaysia or even Singapore, so bring an HI card and consider heading straight for the city's only youth hostel. There's a decent public bus service along the coast roads, but you'll need to rent a car to explore the southern extremities. As Brunei is a strict Muslim country, the sale of alcohol is banned (non-Muslims are allowed to import a very limited amount of alcohol but must declare it) and there's not much to do after nightfall; you should dress modestly (see p.262).

Main attractions

● **The Omar Ali Saifuddien Mosque** The focal point of the Brunei capital, this opulent mosque is constructed from the finest Italian marble, with a dome made from Venetian glass that reflects dramatically in the surrounding lagoon. Non-Muslims are allowed inside the mosque except during prayer times, and you can sometimes persuade the caretakers to let you ride the lift to the top of the minaret, which gives good views over the water villages below.

● **Kampung Ayer** Despite the country's enormous wealth, almost half the population of Bandar Seri Begawan – or around 30,000 people – still live in traditional stilt houses built over the city's three rivers, in the sprawling labyrinth of wooden homes and walkways known as Kampung Ayer. An intriguing and photogenic sight, these "water villages" are best explored by water taxi.

● **Jame 'Asr Hassanil Bolkiah Mosque** Spend a contemplative hour or two in the elegantly manicured gardens of Bandar's enormous mosque, considered by some to be even more impressive than the Omar Ali Saifuddien Mosque.

● **Ulu Temburong National Park** This protected swath of rainforest south of Bandar is crisscrossed by decent trails, and has a treetop-level walkway and observation towers for watching the resident proboscis monkeys, plus occasional guided night walks. On the way here from Bandar, you get to travel through

Mean temperatures (°C) and rainfall (mm)

Average daily temperatures (maximum and minimum °C) and monthly rainfall (mm)

	Jan	Feb	Mar	Apr	May	June	July	Aug	Sept	Oct	Nov	Dec
Bandar Seri Begawan												
max °C	30	30	31	32	33	32	32	32	32	32	31	31
min °C	23	23	23	24	24	24	24	24	23	23	23	23
rainfall mm	133	63	71	124	218	311	277	256	314	334	296	241

the mangrove swamps on the famous "flying coffin" speedboats (so called because of their speed and shape, not their safety record), and can visit an Iban longhouse in Batang Duri.

Also recommended

- **The Brunei Museum** This is the place to bone up on the story behind modern Brunei's economic success and learn about the country's lucrative relationship with oil. There's also a gallery of Islamic art, displaying exquisitely designed antique Korans from all over the Muslim world.

- **Jerudong Park Playground** It may seem strange to travel halfway round the world and end up frittering away your time at a theme park, but the big draw at Jerudong, 25km from Bandar, is the fact that all rides in this huge hi-tech adventure park are paid for by the Sultan. So you can fly as many roller-coasters and spaceship simulators as you like without spending a cent.

- **Stay in a village stilt-house in Sekoloh** The villagers of this remote *kampung* near Bukit Patoi offer home-stay accommodation for tourists, which is a good way to learn about traditional Bruneian life.

- **Kampung Parit** If you don't have time to venture into rural Brunei, this open-air park of twenty replica traditional Brunei dwellings gives a reasonable introduction to local architecture and lifestyles.

Festivals

February 23 *Brunei National Day*. Celebrated with huge parades and firework displays at the National Stadium near Bandar.

July 15 *His Majesty the Sultan of Brunei's Birthday Celebrations*. Begins a fortnight of festivities, including parades, traditional sports competitions and firework displays.

Oct or Nov *Hari Raya Idul Fitri*. To mark the end of the month-long Ramadan fast, the Sultan lets the public inside his fabulous palace, the Istana Nurul Iman, in Bandar.

Routes in and out

Most travellers fly in and out of Brunei's international airport in Bandar Seri Begawan. Bandar is the departure point for international ferries to Lawas and Limbang in Sarawak; or you can reach both towns by bus from Bangar in Temburong District. Boats to Pulau Labuan in Sabah also leave from the capital. Buses to the Sarawak town of Miri leave from Kuala Belait.

Brunei online

Borneo Bulletin – Ⓦ www.brunei -online.com/bb Find out what's happening in the Sultanate from this online version of the English-language daily.

Brunei Travel Information – Ⓦ asiatravel.com/brunei/bruinfo.html Comprehensive rundown of things to see in Brunei, plus some practical information for visitors.

Royal Brunei Airlines Transit Tours – Ⓦ www.bruneiair.com/promotion /transit/index.asp Choose from several short tours of Bandar to alleviate transit-lounge boredom.

Tourism Brunei – Ⓦ www.tourism brunei.com The official site introduces the country, covers the major attractions and has accommodation and tour agency links. It also features details of visa requirements, Brunei embassies and duty-free allowances.

△ Jame'Asr Hassanil Bolkiah Mosque

Books

James Bartholomew *The Richest Man in the World: Sultan of Brunei*. Prepare to be amazed by some mind-boggling statistics, not least concerning the Sultan's 1778-room palace.

Bruneian tourist offices

No overseas tourist office.

Bruneian embassies and consulates

ⓦ www.mfa.gov.bn/missions_abroad /index.htm

Australia and New Zealand 10 Beale Crescent, Deakin ACT 2600, Canberra ☎02/6285 4500, ⓔbruneihc@snetspeed.com.au.
Canada 395 Laurier Avenue East, Ottawa, Ontario K1N 6R4 ☎613-234-5656, ⓔbhco@bellnet.ca.
UK and Ireland 19–20 Belgrave Square, London SW1X 8PG ☎020/7581 0521, ⓔbruhighcomlondon@hotmail .com.
US 3520 International Court NW, Washington DC 20008 ☎202/237-1838, ⓦwww.bruneiembassy.org.

Cambodia

Capital Phnom Penh	**Main religion** Theravada Buddhism
Population 12 million	**Climate** Tropical
Language Khmer	**Best time to go** November–March
Currency Riel (r)	**Minimum daily budget** $10/£5

Cambodia is attracting a burgeoning number of tourists, most of whom are drawn by the prospect of seeing the utterly compelling thousand-year-old temple ruins at Angkor. This city was the epicentre of the ancient Khmer kingdom, a Hindu–Buddhist empire that for almost five hundred years stretched right across Southeast Asia, from Vietnam in the east to China in the north and Burma in the west. These days it is a World Heritage site, and Cambodia's indisputable top attraction. Many of Cambodia's other most famous, and moving, sights are associated with the horrors inflicted by the murderous Khmer Rouge regime, which tried to force communism on its compatriots between 1975 and 1979

and in so doing drove the country back to the Stone Age and caused the deaths of at least a million people. But if you wander further afield you'll also find hill-tribe villages, trekking opportunities, Mekong river trips and beaches, all of which make Cambodia one of southeast Asia's most adventurous destinations.

Twenty-first century Cambodia has still not recovered from the devastations of the 1970s and is one of the poorest countries in the world. Public transport is excruciatingly slow and uncomfortable – though boats between Siem Reap and Phnom Penh, and around the southwest coast, offer a welcome relief from potholed roads – and outside the main tourist centres there is only very basic tourist accommodation. However, there are plenty of cheap guesthouses in Siem Reap, the town closest to Angkor, in the capital Phnom Penh, and in the coastal town of Sihanoukville, and tourists generally get a good reception from the amazingly resilient Khmer people. But you'll probably need a Khmer phrasebook to help you communicate with them outside the main tourist centres.

Until the late 1990s, Cambodia was off the map for all but the bravest travellers, as most people were put off by the reports of continued Khmer Rouge guerrilla activity, bandits, kidnappings and gunpoint muggings. Though safety has improved dramatically and is now generally considered of negligible concern, you should in any case consult newspapers, government travel offices and travellers' Internet forums (see p.420 and p.249) for latest developments. Gun crime continues to be a problem in Phnom Penh, so keep money and valuables hidden if you're walking around the capital after dark. Out in the sticks, landmines left over from the American-Vietnam War and the Khmer Rouge era still pose a major threat to local people, particularly in the provinces along the Thai border. The main tourist areas are clear of mines, but you should never venture off well-used tracks.

Main attractions

● **Angkor** The magnificent ruined Hindu–Buddhist temples and palaces of this ancient Khmer city, built between the ninth and fourteenth centuries, are one of Asia's top five sights – every bit as spectacular and important as better-known lost cities such as Machu Picchu in Peru. Now shrouded in jungle, the crumbling walls, intricate carvings and colossal sculpted faces of Angkor's hundred-plus temples take several days to explore. The biggest draws are the awesome complexes of Angkor Wat and Angkor Thom, but it's well worth exploring the less-visited sights, too, particularly the atmospheric jungle-encrusted remains of Preah Khan, and Kbal Spean where the actual riverbed has been

Mean temperatures (°C) and rainfall (mm)

Average daily temperatures (maximum and minimum °C) and monthly rainfall (mm)

	Jan	Feb	Mar	Apr	May	June	July	Aug	Sept	Oct	Nov	Dec
Phnom Penh												
max °C	31	32	34	35	34	33	32	32	31	30	30	30
min °C	21	22	23	24	24	24	24	25	25	24	23	22
rainfall mm	7	10	40	77	134	155	171	160	224	257	127	45

carved with images of Hindu deities and sacred phalluses.

- **Siem Reap** The town nearest the Angkor temples has retained plenty of charm despite its plethora of guesthouses, tourist restaurants and tour agents. There's decent crafts shopping at the old Psar Chas market, and it's the best place in the country to see performances of traditional Khmer dance. The informal Landmine Museum on the edge of town is a heart-rending testament to the hundreds of limbs and lives that continue to be lost every year to mines hidden in fields and forests. A popular and scenic way to travel between Siem Reap and Phnom Penh is by boat; the journey takes five hours.

- **Phnom Penh** Cambodia's riverside capital is a crazy, eye-popping place to explore, with plenty of markets, temples, French colonial residences, bars, restaurants and museums, and a small but thriving travellers' scene. The main sights are the elegant single-storey buildings of the Royal Palace, which was built in the early twentieth century to a traditional design and is reminiscent of Bangkok's Grand Palace but without the crowds; the glittering Silver Pagoda, whose floor is paved in over five thousand solid-silver tiles; and the National Museum, which has lots of Angkor-related exhibits.

- **The Tuol Sleng Genocide Museum** When Pol Pot's Khmer Rouge seized power in 1975, it turned a Phnom Penh secondary school into Security Prison 21. Over the next four years, an estimated twenty thousand teachers, students, monks and doctors suspected of antirevolutionary behaviour were brought here, often with their wives and children. They were subjected to horrific tortures, and then killed. The prison has been preserved as the very moving Tuol Sleng Genocide Museum, and its thousands of black-and-white mug shots of

ordinary Cambodians who were tortured here will stay with you for a long, long time.

- **The remote province of Rattanakiri** This region, 600km northeast of Phnom Penh, is way out in the sticks, but attracts a steady stream of tourists because of its population of hill tribes and its volcanic scenery. Most people base themselves in the provincial capital, Ban Lung, and everyone takes a tour out to nearby Yeak Laom Lake, to swim in the clear turquoise waters of this forest-encircled volcanic crater.

Also recommended

- **Kratie** Pint-sized Kratie is a little gem of a town, set beside the Mekong River and full of colonial houses and traditional wooden Khmer homes. There's not much to do here except soak up the atmosphere and perhaps make a couple of day-trips into the surrounding countryside; the most popular excursion is to nearby Kampie to see the Irrawaddy dolphins who frequent that part of the Mekong.

- **Sihanoukville** Cambodia's beaches can't compare with those of neighbouring Thailand, but the country's main resort of Sihanoukville is an appealing place, with four decent and not at all crowded beaches, plenty of accommodation, very cheap beer care of the local Angkor brewery, and a fairly lively nightlife.

- **Ream National Park** The best way to enjoy this marine park is to join a tour from Sihanoukville or enlist the help of the park rangers, who can arrange informal boat trips along the mangrove-fringed Prek Toek Sap estuary and to nearby fishing islands.

- **Kampot** Scenic little town that's rich on atmosphere and makes a handy base for trips to Bokor National Park (described below). The misty Bokor mountains provide a picturesque backdrop and pretty, colonial era shophouses line the main thoroughfares.

- **Bokor** A national park full of otherwordly pitcher plants and giant hornbills and the eerie remnants of the deserted adjacent French hill-station and its abandoned hotel, the *Bokor Palace*, make Bokor a memorable place to explore.

- **Battambang** Despite being one of the biggest towns in the country, Battambang is a relaxed place to hang out for a few days, and features appealing colonial architecture. It's a pleasant place to break your journey between Siem Reap and the Thai border: coming from Siem Reap you can also travel by boat.

Festivals

April *Bonn Chaul Chhnam (Khmer New Year)*. As in Thailand and Laos, Buddhist New Year is celebrated with public water fights which symbolize, in theory at least, a spiritual cleansing. Traditional flirtation games are also a common sight in temple grounds and villages.

October or November *Bonn Om Tuk (Water Festival)*. The rainy season officially ends when the waters of the Tonle Sap reverse direction and flow out into the Mekong River again. Celebrations include traditional boat parades and races, and big fireworks displays.

Routes in and out

There are no non-stop long-haul flights to Cambodia, but a number of airlines fly via Bangkok, with connections to and from Phnom Penh and Siem Reap (for Angkor). Elsewhere in Asia, there are non-stop flights to Phnom Penh

and/or Siem Reap from Singapore, Kuala Lumpur, Penang, Shanghai, Kunming, Ho Chi Minh City, Hanoi and Pakxe.

Cambodia's borders are subject to unpredictable regulations, so if you're planning to enter or exit overland check locally first and note that not all border crossings are open to foreigners. From Thailand there are half a dozen entry points open to foreigners; the two most commonly used are at Poipet (six hours by road from Siem Reap), and at Koh Kong (for Sihanoukville and Phnom Penh). There are two border crossings in and out of Vietnam: at Bavet (for Phnom Penh); and at K'am Samnar in the Mekong Delta (for Phnom Penh). The only land border between Laos and Cambodia, at Voen Kham (two hours by boat from Stung Treng), is officially closed but still reportedly used by travellers without incidents; check Internet forums for first-hand accounts.

Cambodia online

Andy Brouwer's Cambodian Tales – ⊛ andybrouwer.co.uk/ctales1.html Famously good and regularly updated collection of travelogues, features and news about Cambodia, plus an active travellers' forum.

The Angkor Guide – ⊛ www .theangkorguide.com Maurice Glaize's seminal 1944 guide to the monuments of Angkor – available online and to download in full, for free.

Bayon Pearnik – ⊛ www.bayon pearnik.com Online Cambodia travel and tourism magazine stacked full of features, tips and travel info.

Beauty and Darkness – ⊛ www .mekong.net/cambodia Concerned mainly with Cambodia's recent history, its people and its refugees. Also covers travel and culture.

△ Angkor Thom

Tales of Asia: Cambodia – ⓦwww .talesofasia.com Very traveller-oriented site with monthly news and features plus a lively forum.

Books

Francois Bizot *The Gate*. The extraordinary account by a French ethnologist of his life in Cambodia during the Khmer Rouge years, first as a captive and later as a negotiator.

Carol Livingston *Gecko Tails*. Funny, touching account of how an aspiring foreign correspondent hangs out in Phnom Penh during the run-up to the 1993 elections waiting for her big break.

Dawn Rooney *Angkor: An Introduction to the Temples*. The most accessible guide, with plenty of pictures as well as temple plans and informative text.

Loung Ung *First They Killed My Father*. Harrowing autobiography of a young girl's childhood during the Khmer Rouge era.

Pin Yathay *Stay Alive, My Son*. The grim and graphic autobiography of a highly educated Cambodian civil engineer who lived through the terrifying Khmer Rouge period.

Films

City of Ghosts (Matt Dillon, 2002). Matt Dillon plays a dodgy New York insurance salesman who flees the FBI and ends up in Phnom Penh to join his business partner in another money-making scam. The eponymous Cambodian capital is the star of the film – by turns seedy, chaotic, enervating and beautiful – with plenty of attention paid to the legacy of its tragic, violent past and to its corrupt, energetic present.

The Killing Fields (Roland Joffé, 1984). The most famous feature film about life under Pol Pot's tyrannical regime centres on journalist Dith Pran who, along with millions of others, was forced to deny his past and work for the Khmer Rouge in labour camps.

Lara Croft: Tomb Raider (Simon West, 2001). Lara Croft leaps out of the video game and on to the big screen, with Angelina Jolie doing her action-hero stuff against a backdrop of some of Angkor's most stunning monuments.

Cambodian tourist offices

ⓦ**www.mot.gov.kh**
No international tourist offices.

Cambodian embassies and consulates

Australia and New Zealand
5 Canterbury Crescent, Deakin, ACT 2600, Canberra ⓣ02/6273 1154, ⓦwww.embassyofcambodia.org.nz/au.htm.

Canada Contact the embassy in Washington.

New Zealand Contact the embassy in Canberra.

UK and Ireland Wellington Building, 28–32 Wellington Rd, London NW8 9SP, ⓣ020/7483 9064, ⓦwww.cambodian embassy.org.uk.

US 4530 16th St, Washington DC 20011 ⓣ202/726-7742, ⓦwww .embassy.org/cambodia.

China

Capital Beijing	**Climate** Tropical in the south; mixed
Population Over 1.3 billion	elsewhere, including temperate
Languages Mandarin, plus scores	(central), desert (northwest) and
of regional languages and dialects	Himalayan (far west); northern and
Currency Yuan (¥) in China;	western winters very cold, southern
Hong Kong dollar (HK$) in Hong	and northwestern summers very hot
Kong; and pataca (M$ or MOP) in	**Best time to go** April–June and
Macau	September–November for most of
Main religions Buddhism,	the country
Confucianism, Daoism and Islam	**Minimum daily budget** $40/£21

As the most populous country on earth, with three thousand years of recorded history and borders encompassing everything from the Himalayan plateau to tropical beaches, China exerts a huge pull on travellers to Asia. The country's scale and complexity, however, can make planning a trip a little daunting. Short visits are best confined to obvious highlights, such as Beijing, Xi'an's Terracotta Army, or the river and hill scenery around Guilin. But with more time, take advantage of the comprehensive (though often uncomfortable) transport network and explore, for example, eastern China's lush landscapes and historic towns, or the country's remoter reaches which – ethnically at least – are not even truly "Chinese".

Wherever you go, take time to try China's classic regional cooking: Northern (featuring hotpots, Peking duck and even lavish Imperial cuisine, which once graced the tables of China's emperors); Eastern (seafood and river-fish delicacies); Sichuan (pungent, spicy dishes using lots of chillies); and Cantonese (little snacks known as *dim sum*, and main courses using just about any ingredient imaginable – as long as it's fresh).

Right now is an exciting time to visit, as the country is changing at breakneck speed, throwing off years of Maoist stagnation with an explosive lust for modernization under a regime that's, in economic terms at least, relatively liberal. Modern skylines are appearing as whole cities are rebuilt; roads and rail lines are spreading everywhere, at an ever more urgent pace in the build-up to the 2008 Beijing Olympics; and the free market is earning people wages which just a generation ago would have been unthinkable. The downsides are rising inflation, leading to poverty for those unable to take part in the boom, ingrained corruption and runaway pollution.

As its infrastructure improves, so China is becoming more accessible to foreigners than it has ever been. Though communication problems can complicate independent travel, you'll usually encounter English-speaking students in the cities who might act as guides in order to improve their language skills, and it's not impossible to learn survival Mandarin even on a brief trip. More

CHINA

KAZAKHSTAN

RUSSIAN FEDERATION

MO

Altay

ALTAI MOUNTAINS

ALMATY   Yining

BISHKEK
KYRGYZSTAN
Torugut Pass

Ürümqi

TIAN SHAN MOUNTAINS

Korla   Turpan   Hami

TAJIKISTAN

Kashgar

Tarim Basin

Tashkurgan

KARAKORAM

Taklamakan Desert

Mogao
Caves   Dunhuang
Jiayuguan

AFGHANISTAN

Sust

Khotan

Khunjerab
Pass

PAKISTAN

KUNLUN MOUNTAINS

Golmud

Qinghai Hu

Xini

Under construction

Ali   ▲ Kailash

Yangzi River

Yellow River

TIBET

Lancang River (Mekong)

DELHI

NEPAL

HIMALAYA

Nu River (Shweli)

Shigatse   Lhasa

Zhangmu
Kodari   Gyantse

KATHMANDU   Everest   THIMPHU

Tiger
Leaping
Gorge

BHUTAN

Lijiang
Dali   Xiagu

INDIA

BANGLADESH

✈ Kunming

Kolkota   DHAKA

Jinghong
(Xishuangbanna)

N

Mo
Har

Bot

BURMA

VIENTIAN

Bay of Bengal

RANGOON

THAIL

0   600 km

BANGKOK

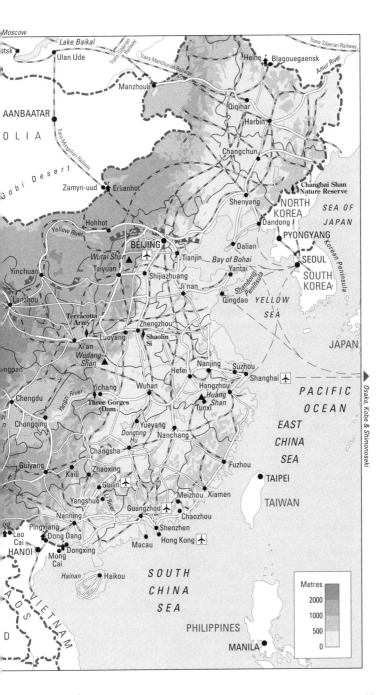

exhausting is a complex bureaucracy which can make even getting a hotel room an achievement; the intensive, unabashed public scrutiny of foreigners; and the stress of trying to see too much in too short a time. If you plan to explore widely, avoid doing so on a rock-bottom budget: when travelling long distances in China, it's worth spending a little bit more on flying or for a comfortable sleeper carriage, so that you'll be refreshed and able to enjoy yourself once you arrive.

Main attractions

• **Beijing** With its skyscrapers and relatively wealthy population, the capital encapsulates the best of modern China but the past survives in some splendid imperial icons, including the elegant palaces of the vast Forbidden City, and the extraordinary, circular Temple of Heaven. Downtown, look for the ever-dwindling number of *hutong*s, the narrow alleyways which make up much of old Beijing. There are also China's foremost restaurants and nightlife to take advantage of – everything from teahouse theatres and acrobatic shows to clubs that only play deepest house. Within easy reach of the capital you'll also find the imperial Summer Palace's spacious and unpolluted parklands, and the stone guardians and chambers of the Ming Tombs.

Mean temperatures (°C) and rainfall (mm)

Average daily temperatures (maximum and minimum °C) and monthly rainfall (mm)

	Jan	Feb	Mar	Apr	May	June	July	Aug	Sept	Oct	Nov	Dec
Beijing												
max °C	1	4	11	21	27	31	31	30	26	20	9	3
min °C	-10	-8	-1	7	13	18	21	20	14	6	-2	-8
rainfall mm	4	5	8	17	35	78	243	141	58	16	11	3
Chongqing												
max °C	9	13	18	23	27	29	34	35	28	22	16	13
min °C	5	7	11	16	19	22	24	25	22	16	12	8
rainfall mm	15	20	38	99	142	180	142	122	150	112	48	20
Hong Kong												
max °C	18	17	19	24	28	29	31	31	29	27	23	20
min °C	13	13	16	19	23	26	26	26	25	23	18	15
rainfall mm	33	46	74	137	292	394	381	367	257	114	43	31
Lhasa												
max °C	7	9	12	16	19	24	23	22	21	17	13	9
min °C	-10	-7	-2	1	5	9	9	9	7	1	-5	-9
rainfall mm	0	13	8	5	25	64	122	89	66	13	3	0
Ürümqi												
max °C	-11	-8	-1	16	22	26	28	27	21	10	-1	-8
min °C	-22	-19	-11	2	8	12	14	13	8	-1	-11	-13
rainfall mm	15	8	13	38	28	38	18	25	15	43	41	10

● **The Great Wall** This extraordinary feat of civil engineering was begun in the 5th century and stretched 6000km across China. The most accessible of its remaining sections are within easy reach of Beijing, including at very popular Badaling and at less commercialized Simatai and Jinshanling.

● **Xi'an** Made rich by the old Silk Road trade, Xi'an was one of China's former capitals. Its most famous sight is the Terracotta Army, life-sized figurines guarding the tomb of the country's first emperor, Qin Shi Huang, but there's much more to Xi'an, including its two 1300-year-old Tang pagodas, and the Neolithic remains at nearby Banpo. The famous kung fu temple, Shaolin Si, is within a day's journey to the east, near Luoyang – packed with visitors, it's a major tourist trap, filled with shops selling weapons and tracksuits, and with *wushu* students showing off their skills.

● **The Li river** Looking exactly like a Chinese scroll painting, a procession of tall, wonderfully weathered limestone peaks flanks 85km of the Li river in southwestern Guangxi province. Base yourself at either the package-tour city of Guilin or the more mellow village of Yangshuo, then cruise around or rent a bicycle and pedal off through the countryside.

● **Shanghai** With over thirteen million residents, Shanghai is the world's most populous city. Its buzzy, style-conscious nightlife is second only to Beijing's, and the shopping is fantastic, with good bargains for tailor-made clothes and plenty of glamorous malls to peruse. Though the city has few unmissable sights, the beautifully presented Shanghai Museum offers the perfect introduction to China's phenomenal artistic heritage. Shanghai also sports pockets of impressive European Art Deco architecture along its riverfront esplanade, a legacy of its time as a former colonial concession, strategically close to the mouth of the Yangzi river.

● **Hong Kong** Hong Kong's cityscape is one of the modern wonders of the world, best seen at night while crossing the harbour on the Star Ferry, though taking the famous tram up to Victoria Peak gives you another classic panorama. Shopping is a major Hong Kong pastime, at the excessively glitzy shopping malls, at the chaotic Temple Street Night Market and in the more traditional Stanley Market. Hong Kong is also the place for unrivalled *dim sum* brunches. Away from the commercial hub, the Ten Thousand Buddha Monastery at Shatin offers fine temple statues and hill views, and there's historic interest at the Qing-dynasty walled village of Kat Hing Wai. Or spend a day or two poking around the less-developed outer islands, exploring Lantau's small beaches and wooded hills or visiting the former Portuguese enclave of Macau.

● **Three Gorges** The latter stage of the 6400-kilometre-long Yangzi River, in Chinese, flows eastwards across central China, and is still used as a transport artery. Catch a ferry through the Three Gorges, between the Sichuanese city of Chongqing and Yichang in Hubei, a three-day 250-kilometre journey past ancient towns, turbulent shoals and spectacular cliff scenery, some of it under threat of submersion from a massive and highly controversial dam project that's due to be completed in 2009.

● **Tibet** The "roof of the world" is a place of red-robed monks and austere monastery complexes set against the awe-inspiring vastness of the Tibetan Plateau. It's also labouring under heavy-handed Chinese military rule, but even the Dalai Lama, exiled in India, encourages people to visit and see the region first-hand. Take your time and, after seeing the mighty Potala Palace – Tibet's foremost tourist sight – in the capital Lhasa, get out to less-touristed monasteries at Shigatse and Gyantse. By 2008 access to Tibet will be possible by what is set to be the spectacular Qinghai–Tibet railway, the highest in the world. It will run over 1100km from Golmud to Lhasa, nearly all of it at an altitude of 4000m or above, using pressurised compartments to prevent altitude sickness.

Also recommended

- **Guangxi and Guizhou** The rural regions of these provinces are among China's poorest, but it's worth exploring the minority communities dotted throughout the fabulously terraced mountains here, especially the Dong village of Zhaoxing, in northern Guangxi. The Miao hilltribe settlements around Kaili in Guizhou host riotous festivals through the year, featuring bull fights, dancing, dragon-boat races and fantastic outfits.

- **Kashgar** An oasis town in China's northwestern deserts, Kashgar is populated by Muslim, Turkic-speaking Uigur people. Its appeal is in its very remoteness from the rest of China – and its Sunday Bazaar, an Arabian-Nights-style affair which draws 100,000 people, including thousands from nearby Kyrgyzstan, Turkistan, Tajikistan and Pakistan, to trade in everything from camels and carpets to plastic buckets.

- **The Silk Road** Follow the ancient Silk Road between China and Central Asia – a 3000-kilometre-long train and bus route from Xi'an to Kashgar. On the way, you can take in remote sections of the Great Wall, the bird-watching lake Qinghai Hu, astonishing eighth-century

Buddhist cave art at Dunhuang, the pleasant oasis town of Turpan and the scorching sands of the Taklamakan desert.

- **Hangzhou and Suzhou** Once a vital trade centre on the 1800-kilometre-long Grand Canal in eastern China, Hangzhou is set around the famed beauty spot of Xi Hu, or West Lake, ringed by pagodas and wooded, hilly parkland, its surface dotted with fishing boats. It's also worth making the haul 60km north to Suzhou, another canal city with a host of traditional Chinese gardens.

- **Changbai Shan Nature Reserve** Set right up on China's frontier with North Korea, Changbai Shan is hard to reach even when the road opens in summer, but the rewards are the stunning blue Tian Chi – "Heaven's Lake" – and the faint chance you may spot Siberian tigers. More likely, you'll get to sample some of the rare fungi and medicinal herbs which locals harvest here and serve up in restaurants; Changbai Shan's ginseng is considered the best in China.

- **Yunnan and Sichuan** China's most varied region, these two provinces stretch from Tibet to the steamy tropical forests of Xishuangbanna, and also share borders with Laos, Vietnam and Burma. Top spots are Sichuan's holy mountain, Emei Shan, where you can sleep and eat in the dozen or more Buddhist temples; the Yunnanese town of Dali, with its ethnic Bai population and vivid mountain and lake scenery; Lijiang, a delightful maze of cobbled lanes and wooden houses, home to the Tibetan-descended Naxi people; and the stark, dramatic scenery of Tiger Leaping Gorge, the deepest canyon in the world, with a drop of 2.5 kilometres.

- **Chaozhou** A self-consciously traditional town in southern Guangdong province, Chaozhou has nineteenth-century streets and even older architecture, including its city walls and beautiful Kaiyuan Temple, which make it a pleasure to explore. Foodies will also need to try out Chaozhou's restaurants, famed for their bitter, refreshing *gongfu* tea and fruit-flavoured sauces.

Festivals

January 5 to February 5 *Ice Lantern Festival*, Harbin. A month-long exhibition of fabulous sculptures carved from snow and ice, including life-size figures and even exact reproductions of Chinese temples.

April or May *Spring Fair*, Dali. A huge gathering from all Yunnan, as crowds pour in to buy and sell horses, watch wrestling matches and socialize, with much dancing and singing.

June/July *Dragon-boat Festival*. Traditional multi-oared dragon boats are raced along waterways in many parts of the country, especially in Hong Kong and in Yueyang in Hunan.

Routes in and out

China's main international airports are in Beijing, Kunming (capital of Yunnan),

Guangzhou (capital of Guangdong), Shanghai and Hong Kong. In addition, Guilin has an airport served by flights from major Chinese cities and from Seoul (South Korea) and Fukuoka (Japan).

You can enter and depart China overland through several designated border crossings. The Trans-Mongolian line of the Trans-Siberian Express runs between Moscow and Beijing via Ulaanbaatar (see p.169) and you can also use local trains to access the border at Erlianhot. There's also a train between Ürümqi in northwestern China and Almaty in Kazakhstan. There are roads from northwestern China into Pakistan (via Tashkurag/Sust) and Kyrgyzstan (via the Torugut Pass) and from Tibet into Nepal (via Zhangmu/Kodari), though regional politics can make using these routes problematic for foreigners. Far easier are the three rail and/or road crossings from north Vietnam, and the single road crossing from Boten in Laos – all of which bring you into China's southwestern provinces of Yunnan and Guangxi, from where there's regular transport to Nanning and Kunming. There are also international ferry services to Japan: between Shanghai and

△ Tiananmen square, Beijing

Kobe and Osaka, from Tanggu near Tianjin to Kobe, and from Qingdao to Shimonoseki.

China online

China the Beautiful – ⓦwww .chinapage.com Wide-ranging cultural site with browsable pages on calligraphy, the appreciation of Chinese painting and poetry, Zen Buddhism, learning Chinese, and extracts from Chinese novels.

The China News Network – ⓦthe chinanews.net The day's headlines, plus news, feature archives and links.

Hong Kong Travel Forum – ⓦhong -kong.travel-information.org Travellers' forum for queries on anything from hotel recommendations to tips on the best tailors' shops.

That's China – ⓦwww.thatschina .net Online version of the lively monthly Beijing and Shanghai magazine whose features cover travel, contemporary culture, traditional heritage and expat life.

Tibet Information Network – ⓦwww .tibetinfo.net News on what's happening in Tibet, political updates, cultural background, plus detailed information on travel to the region, including overland routes, visa information and travel restrictions.

Books

Jung Chang *Wild Swans*. A modern-day classic that charts China's recent history as lived by three generations of women: the author, who grew up in Sichuan during the Cultural Revolution; her mother, who lived through the Japanese occupation of Manchuria and later became a Communist official; and her grandmother, who was a warlord's concubine.

Peter Hessler *River Town*. The funny, touching and illuminating account of a young American Peace Corps volunteer who spent two years as an English teacher in a small Yangzi town in Sichuan province – a town that hadn't been visited by a white foreigner for fifty years.

Peter Hopkirk *Trespassers on the Roof of the World: The Race for Lhasa*. The amazing story of how, at the start of the twentieth century, a group of Brits and Indians charted every nook of the vast High Tibetan Plateau, the most inaccessible – and hostile – place on earth.

Ma Jian *Red Dust*. It is the mid-1980s and, about to become another statistic in the latest Campaign Against Spiritual Pollution, disaffected young Beijing photo-journalist Ma Jian sets off on an arbitrary journey around China. His wanderings, mostly done on foot, last three years and take him to remote villages and ancient minority communities that no foreign traveller could ever hope to penetrate, revealing a country of mind-blowing vastness, diversity and harshness.

Gao Xingjian *Soul Mountain*. The Nobel-prize winning author fashioned this many-voiced novel around a journey he made through remote southern China, weaving in folk tales, true stories and meditations on life, travel, knowledge – and China's recent history.

Films

Crouching Tiger Hidden Dragon (Ang Lee, 2000). Despite having its roots in the martial arts genre that dominates Chinese and Hong Kong TV, this film was a big hit in the West, skillfully blending fantasy, Dao philosophy, awesome aerial stunts and strong female characters. The breathtaking scenery was filmed on location in the Ming-dynasty villages of Xidi and Hongcun in the Huang Shan mountains in eastern China, and in Xinjiang province in the remote northwest.

Farewell My Concubine (Chen Kaige, 1993). An unusual approach to modern

Chinese history, filtering it through the melodramatic and often heart-rending experiences of two (male) stars of the Peking Opera; one a sensitive, gay interpreter of female characters, the other his macho leading man.

Hard Boiled (John Woo, 1993). Probably the most famous of the innumerable bloody, violent Hong Kong guns-and-gangsters action flicks: slick, excessive, and with a ridiculously high body count. Stars Chow Yun Fat.

Red Sorghum (Zhang Yimou, 1987), **Ju Dou** (Zhang Yimou, 1989) and **Raise the Red Lantern** (Zhang Yimou, 1991). Three stunning visual feasts by Zhang Yimou, all of them set in feudal households in rural 1920s' China. They're all variations on a similar theme, concerning a young woman who is sent against her will to marry an elderly and intransigent man, the elderly husbands symbolizing the inflexible Chinese state. Yimou filmed many scenes in the traditional eighteenth-century village homes around Yixian near Tunxi in Anhui province.

Chinese tourist offices

China: Ⓦwww.cnto.org
Hong Kong: Ⓦwww.hkta.org
Australia and New Zealand 11th Floor, 234 George Street, Sydney, NSW 2000 ℡02/9252-9838, Ⓦwww.cnto.org.au. Hong Kong Tourist Board: Level 4, Hong Kong House, 80 Druitt St, Sydney, NSW 2000 ℡02/9283 3083.
Canada 480 University Ave, Suite 806, Toronto, Ontario M5G 1V2 ℡416/599-6636. Hong Kong Tourism Board: 9 Temperance St, Toronto, Ontario M5H 1Y6 ℡416/366-2389.
UK and Ireland 4 Glentworth St, London NW1 5P6 ℡020/7935 9787. Hong Kong Tourism Board: 6 Grafton St, London W1S 4EQ ℡020/7533 7100.
US 350 Fifth Ave, Suite 6413, New York,

NY 10118 ℡212/760-8218; 550 North Brand Boulevard, Suite 910, Glendale, CA 91203 ℡1-800-670-2228. Hong Kong Tourism Board: 10940 Wilshire Blvd, Suite 2050, Los Angeles, CA 90024 ℡310/208-4582; 115 East 54th St, New York, NY 10022, ℡212/421-3382; 130 Montgomery St, San Francisco, CA 94104, ℡415/781-4587.

Chinese embassies and consulates

For Hong Kong visa regulations, see Ⓦwww.immd.gov.hk/ehtml/hkvisas_4.htm.
Australia Ⓦwww.au.chinaembassy.org. 15 Coronation Drive, Yarralumla, ACT 2600 ℡02/6273 4783. Consulates in Melbourne ℡03/9804 3683; and Sydney ℡02/9698 7929.
Canada Ⓦwww.chinaembassycanada.org/eng. 515 St Patrick's St, Ottawa, Ontario K1N 5H3 ℡613/789-3434. Consulates in Calgary ℡403/264-3322; Toronto ℡416/964-8861, Ⓦtoronto.china-consulate.org/eng; and Vancouver ℡604/734-0704.
Ireland 40 Ailesbury Rd, Dublin 4 ℡053/1269 1707, Ⓦwww.chinaembassy.ie.
New Zealand 2–6 Glenmore St, Wellington ℡04/474 9631, Ⓦwww.chinaembassy.org.nz. Consulate in Auckland ℡09/525 1589, Ⓦwww.chinaconsulate.org.nz.
UK Ⓦwww.chinese-embassy.org.uk. 49–51 Portland Place, London W1B 1JL ℡020/7299 4049. Consulate in Manchester ℡0161/224 7480.
US 2300 Conneticut Ave NW, Washington, DC 20008 ℡202/328-2500, Ⓦwww.china-embassy.org. Consulates in Houston ℡713/520-1462, Ⓦwww.chinahouston.org; Los Angeles ℡213/807-808, Ⓦwww.losangeles.china-consulate.org; and New York ℡212/244-9456, Ⓦwww.nyconsulate.prchina.org.

East Timor

Capital: Dili	**Climate**: Tropical
Population: 925,000	**Best time to go**: May–July is when temperatures are mildest, but the dry season runs from June to October
Languages: Tetum and Portuguese	
Currency: US dollar (US$)	
Main religion: Roman Catholic	**Minimum daily budget**: $25/£13

East Timor, or Timor Leste, is the world's newest nation; having finally been give the chance to vote for independence from Indonesia in 1999, the East Timorese finally achieved it on May 20, 2002. For tourists, the fledgling country is very much a new frontier, and with stunning beaches, world-class diving and a ruggedly mountainous interior – not to mention a culture fed by numerous animist cults as well as a strong dose of Portuguese heritage – there's plenty to keep you interested. Plus, being less than 500km west of Australia and just a two-hour flight from Darwin, it makes an ideal final stop on a leisurely overland trip from Europe to Australia. East Timor's dogged courage in the face of its appalling recent history is also part of its appeal to adventurous tourists. Where supporting East Timor was once a question of lobbying for global attention, you can now help the local economy by holidaying there.

As the eastern half of the island of Timor, which sits at the easternmost

point of the Indonesian archipelago, East Timor endured a long history of colonial rule. It was a Portuguese colony for four hundred years (West Timor, meanwhile was bagged by the Dutch and is now part of Indonesia) until 1975 when, just as independence loomed, the world looked the other way as Indonesia invaded. For the next 24 years, the Fretilin resistance movement, led by Xanana Gusmão, now president of East Timor, waged a guerrilla war against the occupiers, and the Indonesians were brutal in their response, killing some 250,000 people. Indonesia finally bowed to global pressure in 1999 and gave East Timor the chance to vote for independence, but even then the Indonesian militia refused to leave quietly, killing hundreds more people, forcing thousands into West Timor as refugees, and systematically destroying the country's infrastructure on their way out – damage that is still evident in places today.

With help from around the world, East Timor is recovering and rebuilding but

Mean temperatures (°C) and rainfall (MM)

Average daily temperatures °C and monthly rainfall (mm)

Dili	Jan	Feb	Mar	Apr	May	Jun	Jul	Aug	Sep	Oct	Nov	Dec
°C	27	27	27	27	27	25	25	24	25	25	27	27
mm	140	128	139	82	77	51	25	13	18	23	64	141

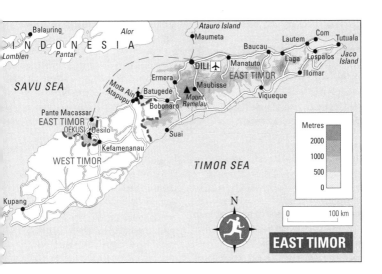

the country is desperately poor. Tourism is in its infancy and facilities are sparse though by no means nonexistent. Hotel accommodation is often fairly pricey for what you get, and is found mainly in the capital, Dili, and at a few beachfront towns along the north coast; for travel elsewhere, a tent would be useful, especially as there are no restrictions on camping on the beach. Public transport is limited so renting a motorbike in Dili is a good idea, though be prepared for some rough rides away from the north coast. Beware of travelling to remote areas in the rainy season (Nov–April) when floods often render parts of central and southern East Timor inaccessible. Though Tetum is the national language, English is widely spoken, as is Portuguese and Indonesian.

Main attractions

● **Atuaro Island** Less than an hour's boat ride from Dili, this island offers fabulous diving for all levels of experience, almost guaranteed dolphin sightings,

great snorkelling and a few accommodation options.

● **Diving** There are unparalleled wall dives off the eastern tip of East Timor, especially around the coast between Com and Tutuala, with plenty of manta rays, sharks and turtles as well as dugongs. Similarly impressive wall dives can be found close to shore along the coast between Dili and Manatuto, and can be organized from Dili.

● **Dili** Embraced by an enormous 27-metre-high statue of Christ at one end and a lighthouse at the other, East Timor's beachfront capital has many battle scars among its faded Portuguese-style houses and wooden homes. One of the most famous legacies of the country's war-torn past is the Santa Cruz cemetery, site of a horrific massacre of pro-independence demonstrators by Indonesian troops in 1991. You can learn about this and other episodes in East Timor's history at the informative Xanana Reading Room. Climb the steps up to the feet of the towering Cristo Rei statue (27 metres high because it was erected by the Indonesians who made East Timor their 27th province) for a grand coastal view. The Tais Market is a great place to browse for East Timor's beautiful textiles, and Dili has the country's best range of restaurants.

● **Maubisse and Mount Ramelau** Even if you don't make the three-hour climb up East Timor's highest peak, Mount Ramelau (2962m), you should definitely take a trip into its foothills for breathtaking upland scenery, beautiful valleys and pretty, traditional villages. This is also the main coffee-growing region in the country. Base yourself at the hill town of Maubisse, which has great views.

● **Com** This burgeoning beach resort has a gorgeous white-sand beach and great diving and snorkelling close by.

Also recommended

● **Ikat textiles** East Timor is justly famous for its beautiful hand-woven heavy cotton textiles whose characteristic dark reds and blue are made from natural plant dyes; the yarn is tie-dyed using the ikat process and the *tais*

(sarongs) often feature stylized figures and animals. Dili market is a good pace to look for *tais*, or try the villages of Viqueque in the southeast or Bobonaro in the west, both of which are especially renowned for their weaving.

● **Baucau** East Timor's second biggest town has an attractive old quarter, a scenic three-kilometre walk through paddies and traditional settlements down to the beach, and a few places to stay, making it a good base for explorations further east. The scenery along the coast road from Dili to Baucau is spectacular.

● **Jaco Island** This tiny islet is fringed with white-sand beaches, breathtakingly pale blue water and rich shallow reefs that are perfect for snorkelling. Catch a lift with a fisherman or join a dive tour.

Routes in and out

The only direct flights into East Timor are with Merpati from Bali in Indonesia and with Airnorth from Darwin in northwest Australia; flights land at Presidente Nicolau Lobato International Airport in Dili. There's a border crossing into West Timor at Batugede, served by buses from Dili

△ Areia Branca Beach, Dili

to Kupang, and you can also cross into Oekusi, the East Timor enclave in West Timor, via Oesilo. Ferries connect Dili with Oekusi and with Atauro Island.

East Timor online

Discover East Timor – Ⓦwww.discover dili.com A handy guide that introduces the main tourist destinations and activities, points you in the right direction for various guesthouses, hotels, bars and restaurants and gives you background info too.

Dive Timor Lorosae – Ⓦwww .divetimor.com Masses of useful info plus tempting under- and above-water pictures on this site belonging to an Australian-run dive shop in Dili.

East Timor Action Network – Ⓦwww .etan.org This US-based grassroots organization has been working in solidarity with the people of East Timor for decades; its website highlights its current campaign issues.

The Unofficial Guide to East Timor – Ⓦwww.osolemedia.com Excellent short guide to all the main sights plus practical info and links.

Books

Luis Cardoso *The Crossing: A Story of East Timor*. Though the author grew up on Atauro Island in East Timor under Portuguese rule, he was studying in Lisbon when Indonesia invaded in 1975 and remained trapped there in exile until Independence. This is the story of his exile and of his father's life in Timor during the 24 years of Indonesian rule.

Irena Cristalis *Bitter Dawn: East Timor – A People's Story*. A Dutch journalist tells the recent history of East Timor's struggle for independence through the life stories of some of the extraordinary people – among them guerilla fighters, nuns, students, politicians and farmers – whom she

met there during Indonesia's final vicious attempt to hold on to the fledgling nation.

Don Greenlees, Robert Garran *Deliverance: The Inside Story of East Timor's Fight for Freedom*. Two Australian journalists flesh out what really happened in the lead-up to Indonesia's bloody retreat from East Timor in 1999.

Timothy Mo *The Redundancy of Courage*. The island of Danu is the barely disguised fictional alter ego of East Timor in this gritty, thought-provoking 1991 novel about a self-serving gay Chinese hotel owner who reluctantly gets drawn in to the brutal guerrilla war against the country's colonial occupiers. Many of the characters are easily identifiable as members of the East Timor resistance.

John Pilger *Distant Voices*. Bestselling 1994 anthology of investigations by the multi-award-winning campaigning journalist. At the heart of the book is an extraordinary exposé of Indonesia's murderous policies in East Timor.

East Timorese tourist offices

Ⓦwww.turismotimorleste.com No overseas offices.

East Timorese embassies and consulates

Ⓦwww.mfac.gov.tp

Australia 25 Blaxland Crescent, Griffith ACT 2603 ☎02/6260-8800, ⒺTL_Emb .Canberra@bigpond.com. Consulates in Melbourne ☎03/9248-1169; and Sydney ☎02/9239-0060.

UK and Ireland Contact the embassy in Portugal: Avenida Infante Santo, 17-6 1350-175 Lisbon ☎00-351-21-393- 3730, Ⓔembaixada.rdtl@mail.telepac.pt.

US and Canada 3415 Massachusetts Ave, NW, Washington, DC 20007 ☎202- 965-1515, Ⓔembtlus@earthlink.net.

India

Capital Delhi	mixed in the north, including
Population Over one billion	temperate (central), desert
Language Hindi, plus fourteen other	(northwest) and Himalayan (far north)
main languages	**Best time to go** October–March
Currency Rupee (Rs)	(except in the southeast); April–
Main religions Hinduism, Islam,	September (for trekking in the
Buddhism and Sikhism	Himalayas, and for the southeast)
Climate Tropical in south India;	**Minimum daily budget** $10/£5

For many travellers, India epitomizes the Asia experience. It brims over with bizarre rituals and extraordinary characters; it holds a wealth of temples, ruined cities and dramatic landscapes; and for tourists everything is bargain-priced. However, it is also more crowded, more hassly and seems to have a lot more visible poverty than many other Asian countries.

With seven major faiths and over fifteen regional languages, India is impossible to pigeonhole. Much of the sub-

Mean temperatures (°C) and rainfall (mm)

Average daily temperatures (maximum and minimum °C) and monthly rainfall (mm)

	Jan	Feb	Mar	Apr	May	June	July	Aug	Sept	Oct	Nov	Dec
Delhi												
max °C	21	24	30	36	41	40	35	34	34	35	29	23
min °C	7	9	14	20	26	28	27	26	24	18	11	8
rainfall mm	25	22	17	7	8	65	211	173	150	31	1	5
Darjeeling												
max °C	8	9	14	17	18	18	19	18	18	16	12	9
min °C	2	2	6	9	12	13	14	14	13	10	6	3
rainfall mm	13	28	43	104	216	589	798	638	447	130	23	8
Mumbai												
max °C	28	28	30	32	33	32	29	29	29	32	32	31
min °C	19	19	22	24	27	26	25	24	24	24	23	21
rainfall mm	3	3	3	0	18	485	617	340	264	63	13	3
Chennai												
max °C	29	31	33	35	38	38	36	35	34	32	29	29
min °C	19	20	22	26	28	27	26	26	25	24	22	21
rainfall mm	36	10	8	15	25	48	91	117	119	305	356	140

continent's cultural history was shaped by the Moguls, an Islamic dynasty who ruled from the sixteenth to the eighteenth century, building majestic forts and exquisite palaces all over the country, many of them now impressively restored. A hundred years later, India came under the sway of the British Empire; known as the Raj, the colonial government built an extensive railway network, introduced a Westernized education system and promoted English as the official state language. Modern-day India is now the world's largest secular democracy, where the Hindu majority is vociferously, and occasionally violently, matched by powerful Muslim and Sikh factions, not to mention countless other religious and political groups. Religious tension occasionally renders some regions temporarily unsafe for visitors, so check official websites (see p.420) and travellers' forums (see p.249) for latest developments; most governments continue to advise against all travel to Jammu and Kashmir, except for the Ladakh region.

A journey from the north of India to the south can seem like a trip across a dozen different countries. More than almost any other destination in Asia, India is a place to return to again and again and not somewhere that rewards a whistle-stop tour. And, because distances are phenomenal and public transport notoriously tardy, it also makes sense to confine yourself to smallish areas – aim to see something in depth and you'll have a far better experience than skittering through countless airports, stations and bus depots.

Many travellers make a beeline for the beaches of Goa and Kovalam, but others head for spiritual centres like Rishikesh and Dharamsala (for more on this, see p.188), or to the palaces and desert landscape of Rajasthan, or the hiking trails and hill stations in the Himalayas.

First-time visitors to India usually worry most about poor sanitation and the prospect of getting sick, but so long as you're sensible and follow the advice outlined in Chapter twelve, you shouldn't find health is much more of an issue here than anywhere else in Asia.

Main attractions

- **Taj Mahal** The world's most famous monument to love features on almost every first-timer's Indian itinerary. Built by the seventeenth-century Mogul emperor Shah Jahan to enshrine the body of his favourite wife, the vast mausoleum stands on the banks of the Yamuna River in the city of Agra, just a couple of hours' train ride from Delhi. It's worth staying in a hotel that's close by the Taj, so you can visit it at sunrise and/or in the moonlight, when the play of light on marble is especially memorable, and the site is less crowded (more than 20,000 visitors a day flock here). Not surprisingly, Agra is one of the worst places for touts, hawkers and hassle, so have your polite rebuffs at the ready.

- **Rajasthan** India's desert state is deservedly the most popular region in the country, with its glorious forts at Jaipur and Jodhpur, magnificent maharajahs' palaces, and flamboyantly clad citizens. Graceful waterside temples, exquisite mansions, and the lovely City Palace make lakeside Udaipur a definite must-see, and the remote desert town of Jaisalmer, built entirely of honey-coloured sandstone, is another gem – and a departure point for overnight camel safaris. When you've tired of forts, palaces and camels, strike out into the state's two most famous national parks; the lakes and swamps of Keoladeo National Park support huge breeding colonies of cranes, storks, flamingos and ibis, while Ranthambore National Park is one of the easiest places in India to see a wild tiger.

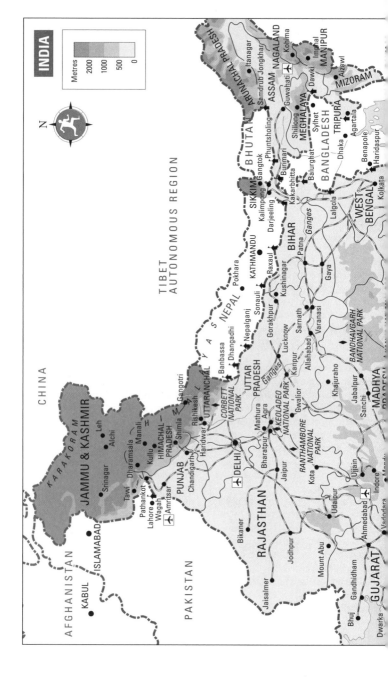

INDIA

Metres
2000
1000
500
0

N

CHINA

AFGHANISTAN
KABUL
ISLAMABAD

PAKISTAN

KARAKORAM

JAMMU & KASHMIR
Leh
Srinagar
Alchi

Tawi
Pathankot
Lahore
Wagah
Amritsar

HIMACHAL PRADESH
Manali
Kullu
Dharamsala
Shimla
Chandigarh

PUNJAB

Haridwar
Rishikesh
Gangotri

UTTARANCHAL

CORBETT
NATIONAL
PARK

DELHI

Mathura
Agra
Bharatpur

KEOLADEO
NATIONAL PARK

Gwalior

RANTHAMBORE
NATIONAL
PARK

Jaipur
Kota

RAJASTHAN

Bikaner

Jodhpur

Jaisalmer

Mount Abu

Udaipur

Bhuj
Dwarka
Gandhidham

GUJARAT
Ahmedabad
Vadodara
Indore
Ujjain

MADHYA
PRADESH

Sanchi
Jabalpur

BANDHAVGARH
NATIONAL PARK

Khajuraho

Allahabad
Kanpur
Lucknow
Sarnath
Varanasi

UTTAR PRADESH

Gorakhpur

TIBET
AUTONOMOUS REGION

HIMALAYAS

NEPAL
Dhangadhi
Banbassa
Nepalganj
Pokhara
KATHMANDU
Sonauli
Raxaul
Kushinagar

Ganges

BIHAR
Patna
Gaya

SIKKIM
Gangtok
Kalimpong
Darjeeling

BHUTAN
Phuntsholing
Samdrub Jongkhar

ARUNACHAL PRADESH
Itanagar

ASSAM
Guwahati

NAGALAND
Kohima

Imphal
MANIPUR

Dawki
MEGHALAYA
Shillong

Aizawl
MIZORAM

TRIPURA
Agartala

Sylhet
Dhaka

BANGLADESH
Benapole
Haridaspur

Balurghat
Karbhitta
Burimari

Kakarbhitta
Lalgola

WEST BENGAL
Kolkata

Ganges

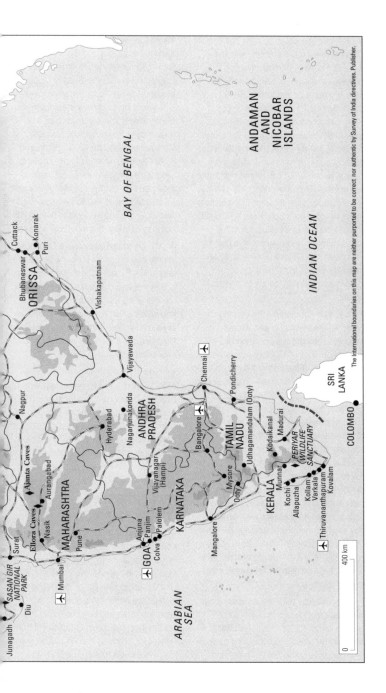

The international boundaries on this map are neither purported to be correct nor authentic by Survey of India directives. Publisher.

BAY OF BENGAL

ANDAMAN
AND
NICOBAR
ISLANDS

INDIAN OCEAN

Cuttack
Konarak
Puri

Bhubaneswar
ORISSA

Vishakapatnam

Vijayawada

Nagpur

Hyderabad

Nagarjunakonda

ANDHRA
PRADESH

Chennai

Pondicherry

Ajanta Caves

Aurangabad

MAHARASHTRA

Ellora Caves

Nasik

Pune

Bangalore

Vijayanagar
(Hampi)

KARNATAKA

Mysore

Ooty

Udhagamandalam (Ooty)

TAMIL
NADU

Kodaikanal

Madurai

SRI
LANKA

COLOMBO

Surat

SASAN GIR
NATIONAL
PARK

Diu

Junagadh

Mumbai

Anjuna
Panjim
GOA
Colva Palolem

Mangalore

KERALA

Munnar

Kochi

Allapuzha

Kollam
Varkala
Kovalam

Thiruvananthapuram

PERIYAR
(WILDLIFE
SANCTUARY)

ARABIAN
SEA

0   400 km

● **Kerala** The south of India has a quite different feel from the north, and the state of Kerala is particularly appealing because it seems less crazy and intense than the rest of the country. Kerala is most famous for its beach resort at Kovalam, and for the more low-key travellers' enclave at Varkala. The other big draw down here is the chance to go boating through the inland waterways near Allapuzha, but the tourist boat-rides are uninspired and overlong, so it's more rewarding to travel through the narrower rivers by local ferry bus. Kerala's delightful old port city of Kochi is full of historic churches and warehouses built by European and Chinese merchants, and regularly stages traditional, elaborately costumed Kathakali dance performances.

● **Ladakh** Cradled by the soaring peaks of the Himalaya and Karakoram ranges, Ladakh is a fascinating high-altitude outpost of Tibetan culture and religion. One of the furthest-flung parts of the country, this arid, stark, mountainous region, dotted with tiny pockets of fertility, offers some of the best trekking in India, from easy two-day strolls to treks of several weeks across the exceptionally remote and spellbindingly beautiful Zanskar region. The other highlights are the temples; Alchi, Tikse and Hemis are the best known, the last of these especially famed for its masked dances at festival time. The popular two- or three-day road journey from the lively hill town of Manali to Ladakh's main town, Leh, is one of the great Asian road trips, with high-altitude passes and stunning scenery (for more, see p.321).

● **City life** Any huge Indian metropolis can scare the life out of a first-timer, but all visitors should have, and will probably be unable to avoid, the city experience at some point. The chaotic capital of Delhi boasts Mogul palaces inside the Red Fort, sweeping thoroughfares in New Delhi and the ultramodern Baha'i Temple, which is often favourably compared to the Sydney Opera House. Kipling's "city of dreadful night", Kolkata, is famously warm-hearted and literary with dozens of bookshops and a reputation for intellectual liveliness. Varanasi lines the banks of the sacred River Ganges, where pilgrims immerse themselves in the waters and cremate their dead on the banks. Mumbai boasts a Louis Vuitton store, some of the best, and most expensive, food in the country, but also some of the most awful poverty.

● **Go on safari** India has a fabulous variety of wildlife including wild elephants and leopards, but its real claim to fame is that it is one of the best places on the planet to spot tigers. The best known national parks are Ranthambore in Rajasthan and Kanha in Madhya Pradesh, but the newer park of Pench, near Nagpur, is a less crowded option.

● **Goa** The beachfront raves are no more but the 100-kilometre-long strip of beaches has something for everyone. And don't forget to venture inland to the palm groves, rice fields, markets and Portuguese-style facades that characterize the heart of the Goan state.

Also recommended

● **Cool out in a hill station** Get away from the steamy heat of the plains in Kodaikanal in the Western Ghats, Ooty (Udhagamandalam) in the Nilgiri Hills, Munnar in Kerala or Darjeeling in the Himalayan foothills; fine scenery (stunning vistas of Kanchenjunga, the third-highest mountain in the world from Darjeeling), trekking, tea and often quaint journeys all add to the character and charm.

- **Dharamsala** Through the high profile of one resident, the Dalai Lama, and as a result of the Chinese occupation of Tibet, Dharamsala – the seat of the Tibetan government in exile – is now world famous. Thanks to the large Tibetan population and influence in the area, this is a great place to take meditation courses, shop for Tibetan trinkets, see Tibetan folk opera and even, if you get lucky, shake hands with the Dalai Lama himself. It is also a good place to arrange local treks into the Dhauladhar range.

- **Amritsar** At the heart of the holy city of the Sikhs stands the sumptuous sixteenth-century Golden Temple, encircled by a sacred lake and constantly thronged by pilgrims in their finest ceremonial dress. You can easily spend half a day absorbing the ritual goings-on of the temple: arrive here at sunrise for the most awesome effect of gilt on water, then walk slowly through the long white marble colonnades that frame the lake; cross the causeway to enter the Golden Temple itself; and finally join the pilgrims for the free meal of chapatti and dhal, dished out to all visitors twice a day.

- **Khajuraho** The 25 Hindu and Jain temples here date back to the tenth century and are built of sandstone, with almost every facade carved into exuberantly erotic sculptures and friezes, depicting in graphic and beautiful detail a whole encyclopedia of *Kama Sutra*-like entanglements.

- **Gangotri Glacier trek** The sacred frozen source of the River Ganges is spectacularly positioned amid spiky snow-clad peaks at 5000m above sea level, but is fairly easily reached along a seventeen-kilometre pilgrims' route.

- **Play an extra in an Indian film** India's film industry, known as Bollywood, is based in Mumbai and produces twice as many movies as Hollywood each year. Non-Indians are invariably needed to pad out the cast, so hang out at the city's Salvation Army Red Shield Hostel, where many movie hopefuls are recruited.

- **Snorkelling and diving in the Andaman islands** This rarely visited archipelago of two hundred picture-perfect islands lies 100km off India's east coast. Tourism is a growing industry and the main areas were unaffected by the 2004 tsunami – it's still about as far off the beaten track as you can get in India.

Festivals

December/January *Kumbh Mela*. A major three-yearly festival held in turn in the four holy cities – Nasik, Ujjain, Haridwar and Prayag – where drops of nectar fell from Vishnu's pot. Each draws millions of pilgrims, including huge numbers of sadhus, to bathe in the holy river at auspicious moments. The Great Kumbh Mela held every twelve years in Allahabad (next in 2013) is the largest of all – in 2001 seventeen million pilgrims came.

April/May *Thrissur Puram*. Kerala's biggest temple festival involves a procession with more than a hundred fabulously ornamented elephants.

June/July *Hemis Festival*. Celebrating the victory of Buddhism over evil at the temple of Hemis in Ladakh; highly unusual masked dances (*chaam*) are the centrepiece.

June/July *Rath Yatra*. Puri and other Southern Indian temples celebrate Krishna's journey to Mathura; three gigantic chariots bedecked with coloured canopies are pulled through the streets by devotees.

November *Pushkar Camel Fair*. The largest livestock market in the world draws more than 200,000 people. The fair coincides with a Hindu pilgrimage to Pushkar, one of the holiest of Hindu cities.

△ Taxi driver, Kolkata

Routes in and out

There are international airports in Delhi, Ahmedabad, Amritsar, Bangalore, Chennai, Cochin, Goa (Dabolim Airport), Guwahati, Kerala (Thiruvananthapuram Airport), Kolkata and Mumbai. Local politics permitting, you can also enter and depart India overland at the border crossings with Pakistan (near Amritsar); Nepal (from Banbassa, Gorakhpur and Raxaul, and at the Nepalese towns of Kakarbhitta, Nepalganj and Dhangadhi, which are less accessible); Bangladesh (from Haridaspur to the northeast of Kolkata, Dawki in Assam, Burimari in West Bengal, Agartala in Tripura, Balurghat in West Bengal and Lalgola in West Bengal). You cannot take a ferry to or from Sri Lanka, which is currently only accessible by air.

India online

123India – ⓦwww.123india.com Scores of links to all manner of India-related sites, including those covering the arts, culture and news, as well as introductions to every region and major city in the country and listings of upcoming festivals.

Discover India – ⓦwww.pugmarks .com/d-india This fabulously colourful monthly travel magazine reaches every corner of the country and has something for every interest.

India Travelogue – ⓦwww.indiatravel ogue.com Magazine-style site with well-written, travel-orientated features, profiles and travelogues, plus plenty on destinations and activities.

The Times of India – ⓦwww.timesof india.com Daily news and the best features from the highly respected English-language daily.

Travel Intelligence – ⓦwww.travel intelligence.net This is a global travel site partly dedicated to great travel writing. Search the "Destinations" for pieces on India by writers such as William Dalrymple, Isabella Tree and Justine Hardy.

Books

Elizabeth Bumiller *May You Be the Mother of a Hundred Sons.* The life stories of many different Indian women – young brides, housewives, films stars, a traffic cop – are drawn together in this book by an American journalist.

William Dalrymple *White Moghuls*. Dalrymple is an excellent modern writer on India, and this story – of the early European colonials who married Indian women, paralleled by the story of the author's researches – is an excellent introduction to his work, told with pace and panache.

Arundhati Roy *The God of Small Things*. Evocative, beautifully written story of caste, colonialism and personal tragedy in Kerala that successfully creates the dreamlike quality of the country.

Salman Rushdie *Midnight's Children*. The life story of a man born at the moment of India's independence mirrors the birth pangs of the new nation. The sheer exuberance of the language and the story-telling capture the wild energy of so much of the country perfectly.

Vikram Seth *A Suitable Boy*. The rollicking saga of a young Indian woman, her extended family and all their acquaintances. Hilarious and gripping, it's full of characters that you'll bump into all over India, though at more than a thousand pages you might think twice about carrying it around on your trip.

Films

The Bandit Queen (Shekhar Kapur, 1994). Harrowing story of the early life of Phoolan Devi, a woman who fought back against her terrible life experiences to lead a bandit gang. She was eventually jailed and, on release, became a politician before her murder in 2001.

Lagaan (Ashutosh Gowariker, 2001). Smash hit Bollywood movie that made a successful cross over to the West, featuring one of the usual Bollywood themes, good versus evil, heroes versus villains.

A Passage to India (David Lean, 1984). Moody, atmospheric film about the colonial tensions in India in the early twentieth-century and the overwhelming strangeness of India that has struck visitors throughout history.

Salaam Bombay (Mira Nair, 1988). A harrowing depiction of the fight for survival by Krishna, a 10-year-old boy, who is tutored by a prostitute and drug addict.

Sholay (Ramesh Sippy,1975). Arguably the best Bollywood film ever made, its contemporary cops and robbers story broke all box office records. A great conversation subject on long journeys.

Indian tourist offices

Ⓦ**www.incredibleindia.org**
Ⓦ**www.tourismofindia.com**
Australia Level 2 Piccadilly, 210 Pitt St, Sydney, NSW 2000 ☎02/9264 4855, Ⓕ02/9264 4860.

Canada 60 Bloor St W #1003, Toronto, Ontario M4W 3B8 ☎416/962-3787, Ⓕ416/962-6279.

New Zealand Contact the Sydney office or the embassy in Wellington.

UK 7 Cork St, London W1X 2AB 020/7437 3677, Ⓕ020/7494 1048.

US 1270 Ave of the Americas #1808, New York, NY 10020 ☎1-800-953-9399, Ⓕ212/582-3274; 3550 Wilshire Blvd, Room 204, Los Angeles, CA 90010 ☎213/380-8855, Ⓕ213/380-6111.

Indian embassies and consulates

Australia 3–5 Moonah Place, Yarralumla, Canberra, ACT 2600 ☎02/6273 3999, Ⓦwww.highcommissionofindiaaustralia.org. Consulates in Sydney ☎02/9223 9500, Ⓦwww.indianconsulatesydney.org;

Perth ☎08/9221 1485; and Melbourne ☎03/9384 0141.

Canada 10 Springfield Rd, Ottawa, Ontario K1M 1C9 ☎613/744-3751; ⓦwww.hciottawa.ca. Consulates in Toronto ☎416/960-0751, ⓦwww.cgitoronto.ca; and Vancouver ☎604/662-8811, ⓦwww.cgivancouver.com.ca.

Ireland 6 Leeson Park, Dublin 6 ☎1/4970 959, ⓕ1/4978 074.

New Zealand 180 Molesworth St, Wellington PO Box 4045 ☎04/473 6390.

UK India House, Aldwych, London WC2B 4NA ☎020/7836 8484, visa line ☎0900/188 0800, ⓦwww.hcilondon.org. Consulates in Birmingham ☎0121/212 2782; and Edinburgh ☎0131/229 2144.

US 2536 Massachusetts Ave NW, Washington, DC 20008 ☎202/939-9806, ⓦwww.indianembassy.org. Consulates in Chicago ☎312/595-0405, ⓦwww.indianconsulate.com; Houston ☎713/626-2355, ⓦwww.cgihouston.org; New York ☎212/774-0600, ⓦwww.indiacgny.org; and San Francisco ☎415/668-0662, ⓦwww.indiacgny.org.

Indonesia

Capital Jakarta
Population 200 million
Language Bahasa Indonesia is the national language, with an estimated five hundred or more local languages and dialects
Currency Rupiah (Rp)
Religion Predominantly Muslim, though animism is indigenous and widespread; there are also Buddhist, Hindu and Christian minorities
Climate Tropical throughout, with nominal wet and dry seasons
Best time to visit During the dry season (May–Oct for most of the country, but Nov–April in northern Sumatra and central and northern Maluku)
Minimum daily budget $10/£6

For scale and variety, Indonesia, the world's largest archipelago, is pretty much unbeatable. The fabulously varied scenery (from equatorial rainforest and volcanoes to idyllic white-sand beaches and desert terrain), the equally diverse flora and fauna, and the generally friendly and welcoming people make Indonesia one of Asia's most rewarding destinations. Given the country's sheer enormity, though, you must be selective – with too little time and too much travel your trip could turn into a miserable, stressful race between islands, looking at the clock and cursing all the way.

There's an immensely rich melange of peoples, religions and cultures across the archipelago, and the ancient monuments are some of the most dramatic sights of Indonesia. Within this one country it's possible to encounter Westernized city dwellers with mobile phones and plush apartments, as well as hunters armed with bows and arrows, clad in penis gourds and feathered head-dresses. Each ethnic group has its own artistic heritage, and their textiles, music, arts, crafts and dance add a rich cultural dimension to most visits to the islands.

Perhaps predictably, the problems of melding such diversity into one nation have resulted in violence and unrest. In recent years there have been civil disturbances, some lasting a couple of days, others long-running, in Maluku, Aceh, West Papua and Sulawesi. The 2002 and 2005 terrorist attacks on Bali further emphasized Indonesia's vulnerability to manmade disaster, while the Asian tsunami in December 2004, which destroyed whole swathes of Northern Sumatra, was only the most recent in a long history of natural catastrophes.

However, it is important not to overstate the risks of a visit. Given the vastness of the country, difficulties in one region often barely affect another a few hundred kilometres away. Before you travel, it's vital to get up-to-date information from newspapers and the official websites listed on p.420. It's also worth noting that travel through Muslim areas (this doesn't include Bali) during Ramadan, the traditional month of fasting, can be hard going as local people don't eat, drink or smoke during daylight hours.

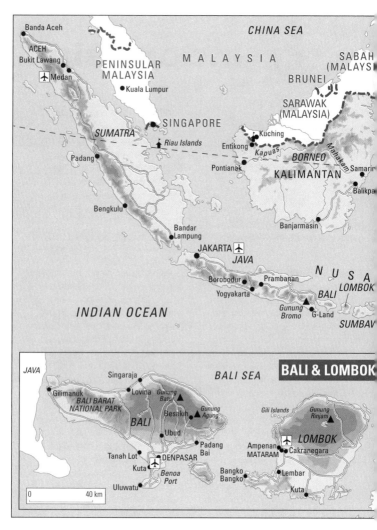

MALAYSIA · **CHINA SEA** · Banda Aceh · **ACEH** · Bukit Lawang · ✈ Medan · **PENINSULAR MALAYSIA** · **SUMATRA** · Kuala Lumpur · **SINGAPORE** · Riau Islands · Padang · Bengkulu · Bandar Lampung · **SABAH (MALAYS)** · **BRUNEI** · **SARAWAK (MALAYSIA)** · Kuching · Entikong · *Kapuas* · Pontianak · **BORNEO** · **KALIMANTAN** · *Mahakam* · Samarin · Balikpa · Banjarmasin · **JAKARTA** ✈ · **JAVA** · Borobodur · Prambanan · Yogyakarta · Gunung Bromo · **INDIAN OCEAN** · **N U S A** · **BALI** · **LOMBOK** · G-Land · **SUMBAV**

BALI & LOMBOK

JAVA · Singaraja · **BALI SEA** · Gilimanuk · Lovina · *Gunung Batur* · **BALI BARAT NATIONAL PARK** · Besakih · *Gunung Agung* · **BALI** · Ubud · Tanah Lot · **DENPASAR** · Kuta · Padang Bai · Benoa Port · Uluwatu · Gili Islands · *Gunung Rinjani* · Ampenan · **MATARAM** · Cakranegara · ✈ **LOMBOK** · Bangko Bangko · Lembar · Kuta

0 —————— 40 km

Main attractions

- **Bali** With its alluring mix of beaches, volcanoes, temples, stunning scenery and artistic and cultural wealth, the island has long been the jewel in the

Indonesian tourism crown. Bali is the enclave of a unique and colourful form of Hinduism, and of its thousands of temples Besakih, Tanah Lot and Uluwatu are the three most impressive. The festivals celebrated at all these shrines are a colourful and vibrant celebration of the devout traditional lifestyle that has

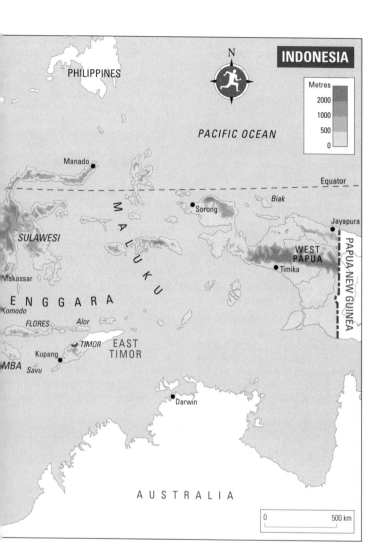

INDONESIA

PHILIPPINES

N

PACIFIC OCEAN

Manado

Equator

Biak

Sorong

Jayapura

SULAWESI

M
A
L
U
K
U

WEST
PAPUA

Timika

PAPUA-NEW GUINEA

Makassar

E N G G A R A

Komodo

FLORES   Alor

TIMOR   EAST
TIMOR

Kupang

MBA   Savu

Darwin

A U S T R A L I A

0   500 km

drawn tourists to the island for decades. Most visitors also go to the southern beach resorts that have developed around Kuta, a heady, hedonistic mix of hotels, shops, restaurants and nightlife, but there are plenty of quieter resorts around the coast, and a few secluded spots remain for total relaxation. Those interested in art, crafts, music and dance usually head for Ubud, a cool, laid-back town with galleries, studios, perform-ances and classes galore and plenty of local walks among the rice-terraces to engage the more energetic. The still-smoking Gunung Batur, in the volcanic centre of the island, is a popular climb, usually done in the pitch dark so as to arrive at the top in time to admire the glowing sunrise.

● **Gunung Bromo** The obligatory sunrise views of this mountain in east Java, with the peak and its equally stunning neighbours rising from an almost otherworldly sea of sand, are simply spellbinding. There are also plenty of walks to enjoy in this cool, attractive region.

● **Borobodur** Java's number-one tourist attraction, this colossal, multi-tiered temple is the world's largest Buddhist stupa. Over a thousand years old, the temple, though now ruined, is still surprisingly evocative, with over three thousand reliefs detailing scenes from everyday life and the path followed by the soul to enlightenment, along with ancient tales illustrating the journey.

● **Lake Toba** In northern Sumatra, this is Southeast Asia's largest freshwater lake. Its central island, Samosir, is the heartland of the Toba Batak people and offers great scenery, trekking and relaxation, with the option of visiting megalithic stone complexes, local villages and hot springs.

● **Orang-utans** The animals at the orang-utan rehabilitation centre at Bukit Lawang in Sumatra are arguably the most famous example of Indonesia's wildlife. The centre aims to reintroduce into the wild orang-utans that have been rescued from captivity; visitors here are welcome to watch the twice-daily feeding sessions.

● **Komodo Dragons** An apparent throwback to the age of dinosaurs, these creatures, actually the world's largest lizards, live on Komodo in Nusa Tenggara, the chain of islands stretching between Bali and West Papua. The largest ever recorded was more than 3m long and weighed in at 150kg, though most of the dragons aren't quite so enormous.

● **Diving** The highlight of many visits, Indonesia's marine life is startling in its diversity. Current centres for diving are Bali, the Gili islands off Lombok, and Sulawesi.

● **Tanah Toraja** This region of Sulawesi is home to the Torajan people, who have a wealth of traditional architecture and ceremonies, most famously

Mean temperatures (°C) and rainfall (mm)

Average daily temperatures (maximum and minimum °C) and monthly rainfall (mm)

	Jan	Feb	Mar	Apr	May	June	July	Aug	Sept	Oct	Nov	Dec
Jakarta (Java)												
max °C	29	29	30	31	31	31	31	31	31	31	30	29
min °C	23	23	23	24	24	23	23	23	23	23	23	23
rainfall mm	300	300	211	147	114	97	64	43	66	112	142	203
Makassar (Sulawesi)												
max °C	29	29	29	30	31	30	30	31	31	31	30	29
min °C	23	24	23	23	23	22	21	21	21	22	23	23
rainfall mm	686	536	424	150	89	74	36	10	15	43	178	610
Padang (Sumatra)												
max °C	31	31	31	31	31	31	31	31	30	30	30	30
min °C	23	23	23	24	24	23	23	23	23	23	23	23
rainfall mm	351	259	307	363	315	307	277	348	152	495	518	480

funerals. Also on offer are plenty of opportunities for trekking in the scenic highlands.

● **Yogyakarta** The city is the heartland of Javanese arts; exhibitions of art and batik, and performances of music, drama, puppetry and dance abound, with courses available for visitors. The Kraton, the old walled city, is well preserved for architecture buffs, and Yogyakarta is ideally placed for excursions into the surrounding countryside and – if it hasn't blown its lid recently – treks up Gunung Merapi, Indonesia's most volatile volcano.

Also recommended

● **Nusa Tenggara** The most westerly of this string of islands, Lombok, is a great antidote to its more developed neighbour, Bali. Its highlights include Gunung Rinjani, Indonesia's second highest mountain, with a huge crater lake; the tiny Gili Islands off its northwest coast; and the unspoilt southcoast beaches. The further east you go through Nusa Tenggara, the less tourist infrastructure there is, so the more time you'll need; highlights here include Sumba's unspoilt beaches and traditional *ikat* weaving and the three-coloured lake of Keli Mutu on Flores.

● **Baliem Valley in West Papua** It's time-consuming and expensive to get here, and to really explore the area you'll need to trek long distances and often sleep extremely rough. But the scenery is dramatic and splendid, and the tribes of the area are managing to retain an age-old lifestyle and culture, often despite considerable pressure from outsiders.

● **Surfing** G-Land off the south coast of Java and Desert Point off the southwest coast of Lombok at Bangko

Bangko are just two of many legendary Indonesian surf spots.

● **Staying in a longhouse** The indigenous Dyak peoples in the interior of Kalimantan have retained their traditional beliefs and ways of life to varying degrees. Their communal longhouse dwellings – long wooden structures raised on stilts – have survived and are being restored, and many welcome visitors.

● **The Prambanan temple complex** The Hindu temples here, accessed from Yogyakarta in Java, are soaring, intricately carved structures dating from the ninth century AD. Visits at dawn and dusk are especially atmospheric.

Festivals

February/March *Nyale*. Hundreds of thousands flock to the coasts in search of an aphrodisiac seaworm in this festival celebrated on the islands of Lombok, Sumba and Savu.

February/March *Sumba Pasola*. Occurring simultaneously with Nyale on the coast, the *pasola* features battles between hundreds of fabulously attired horsemen, and takes place to balance the sphere of the heavens and the sphere of the sea by the spilling of blood.

June–September *Torajan funerals*. Taking place over several days, funerals in Tanah Toraja in Suluwesi are accompanied by ceremonies, buffalo fights and sacrifices.

All year *Bali temple festivals*. Featuring gorgeously clad worshippers, offerings and gamelan music, temple festivals in Bali occur throughout the year.

All year *Bali cremations*. Ceremonial music, dance and the spectacular burning itself make this the most dramatic manifestation of religious observance on the island. Visitors are welcomed to these ceremonies as long as they observe cultural guidelines.

Routes in and out

There are 35 designated gateways for foreigners entering and leaving Indonesia. However the visa situation remains in a state of flux, and potential visitors should check the current situation prior to travel. Indonesia boasts a huge choice of international airports, the busiest of which are in Jakarta, Denpasar (on Bali) and Medan. There are fast and frequent passenger ferries from Malaysia and Singapore, mostly arriving in the Riau islands to the east of Sumatra; and an overland route from Malaysia into Kalimantan at Entikong.

Indonesia online

Bali Paradise Online – ⓦwww.bali -paradise.com Wide-ranging site covering everything from traditional architecture to nightlife recommendations. There's also a travellers' forum.

Forum Makassar Straits – ⓦwww .forumms.com Questions, messages, articles and photos about the coastal areas of South Sulawesi – picturesque and inspiring.

Inside Indonesia – ⓦwww.inside indonesia.org The online version of this topical magazine, published quarterly in Australia and detailing politics, government shortcomings and human rights and social issues across the country. A variety of articles are available online.

Jakarta Post – ⓦwww.thejakarta post.com This is the online version of the daily English-language newspaper that, despite its name, covers the entire country. It is superb for up-to-the-minute news, analysis and in-depth features and has a limited archive of previous articles.

The Orangutan Foundation – ⓦwww.orangutan.org This international organization is involved in the preservation of orang-utans and supports the work at Camp Leakey, a rehabilitation

△ Borobudur, Java

centre in Tanjung Puting National Park in Kalimantan. Their website is an excellent starting point for information on this remarkable creature and there are dozens of links to follow.

Books

Benedict Allen *Hunting the Gugu*. Beguiled by stories of black-maned ape men, Allen heads into the Sumatran Highlands with the aboriginal Kubu people in search of the creature itself.
Giles Milton *Nathaniel's Nutmeg*. The competition between England and Holland for control over the spice-producing islands of Southeast Asia in the sixteenth and seventeenth centuries is a tale of intrigue and high adventure.
Pramoedya Ananta Toer *All That is Gone*. A wonderful introduction to an Indonesian icon, this collection of eight short stories draw on the author's childhood in east Java. Later in life he was imprisoned by the Dutch, and then for fourteen years under Suharto. His 37 books and essays have been translated into 37 languages.
Simon Winchester *Krakatoa*. fine account of how and why the great volcano off the coast of Java erupted in 1883 and what happened afterwards.

Films

Arisan (Nia Dinata, 2004). An ensemble piece about a group of rich thirty-something Jakartans, including, rather bravely for Indonesia, two gay characters. The movie quickly dispels any idea that everyone in Indonesia is poor and needy.
Looking for Madonna (John De Rantau, 2004). A powerful mix of drama and documentary woven around HIV/AIDS in West Papua, which has the highest rates of these diseases in the country.

Pasir Berbisik (Whispering Sands; Nan T Achnas, 2001). One of the few female film directors working in Indonesia produced this dramatic film of death, destruction and violence, as a single mother and her teenage daughter flee across the desert in search of a new life.
The Year of Living Dangerously (Peter Weir, 1983). Adapted from a novel by Christopher Koch, this moody film focuses on a group of Western journalists and photographers in Indonesia to cover the upheavals of 1965, and superbly delineates the tensions and undercurrents in the country.

Indonesian tourist offices

Ⓦ**www.tourismindonesia.com**
Contact the information desk at the nearest embassy.

Indonesian embassies and consulates

Ⓦ**www.deplu.go.id**
Australia 8 Darwin Ave, Yarralumla, Canberra, ACT 2600 ℡02/6250 8600, Ⓦwww.kbri-canberra.org.au; 20 Harry Chan Ave, Darwin, NT 0801 ℡08/8941 0048; 72 Queen Rd, Melbourne, VIC 3004 ℡03/9525 2755, Ⓦwww.kjri -melbourne.org; 134 Adelaide Terrace, East Perth, WA 6004 ℡08/9221 5858, Ⓦwww.kri-perth.org.au; 236 Maroubra Rd, Maroubra, Sydney, NSW 2035 ℡02/9344 9933, Ⓦwww.kjri-sydney.org.
Canada 55 Parkdale Ave, Ottawa, Ontario K1Y 1E5 ℡613/724-1100, Ⓦwww.indonesia-ottawa.org; 129 Jarvis St, Toronto, Ontario M5C 2H6 ℡416/360-4020, Ⓦwww.indonesiatoronto .org; 1630 Alberni St, Vancouver, BC V6G 1A6 ℡604/682-8855, Ⓦwww .indonesiavancouver.org.
New Zealand 70 Glen Rd, Kelburn, Wellington ℡04/475 8697,

@www.indonesianembassy.org.nz; 2nd floor, Beca Carter Hollings Femer Ltd, 132 Vincent St, Auckland ℡09/308 0842.

UK and Ireland 38 Grosvenor Sq, London W1X 9AD (personal callers: 38 Adams Row, W1) ℡020/7499 7661, @www.indonesianembassy.org.uk. Recorded visa information ℡0906/550 8962.

US 2020 Massachusetts Ave NW, Washington, DC 20036 ℡202/775-5200, @www.embassyofindonesia.org; 72 E Randolph St, Chicago, IL 60601 ℡312/345-9300, @www.indonesia chicago.org; 10900 Richmond Ave, Houston, TX 77057 ℡713/785-1691; 3457 Wilshire Blvd, Los Angeles, CA 90010 ℡213/383-5126; 5 E 68th St, New York, NY 1002 ℡212/879-0600-15; 1111 Columbus Ave, San Francisco, CA 94133 ℡415/474-9571, @www .kjrisfo.org.

Japan

Capital Tokyo	**Climate** Temperate
Population 127 million	**Best time to go** March–May and
Language Japanese	September–November, with cherry
Currency Yen (¥)	blossom time (April) and maple leaf
Main religions Shintoism and	season (Nov) the most rewarding
Mahayana Buddhism	**Minimum daily budget** $65/£34

Lying east off continental Asia, across the Sea of Japan from Russia, China and Korea, the Japanese archipelago comprises over six thousand volcanic islands, though the bulk of the population lives on the main island of Honshu, which is linked by bridges and tunnels to the other three main islands of Hokkaido, Kyushu and Shikoku.

Many Westerners imagine this isolated island nation to be a cold-hearted country of futuristic machinery and an obsessive work ethic, but beneath the label-conscious, hi-tech veneer, Japan is still a very traditional society, with an absorbingly ancient culture to investigate, from Zen temples to fire festivals, and tea ceremonies to sumo wrestling matches. Some of the most arresting sights are the majestic Buddhist temples and the contrastingly kitsch Shinto shrines; the latter in particular are still an important focus of daily life, with devotees coming here to pray for everything from a new baby to respectable exam results. Twenty-first century Japan, meanwhile, provides the perfect contrast, full of sleek architecture, crazy fashions and intriguing technological innovations.

As the archipelago stretches over 3000km from north to south, running from the chilly end of the temperate zone to tropical Okinawa in the south,

there are varied and plentiful hiking opportunities – in Honshu's Japan Alps; in the mountains, gorges and lakes of the northern island of Hokkaido; and in the national parks on the southern island of Kyushu.

Foreign tourists are rare outside the main cultural centres, but are generally welcomed warmly. Language is a problem for visitors to Japan, but foreigners usually find they can make themselves understood without too much difficulty and there is an increasing number of signs in Roman script. Public transport is fast, efficient and extensive (this is after all, the home of the Bullet Train).

Despite all its attractions, very few budget travellers make it to Japan, for the simple reason that they can't afford it. The recent economic downturn has made accommodation and transport much cheaper for visiting Westerners, but the cost of living is still high compared with the rest of Asia, so for backpackers, one of the best ways to experience the country is to get an English-teaching job here for a few months (see p.242 for advice on this). Otherwise, buy a train pass, bring a tent and don't hang out in too many coffee shops or pinball parlours.

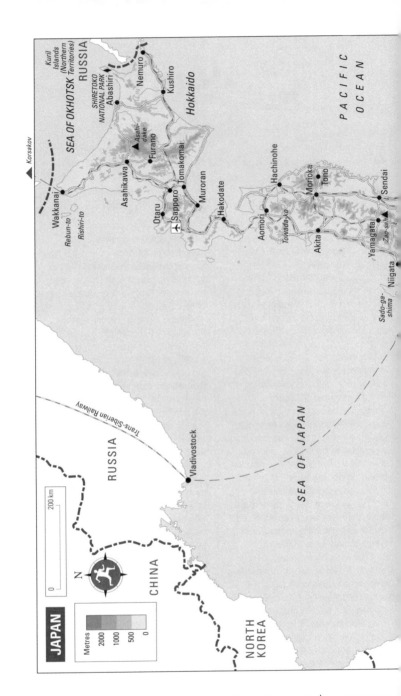

JAPAN

Metres
2000
1000
500
0

0   200 km

N

CHINA

NORTH
KOREA

RUSSIA

Trans-Siberian Railway

Vladivostock

SEA OF JAPAN

Sado-ga-
shima

Niigata

Yamagata

Zao-san

Akita

Aomori

Towada-ko

Sendai

Tono

Morioka

Hachinohe

Hakodate

Muroran

Sapporo

Otaru

Tomakomai

Asahikawa

Furano

Asahi-
dake

SHIRETOKO
NATIONAL PARK

Abashiri

Kushiro

Nemuro

Hokkaido

PACIFIC
OCEAN

SEA OF OKHOTSK

Korsakov

Kuril
Islands
(Northern
Territories)

RUSSIA

Wakkanai

Rebun-to

Rishiri-to

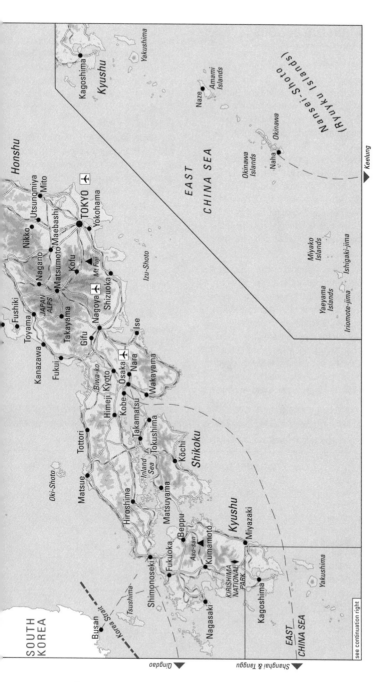

SOUTH
KOREA

Busan

Korea Strait

Tsushima-

Shimonoseki
Fukuoka
Nagasaki

Beppu
Asa-San
Kumamoto
KIRISHIMA
NATIONAL
PARK
Kagoshima

EAST
CHINA SEA

Yakushima

Matsuyama

Matsue

Oki-Shoto

Tottori

Hiroshima

Inland
Sea

Kochi

Shikoku

Takamatsu
Tokushima
Kobe
Himeji Kyoto
Osaka
Nara
Wakayama

Biwa-ko

Fukui
Gifu
Takayama

Kanazawa

JAPAN
ALPS

Toyama

Fushiki

Nagano
Matsumoto Maebashi
Nikko
Utsunomiya

Mt Fuji

Shizuoka
Nagoya
Ise

Izu-Shoto

TOKYO
Yokohama

Mito

Honshu

Kyushu
Kagoshima

Miyazaki

Kyushu

Yakushima

EAST
CHINA SEA

Naze
Amami
Islands

Okinawa Islands

Naha
Okinawa

Miyako
Islands

Yaeyama
Islands
Ishigaki-jima

Iriomote-jima

Nansei-Shoto
(Ryukyu Islands)

Keelung ▶

▶ Qingdao

▶ Shanghai & Tanggu

see continuation right

Main attractions

● **Kyoto** This historic former capital city should be at the top of every visitor's list. It has scores of breathtaking Buddhist temples, some of the country's finest Zen gardens, and lovely neighbourhoods of wooden homes and traditional tea houses. Don't miss the 1001 gilded statues of Buddha at Sanjusanngen-do temple, Ginkakuji's Temple of the Silver Pavilion, or the inspirational Ryoan-ji rock garden. The modern face of Kyoto is energetic and youthful, with good bars, clubs and restaurants, and there are invigorating hill walks within day-tripping distance.

● **Tokyo** Japan's modern-day capital lacks the refined aesthetic of Kyoto, or the tranquillity of Nara, but comes up trumps with its contemporary icons, like the forest of sci-fi skyscrapers that dominates the Shinjuku district, the ever-changing gadgets exhibited in the Sony Building and the hyper-trendy street fashions and boutiques of Harajuku. Historic highlights include the country's most venerated Shinto shrine, Meiji-jingu, and the impressive Senso-ji temple, while the old-style early-morning Tsukiji fish market makes a lively contrast with the shopping malls of super-chic Ginza, the latest gadgets on sale in Akihabara's "Electronics Town" and the cutting-edge clubs in Roppongi.

● **Hiroshima** Many visitors to Japan make a pilgrimage to Hiroshima's excellent Peace Memorial Museum, a balanced commemoration of the dropping of the atomic bomb here on August 6, 1945, and its horrific repercussions. The regenerated city has a breezy, upbeat atmosphere and is a pleasure to explore. Just a twenty-minute ferry ride away is the little island of Miyajima, site of one of Japan's most scenically located Shinto shrines.

● **Mount Fuji** Although the walk to the top of Japan's iconic snow-capped peak takes a gruelling six hours, thousands of people make it up to the 3776-metre summit every summer. Unfortunately, the tracks are always heaving with hikers, the mountainside is strewn with

Mean temperatures (°C) and rainfall (mm)

Average daily temperatures (maximum and minimum °C) and monthly rainfall (mm)

	Jan	Feb	Mar	Apr	May	June	July	Aug	Sept	Oct	Nov	Dec
Tokyo												
max °C	10	10	13	18	23	25	29	31	27	21	17	12
min °C	1	1	4	10	15	18	22	24	20	14	8	3
rainfall mm	110	155	228	254	244	305	254	203	279	228	162	96
Sapporo												
max °C	2	2	6	13	18	21	24	26	22	17	11	5
min °C	-10	-10	-7	-1	3	10	16	18	12	6	-1	-6
rainfall mm	25	43	61	84	102	160	188	155	160	147	56	38
Nagasaki												
max °C	9	10	14	19	23	26	29	31	27	22	17	12
min °C	2	2	5	10	14	18	23	23	20	14	9	4
rainfall mm	71	84	125	185	170	312	257	175	249	114	94	81

unattractive volcanic debris and, due to persistent haze, the views are rarely spectacular. A better way to appreciate Fuji-san is to climb nearby Mount Tenjo, which you can do in just 45 minutes, giving you the chance to admire Mount Fuji from a more interesting perspective. Or, more leisurely still, take a slow train ride through the surrounding Hakone region, an area of lakes and hot springs which also offers fine views of the sacred peak.

● **Himeji castle** With its five-tiered roofs, elegant proportions and chilly interiors, imposing Himeji castle looks much as it would have done when it housed the local lord and his samurai in the seventeenth century. Take the free guided tour to discover the castle's secret defences – like floors that were designed to creak and a labyrinthine network of corridors.

Also recommended

● **The Tono valley** For a glimpse of traditional life in rural Japan, hire a bike for a day's cycling here, visiting some of the restored eighteenth-century farmhouses and stopping in at one of the local folk museums.

● **Kenrokuen in the city of Kanazawa** Japanese gardens have inspired designers all over the world, and Kenrokuen, the country's top garden, is a classic composition of ponds, pine trees, contemplative vistas and graceful teahouses.

● **Nikko** Set in a huge forested park of mountains, lakes and waterfalls, this complex of elaborately carved and gaudily painted shrines and temples looks especially fantastical in the snow.

● **Nara** A popular side-trip from Kyoto, and also a former capital, Nara is dotted

with venerable temples and shrines, in particular the historic Todai-ji temple, housing a fifteen-metre-high bronze Buddha.

● **Hiking in Kirishima National Park** The southern island of Kyushu boasts the most dramatic volcanic scenery in the country, nowhere more so than in Kirishima National Park, which has 23 peaks within its boundaries. There are plenty of bracing mountain trails here, plus waterfalls, an impressive gorge and an outdoor hot spring.

● **Hokkaido** The northernmost of Japan's four main islands is also its wildest and least populated. The volcanic landscape is dotted with lakes and forests, which makes it perfect hiking country: Shiretoko National Park is especially rewarding, with five lakes linked by forest paths, plus natural hot springs and challenging trails.

● **A night in a ryokan** These traditional inns are like a genuine step backwards in time; the rooms have *tatami* mat floors, sumptuous futons, sliding paper doors and views onto traditional Japanese gardens. Everyone pads around in their socks, and you can often ask to have dinner served on low tables in your room.

● **A session at the onsen** Bathing in outdoor hot springs is a big thing in Japan and there are many lovely spots to enjoy some communal soaking, including popular Beppu on the southern island of Kyushu.

Festivals

February 5–11 *Yuki Matsuri* (*Snow Festival*), Sapporo. The snow sculpture competition is the highlight of this genuinely winter-wonderland event, with hundreds of extraordinary carvings of life-sized buildings and figurines made from snow and ice.

March–May *Cherry blossom viewing.*
When the cherry trees flower there are
blossom-viewing parties under the trees
in every park across the country and a
nightly cherry-blossom forecast on the
TV shows how far the pink wave has
progressed up the country.

July 16–17 *Gion Matsuri*, Kyoto. Japan's
cultural capital celebrates with a grand
pageant of 32 sumptuously decorated
six-metre-high shrines which are pulled
through the streets by men dressed in
traditional costumes.

August *Kodo Drummers' Earth
Celebration*, Sado-ga-shima Island. The
world music and dance event held over
three days every August makes the
perfect excuse to visit this remote island,
home to the famous drumming troupe,
whose muscular performances at their
colossal *taiko* drums are an amazing
spectacle that's well worth catching.

Routes in and out

Japan's main international airports are
in the Tokyo and Osaka areas, the latter convenient for Kyoto, and there are
smaller international airports in Nagoya
and Sapporo. You can also arrive and
depart by sea, with boats from Busan in
South Korea to Fukuoka (Kyushu) and
Shimonoseki (Honshu); and from China
there are ferry services from Shanghai to
Osaka/Kobe, from Tanggu near Tiangin to
Kobe, and from Qingdao to Shimonoseki.
There are also ferries from Keelung in
Taiwan to Okinawa (Japan's southernmost
island); from Vladivostok (the terminus of
the Trans-Siberian rail line in Russia; see
p.169) to Fushiki, near Toyama; and from
the Russian port of Korsakov to Wakkanai
(northern Hokkaido; July–Sept only).
Consult the Japan National Tourist Office
website (Ⓦ www.seejapan.co.uk/transport/
sea/international.html) for a comprehensive rundown of timetables and operators.

Japan online

Jan Dodd's Japan – Ⓦ **www.jandodd
.com/japan** The co-author of *The
Rough Guide to Japan* spills the beans
on her favourite destinations, supplies an
exhaustive collection of links and reviews
Japan-related books and films.
Japan Guide – Ⓦ **www.japan-guide
.com** Amazingly detailed coverage of

△ Otorii Gate, Miyajima Island

sights, culture and shopping, plus hostel-booking and a forum.

Outdoor Japan – Ⓦwww.outdoor japan.com Everything from cycling routes to wakeboarding outfits is covered on this comprehensive site to outdoor activities in Japan.

Randy Johnson's Japan Page – Ⓦwww.ease.com/~randyj/japan .htm Extensive homepage with an especially good section on getaways in rural Japan, complete with descriptions, accommodation ideas and directions. Also interesting stuff on sushi and art, plus decent links.

Teaching English in Japan – Ⓦwww .wizweb.com/~susan/japan Useful resource that covers many aspects of teaching in Japan, from finding a job to living in the country. Aimed at Americans, but applies equally to other nationalities.

Books

Shoichi Aoki *Fresh Fruits*. Teen streetfashion portraits from the famously creative and style-conscious streets of Harajuku in Tokyo, culled from the cult Japanese fanzine of the same name.

Alan Booth *The Roads to Sata: A 2000-mile Walk Through Japan*. The classic travel book on Japan, written with humour, affection and occasional irritation by a long-time resident who literally walked the length of the country.

Will Ferguson *Hokkaido Highway Blues*. The opinionated Canadian English teacher author proves to be good company as we follow him on his journey across Japan, hitchhiking from the southern tip of Kyushu to northern Hokkaido in the wake of the cherry blossom wave.

Haruki Murakami *The Wind-up Bird Chronicle*. The most famous of the novels written by Japan's best known contemporary novelist follows an

increasingly disoriented modern-day Japanese Everyman through a bizarre chain of mysterious encounters.

Mark Schilling *The Encyclopedia of Japanese Pop Culture*. All the famous late twentieth-century innovations are here, from instant noodles to manga characters.

Films

Akira (Katushiro Otomo, 1988). Groundbreakingly slick – and gory – animé based on a hugely popular manga series, involving delinquent biker boys, supernatural powers and corrupt powermongers fighting it out in post-World War III neo-Tokyo.

Lost in Translation (Sophia Coppola, 2004). Despite the sleek, energetic scenes of downtown Tokyo this moderately interesting tale of alienation and dislocation is depressingly thick with Japan clichés.

Rashomon (Akira Kurosawa, 1950). Akira Kurosawa's classic and hugely influential drama in which a rape and a murder are described from the four protagonists' different points of view.

Sonatine (Takeshi Kitano, 1993). Often labelled the Japanese Tarantino, cult director Takeshi Kitano here uses his trademark blend of extreme violence and off-beat comedy to tell the story of a gangster who flees to Okinawa.

Tokyo Story (Ozu Yasujiro, 1954). This slow, rather mournful meditation on changing values in modern Japan follows an elderly couple as they pay an extended visit to their grown-up children in Tokyo.

Japanese tourist offices

Ⓦwww.jnto.go.jp
Australia and New Zealand Level 18, Australia Square Tower, 264 George St,

Sydney, NSW ☎02/9251 3024, 🌐www
.jnto.go.jp/syd/index.html.
Canada 165 University Ave, Toronto,
Ontario M5H 3B8 ☎416/366-7140.
UK and Ireland Heathcote House,
20 Savile Row, London W1S 3PR
☎020/7734 9638, 🌐www.seejapan
.co.uk.
US 🌐www.japantravelinfo.com. 1
Daniel Burnham Court, Suite 250C, San
Francisco, CA 94109 ☎415/292-5686;
515 South Figueroa St, Suite 1470, Los
Angeles, CA 90071 ☎213/623-1952;
One Rockefeller Plaza #1250, New York,
NY 10020 ☎212/757-5640.

Japanese embassies and consulates

Australia 112 Empire Circuit, Yarralumla,
Canberra, ACT 2600 ☎02/6273
3244,🌐www.japan.org.au. Consulates
in Brisbane ☎07/3221 5188, 🌐www
.brisbane.au.emb-japan.go.jp; Melbourne
☎03/9639 3244, 🌐www.melbourne
.au.emb-japan.go.jp; Perth ☎08/9480
1800, 🌐www.perth.au.emb-japan.go.jp;
and Sydney ☎02/9223 4027, 🌐www
.sydney.au.emb-japan.go.jp.
Canada 255 Sussex Drive, Ottawa,
Ontario K1N 9E6 ☎613/241-8541,

🌐www.ca.emb-japan.go.jp. Consulates
in Calgary ☎403/294-0782, 🌐www
.calgary.ca.emb-japan.go.jp; Montreal
☎514/866-3429, 🌐www.montreal
.ca.emb-japan.go.jp; Toronto ☎416/363-
7038, 🌐www.toronto.ca.emb-japan
.go.jp; and Vancouver ☎604/684-5868,
🌐www.vancouver.ca.emb-japan.go.jp.
Ireland Nutley Building, Merrion Centre,
Nutley Lane, Dublin 4 ☎01/202 8300,
🌐www.ie.emb-japan.go.jp.
New Zealand Level 18, Majestic
Centre, 100 Willis St, Wellington 1
☎04/473-1540, 🌐www.nz.emb-japan.
go.jp. Consulates in Auckland ☎09/303-
4106, 🌐www.nz.emb-japan.go.jp/auck-
land; and Christchurch ☎03/366-5680,
🌐www.nz.emb-japan.go.jp/christchurch.
UK 101 Piccadilly, London W1V 9FN
☎020/7465 6500, 🌐www.uk
.emb-japan.go.jp. Consulate in
Edinburgh ☎0131/225 4777, 🌐www
.edinburgh.uk.emb-japan.go.jp.
US 2520 Massachusetts Ave NW,
Washington, DC 20008 ☎202/238-
6700, 🌐www.us.emb-japan.go.jp.
Consulates in Chicago ☎312/280-0400,
🌐www.chicago.us.emb-japan.go.jp; Los
Angeles ☎213/617-6700, 🌐www.la.us
.emb-japan.go.jp; New York ☎212/371-
8222, 🌐www.cgj.org; and San Francisco
☎415/777-3533, 🌐www.cgjsf.org.

Laos

Capital Vientiane	**Main religion** Theravada Buddhism
Population 6 million	**Climate** Tropical
Language Lao	**Best time to go** November–March
Currency Kip (K)	**Minimum daily budget** $10/£5

Laos is the most traditional corner of Southeast Asia, much less well known to the outside world than neighbouring Thailand and Vietnam. Though ruled by France as part of its Indochinese empire for the first half of the twentieth century, and then fatefully embroiled in the American-Vietnam War of the 1960s and 70s, Laos faded from view between 1975 and 1989 when a revolutionary communist government took over, forbidding contact with the outside world and imposing dogmatic political and economic reforms. Great hardship ensued and, despite recent liberalization, Laos continues to be much poorer and less developed than other Southeast Asian nations.

For visitors, however, the old-fashioned lifestyles and traditional rural ways of the Lao people hold great appeal, not least because tourism is still in its infancy. There are few tourist facilities outside the two main cities of Vientiane and Louang Phabang, and with no beaches and few historical gems to write home about, it's not everyone's idea of a great holiday destination. But those who do make it here rave about the dramatic river landscapes, the easy-going, unhurried pace of daily life, and the chance to experience a culture that's still relatively unchanged by the tourist industry. If you do venture out into the sticks, you'll need to learn some Lao phrases, but you can get by in English in the main towns.

Because it has borders with Thailand, Vietnam and China, Laos works well as part of a leisurely overland trip. Indeed, journeys in Laos generally have to be leisurely, because public transport is frustratingly slow. Travelling in Laos is hard, not least because of the buttock-crunchingly potholed roads; worse still, bandits render some roads too dangerous for tourists to use. Many visitors stick to the rivers – a more scenic, though not always more comfortable, way of getting between towns. Unfortunately, the domestic airlines are not the answer either, as they have a poor safety record on many routes, and run to an erratic schedule.

Many areas of Laos were very heavily bombed during the American-Vietnam War and, away from the main tourist areas, there is a real danger of stepping on unexploded ordnance and land mines. Always stick to well-trodden paths, and pay attention to warning signs. Anti-government groups of ethnic Hmong tribespeople occasionally set off bombs in Vientiane and have also targeted other places including the Friendship Bridge into Thailand so you should check the current security situation with government travel advisories (see p.420) and travellers' forums on the Internet (see p.249).

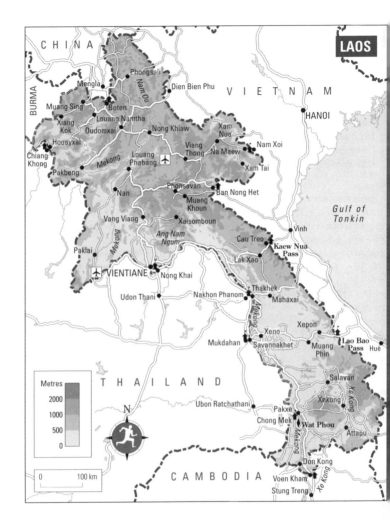

LAOS

Main
attractions

- **Louang Phabang** The former Lao
capital is the most elegant and attractive
city in the country, an almost village-like
place whose riverbanks and cobble-
stoned lanes are lined with the graceful
gilded spires of dozens of Buddhist

temples. Other highlights include the
Royal Palace Museum, which was home
to the Lao royal family right up until their
exile in 1975; the markets; and the view
of the city from the north bank of the
Mekong river. The city is stacked full of
guesthouses, and there are waterfalls
and caves within day-tripping distance.

- **The slow boat down the Mekong
from Houayxai to Louang Phabang**

Average daily temperatures (maximum and minimum °C) and monthly rainfall (mm)

	Jan	Feb	Mar	Apr	May	June	July	Aug	Sept	Oct	Nov	Dec
Vientiane												
max °C	28	30	33	34	32	32	31	31	31	31	29	28
min °C	14	17	19	23	23	24	24	24	24	21	18	16
rainfall mm	5	15	38	99	267	302	267	292	302	109	15	3
Louang Phabang												
max °C	28	32	34	36	35	34	32	32	33	32	29	27
min °C	13	14	17	21	23	23	23	23	23	21	18	15
rainfall mm	15	18	31	109	163	155	231	300	165	79	31	13

Despite the obvious drawbacks – the trip takes two days and the boats are designed to carry cargo, not passengers – this continues to be one of the most popular journeys in Laos, chiefly because of the fine river scenery and glimpses of traditional rural Southeast Asian life, and because Houayxai is a designated border crossing point with Thailand.

● **Vientiane** The Lao capital is surprisingly gentle and, though lacking sights, gives a pleasant introduction to the country. Make the most of its eateries, as the city serves the best food in the country – its bakeries, fruit-juice bars, Lao, Thai and Indian restaurants are a world away from those in other parts of Laos.

● **The ruins of Wat Phou** This seventh-century temple, built by the ancient Khmers in similar style to their temples at Angkor in Cambodia, sits in a gloriously lush river valley near Pakxe, surrounded by forested mountain peaks. It's an atmospheric place, with many of the sculptures and walls half-buried, but also plenty of intact Hindu and Buddhist carvings.

● **Muang Sing** This remote little northwest town is mainly of interest for its population of hill tribespeople, who trade at the now rather overtouristed morning market and whose nearby villages are a major highlight of the burgeoning local trekking industry. There are plenty of guesthouses catering for the growing number of backpackers who visit, though the authorities have clamped down hard on the availability of opium, which is grown and smoked by local tribespeople and used to be the big draw.

● **The Plain of Jars** Drawing its name from the hundreds of mysterious two-thousand-year-old stone funerary urns that lie scattered across the uplands of Xieng Khuang, the Plain of Jars is best appreciated from the air. Flying in from Vientiane gives you a gripping view of the plain's dramatic karst scenery and some of the most scarred landscape in Laos – the result of relentless bombing, mostly by the Americans, in the 1964–73 war. Ground-level tours across the plain leave from nearby Phonsavan, but the history of the jars is more interesting than the urns themselves – if time is tight, it's not really worth making a special effort to get here.

Also recommended

● **Vang Viang** Set in a spectacular landscape of limestone karst, this laid-back little riverside town is a backpackers' haven. Not far from Vientiane, it offers good-value guesthouses, interesting caves nearby and the chance to soak up the scenery while floating downriver in a huge inner tube.

- **Don Khong** Traditional village life on this tiny island (part of the Si Phan Don island group) in the Mekong River has remained almost unchanged for hundreds of years. There are only two main settlements and hardly any traffic, so renting a bicycle for the twenty-kilometre circuit is the best way to apppreciate the scenery of ricefields, bamboo forests and wooden homes. You can also take trips out into the Mekong to see the famous freshwater dolphins.

- **Attapu** Spend a night or two in this remote southern "garden city", where coconut palms and banana trees shade spacious wooden houses with capacious balconies, high on stilts. The journey there, along the scenic Xe Kong River, is a gem.

- **Herbal sauna and traditional massage** Sweat out all your impurities at the Buddhist monastery of Wat Sok Pa Louang in Vientiane. In between

sessions, you can sip restorative teas brewed from carambola, tamarind, eucalyptus and citrus leaves.

Festivals

April 13–16 *Pi Mai Lao* (Lao New Year). As in Thailand and Cambodia, the new year is heralded with water fights in the street and much public splashing. In Louang Phabang there's a huge parade through towns and pagodas made of sand are built in temple grounds.
October *Lai Heua Fai* (Festival of Lights). Nationwide, communities decorate floats with lights and then float them on the nearest body of water to mark the end of the rainy season; it's especially pretty in Louang Phabang where each neighbourhood takes their float down to the Mekong and a fleet of boats parades them down the river.

Routes in and out

Most international flights arrive in Vientiane, via Bangkok, though it's also possible to fly to Louang Phabang from the northern Thai city of Chiang Mai.

△ Vang Viang

Vientiane also has international connections with Kunming, Phnom Penh, Siem Reap, Hanoi and Ho Chi Minh City. Many travellers arrive overland from Thailand, most commonly at the Nong Khai/Vientiane crossing. There are four other land crossings from Thailand; four from Vietnam; one from Cambodia at Voen Kham, near Don Khong (though this is not officially open, travellers reportedly use it without incident); and one from China at Boten (near Louang Namtha). Pay close attention to visa requirements, which differ at every entry point.

Laos online

The Boat Landing – Ⓦ**www.theboat landing.laopdr.com** This Louang Namtha guesthouse website is much more than a puff for their accommodation. Loads of useful info, including on overland travel into China, regional attractions and Louang Phabang boat journeys. Excellent links.
Internet Travel Guide – Ⓦ**www .Pmgeiser.ch/laos** A general introduction to the country, plus pages on sights, visas and transport options.
Lao Connection – Ⓦ**laoconnection .com** Wide-ranging and frequently updated Lao-operated site with lots of useful background, advice and links on Lao life, culture and travel.
The Vientiane Times – Ⓦ**www .vientianetimes.com** The online version of Laos's only English-language newspaper features headline stories as well as masses of links.
Visit Laos – Ⓦ**www.visit-laos.com** General Laos travel site, with handy planning advice, a roundup of destination highlights, travelogues and links.

Books

Natacha Du Pont De Bie *Ant Egg Soup: The Adventures of a Food Tourist in Laos*. Is deep-fried cricket really all that bad, and how should one respond to the offer of a cup of fresh turkey blood? These and many other pressing foodie questions are answered in this funny, original tour of Laos and its cuisine.
Christopher Kremmer *Stalking the Elephant Kings: In Search of Laos*. One of very few relatively recent travelogues about Laos, this one sees the author traipsing round the country in the 1990s looking for information about the Lao royal family, missing since the 1975 communist takeover, and testing the current political temperature.
Norman Lewis *A Dragon Apparent: Travels in Cambodia, Laos and Vietnam*. An elegant portrait of Laos in the 1950s from a veteran travel writer of the old school.
Christopher Robbins *The Ravens: Pilots of the Secret War of Laos*. A British journalist tells the explosive story of America's clandestine campaign in Laos during the American-Vietnam War, based on interviews with the American pilots involved.

Lao tourist offices

No overseas tourist office.

Lao embassies and consulates

Australia and New Zealand 1 Dalman Crescent, O'Malley, Canberra ACT 2606 Ⓣ02/6286 4595, Ⓔclao1@cyberone .com.au.
UK and Ireland Contact the embassy in France: 74 Ave Raymond Poincaré, Paris 75116 Ⓣ01/45 53 02 98, Ⓔambalaoparis@wanadoo.fr.
US and Canada 2222 S Street, NW, Washington DC 20008 Ⓣ202/332-6416, Ⓦwww.laoembassy.com.

Malaysia

Capital Kuala Lumpur
Population 23 million
Language Malay
Currency Ringgit (RM), aka
Malaysian dollar (M$)
Main religion Islam, with significant

Buddhist, Hindu and Christian
minorities
Climate Tropical
Best time to go March–July (Dec–
Feb for peninsular west coast)
Minimum daily budget US$15/£8

The history of Malaysia is dominated by a succession of Portuguese, Dutch and British colonists, which means that the country's major sights tend to be rather low-key and quaintly European. Instead, the real interest comes from contemporary Malaysia's remarkably heterogeneous population, half of whom are Malays (whose culture originated in Indonesian Sumatra), a third ethnic Chinese, a tenth Indians (from the subcontinent) and seven percent indigenous tribal people. This dynamic mix gives great energy to the stuff of everyday life in Malaysia, with

huge variety in everything from food to festivals, places of worship to dress.

An ideal destination for first-time over-landers, Peninsular Malaysia has good transport connections with neighbouring Thailand, Singapore and Sumatra, and a well-developed tourist infrastructure. English is widely spoken, local transport is efficient, and the standard of living is among the highest in Southeast Asia. The peninsula's coast is graced with some of the most idyllic white-sand beaches in the region and plenty of rewarding offshore reefs; inland, chunks of jungle are accessible to hikers via well-maintained national-park trails and animal hides.

Six hundred kilometres east across the South China Sea from the peninsula, the East Malaysian states of Sarawak and Sabah offer a more adventurous – and more expensive – experience. They share the huge, thickly forested island of Borneo with Indonesia's Kalimantan province and the tiny sultanate of Brunei, and are only accessible from Peninsular Malaysia by plane. Once there, travel into the interior is mainly by river, particularly if you want to visit the longhouses – traditional communal homes – of the tribal peoples, which usually stand in a remote jungle clearing beside the riverbank. Staying in a longhouse is a highlight of trips to East Malaysia, as are jungle hikes. Most travellers to Sabah also attempt to climb the fearsomely high Gunung Kinabalu.

Main attractions

- **The beaches** Peninsular Malaysia's beaches compare well with those found in southern Thailand. The biggest, most

developed resorts are on the beautiful islands of Pulau Langkawi and Pulau Tioman, but backpackers generally prefer the cheaper, more chilled-out Perhentian Islands, which are also great for snorkelling; the bay at Cherating, where you stay in village-style huts on stilts; and the tiny Pulau Kapas. Your best bet for a beach break from the capital is Pulau Pangkor, a six-hour journey from KL.

- **Taman Negara National Park** The peninsula's biggest and most popular national park offers something for most outdoor enthusiasts. There's a spectacular canopy walkway through the tree tops, and plenty of day-hikes on well-marked trails. You could spend a night in a hide trying to spot elephants and leopards, or opt to do the guided nine-day trek through the park to the summit of 2187-metre-high Gunung Tahan, the peninsula's highest peak.

- **The Cameron Highlands** Tea plantations, colonial residences and, above all, the chance to cool down draw scores of travellers to the hill station here. The rolling green fields are dotted with farms and country cottages, and there are plenty of gentle walking trails through this rather quaint pastoral idyll.

- **Kuala Lumpur** There's nothing particularly appealing about the shrub-lined boulevards and rather bland malls of the Malaysian capital, Kuala Lumpur, though you'll probably find yourself passing through at some point. The variety of architectural styles, however, is intriguing – from the traditional elegance of the Masjid Jamek mosque and its ultra modern counterpart Masjid Negara through to the extraordinary Anglo-Indian Railway Station and the gleamingly hi-tech 88-storey Petronas Towers, one of the tallest buildings in the world. Shopping is pretty good, too, especially at the

handicraft stalls crowded into the covered Art Deco-style Central Market and in the fashion boutiques and electronic emporia of the Golden Triangle. At the Forest Institute of Malaysia, on the outskirts of the city, you can stroll through the tree tops on a Taman-Negara-style walkway that gives you elevated views of the skyscrapered skyline.

- **Georgetown** Despite being Malaysia's second largest city, this former British trading post on the island of Penang still exudes great historical charm. The elegant old European-style churches, forts and warehouses contrast appealingly with the atmospheric traditional shuttered shophouses, temples and markets of the local Chinese community. And within easy reach of the city there's an impressive rope-and-wire canopy walkway through the treetops, bringing you close to monkeys, hornbills and clouds of butterflies.

- **Sarawak** Sarawak's most outstanding attractions are its river systems and the chance to travel by longboat along these jungle waterways, staying in tribal longhouses along the way. Gunung Mulu National Park conserves a dramatic landscape of limestone pinnacles and the largest limestone cave system in the world, with heaps of hiking and climbing potential, while the Bario Loop is a challenging five-day trek through the thick jungle of the Kelabit tribal highlands near the Kalimantan border. The state capital, Kuching, is an appealing old waterside colonial outpost with excellent ethnographic collections at its Sarawak Museum.

- **Sabah** At 4101m, Gunung Kinabalu, in Kinabalu National Park, is Sabah's biggest draw; its summit is accessible to any reasonably fit hiker willing to undertake the day-and-a-half's climb up. Sabah's other highlights are the Sepilok Orang-Utan Rehabilitation Centre, where

Mean temperatures (°C) and rainfall (mm)

Average daily temperatures (maximum and minimum °C) and monthly rainfall (mm)

	Jan	Feb	Mar	Apr	May	June	July	Aug	Sept	Oct	Nov	Dec
Kuala Lumpur												
max °C	32	33	33	33	33	32	32	32	32	32	31	31
min °C	22	22	23	23	23	23	23	23	23	23	23	23
rainfall mm	159	154	223	276	182	119	120	133	173	258	263	223
Mersing												
max °C	28	29	30	31	32	31	31	31	31	31	29	28
min °C	23	23	23	23	23	23	22	22	22	23	23	23
rainfall mm	319	153	141	120	149	145	170	173	177	207	359	635
Kuching												
max °C	30	30	31	32	33	33	32	33	32	32	31	31
min °C	23	23	23	23	23	23	23	23	23	23	23	23
rainfall mm	683	522	339	286	253	199	199	211	271	326	343	465
Kota Kinabalu												
max °C	30	30	31	32	32	31	31	31	31	31	31	31
min °C	23	23	23	24	24	24	24	24	23	23	23	23
rainfall mm	133	63	71	124	218	311	277	256	314	334	296	241

you can watch the baby orang-utans learning to swing and swagger, the forests around the Kinabatangan river, famous for their proboscis monkeys, and the chance to shoot the rapids on the Sungei Padas, near Beaufort.

● **Diving and snorkelling off Pulau Sipadan** Exceptionally rich reefs and marine life grace the waters around this island off eastern Sabah, where highlights include fabulous shore diving, underwater caves, barracudas, white-tip sharks and masses of turtles.

Also recommended

● **Riding the jungle railway** If you have plenty of time, it's worth travelling the entire length of this fourteen-hour route, which starts in Gemas, near Melaka, and meanders through the mountainous landscapes of the peninsula's scenic jungle interior all the way up to Kota Bharu. But most people break the journey at Jerantut, which is three hours from Gemas and convenient for Taman Negara National Park.

● **Melaka** This cosmopolitan old port town wears its history on its sleeve, with self-consciously prettified churches and town squares from its days under Portuguese and then Dutch colonial rule. More interesting, for Western visitors at least, are the 300-year-old ancestral homes and temples of the Peranakan, the name given to the descendants of the Chinese merchants who settled here and married local Malay women. The finest Peranakan homes were lavishly furnished with the most exquisite artefacts from China, Europe and Malaysia; some are still inhabited by family members and open for the public to visit. Peranakan culture continues to thrive on the peninsula, and Melaka is a great place to sample Peranakan cuisine, known for its distinctive blending of sour sauces and coconut milk.

- **Turtle-watching at Rantau Abang** Every year, from May through to September, a few giant four-hundred-kilogram leatherback turtles lumber ashore here, the east-coast beach where they themselves were born, to lay their eggs. Leatherbacks are an endangered species now, so the whole event is supervised by national park rangers, but it's such a fine sight that local guesthouse managers wake up tourists in the middle of the night as soon as a turtle's been spotted in the area.

- **Kota Bharu** Located close to the Thai border, this small town is renowned for its cultural traditions and makes an interesting place to watch shadow-pup-

pet plays and traditional sports like top-spinning. The town's night market is one of the best in the country, serving everything from freshly barbecued chicken in coconut sauce to fried purple rice and sugar-cane juice.

Festivals

January or February *Thaipusam*, Batu Caves, Kuala Lumpur. Devout Hindus do penance for past sins by parading to the Batu Caves with skewers and other spiked objects hooked through their flesh.

January or February *Chinese New Year*. Across Malaysia, Chinese communities welcome in their new year with parades of lion dances, street performances of Chinese opera and special food.

June *Gawai Dayak* (Harvest Festival), Sarawak. The Iban people celebrate the end of the rice harvest with rowdy

△ The nineteenth-century Sultan Abdul Samad building, Kuala Lumpur

parties and excessive drinking at their open-to-all longhouses.

October or November *Kota Belud Tamu Besar*, Kota Belud, Sabah. The huge annual version of the weekly market draws big crowds of tribespeople from across the region and is a good chance to buy handicrafts and catch cultural performances.

Routes in and out

Malaysia's main international airport is near Kuala Lumpur, but some travellers fly in or out of Singapore, which is a short bus ride from the southern Malaysian city of Johor Bahru. Penang airport runs planes to and from Thailand and Indonesia. Peninsular Malaysia has several land border crossings with Thailand, with buses and trains connecting the cities and tourist spots of the two countries. There are good boat connections between west-coast Peninsular Malaysia and the Indonesian island of Sumatra, as well as a service between Sandakan, in Sabah, and Zamboanga in the southern Philippines. Most people fly to Sabah and Sarawak from Kuala Lumpur or Singapore, but you can also cross overland from Brunei and Indonesian Kalimantan.

Malaysia online

Interknowledge: Malaysia – Ⓦ**www .interknowledge.com/Malaysia** The New York Malaysian tourist board offers an in-depth look at many interesting aspects of the country, including life in a longhouse, the Malaysian cultural mix, and overnighting in Taman Negara.

Sabah Tourism – Ⓦ**sabahtourism .com** The official Sabah tourism website features info on upcoming festivals, diving and trekking destinations, info on climbing Mount Kinabalu, plus general travel tips and links.

Sarawak Tourism – Ⓦ**www.sarawak tourism.com** Includes especially good pages on Sarawak's national parks.

The Star – Ⓦ**www.thestar.com.my** Find out what's happening in Malaysia with the online version of one of Malaysia's English-language dailies.

Wild Asia – Ⓦ**www.wildasia.net** Although it covers nature conservation and responsible tourism across the whole of Southeast Asia, this site is particularly strong on Malaysia. It includes feature articles, short guides to wilderness areas of Malaysia, and tips on eco-friendly accommodation.

Books

Lloyd Fernando *Green is the Colour*. One of Malaysia's most famous novelists explores the social and political issues that led to the Kuala Lumpur race riots in 1969.

CS Godshalk *Kalimantaan*. A gripping, sweeping novel about ambitious, empire-building British colonials in tribal, nineteenth-century Borneo that painstakingly re-creates the world of James Brooke, the first White Rajah of Sarawak.

KS Maniam *The Return*. A wry, incisive novel about the immigrant experience in Peninsular Malaysia in the years before and after Independence in 1957, in which a young Tamil man returns to Malaysia after studying abroad.

Redmond O'Hanlon *Into the Heart of Borneo*. The hilarious true story of two erudite, but not terribly fit, Englishmen as they search the impenetrable Borneo jungle for the elusive two-horned rhinoceros. There's a memorable passage on a typical Dyak party (involving much drunkenness and buffoonery) and off-puttingly graphic descriptions of leeches, Dyak cuisine and jungle trekking.

Film

Entrapment (Jon Amiel, 1999). Hi-tech pre-Millennium bank-heist caper starring Catherine Zeta Jones, Sean Connery – and Kuala Lumpur, where much of the action takes place, leaving room for plenty of glamorous shots of the slinky Petronas Towers.

Return to Paradise (Joseph Ruben, 1998). Three young Americans party together in Malaysia and then go their separate ways. One stays on to do some conservation work with orang-utans but gets busted for the group's stash of recreational hash and ends up on Death Row. Will the other two acknowledge their responsibility and return to paradise to face the music, share the jail term and get him off Death Row?

Malaysian tourist offices

Ⓦwww.tourism.gov.my
Australia and New Zealand
Level 2, 171 Clarence Street NSW 2000 Ⓣ02/9299-4441, Ⓔmtpb
.sydney@tourism.gov.my; 56 William St, Perth, WA 6000 Ⓣ09/481-0400, Ⓔmtpb.perth@tourism.gov.
Canada 1590-1111, West Georgia St,

Vancouver, BC V6E 4M3, Ⓣ604/689-8899, Ⓦwww.malaysiatourism.ca.
UK and Ireland 57 Trafalgar Square, London WC2N 5DU Ⓣ020/7930 7932, Ⓦwww.malaysiatrulyasia.co.uk.
US Ⓦwww.interknowledge.com /malaysia. 818 West 7th St Suite 970, Los Angeles, CA 90017 Ⓣ213/689-9702; 120 East 56th St, Suite 810, New York, NY 10022 Ⓣ212/754-1113.

Malaysian embassies and consulates

Australia 7 Perth Ave, Yarralumla, Canberra, ACT 2600 Ⓣ02/6273 1543, Ⓔmalcnbera@netspeed.com.au.
Canada 60 Boteler St, Ottawa, Ontario K1N 8Y7 Ⓣ613/241-5182, Ⓦhome.istar .ca/~mwottawa.
New Zealand 10 Washington Ave, Brooklyn, Wellington Ⓣ04/385 2439, Ⓔmwwelton@xtra.co.nz.
UK and Ireland 45 Belgrave Square, London SW1X 8QT Ⓣ0870/005 6957, Ⓦmalaysia.embassyhomepage.com.
US 3516 International Court, NW, Washington, DC 20008 Ⓣ202/572-9700, Ⓔmalwashdc@kln.gov.my. Consulates in Los Angeles Ⓣ213/892-1238, Ⓔmwla@pacbell.ne; and New York Ⓣ212/490-2722, Ⓔmalnycg@kln.gov.my.

Mongolia

Capital Ulaanbaatar (also spelt Ulan Bator)
Population 2.5 million
Language Mongolian
Currency Tug
Religion Mahayana Buddhist. There is a small minority of Muslims in the Kazakh population.
Climate Extreme continental. Very cold winters of minus 20–40°C. Warm/hot summers of plus 20–40°C.

Best time to visit June to September.
Minimum daily budget In Ulaanbaatar it's possible to survive on $15 per day, but if you want to experience the real Mongolia it is necessary to travel outside the capital and book with a tour company, for which you'll pay $80–150 per day (all inclusive).

Having only opened up to tourism just over a decade ago, Mongolia remains one of the least visited tourist destinations in Asia. The nomadic lifestyle, little changed since the days of Genghis Khan, is still the way of life of nearly half the population. Even in the cities (of which there are only three) many of the people prefer to live in traditional "gers", round white felt tents, rather than the concrete blocks with amenities that were introduced during eighty years of socialist (Russian) development. If your intention is to get as far from the twenty-first century as possible, then this is the place for you. In a country the size of Western Europe, there are one and a half people per square kilometre. You can travel for hours meeting only a few horsemen, a family on a motorbike, or the occasional truck overloaded with sheepskins travelling towards the capital.

Ulaanbaatar has fine temples, art galleries and museums, but the glory of Mongolia lies outside the city in the vast open landscapes – the mountains, desert and open steppe, inhabited only by nomadic families with their herds of horses, camels and yaks. Hospitality is an important tradition in this sparsely populated land, and anyone passing by, be they Mongolian or foreign, will be invited in for a bowl of "airag" (fermented mare's milk) or yoghurt. The Mongolians are a proud race, able to live a self-sufficient existence with or without foreign assistance, and guests are treated with respect according to their age rather than their wealth or profession.

For many visitors one of the greatest pleasures is the lack of other tourists. Foreigners are never hassled; the local people are delighted to show off their beautiful country and heritage, and they still do not expect to be paid for this. Although much of the country is open grassy steppeland, each province has its own ancient monuments, unusual geographical features or rare wildlife that make it worth visiting. In the south next to the border with China lies the fabled Gobi Desert where dinosaur remains are frequently found. In the west is the high Altai mountain range, and in the central

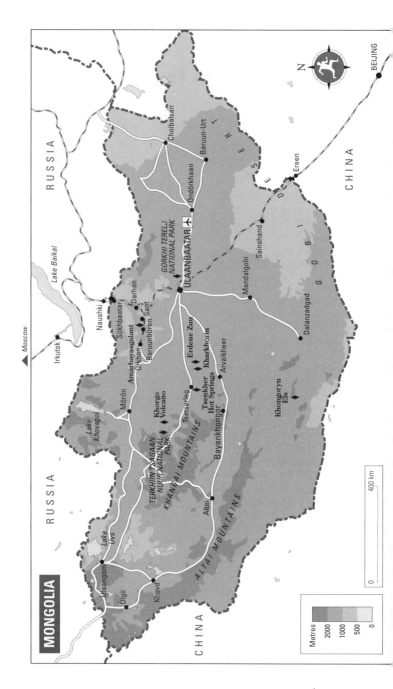

MONGOLIA

RUSSIA

CHINA

BEIJING

N

RUSSIA

Lake Baikal

Moscow

Irkutsk

Naushki

CHINA

Choibalsan

Baruun-Urt

Öndörkhaan

Ereen

Sainshand

Mandalgobi

GORKHI TERELJ
NATIONAL PARK

ULAANBAATAR

Darhan

Sükhbaatar

Amarbayasgalant

Orhon

Baruunbüren Sant

Erdene Zuu

Kharkhorin

Arvaikheer

Dalanzadgad

GOBI DESERT

Mörön

Lake Khovsgol

Khorgo
Volcano

Tsetserleg

Tsenkher
Hot Springs

Bayankhongor

Khongoryn
Els

TERKHIIN TSAGAAN
NUUR NATIONAL
PARK

KHANGAI MOUNTAINS

Altai

ALTAI MOUNTAINS

Lake
Uvs

Ulaangom

Ölgii

Khovd

Metres

2000
1000
500
0

0   400 km

92   First Time Asia | WHERE TO GO

Mean temperatures (°C) and rainfall (mm)

Average daily temperatures (maximum and minimum °C) and monthly rainfall (mm)

	Jan	Feb	Mar	Apr	May	June	July	Aug	Sept	Oct	Nov	Dec
Ulaanbaatar												
max °C	-19	-13	-4	7	13	21	22	21	14	6	-6	-16
min °C	-32	-29	-22	-8	-2	7	11	8	2	-8	-20	-28
rainfall mm	0	0	3	5	10	28	76	51	23	5	5	3

region the Khangai mountains. On the northern border with Siberia is "Mother Ocean", Lake Khovsgol, which is outstandingly peaceful and beautiful.

This is a difficult country for backpackers. Although it is not hard to find a local driver and agree a reasonable price for where you want to go, the chances that his vehicle is reliable, and that he doesn't have a bottle of vodka hidden under his seat, are slim. The best way to enjoy Mongolia fully is to organize your trip before you go, either with one of the local travel companies in Ulaanbaatar, or with a foreign travel company; most of the latter can be found on the Internet. Be prepared for long-distance travel, either by plane or by jeep. In the most important visited and beautiful places, traditional ger camps with toilet and washing facilities have been set up for travellers. Elsewhere camping is the only option, with rivers or lakes to cleanse yourself and minimal toilet facilities. Expect a wild trip!

Main attractions

● **Gobi Desert** Straddling the southern border between Inner Mongolia (an autonomous region of China) and Outer Mongolia, this vast expanse of sparsely populated wilderness is the habitat of a surprising variety of wildlife, including several rare species such as snow leopards, Gobi bears, wild sheep and camels. Apart from the handful of sites visited by most tourists (which include an ice-filled canyon in the mountains of the Gurvansaikhan Nuruu, and the "flaming red cliffs" at Bayanzag where many dinosaur remains have been discovered) the main attraction of the Gobi lies in the astonishing amount of empty space. It is a one-and-a-half-hour flight from Ulaanbaatar, or a gruelling two-day journey (each way) by jeep.

● **Kharkhorin** This quiet valley was once the centre of the great Mongol Empire. On the site where Genghis Khan built his capital in the thirteenth century, a monastery was later founded which became the centre of Buddhism in Mongolia. Erdene Zuu monastery is now the main attraction in this otherwise unexceptional town, and is visited by foreigners and Mongolians throughout the year. It can be visited in three days from Ulaanbaatar (it's a full day's drive in each direction).

● **Lake Khovsgol** Situated on Mongolia's northern border with Siberia, this huge inland sea is surrounded by mountains, forests and meadows of wild flowers. It's a perfect place to relax, or to enjoy a few days trekking, horse-riding, mountain biking, fishing or boating. Along the western shore are a growing number of facilities for tourists, including ger camps and lodges located at the water's edge. Flights from Ulaanbaatar to Mörön, the provincial capital, take one and a half hours, then it's a further three- or four-hour drive north to Lake Khovsgol.

• **Terelj** Only 80km from Ulaanbaatar, the Gorkhi Terelj National Park boasts granite mountains, lush green valleys and fast-flowing rivers. Towards the end of the road are several ger camps tucked away in the side valleys, but beyond this it is as remote as anywhere in Mongolia.

Also recommended

• **Hot springs** There are many hot mineral springs dotted about the country, visited mainly by Mongolians for their health-giving properties. Relatively accessible is Tsenkher in Arkhangai province where you can stay in traditional gers and relax in outdoor hot pools while admiring the surrounding forested mountains.

• **Riding** Take the opportunity to ride, whether it be mountain bikes, horses, camels, yaks or even reindeer – check with travel companies to see what they can offer. Gallop across the open steppe like one of Genghis Khan's warriors or ride over the mountains in a yak and cart.

• **Amarbayasgalant Monastery** More spectacular and remote than Erdene Zuu in Kharkhorin, this monastery is a good eight-hour drive northeast of Ulaanbaatar. The temples and pavilions were largely spared the fate of other similar institutions during the Stalinist purges of the 1930s.

• **Khongoryn Els** If you are going as far as the Gobi Desert, make a little extra effort to travel to the western side – beyond the normal tourist route – where big golden sand dunes meet the end of the high Altai mountain range. The sight

of herds of Bactrian camels against the sunset here is particularly photogenic.

Festivals

End January–March *Tsagaan Sar*. The forced consumption of deliciou, *buuz* (steamed dumplings) and vodka marks the Lunar New Year, the end of winter and the beginning of spring.

July *Naadam*. Three-day annual festival celebrating "the three sports of men" (horseracing, archery and wrestling), held in every town or village on or around July 11.

Routes in and out

Buyant-Ukhaa Airport, just outside Ulaanbaatar, receives international flights. An alternative is to enter Mongolia on the Trans-Mongolian Railway, a branch line of the Trans-Siberian Railway between Ulan-Ude and Beijing. There are established overland borders between Ereen (China) and Zamyn-Uud, and between Naushki (Russia) and Sukhbaatar. It's possible that other land crossings between Russia and Mongolia are open and accessible to foreigners, but information is extremely sparse, and the best advice is to check government sources, local travel agents and travellers' bulletin boards.

Mongolia online

Blue Peak – ⊛ **www.bluepeak.net** The site of photographer Roger Gruys who lived and travelled extensively in Mongolia. The images are fabulous and there's interesting background and travel information as well.

Ganden Tegchinlen Monastery – ⊛ **http://baatar.freeyellow.com /mongandan.html** Dedicated to this

Buddhist monastery in Ulaanbaatar, with good historical information. It has links to other sites for Mongolian history, Buddhism and city information.

Mongolia Mountainbike Expedition – Ⓦwww.mountainbike-expedition -team.de/Mongolia/mongo.htm Although it took place some years ago, this account of a seven-week mountain-biking expedition through the country is fascinating, and there are plenty of up-to-date practical tips, plus some useful links to other bike trips and general Mongolian sites.

Mongolian Art and Culture – Ⓦwww.mongolart.mn Excellent introduction to all aspects of Mongolian art, music, theatre, dance, film, entertainment and museums, although the site's not fully completed yet.

Ulaanbaatar – Ⓦwww.ulaanbaatar .net A gateway to the city, including news, background and practical stuff.

△ Horsemen and camels, Altai mountains

Books

Benedict Allen *Edge of Blue Heaven*. A fine travelogue detailing the adventurous author's intrepid horse trek in the west of the country and a solo camel trek across the Gobi.

Stephen J Bodio *Eagle Dreams: Searching for Legends in Wild Mongolia*. This renowned naturalistic, hunter and writer traces his fascination with the eagle-hunters of Mongolia and the realization of his dream to hunt with them.

John Man *Genghis Khan*. Popular, recent history of the most famous character in Mongolian history.

Stanley Stewart *In the Empire of Genghis Khan*. This prize-winning account of the author's 1000-mile journey across Mongolia brilliantly melds history and anecdote.

Louisa Waugh *Hearing Birds Fly*. Having spent two years in Ulaanbaatar, Louisa Waugh heads off to experience the harshness of village life in remote western Mongolia, living in a ger, breaking the ice in winter for her daily wash, and moving up into the Altai mountain pastures to help care for the sheep and goats in the summer.

Films

Chinggis Blues (Roko & Adrian Belic, 1999). This documentary traces the journey of a blind American blues singer from the West Coast to the wilds of Mongolia in search of the secret of *khoomi* (throat singing).

Nohoi Oron (*State of Dogs*; Peter Brosens & Dorjkhandyn Turmunkh,

1998). Prize-winning mystical travelogue following the life of Bassar, one of the 12,000 stray dogs in Ulaanbaatar.

The Story of the Weeping Camel (D Byambasuren & Luigi Falami, 2004). Documentary that mixes drama, nature film and enthnographical study as it follows a Mongolian nomad family seeking to reunite a baby camel with its mother. This film made it into cinemas in the West to considerable acclaim.

Wild East: Portrait of an Urban Nomad (Michael Haslund-Christensen, 2002). Set in Ulaanbaatar, this documentary traces two friends, Jenya and Sasha, as they try to find work. It explores issues of identity, tradition versus modernity, science versus religion and the struggle of life under the new capitalism.

Mongolian tourist offices

Ⓦ **www.mongoliatourism.gov.mn** No overseas tourist office.

Mongolian embassies and consulates

Ⓦ **www.extmin.mn** or Ⓦ **www.un.int /Mongolia**

Canada 151 Slater Street, Suite 503, Ottawa, K1P 5H3 ☏613/569-3830, Ⓦ www.mongolembassy.org.

UK 7 Kensington Court, W8 5DL ☏020/7937 0150, Ⓦ www .embassyofmongolia.co.uk.

USA 2833 Main Street NW, Washington, DC 20007 ☏202/333-7117, Ⓦ www .mongolianembassy.us.

Nepal

Capital Kathmandu
Population 24 million
Language Nepali plus 47 other languages and dialects spoken by the 55 separate ethnic groups that make up the population
Currency Rupee (Rs)

Religion Hindu and Buddhist
Climate Monsoonal
Best time to visit Autumn (Oct & Nov) and spring (Feb to mid-April)
Minimum daily budget $10/£6, though organized treks and adventure sports add significantly to the cost

Sandwiched between the enormous land masses of Tibet and India, Nepal is a relatively small country, but what it lacks in size it more than makes up for in dramatic scenery and the vast range of experiences on offer. Nepal contains a huge stretch of the Himalayas, the highest mountain range in the world, as well as dozens of equally dramatic peaks. Trekking is the main draw, but other attractions include Kathmandu, whose very name conjures up images of mountains and mysticism; the wildlife reserves of the lowland jungles in the south; Buddhist and Hindu temples and festivals; and white-water rafting. Many visitors also come in pursuit of bodily calm and spiritual truth, and Nepal has plenty of practitioners of massage, Ayurvedic and Tibetan medicine and astrology, plus courses in meditation and yoga.

Nepal remains one of the poorest countries in the world, facing not just a population explosion but also enormous environmental degradation, including the deforestation of much-tramped treks; visitors should do what they can (see the KEEP website listed on p.108 for suggestions) to avoid further damage to the fragile mountain ecosystem.

Tourism provides an important source of foreign exchange but tourist numbers have plummeted in the wake of the Maoist rebels' battle against the government, which began in 1996 in the far west of the country, spreading violence and potential instability. The situation was only made worse in June 2001 when Crown Prince Dipendra shot nine members of his immediate family including his parents (the king and queen), and then himself. Since then, there have been umpteen theories about the event. The brother of the previous king, Gyanendra, is now the monarch, with his unpopular son, Paras, next in line.

The Maoists declared a three-month unilateral ceasefire in September 2005; it remains to be seen whether this is the beginning of a lasting peace. Potential visitors should check the security situation before finalizing plans for a visit (see p.396).

Main attractions

● **Kathmandu** Nepal's bustling, sprawling capital city is noisy, traffic-clogged and appallingly polluted, but also vibrant, excellent for shopping and eating and a great place to arrange trips out into the wilderness. Durbar Square, in the heart of the city, is the location

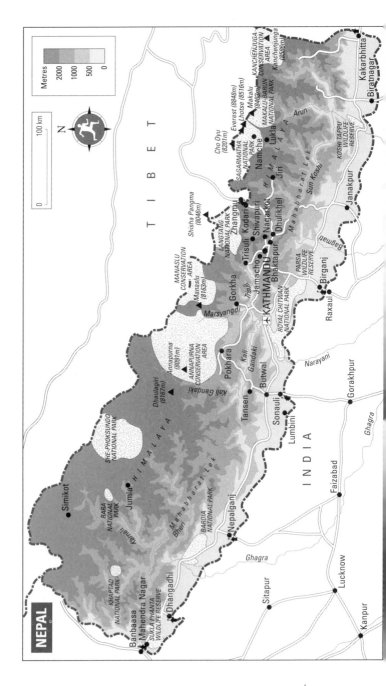

of innumerable temples and ancient monuments, most notably the Old Royal Palace and the Kumari Chowk; the latter is the home of Nepal's own living goddess, the Kumari, a prepubescent girl worshipped as the living incarnation of the Hindu goddess Durga. The other obligatory sight, on a hill west of the centre, is the huge Buddhist stupa at Swayambunath, from where the stylized eyes of the Buddha gaze out in all directions on the world. There are great views over the city from here, and the site draws an endless stream of pilgrims – one act of worship here is said to carry 13 billion times more merit than elsewhere.

● **Kathmandu Valley** Some of the best-preserved historic buildings and temples in the area are found in the ancient city of Bhaktapur, which has its own Durbar Square, featuring the five-storey Nyatapola pagoda. Patan, just south of Kathmandu, is the valley's most Buddhist city, with a calmer, less frantic feel than elsewhere; there's yet another Durbar Square here, with a fine Royal Palace dating from the seventeenth century and a number of temples. A trip out to the valley rim at Shivapuri or Jamacho is rewarded with some fine views of the Himalayas. Easily accessible from Kathmandu, although strictly speaking outside the valley itself, are Nagarkot and Dhulikel, both great excursions for even better mountain views, and excellent bases for treks.

● **Pokhara** One of the most popular destinations in Nepal, Pokhara is excellent for simply relaxing amid great scenery and in plenty of comfort; the views of the unforgettable Machhapuchhre (or "fish-tail peak"), the Annapurna mountain and Manaslu ranges are stunning. There are also plenty of local excursions, including hikes to the mountain viewpoint of Sarangkot or up to the World Peace Pagoda, on a ridge overlooking pretty Phewa lake.

● **Trekking** Nepal has an enormous variety of treks on offer, varying in length and difficulty; some have comfortable accommodation all along the way, while others require you to be totally self-reliant. It's worth researching the options, especially if you want to get away from the most popular routes. The three-week Annapurna circuit involves climbing up to a heady 5380m, passing through gloriously diverse scenery; you'll need to be reasonably fit to tackle it, though there's plenty of accommodation and eating places serving Western food en route, and other trekkers for company. The ten-day Jomosom trek is also highly commercialized, though this doesn't detract from the many small, ethnically diverse villages along the route. Everest treks, which get you close to the world's tallest peak, are very strenuous, the cold and high altitude being serious concerns; you'll need to allow three or four weeks to do one of these, unless you fly into or out of Lukla, partway along the

Mean temperatures (°C) and rainfall (mm)

Average daily temperatures (maximum and minimum °C) and monthly rainfall (mm)

	Jan	Feb	Mar	Apr	May	June	July	Aug	Sept	Oct	Nov	Dec
Kathmandu												
max °C	18	19	25	28	30	29	29	28	28	27	23	19
min °C	2	4	7	12	16	19	20	20	19	13	7	3
rainfall mm	15	41	23	58	122	246	373	345	155	38	8	3

route. Those with less time or inclination may want to consider the three- to five-day Royal Trek from Pokhara, or spending seven to twelve days on the Langtang trek closer to Kathmandu.

● **Chitwan National Park** On the plains in the far south of the country, the park is the jungle home of the famed Bengal tiger and the Indian rhinoceros, as well as plenty of deer and wild oxen, crocodiles and over 450 species of birds – among other creatures. Elephant rides, jeep tours, canoe trips and walks are all available, though Chitwan's fame and accessibility mean that it can be hard to escape the crowds.

● **White-water rafting and kayaking** Nepal's picturesque rivers offer both beginners and the more advanced plenty of opportunities to try these activities. Two- or three-day trips on the Trisuli river west of Kathmandu, and three- or four-day excursions out of Pokhara or on the upper Kali Gandaki are among the most popular. Agents who arrange trips can be found in both Kathmandu and Pokhara.

Also recommended

● **Mountain flights** On these excursions, which leave daily from Kathmandu between May and September, you pass just 25km from Everest and get to eyeball a couple of dozen of the world's highest peaks.

● **Bardia National Park** In the west of the country, the park doesn't have as many rhinos as Chitwan, but offers a greater chance of spotting tigers. Recent estimates suggest that there are around sixty breeding adult tigers in Chitwan, and 35 in the smaller area of Bardia – so do bear in mind that a sighting is remarkable rather than predictable.

● **Courses in meditation, yoga or Nepali** The Kathmandu valley, and to a lesser extent Pokhara, are ideal places to enrol yourself.

● **Lumbini** A place of pilgrimage for devotees from across the globe, the spot where Buddha was born in 543 BC has ancient archeological monuments as well as modern Tibetan and Theravadan monasteries.

● **Mountain biking** Organized tours, geared to any level of fitness and ability, provide all equipment and accommodation – and a lift if you get tired. Kathmandu and Pokhara are the main centres to arrange trips.

Festivals

February/March *Shiva Raatri*. Nepal's best known religious fair or *mela*, "Shiva's Night" attracts thousands of pilgrims and sadhus (Indian ascetic holy men) to Pashupatinath on the eastern edge of Kathmandu for worship and mind-boggling yogic demonstrations.
August/September *Indra Jatra*. An eight-day confection of music, dance and drama, in which the living goddess, the Kumari, is towed in a chariot through Kathmandu.
September/October *Dasain*. Nepal's longest and biggest festival lasts fifteen days. The best day for onlookers is Bijaya Dasami, the tenth day, which celebrates the hero Rams's victory over the evil king Ravana, as detailed in the great Hindu epic, the Ramayana; it is marked by processions and masked dances.

Routes in and out

Kathmandu's international airport, Tribhuvan, is served by several major carriers. There are a handful of well-used overland routes from India, arriving into Mahendra Nagar (from Banbassa; convenient if you're coming from Delhi), Sonauli (from Gorakhpur; convenient from Delhi or Varanasi), Birganj (from Raxaul; convenient from Kolkata and Patna) and Kakarbhitta (convenient from Darjeeling and Kolkata). Crossings between India and Nepal are also open at Nepalganj (north of Faizabad) and Dhangadhi (north of Sitapur) but are less convenient and little used by foreign visitors. The crossing from Tibet is between Zhangmu and Kodari; however, only tour groups are allowed into Tibet via this route (though independent travellers can leave Tibet this way) – check the situation at the time of travel.

Nepal online

Everest News – Ⓦwww.everestnews .com This site offers up-to-date and extensive coverage of news from Everest and the other big Himalayan peaks. There's a huge amount of information here about current expeditions, plus plenty of detail about history, facts, gear – almost everything you'd want to know about the highest mountain on earth.
Himalayan Art – Ⓦwww.himalayan art.org Fabulous site dedicated to Himalayan art that displays more than 19,000 images from museum, university and private collections around the world, including paintings, sculpture and textiles. There's excellent information on all the images here as well.
International Porter Protection Group – Ⓦwww.ippg.net This group campaigns for a safe and fair deal for porters who work in the trekking business. Their thought-provoking site has plenty of sad examples of what can go wrong for the people who carry the loads and advice on how to prevent them.

Kathmandu Environmental Education Project (KEEP) – Ⓦwww.keepnepal .org Excellent site for tourist information, plus images of some popular treks. There are brilliant links to other environmental organizations and plenty of good ideas about how to visit Nepal without doing more harm than good. Volunteer opportunities are also listed.
Yeti Zone Web Himalayan Trekking Guide – Ⓦwww.yetizone.com Offers brilliantly detailed, day-by-day accounts of the Annapurna Circuit and Sanctuary, Everest and Khumbu regions, Langtang and Helambu treks, plus ample inspirational images. You can order DVD or MPEG versions or simply read it all on the site, which is packed with information and also features a bulletin board if you're looking for a trekking partner. Check out the Yeti Cam to search for the elusive creature.

Books

Eva Kipp *Bending Bamboo, Changing Winds: Nepali Women Tell Their Life Stories*. Moving oral histories and photographs from across the country detailing every aspect of women's lives.
Jon Krakauer *Into Thin Air*. Harrowing and thought-provoking description of the events of May 1996, the deadliest season ever on Mount Everest.
Peter Matthiessen *The Snow Leopard*. Fabulous, and now classic read, describing the author's two-month hike into the remote Inner Dolpo region of northwest Nepal. Alongside beautiful descriptions, Matthiessen talks about his emotional ups and downs, as he oscillates between exhaustion and exhilaration and tries hard to make sense of his Zen Buddhist training.
Samrat Upadhyay *Arresting God in Kathmandu*. This is a volume of short stories by one of the first Nepalese

△ Sadhu, Durbar Square, Kathmandu

authors to be published in the West; tales of traditional expectations are set against a Kathmandu backdrop of urban life and a changing society.

Amy Willesee & Mark Whittaker *Love and Death in Kathmandu: A Strange Tale of Royal Murder*. An attempt to unfathom the events of June 1, 2001, when Crown Prince Dipenda mowed his family down before turning his gun on himself as a result of his affair with Devyani Rana whom he was forbidden to marry.

Films

Himalaya (Eric Valli, 2000). The story of a struggle for power between the generations in an isolated mountain village in the Dolpo region, played out on the annual salt trek across the Himalayas.
Starkiss Circus Girls in India (Chris Relleke & Jascha de Wilde, 2003). Documentary detailing the lives of girls from desperately poor Nepalese families who are essentially sold to the Great

Rayman Circus, the oldest in India. It's a bleak look at their lives, work and future options.

Nepalese tourist offices

Ⓦ www.welcomenepal.com
No overseas tourist office.

Nepalese embassies and consulates

Ⓦ www.immi.gov.np/location.php
Australia and New Zealand Contact Tokyo embassy: 7-14-9 Todoroki Setagaya-ku, Tokyo 158-0082 Ⓦ www.nepal-embassy.org.
Canada Contact US embassy.
UK 12A Kensington Palace Gardens, London W8 4QU ☎ 020/7229 1594, Ⓦ www.nepembassy.org.uk.
US 2131 Leroy Place NW, Washington, DC 20008 ☎ 020/667-4550, Ⓦ www.nepalembassy.org; consulate in New York ☎ 212/370-3988.

Pakistan

Capital Islamabad
Population 151 million
Language Urdu is the official language, though it is largely used as a second language alongside other native tongues, including Punjabi, Sindhi, Pashto and Baluchi
Currency Pakistani Rupee (Rs)
Religion Most of the population are Muslim, with small Christian, Hindu, Sikh and Parsee minorities
Climate There are three climatic zones: dry (which covers most of the country), humid subtropical (from Lahore to Peshawar) and highland (the climate of the northern mountains)
Best time to visit The south is best from November to March, when it is cooler; the north is best from April to October (main trekking season June–Sept), which avoids the harshest winter snows
Minimum daily budget $10/£6

Relatively few tourists make it to Pakistan, but those that do generally describe it as being like Nepal without the crowds or like India without the hassles. The country has many attractions, including spectacular mountain and desert landscapes, and ancient ruins and fabulous mosques – the legacy of prehistoric civilizations and successive Persian, Arab, Mogul and Sikh empires. Travellers generally head for the north, either using the Karakoram Highway and its offshoots, or visiting Peshawar, the Khyber Pass and Chitral. Hiking is the most popular activity, and there are plenty of treks to suit all levels of fitness and aspiration.

Although the tourist industry in Pakistan is embryonic, there's a fair choice of hotels, especially in towns and cities, but electricity and water supplies can be unreliable. Trains and buses are generally slow, and can be uncomfortable. English is spoken by most educated Pakistanis, and foreigners who respect the local culture are warmly welcomed as honoured guests. Women should dress appropriately for a Muslim country, in long loose clothes. During Ramadan, the Islamic month of fasting, eating, drinking and smoking are banned during daylight hours; many restaurants are closed, offices work short hours and tempers can get rather frayed.

Some parts of Pakistan are considered dangerous for travellers, most notably rural Sindh, the tribal areas of the Northwest Frontier province and Balochistan, and rural areas of Punjab. However, the situation can change very fast, and travellers planning to visit Pakistan should check the current situation with their own government advisory body before they go (see p.420) and, once in the country, with local tourist offices and/or the police.

Main attractions

- **Islamabad and Rawalpindi** Built in the 1960s, Islamabad, Pakistan's planned capital, is laid out on a grid design, without the chaos (and the character) usually associated with Asian cities. Its Faisal

Masjid, one of the largest mosques in the world, is worth a visit, as are the nearby Margalla hills, which offer opportunities for walks and treks. Just 15km away, the traditional city of Rawalpindi has both chaos and character aplenty and is expanding fast. Rajah Bazaar, the commercial heart of its old market area, is a maze of tiny alleyways lined with shops and workshops of every type. Although the two cities have little to detain visitors for long, they do make a convenient gateway to Pakistan if you're visiting the north.

● **Trekking in Northern Pakistan**
The meeting point of the Himalaya, Karakoram and Hindu Kush mountain ranges, the region offers some of the best trekking in the world, ranging from gentle day-long strolls to extremely strenuous affairs lasting several weeks and involving glaciers, fast-flowing rivers and passes 5500m up. Trekking centres are Shigar near Skardu, Gilgit, Chitral and, further afield, the Hunza, Nagar and nearby valleys. As the trekking infrastructure is much less developed than in Nepal, the need for self-sufficiency is far greater, though the organized treks now offered by some companies are a viable alternative to going it alone. Be sure to read p.366 for information on acclimatisation to altitude.

The accession of Jammu and Kashmir to Pakistan or India remains to be decided.

Average daily temperatures (maximum and minimum °C) and monthly rainfall (mm)

	Jan	Feb	Mar	Apr	May	June	July	Aug	Sept	Oct	Nov	Dec
Islamabad												
max °C	16	19	24	31	37	40	36	34	34	32	28	20
min °C	2	6	10	15	21	25	25	24	21	15	9	3
rainfall mm	64	64	81	42	23	55	233	258	85	21	12	23

● **Peshawar** Though it's long had a reputation as a frontier town, Peshawar these days is a thriving city. The buzz and excitement of the twisting alleyways and bazaars of the Old City remain, though. A popular excursion from Peshawar is 40km south to the village of Darra Adam Khel (usually just called Darra), centre of arms manufacture and trading in the region. Here, gunsmiths' shops line the road, and you'll be invited to test-fire home-made imitation Kalashnikovs.

● **Khyber Pass** In Western minds, the pass has mystical status, symbolizing a time when travellers were real adventurers. Travel there by road or steam train from Peshawar, and gaze down into Afghanistan through the barren, desolate hills. The pass may be closed if security concerns are high.

● **Lahore** The most worthwhile of Pakistan's cities, Lahore has numerous fine examples of Mogul architecture, while a walk through the atmospheric alleyways of the Old City takes in mosques, bazaars and markets. The Lahore Museum is a treasure trove of items from throughout Pakistan's history.

● **Karakoram Highway** To travel along this 1300-kilometre-long road – linking Islamabad with Kashgar in China (see p.46) via the Khunjerab Pass – is to experience some of the most spellbinding scenery in the world, as the highway weaves between towering mountains,

over huge passes, beside thundering rivers and along apparently impenetrable valleys. With a visa for China and a double-entry Pakistan visa, you could travel the full length of the highway and spend a few days sightseeing in Kashgar to recover before heading back.

● **Moenjo Daro** The Indus Valley civilization, at its peak four thousand years ago, was centred here; a great deal remains of the original city, much of it brilliantly preserved and well restored.

Also recommended

● **Tombs of Uch Sharif** These are some of the most beautiful – albeit partially ruined – tombs in the country. Fabulously decorated, the tombs, the oldest of which is thought to date from the tenth century, are lasting memorials to the prominent figures of Sufi Islam who are buried here.

● **Camel safari** Venturing into Pakistan's largest desert, the Cholistan Desert, by camel, you'll visit desert forts built along the ancient trading route across the sands, most famously the eighteenth-century Fort Derawar.

● **Mountain flights** Take a flight from Islamabad to Gilgit or Skardu, or from Peshawar to Chitral; the planes fly between rather than above the peaks, so you get fantastic views – especially as the pilots are only allowed to fly in fine weather.

● **Take the road between Gilgit and Chitral** The two- to three-day journey, crossing the Shandur Pass, is one of the roughest but most impressive in the country, with awesome mountain scenery. The most flexible way to do it is by hiring a jeep, and there are some great spots along the way to camp rough.

Festivals

July *Shandur polo tournament*. Annual event between Gilgit and Chitral, played out among fabulous, remote scenery at the world's highest polo ground, 3775m up on the Shandur Pass. Some authorities claim the game was invented in the north of the country, and matches in Pakistan are far more enthusiastic and raucous than in the West. The Shandur polo tournament is accompanied by cultural events and golf and fishing tournaments.

October *Lok Virsa*, Islamabad. Pakistan's annual folk festival is held over ten days and showcases the best of Pakistani culture, food and music from every corner of the country, and also features groups from overseas.

December *Chaomos*. The solstice festival of the Kalasha people in Chitral region features feasting, sacrifices and dancing.

Routes in and out

Karachi, Islamabad, Lahore, Quetta and Peshawar have international airports, the first three offering the most worldwide connections. Overland routes link Pakistan with China (via the Karakoram Highway); India (the only crossing is between Wagah on the Pakistani side and Attari on the Indian side); Iran (the only official crossing is at Taftan, more than 600km west of Quetta); and Afghanistan (between Torkham on the Khyber Pass and Jalalabab, and at Chaman between Quetta and Kandahar).

Pakistan online

Dawn – ⓦ www.dawn.com The Internet edition of Pakistan's most widely

△ Hunza Baltit hotel

available English-language newspaper is an excellent introduction to the news and current preoccupations in Pakistan.

The Karakoram Highway and beyond – ⓦhttp://home.hkstar.com/~roz /Index.ht Incredibly detailed, useful and inspirational site for anyone contemplating cycling the Karakoram Highway (allow at least six weeks for the whole thing). Distances, times, gear, food, nuisances – it's all covered, although sadly the site has no photographs.

Pakistan Positive – ⓦwww.pak positive.com Operated by a Pakistani living in Karachi, this site specializes in ordinary news from around the country – it's a great antidote to all the bad media the country gets.

Travel and Culture – ⓦwww.travel -culture.com This 800-page Pakistani travel agent's website contains a wealth of well-presented information about the country, including a lot of hard facts and some good articles.

Women of Pakistan – ⓦwww.jazbah .org This site celebrates the achievements of Pakistani women and includes plenty of profiles, articles, essays, interviews and suggestions of books worth reading.

Books

Peter Hopkirk *The Great Game*. Rip-roaring history of the struggles for power between Victorian England and Tzarist Russia played out in northern India and Central Asia during the nineteenth century. The area that is now Pakistan was the heart of these struggles.

Kathleen Jamie *The Golden Peak: Travels in Northern Pakistan*. Not a great deal happens on the author's journey through Pakistan but this woman is a poet and it shows in her fabulous descriptions.

Eric Newby *A Short Walk in the Hindu Kush*. This book's iconic status as a classic of travel writing is well deserved as the author details his adventures in the Hindu Kush. It's a great tale, told hilariously and is pretty much a handbook on how not to venture into the mountains.

Kamila Shamsie *Kartography*. Set in Karachi in the 1980s and 90s, in the years after the civil war of 1971, which created an independent Bangladesh, this is the story of Raheen and Karim and childhood friendship growing into adult love.

Khushwant Singh *Train to Pakistan*. One of the best books about the awful human cost of the 1947 Partition of the continent into Hindu India and Muslim Pakistan. Ten million people were relocated and by the end of it a million had been slaughtered in the accompanying bloodshed.

Films

Choorian (Syed Noor, 1998). This smash hit single-handedly revived Punjabi film-making, although the story of good versus evil is pretty standard "Lollywood" fare (the Pakistan film industry being based in Lahore).

Khamosh Pani (*Silent Water*; Sabiha Sumar, 2003). Set in 1979, just as Pakistan is subject to martial law, with flashes back to the time of Partition. This is the tale of the village of Charkhi in the Punjab and the widow Ayesha whose son becomes a fundamentalist. As Sikh visitors seek to unearth the hidden past, current tensions form an eloquent backdrop.

Maula Jat (Yunus Malik, 1979). This story of a blood feud is often described as unrealistic, badly filmed and totally exaggerated, but it remains the most successful film ever made in Pakistan and it spawned apparently endless sequels.

Yeh Dil Aap Ka Hua (Javed Sheik, 2004). Love, marriage and business rivalry are the themes of this modern smash hit. A great topic of conversation for those long bus journeys.

1947: Earth (Deepa Mehta, 1999). An adaptation of the novel *Cracking India* (or *The Ice Candy Man*) by well-regarded Pakistani novelist Bapsi Sidhwa, this film looks at Partition through the eyes of a young Parsi girl in Lahore.

Pakistani tourist offices

ⓦ **www.tourism.gov.pk**
No overseas tourist office.

Pakistani embassies and consulates

Australia 4 Timbarra Crescent, O'Malley, Canberra, ACT 2606

ⓣ 02/6290 1676, ⓦ www.pakistan.org.au.

Canada 10 Range Road, Ottawa, Ontario K1N 8J3 ⓣ 613/238-7881, ⓦ www.pakmission.ca. Consulates in Montreal ⓣ 514/845-2297; Toronto ⓣ 416/250-1255.

New Zealand Contact the embassy in Canberra.

UK 35–36 Lowndes Square, London SW1 9JN ⓣ 020/7664 9200, ⓦ www.pakmission-uk.gov.pk. Consulate in Bradford ⓣ 01274/721921.

USA 3517 International Court NW, Washington DC, 20008 ⓣ 202/243-6500, ⓦ www.embassyof pakistan.org. Consulates in Chicago ⓣ 312/781-1831; Houston ⓣ 281/890-2223; Los Angeles ⓣ 310/441-5114; and New York ⓣ 212/879-5800.

Philippines

Capital Manila	**Best time to go** November–April for
Population 87 million	the western half of the archipelago,
Language Tagalog	but avoid the eastern islands
Currency Peso (P)	between November and January
Main religion Roman Catholic	**Minimum daily budget** $15/£8
Climate Tropical	

The Philippines is an outdoors destination, with world-class – and good-value – diving off many of its 7107 islands, as well as plenty of white-sand beaches and hundreds of hiking trails across its lush volcanic terrain. Because of its Spanish colonial history, which lasted over 300 years, its subsequent half-century as an American colony, and its Catholic heritage, there are fewer indigenous cultural sights here than in Indonesia or Thailand, but this is more than compensated for by the exuberant, easy-going Filipino attitude to life, once summed up as "that rare blend of Asian grace and Latin fire". The Filipinos hold great fiestas – their calendar is packed with religious occasions that are celebrated with pageants, fancy-dress parades, music and dancing in the streets, the inevitable beauty-queen contest, and plenty of beer and spit-roasted pork; foreigners are warmly welcomed at these events and offered characteristic Filipino hospitality.

In spite of its obvious attractions, the Philippines are still a relatively unusual backpackers' destination, in part because accommodation and travel are about fifty percent more expensive than in Thailand, but also because you can't get to the archipelago overland. For many travellers, this comparatively low-key tourist development is a big plus, and a welcome relief from some of the more clichéd Southeast Asian havens. Conveniently for the traveller, English is widely spoken and the transport system is generally easy to fathom, if a bit flexible in its timetabling, though you'll be spending a lot of time on boats unless you budget for a few fast but pricey internal flights.

The last few years have seen an alarming number of kidnappings in the Philippines, many of them by Muslim separatist groups. Most governments are currently advising against travel to central, southern and western Mindanao, where the separatists are most active, and to the Sulu archipelago, so check with official travel advisories (see p.420) and travellers' forums (see p.249) before your visit.

Main attractions

- **The beaches** Filipino beaches are some of the finest in Asia, and with almost 60,000 km of coastline, there's plenty to choose from. You'll find the very best in the chain of islands known as the Visayas, which stretches from the southern tip of Luzon all the way down to Mindanao, and includes the

THE PHILIPPINES

Metres
2000
1000
500
0

0   200 km

N

Batanes
Islands

Luzon Strait

Babuyan
Islands

Laoag
Vigan

SOUTH
CHINA
SEA

Sagada   Bontoc
          Batad
San Fernando Banaue
       Baguio
     Dagupan
     Luzon

SIERRA MADRE

PHILIPPINE SEA

Angeles
San Fernando
Mount Pinatubo
Olongapo   MANILA
Corregidor   Pagsanjan Falls
                 Daet   Catanduanes
        Arilao Lucena
Puerto Galera Batangas Naga
               City   Mount Mayon
        Calapan   Legaspi
Apo Reef Mindoro Marinduque
                   Donsol
Busuanga   Romblon
                  Masbate   Catarman Samar
Calamian   Boracay
Islands   Kalibo   Masbate
                  Roxas
El Nido   Bantayan   Tacloban
        Cuyo   Panay VISAYAS
        Islands Iloilo City Cebu Ormoc Leyte
                 Bacolod
Palawan   Cebu City   Dinagat
        Honda Bay   Mount Kanlaon   Siargao
        Puerto Princesa Moalboal Bohol Surigao
                 Negros Panglao Camiguin
        SULU SEA Dumaguete   Bohol
                          Dipolog Sea   Butuan
Brooke's Point Tubbataha
                Reef   Cagayan
                                  de Oro
Balabac   Mindanao
                          Cotabato Mt Apo
                          Zamboanga City   Davao
Sandakan   Jolo Jolo Basilan
                              General
MALAYSIA   Tawi-Tawi   Santos
(SABAH)   Sulu Archipelago CELEBES SEA

Sulawesi

major islands of Samar, Leyte, Bohol, Cebu, Negros and Panay, as well as hundreds of alluring pint-sized islets in between. The most famous island in the whole set is tiny Boracay, a beautiful but pricey resort island. Quieter, equally lovely Visayan islands include Romblon, Bantayan, Panay, Bohol, Malapascua and Panglao, all of which offer the perfect combination of luxuriously soft sand, a decent choice of beachfront accommodation, and laid-back fishing villages.

● **Diving** With all that fabulously clear tropical water around, it's not surprising that the Philippines is one of Asia's premier diving destinations. You'll find some of the richest reefs off Boracay, Palawan and Mindoro, but there are also spectacular underwater walls, drop-offs and coral arches at Moalboal on Cebu, and hammerhead sharks and manta rays near Panglao and Cabilao islands, off Bohol.

● **Manila** Cursed with traffic and pollution that make Bangkok seem like a nature reserve, Manila is one of those capitals that just has to be endured between flights or ferry connections. You can cheer yourself up, though, with a visit to the Chinese cemetery – it's literally a ghost town, with streets and two-storey houses for the departed, many of them furnished with kitchens, bathrooms, electricity and air-conditioning. Elsewhere, parts of Intramuros, the Old City, date back to the sixteenth century and the early years of Spanish occupation and combine well with a browse around the galleries of the twin national museums in Rizal Park, which focus on tribal people, including the Ifugao, and colonial history. Otherwise, Manila is best for shopping and drinking, with colossal malls in every neighbourhood, and a trendy nightlife scene in Malate.

Mean temperatures (°C) and rainfall (mm)

Average daily temperatures (maximum and minimum °C) and monthly rainfall (mm)

	Jan	Feb	Mar	Apr	May	June	July	Aug	Sept	Oct	Nov	Dec
Manila												
max °C	30	31	33	34	34	33	31	31	31	31	31	30
min °C	21	21	22	23	24	24	24	24	24	23	22	21
rainfall mm	23	13	18	33	130	254	432	422	356	193	145	66
Iloilo												
max °C	29	31	31	33	33	32	31	31	31	31	31	30
min °C	23	23	23	24	25	24	24	24	24	24	24	23
rainfall mm	64	46	33	43	158	264	447	386	315	269	211	119
Surigao												
max °C	28	29	29	31	31	31	31	31	31	31	29	28
min °C	23	23	23	23	24	24	24	24	24	24	24	23
rainfall mm	544	376	506	254	158	125	178	130	168	272	427	620
Zamboanga												
max °C	31	31	32	31	31	31	31	31	31	31	31	32
min °C	23	23	23	23	24	24	23	24	23	23	23	23
rainfall mm	64	46	33	43	158	264	447	386	315	269	211	119

- **Puerto Galera** With stunning beaches, thirty major dive sites along a reef so rich in marine life that it's Unesco-listed, and heaps of reasonably priced accommodation, Puerto Galera, on the north coast of Mindoro, is the perfect beach break away from Manila.

- **Banaue** This little town in northern Luzon occupies a stunning landscape of mountains, steep-sided valleys, and breathtakingly beautiful amphitheatres of sculpted rice-terraces. First cut from the hillsides 2000 years ago by Ifugao tribespeople, whose descendants still live in the area, the terraces are so spectacular that they've been given World Heritage status. To make the most of the scenery, follow the popular walking trail from Banaue to the traditional village of Batad. The bus journey up to Banaue is a scenic highlight in itself, as it takes you along the Halsema Highway, one of the most awesome roads in Southeast Asia.

- **Palawan** Graced with peaceful shores, thickly forested crags and a gorgeous rugged natural beauty, the large, remote island of Palawan is probably the single most rewarding destination in the Philippines. It's got everything: snow-white beaches at El Nido, Taytay, Port Barton, Sabang and Roxas, unrivalled diving at El Nido and Tubbataha Reef Marine Park, hiking trails through the jungle, intact tribal culture, and a noticeable lack of tourists. And there's also the famous eight-kilometre boat ride through the spooky, bat-infested caves of the Underground River in Saint Paul's Subterranean Cave.

- **Sagada** This charming hill village in northern Luzon is the home of the Igorot tribe, who are famous for their hanging coffins – suspended high in caves out of the reach of wild animals – as well as for their weavings. There are plenty of hiking possibilities around here too, and a distinctly bohemian ambience to the village,

all of which make it a really nice place to hang out for a few days.

Also recommended

- **Siargao Island** Kayaking is the perfect way to explore the shapely coastline of this undeveloped island off northeastern Mindanao, with its secret coves, hidden lagoons and peaceful crystal-white beaches. There's good surfing here too and a rustic interior full of coconut palms and tiny villages.

- **Camiguin Island, off northern Mindanao** Famous for its exceptionally sweet and succulent *lanzone* (lychee) fruits, this little gem of an island offers heaps of variety, including sugar-fine beaches, seven volcanoes, exceptional trekking and rock-climbing, hot springs and waterfalls.

- **Shooting the rapids at Pagsanjan Falls** The scenery along this stretch of the Bombongan River is impressively dramatic, and it's a genuine thrill to race the fourteen rapids as you squeeze between the jungle-clad canyon walls. If you get a sense of déjà vu, it's because the final scenes of *Apocalypse Now* were filmed here. This is an immensely popular day-trip from Manila, but you can avoid the crowds by staying nearby and doing an early-morning boat ride before the coaches pitch up. Be wary though, as the touts here are the most aggressive in the country.

Festivals

January *Ati-Atihan*, Kalibo, Panay Island. Everyone dresses up in outrageous costumes for Southeast Asia's biggest three-day street party, which is held in honour of the Holy Infant Jesus and climaxes with a masquerade ball.

March or April *Holy Week Crucifixions*, Pampagna province, Luzon.
Held every year near San Fernando, these are real crucifixions of real people. Under the rapt gaze of hundreds of spectators, a dozen or so pious penitents flagellate themselves before being nailed onto crosses, believing that this earthly suffering will ease their eventual passage into heaven. Although the penitents are taken off the crosses after only a few seconds, it's a disturbing spectacle with plenty of genuine blood – and an act of piety that is not endorsed by the Catholic Church.

October *Lanzones Festival*, Camiguin Island. Ribald festival in honour of the lychee, Camiguin's most famous product, which sees islanders parading through the streets dressed only in lychee leaves.

Routes in and out

Most long-haul travellers fly into the Philippines via Hong Kong and land in Manila, though some Southeast Asian airlines also run international flights to and from Cebu and a few serve Davao. There are international ferry routes from Sandakan in Sabah (East Malaysia) to Zamboanga, and from Bitung in northern Sulawesi (Indonesia) to General Santos in Mindanao, but some routes are served by cargo boats (many of them unlicensed and overloaded) and are considered unsafe due to pirate attacks in local waters: see government travel warnings and Internet forums for current advice.

Philippines online

Bundok Philippines – ⓦwww .geocities.com/Yosemite/3712 Site specializing in hiking opportunities in the Philippines, featuring hikers' travelogues, slide shows and some maps.

Jens Peters' Philippines Guide – ⓦwww.travelphil.de Comprehensive travel site created by a travel guide author. Alongside links and summaries on everything from hiking to motorcycling, there's also a fun "Who's Who" section with links to homepages and biogs of dozens of Filipino bands, actors, writers and other current celebs.
The Philippine Diver – ⓦwww.diver .com.ph Online version of this glossy quarterly comes up trumps with hundreds of divers' reports on the archipelago's best dives. Also has links to dive centres and courses.
The Philippine Star – ⓦwww.philstar .com The national daily newspaper has the day's headline stories plus a stack of archived ones.
Tanikalang Ginto – ⓦwww .filipinolinks.com Links to scores of interesting Philippines-related sites, including travel, airport info, unusual destinations, books and hotels.

Books

Alan Berlow *Dead Season: A Story of Murder and Revenge*. Famously gripping account of the real facts behind three murders – of a soldier, a peasant and a plantation owner – on the sugar-producing island of Negros, which reveals a depressing picture of the powerlessness of ordinary Filipinos in the face of entrenched interests and far-reaching corruption.
Jessica Tarahata Hagedorn *Dogeaters*. Gritty contemporary novel by a Filipino–American set in Marcos-era Manila and peopled by a cast of underworld characters, prostitutes, DJs, clubbers and hustlers.
James Hamilton-Paterson *Playing With Water: Passion and Solitude on a Philippine Island*. The beautifully lyrical account of the several extended periods

△ Pagsanjon Falls

the author spent living alone on a tiny uninhabited island near Marinduque, befriended by local fishermen and learning to dive and fish as they did – often at night with a spear and the most rudimentary breathing apparatus. His descriptions of these underwater forays are breathtaking.

First Time **Asia** | **WHERE TO GO**

Hiroo Onoda *No Surrender: My Thirty-Year War*. The incredible true story of the Japanese lieutenant who did not know World War II was over until he emerged from the jungle on Lubang Island (north-west off Mindoro) almost thirty years later, in 1974. His account tells how he continued to wage his one-man guerilla campaign in the Philippines, despite repeated rescue attempts, including by his own relatives, all of which he dismissed as trickery and enemy propaganda.

Films

Back to Bataan (Edward Dmytryk, 1950). Patriotic dramatization of the infamous Bataan Death March in World War II, when 70,000 Filipino and US POWs were marched by their Japanese captors from Mariveles to San Fernando, an arduous trip of 100km across the Batan Peninsula west of Manila. Some 7000 soldiers died along the way, with around another 7000 escaping into the jungle. John Wayne takes the role of the US soldiers' leader, opposite Anthony Quinn as leader of the Filipino guerilla fighters.
Manila in the Claws of Neon (Lino Brocka, 1975). Classic noir depiction of a hellish Manila by the Philippines' most famous film director, as a young, bewildered innocent from the provinces heads to the scary metropolis in search of his beloved.
Woman of the Breakwater (Mario O'Hara, 2003). By turns a warm, funny, depressing and heart-warming story of life on the streets for the slum-dwellers of Manila Bay.

Philippines tourist offices

ⓦ **www.tourism.gov.ph**
ⓦ **www.wowphilippines.com.ph**

Australia and **New Zealand** Level 1, Philippine Centre, 27–33 Wentworth Ave, Sydney, NSW 2000 ☎02/9283 0711, ⓔpdotsydney@ozemail.com.au.
Canada 151 Bloor Street, West Suite 1120, Toronto, Ontario M5S 1S4 ☎416/924-3569, ⓦwww.wow philippines.ca.
UK and Ireland 146 Cromwell Rd, London SW7 4EF ☎020/7835 1100, ⓦwww.wowphilippines.co.uk.
US 30 North Michigan Ave, Suite 913, Chicago, IL 60602 ☎312/782-2475, ⓔpdotchi@aol.com; 556 Fifth Ave, New York, NY 10036 ☎212/575-7915, ⓔpdotny@aol.com; 447 Sutter St, Suite 507, San Francisco, CA 94108 ☎415/956-4060, ⓔpdotsf@aol.com.

Philippines embassies and consulates

Australia ⓦwww.philembassy.au.com. 1 Moonah Place, Yarralumla, Canberra, ACT 2600 ☎02/6273 2535. Consulate in Sydney ☎02/ 9262 7377.
Canada 130 Albert St, Suite 606–608, Ottawa, Ontario K1P 5G4 ☎613/233-1121. Consulate in Toronto ☎416/922-7181, ⓦwww.philcongen-toronto.com.
New Zealand 50 Hobson St, Thorndon, Wellington ☎04/472 9848, ⓔembassy@wellington-pe.co.nz.
UK and Ireland 9a Palace Green, London W8 4QE ☎0870 005 6968, ⓦphilippines.embassyhomepage.com.
US 1600 Massachusetts Ave NW, Washington, DC 20036 ☎202/467-9300, ⓦwww.philippineembassy-usa .org. Consulates in Chicago ☎312/332-6458, ⓦwww.chicagopcg.com; Honolulu ☎808/595-6316, ⓦwww .geocities.com/pcghawaii; Los Angeles ☎213/639-0980, ⓦwww.philcongenla .org; and New York ☎212/764 1330, ⓦwww.pcgny.net.

Singapore

Population 2.7 million	Hinduism, Sikhism, Christianity
Language Mandarin, Malay, Tamil and English are the official languages; various Chinese dialects also spoken	**Climate** Tropical
	Best time to visit Singapore is extremely hot and humid all year; November–January is slightly cooler, but also has the highest rainfall
Currency Singapore dollar (S$)	
Religion Buddhism, Islam,	**Minimum daily budget** US$35/£20

Though some monuments and buildings from its British colonial days remain, Singapore is more a showcase for gleaming modern architecture than a memorial to times past; the speed and ruthlessness of development on the tiny island are quite breathtaking. Most visitors to Southeast Asia pass through here at some point, it being the region's transport hub. While many love the orderly efficiency of the place after a few weeks in wilder parts, others miss the feel of "real" Asia among the high-rises, shopping centres, seamless transport systems and booming economy.

It's easy to mock the authoritarian regulations that have accompanied Singapore's development – don't bring in any chewing gum, don't jaywalk and always flush the toilet after use – but Singapore is the Asia that most Asian nations aspire to, a well-ordered and safe environment both day and night for residents and foreigners alike. It isn't cheap, though, and anyone on a tight budget should try to stay as short a time as possible. Fortunately, the island is compact enough that you can explore the highlights – downtown Singapore, the zoo and Sentosa – in just a few days, eating great meals every few hours along the way; Singapore has a well-deserved

reputation as a foodie mecca, which owes much to the different cuisines of the rich ethnic mix on the tiny island, with Chinese in the majority and sizeable minorities of Malays and Indians.

Main attractions

● **Chinatown Little India, the Arab Quarter** Towered over by the new Singapore skyline, these remaining ethnic enclaves are relatively untouched by modern development. Some of their tiny, terraced shophouses are still in operation – the shop operates from the front downstairs rooms, while the inhabitants live behind and above. Not surprisingly, traditional places of worship remain most evocative of times past. The Sri Mariamman Hindu temple, with its exuberant carvings; the graceful domes and dignified interior of the Sultan Mosque; and the Thian Hock Keng Chinese temple are especially atmospheric and picturesque.

● **The zoo** A shining example: most of the bigger animals are kept in huge enclosures, separated from visitors by deep moats. Also on offer is a brilliant Night Safari for viewing nocturnal animals.

● **Food** Head for the food courts, lined with numerous stalls selling their own specialities; you put your meal together from whichever stalls take your fancy. The surroundings at these places may be pretty uninspiring, but the range of Asian cuisines on offer is amazing, from Malay satay to Indian biriyanis via Thai *tom-yam* soup. Those missing more familiar tastes will be pleased to find that Singapore also offers everything from Italian and French to Mexican, and American coffee-bar chains have hit the city big-time.

● **Raffles Hotel** The luxurious atmosphere of this colonial-era institution is still much in evidence, and a visit is considered a must for tourists, though much of the site has been turned into a shopping arcade. You can even have a Singapore Sling at the very bar where the cocktail was created – though it'll cost you more than a night in one of the city's budget guesthouses (Ⓦwww.raffleshotel.com).

● **Shopping** Singapore's number-one hobby. The island's shopping malls are certainly on a grand scale, and boast aggressive air-conditioning – useful if the heat gets too much. You'll find the greatest concentration of malls along Orchard Road. If you're on a wider trip through Asia, though, you'll usually find better prices elsewhere.

● **Sentosa** This offshore-island amusement park has plenty of rides, exhibitions and museums. Underwater World, where a moving walkway carries you through a transparent underwater tunnel with sharks and other sea creatures swimming around outside, is hard to beat, as are the views of the city's skyscrapers you get as you ride the cable car here.

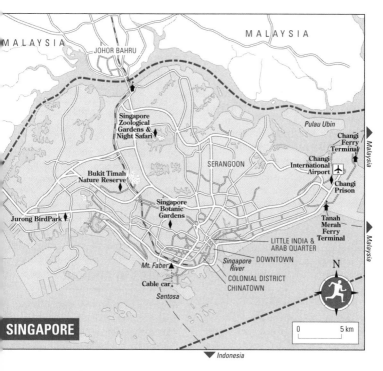

Average daily temperatures (maximum and minimum °C) and monthly rainfall (mm)

	Jan	Feb	Mar	Apr	May	June	July	Aug	Sept	Oct	Nov	Dec
Singapore												
max °C	31	32	32	32	32	32	31	31	31	31	31	30
min °C	21	22	23	23	23	23	22	22	22	22	22	22
rainfall mm	146	155	182	223	228	151	170	163	200	199	255	258

● **Jurung Bird Park** In the west of the main island, the park contains over six hundred species of bird, including, remarkably, Antarctic penguins. There's also a gigantic walk-in aviary so visitors can stroll among the birds.

Also recommended

● **A cruise on the Singapore River** A chance to see the city's fabulously modern high-rises, gentrified warehouses and Chinese shophouses from a different angle.

● **Bukit Timah Hill** Singapore's highest peak (at a mere 162.5m) is home to the island's last pocket of primary rainforest, the habitat of macaques, butterflies and flying lemurs. It's said there are more plant species here than in the whole of North America.

● **Drink at the Swissotel's City Space Bar** So high up in the stratosphere, you can see as far as Indonesia to the south and Malaysia to the north.

● **Pulau Ubin** Just 7km long and 2km wide, this tiny island tucked into the waters between Singapore and Malaysia gives a glimpse into a rural Singapore long gone elsewhere, with Malay stilt houses and little tracks.

● **Asian Civilizations Museum** If you're looking for inspiration for the next leg of your journey you'll surely find it

here, in this stylish, perfectly judged introduction to the cultures, arts and faiths of Southeast Asia, the Indian subcontinent, China and Islamic Asia.

● **Esplanade** Singapore's high profile entertainment complex is a must, not least for the startlingly futuristic design.

Festivals

January/February *Thaipusam*. In honour of the Hindu god of bravery, Lord Murugu, devotees have their bodies pierced and are encased in *kavadi*, heavy metal spiked cages.

January/February *Chinese New Year*. Dragon and lion dances plus a riverside carnival, including Dragon Boat Races, ends with the Chingay Parade, Singapore's biggest, in which floats, martial arts troops and stilt walkers parade through the streets.

October/November *Thimithi*. At the Sri Mariamman Temple, Hindu devotees sprint across burning coals in honour of Draupathi, a legendary heroine. The night before a silver chariot honouring her is pulled from here to the Sri Srinavasa Temple.

Routes in and out

Singapore's Changi airport is one of the busiest in Asia and is served by all major international carriers. As well as long-haul flights, there are excellent links to all parts of Asia. A causeway connects Singapore with the Malaysian city of Johor Bahru, and there are direct buses to destinations throughout Malaysia and on to Hat Yai and Bangkok in Thailand; trains also link Singapore with destinations in Malaysia. There are ferries to Tanjung Belungkor and Pengerang in Malaysia, and to the Riau Archipelago of Indonesia, from where there are connections to Sumatra.

Singapore online

Esplanade – Ⓦ www.esplanade.com Singapore's newest arts complex hosts a great website, detailing everything you can do here – and there's a lot.
Makansutra – Ⓦ www.makansutra .com Leaving no doubt that Singapore is foodie heaven, this monthly magazine features articles, reviews and listings about every aspect of eating in Singapore – there's also an excellent discussion forum where you can ask specific advice on where to eat.
Post Colonial Web – Ⓦ www.post colonialweb.org Singapore is only one of many countries featured here but the site's a great resource for up-to-date information on all areas of the arts and there are tons of links to follow up.
Singapore Infomap: the National Website – Ⓦ www.sg Awesome in its scope and efficiency, this portal has links to more than 16,000 Singaporean sites on every imaginable aspect of Singapore and is updated daily – if it isn't here, the chances are it doesn't exist.

Books

Maurice Collis *Raffles*. This biography describes the amazing life of Raffles, the British founder of modern Singapore.
Su-chen Christine Lim *A Bit of Earth*. Following the friendship between a Malay chef and a Chinese refugee, this moving novel, by one of Singapore's best known novelists, subverts the stereotypes that exist within the culture.
Vyvyane Loh *Breaking the Tongue*. The Fall of Singapore is told from a local perspective in this chilling story. The Chinese central character, Claude Lim, has been brought up to be British, and this book is also about identity, as relevant to Singapore today as it was at that time. In some ways a gruesome read, there is hope in the midst of the chaos and conflict.

△ Singapore skyline

Lau Siew Mau *Playing Madam Mao*. The complex plot involves an actress, Chang Ching, who shares a name with Mao's third wife and also plays her on the stage. The instability of identity is set against the backdrop of uncertainties in Singapore in the 1980s – including media censorship and the repression of political opposition.

Hwee Hwee Tan *Foreign Bodies*. One of Singapore's best known authors tackles nine frenetic days in the lives of the three central characters taking on culture clash in the city-state head on.

Films

Chicken Rice War (Cheah Chee Long, 2001). A riff on Romeo and Juliet, this tells the story of Fenson Wong and Audrey Chang whose feuding parents operate neighbouring stalls in a hawker centre.

Eating Air (Zhi Feng, 1999). This is the story of less than model Singaporeans, the tatooed bikers who smoke, drink, trade porn and drive fast motorbikes. But there's a touching love story here as well – and a rousing rock soundtrack.

I Not Stupid (Jack Neo, 2002). A big box office success in Singapore, this comic drama tells the story of three 12-year-old classmates and their families.

Money No Enough (Tay Teck Lock, 1998). A pointed look at the materialism of modern Singapore society, this film garnered praise, and a huge box-office income, at home.

Twelve Storeys (Eric Khoo, 1997). The lives of ordinary Singaporeans are dissected in this scathing criticism of the island's heart and soul. An oldest son, an elderly lady and a henpecked husband tell their tales and illustrate the dark side of Singaporean culture and life.

Singaporean tourist offices

Ⓦ www.visitsingapore.com
Australia Level 11, AWA Building, 47 York St, Sydney, NSW 2000 Ⓣ07/9290 2888, Ⓕ02/9290 2555; 15 Lawrence Avenue, West Perth, WA 6005 Ⓣ08/9226 5666, Ⓕ08/9226 2444.
Canada Contact the closest US office.
New Zealand Suite 10K, 18 Ronwood Avenue, Manukau City, Auckland 1702 Ⓣ09/262 3933, Ⓕ09/262 3937.
UK 1st floor, Carrington House, 126–130 Regent St, London W1B 5JX Ⓣ020/7437 0033 or Ⓣ0800/65 65 65, Ⓕ020/7734 2191.
US 4929 Wilshire Blvd #510, CA 90010 Ⓣ323/677-0808, Ⓕ323/677-0801; 1156 Avenue of the Americas #702, New York 10036, Ⓣ212/302-4861, Ⓕ212/302-4801.

Singaporean embassies and consulates

Ⓦ www.mfa.gov.sg/internet/
Australia 17 Forster Crescent, Yarralumla, Canberra, ACT 2600 Ⓣ02/6273 3944, Ⓦ www.mfa.gov.sg/canberra.
Canada Contact US embassy.
New Zealand 17 Kabul St, Khandallah, Wellington Ⓣ04/470 0850, Ⓦ www.mfa.gov.sg/wellington.
UK 9 Wilton Crescent, London SW1X 8SP Ⓣ020/7235 8315, Ⓦ www.mfa.gov.sg/london.
US 3501 International Place NW, Washington, DC 20008 Ⓣ202/537-3100, Ⓦ www.mfa.gov.sg/washington; consulates in Chicago Ⓣ312/853-7555; Miami Ⓣ305/858-4225; New York Ⓣ212/223-3331; and San Francisco Ⓣ415/543-4775.

South Korea

Capital Seoul
Population 48 million
Language Korean
Currency Won (W)
Main religions Mahayana Buddhism and Christianity

Climate Temperate
Best time to go September–November; also April–June
Minimum daily budget $35/£19

Overshadowed as a tourist destination by neighbouring China and Japan, South Korea features on backpackers' itineraries more as a place to find work than as somewhere to explore for its own sake. English-teaching jobs are fairly easy to land in Seoul and Busan (check the adverts in the local English-language newspapers), and the cost of living is less prohibitive than in Japan, though still a lot higher than nearly everywhere else in Asia. Being so close to China and Japan, South Korea also works well as part of a journey between the two, and there are useful ferry services in both directions.

The same is not true of its immediate neighbour, North Korea, with whom virtually all contact – including transport links – has been banned since 1950, when civil war erupted between the communist, Soviet-backed North and the US-backed South. Though overt hostilities ended in 1953, no peace agreement has yet been signed, so the two countries are still theoretically at war. Indeed the ceasefire line between them – the Demilitarized Zone (DMZ) – is a major tourist attraction. Encouragingly, the new millennium has seen unprecedented dialogue between the two governments and a few of the eleven million separated North–South families have been reunited for the first time in fifty years. However, North Korea is still a very difficult and expensive place to visit: visas are not granted to nationals of South Korea or the US; other nationalities must apply two months ahead and are obliged to be accompanied by a tour guide throughout their stay in this reclusive, autocratic, communist state. Access is generally by plane or train from Beijing but, should North–South relations thaw further, restored rail links between the two countries would make South Korea accessible by rail all the way from Europe, via the Trans-Siberian terminus in Vladivostock.

The dominant force in contemporary South Korean culture is Confucianism; more of a philosophy than a religion, it originated in China 2500 years ago and is essentially a moral code of family duty and social obligations. The most widespread religion in South Korea is Mahayana Buddhism, and you will find traditional Buddhist temples all over the country, in the heart of the city as well as hidden away on remote mountain sides.

For tourists, South Korea's greatest attractions are the thousands of hiking trails through the forests of its mountainous national parks. Around seventy percent of the country is mountainous, and the autumn colours on the trees that

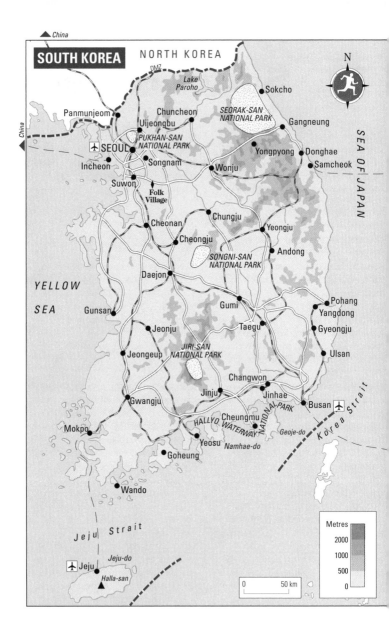

SOUTH KOREA

carpet the mountains are at their most spectacular in late October; springtime brings a similarly impressive display of

cherry blossom, followed soon after by azaleas. Try to avoid major sights, national parks and hiking trails at

First Time Asia | WHERE TO GO

weekends, when you'll be competing for space with thousands of city dwellers. Public transport within South Korea is fast and efficient, and the country is so compact that you can cross from coast to coast in half a day.

Main attractions

- **Gyeongju** Korea's ancient capital, Gyeongju, is the country's big must-see, and rates as one of the ten most important ancient cultural cities in the world. In among the shops and markets of the modern-day city you'll find abundant relics of its two-thousand-year history, including colossal fifth-century tombs and burial mounds, a seventh-century stone observatory, and the royal pleasure gardens of Anapji, which were designed in 674 AD. Other quarters of Gyeongju are rich with elegant pagodas and historic wooden Buddhist temples, and numerous trails take you up the slopes of the sacred mountain, Nam-san, which dominates the south of the city.

- **Hiking in the national parks** South Korea is full of exhilarating national parks, all of which are crisscrossed by clearly marked trails and dotted with good camping spots (and the occasional mountain hut). The cream of the crop is Seorak-san, and in particular Naeseorak (Inner Seorak), an exceptionally tranquil stretch of forested peaks, rivers, waterfalls and Buddhist temples – and some established rock climbs too. Also well worth seeking out are Jiri-san, which boasts a 65-kilometre-long ridge trail and lots of historic temples; the popular and fairly gentle trails of Songni-san; and Bukhan-san, which is on the edge of Seoul.

- **Seoul** South Korea's modern-day capital has a reasonable number of sights to keep you entertained for a few days. Most interesting are the five imposing royal palaces, some of which date back to the fifteenth century. Inside the Changdokkung Palace you'll find one of South Korea's loveliest gardens, the Piwon, a beautifully landscaped haven of ponds and pavilions. In the modern part of town, check out the Kimchi Museum, dedicated to the fiery pickled cabbage that is South Korea's national dish, browse the cutting-edge Leeum Museum of Modern Art, and spend the evening in the trendy nightlife district of Sinchon.

- **Panmunjeom** On the 38th parallel, the 1953 ceasefire line between North and South Korea – a four-kilometre-wide strip of land spiked with guardposts

Mean temperatures (°C) and rainfall (mm)

Average daily temperatures (maximum and minimum °C) and monthly rainfall (mm)

	Jan	Feb	Mar	Apr	May	June	July	Aug	Sept	Oct	Nov	Dec
Seoul												
max °C	0	3	8	17	22	27	29	31	26	19	11	3
min °C	-9	-7	-2	5	11	16	21	22	15	7	0	-7
rainfall mm	31	20	38	76	81	130	376	267	119	41	46	25
Busan												
max °C	6	7	12	17	21	24	27	29	26	21	15	9
min °C	-2	-1	3	8	13	17	22	23	18	12	6	1
rainfall mm	43	36	69	140	132	201	295	130	173	74	41	31

– is still in force today, and the village of Panmunjeom, which stands on the DMZ just 56km north of Seoul, is a popular day-trip from the capital. Unless you can afford the cost of joining an organized tour around North Korea this is the closest you can get to the repressive, desperately impoverished totalitarian state. There's no border crossing here (or anywhere between the two countries) but Panmunjeom attracts busloads of tourists, all of whom are required to dress smartly (no jeans, T-shirts or miniskirts) and, if male, to have a respectable haircut!

● **The Korean Folk Village** It may sound like a coach-tour nightmare, but the Korean Folk Village is well worth a day-trip from Seoul, especially if you've not got time to explore the rest of the country. A reconstruction of a typical nineteenth-century village, it's complete with Buddhist temple, Confucian school, pottery and weaving workshops, blacksmiths and traditional farmhouses. The people you see in the village do actually live and work here, even if they might look like actors dolled up in traditional outfits.

● **Jeju-do** This southern island has maintained traditions that have long disappeared from the mainland and is now a popular tourist destination as well as a favourite with local honeymooners. Highlights here include mysterious Easter Island-like statues, hikes to the summit of Halla-san (South Korea's highest volcano), and a seven-kilometre-long lava-tube cave. The climate down here is warmer and wetter than in the rest of the country, but don't come specifically for the beaches, as you'll find them crowded and disappointingly scruffy.

Also recommended

● **The three-hour boat ride from Busan to Yeosu** This is one of the most scenic journeys in the country, with fine views of the crenellated coastline and myriad islets. It's so attractive round here that the whole area has been conserved as Hallyo Waterway National Park.

● **The island of Ullung-do** Rugged, remote and starkly beautiful, this tiny volcanic outcrop – accessed by ferry from Samcheok – has hardly any roads and is best explored on foot. It takes two days to walk right round the island, giving you ample opportunity to enjoy the temples, forested ridges, waterfalls and famous 2000-year-old juniper tree.

● **Taking an open-air bath with a view at Seorak Waterpia** Soak up the glorious mountain vista while wallowing in the natural hot springs at this spa resort in Seorak-san National Park, where you can also bathe in a lemon-flavoured pool, go skinny-dipping, and brave a shower under a near-boiling waterfall.

● **The fifteenth-century village of Yangdong** Prettily set beside a river and beneath a wooded hill, Yangdong is of such historic importance that villagers are forbidden to modify or knock down their antique wooden houses, many of which are magnificent structures, with sweeping roofs, beautifully carved beams and capacious verandahs.

● **Bargain-hunting at Namdaemun Night Market in Seoul** Opening every night at around 10.30pm and running through till just before dawn, the enormous Namdaemun Market sells everything from handicrafts to saucepans, ginseng to live fish. It's a great place to while away the evening, not least because of all the cheap food stalls that dish up hot snacks through till morning.

● **Staying in a yogwan** If you're on a budget, make a beeline for these ubiquitous traditional guesthouses: they're cheap, family-run, and usually have lots of character. You sleep on a futon on the floor – a special treat in winter when the underfloor heating system kicks in and acts like a huge electric blanket.

● **Snowboarding and skiiing at Yongpyong** There are over thirty runs for skiers and snowboarders at this trendy ski resort on the slopes on Mount Balwang, plus floodlit night-skiing, a sledging park and cross-country trails. Also holds a snow-sculpture festival in February.

Festivals

March or April *Jinhae Cherry Blossom Festival*, Jinhae, near Busan. The cherry blossoms are particularly gorgeous in Jinhae, where they're celebrated with a week of parades and blossom photo contests, but you also get a good show in Incheon and in Seorak-san National Park.
May or June *Dano Festival*, Namdaecheon, near Gangneung. Very traditional festival of the spirits in which shamen pray for a good harvest and there are public displays of traditional wrestling, martial arts, dance and masked drama.

October *Chungju World Martial Arts Festival*. Groups from across the world gather to demonstrate their special martial arts skills in this week-long sporting spectacle in Chungju, credited as the spiritual home of modern tae kwon do.

Routes in and out

Most international flights arrive at Seoul's Incheon Airport, 60km west of the capital. There are also flights from Japan into Busan and Jeju-do airports. South Korea has good international ferry connections with Japan and China. Ferries and hydrofoils to and from Japan run between Shimonoseki and Busan, and between Fukuoka and Busan, and there's a handy combination rail and hydrofoil ticket from Osaka all the way through to Seoul, via Fukuoka and Busan. Ferries to China all arrive at and depart from Incheon (near Seoul), running regularly to Tianjin (near Beijing), Qingdao and Weihai (both in Shandong), and Dalian and Dandong (both in Liaoning). See ⓦwww.seoulsearching .com/transportation/boat for international ferry timetables.

△ Sculptures at Kyongbokkung, one of Seoul's five historic palaces

There has been no legal border crossing between South and North Korea since the Korean War; this may change, however, if relations continue to thaw.

South Korea online

ELT Bank Cool Connection: Korea – Ⓦ www.eltbank.com/cool_con /before_coming_to_korea/1.html Carries lots of posts from English teachers, with different views on the ELT experience in Korea.

The Korean Blog List – Ⓦ korea .banoffeepie.com Over two hundred blogs about Korea, written in English by expats, emigrés and tourists.

National Parks – Ⓦ www.npa.or.kr Check out the how and where of Korea's most scenic national parks, or book a campsite or mountain lodge.

North Korea Zone – Ⓦ www.nkzone .org Forum and headline feeds on North Korea, plus a dedicated travel section.

Seoul Selection – Ⓦ www.seoul selection.com Weekly roundup of cultural events in the capital, plus background features, a forum, and Korean books and films for sale.

Books

Kang Chol-Hwan *The Aquariums of Pyongyang: Ten Years in the North Korean Gulag.* The horrifying account of Kang Chol-Hwan's childhood, which was spent from ages 9 to 19 in a North Korean labour camp, because his grandfather was suspected of harbouring counter-revolutionary tendencies. The family was released in 1987 and the author, a journalist, now lives in South Korea.

Bruce Cumings *North Korea: Another Country.* Intelligent, very current analysis of life in the North Korea, focusing particularly on North Korea's

tortured relationship with the US, from the American–Korean War to America's branding of the country as part of the "axis of evil".

Clive Leatherdale *To Dream of Pigs: Travels in South and North Korea.* One of very few travelogues about Korea, this one charts a journey rounds South Korea in the late 1980s and a trip to North Korea in 1992.

Shawn Matthews *Island of Fantasy: A Memoir of an English Teacher in Korea.* An American teacher reveals all about his year spent teaching in a small private school on the island of Koje-do, off Busan. The author now teaches in Seoul and posts his blogs at Ⓦ korealife .blogspot.com.

Simon Winchester *Korea: A Walk Through the Land of Miracles.* An updated version of a 1988 journey around South Korea by one of Britain's most erudite travel writers.

Films

Ⓦ **koreanfilm.org**
Chihwaseon: Strokes of Fire (Im Kwon-Taek, 2002). Beautifully shot story of the troubled life and loves of an impassioned, alcoholic nineteenth-century artist. It won the already famous Korean director Kwon-Taek Im best director award at the Cannes Film Festival.

Memories of Murder (Boon Jun-Ho, 2003). Phenomenally popular, way above-average suspense thriller based on the real unsolved case of ten serial rapes and murders in a small village in the late 1980s.

Shiri (Kang Je-Kyu, 1999). A huge smash at the Korean box office, this pertinent North-South action thriller involves Southern secret agents, a slinky female assassin from North Korea and a North–South football match during which the two leaders shake hands...

Spring, Summer, Autumn, Winter... and Spring (Kim Ki-Duk, 2004). Gentle Buddhist fable about a troubled young man and an elderly monk who live in a floating temple on a lake encircled by forested slopes. The breathtakingly beautiful setting – Juwangsan National Park – is stunning, shot in its different seasonal guises.

A Tale Of Two Sisters (Kim Ji-Woon, 2004). Scary, brilliantly crafted psycho-supernatural thriller about two sisters returning to live with their father and cruel stepmother after a stint in a mental-health hospital. Updated version of a traditional ghost story.

South Korean tourist offices

ⓦ www.tour2korea.com
Australia and New Zealand Level 40, Australia Square Tower, 264 George St, Sydney, NSW 2000 ☏02/9252 4147, ⓦwww.knto.org.au.
Canada 700 Bay St, Suite 1903, Toronto, Ontario M5G 1Z6 ☏416/348-9056, ⓦwww.knto.ca.
UK and Ireland 3rd floor, New Zealand House, Haymarket, London SW1Y 4TE ☏020/7321 2535, ⓔlondon@mail.knto .or.kr.
US ⓦwww.kntoamerica.com. Two Executive Drive Suite 750, Fort Lee, NJ 07024 ☏201/585-0909; 737 N. Michigan Ave, Suite 910, Chicago, IL

60611 ☏312-981-1717; 4801 Wilshire Blvd, Suite 103, Los Angeles, CA 90010 ☏323/634-0280.

South Korean embassies and consulates

ⓦ www.mofat.go.kr
Australia 57 Culgoa Circuit, O'Malley, ACT 2606 ☏02 6286 4770, ⓔdprkembassy@hotmail.com. Consulate in Sydney ☏02/9221 3866.
Canada 150 Boteler St, Ottawa, Ontario K1N 5A6 ☏613/244-5010, ⓦwww .emb-korea.ottawa.on.ca. Consulates in Toronto ☏416-920-3809, ⓦwww .consulatekorea-tor.org; and Vancouver ☏604-685-9577.
Ireland 15 Clyde Road, Ballsbridge, Dublin 4 ☏01/660-8800.
New Zealand 11th Floor, ASB Bank Tower, 2 Hunter Street, Wellington, ☏04/473 9073, ⓔkoreaemb@world-net .co.nz.
UK 60 Buckingham Gate, London SW1E 6AJ ☏020/7227 5505, ⓦkorea .embassyhomepage.com.
US 2320 Massachusetts Ave NW, Washington, DC 20008 ☏202/ 939-5661, ⓦwww.koreaembassyusa.org. Consulates in Houston ☏713-961-0186, ⓦwww.koreahouston.org/e/; Los Angeles ☏213-385-9300, ⓦkoreanconsulatela.org; New York ☏646-674-6000, ⓦwww.korean consulate.org; and San Francisco ☏415-921-2251, ⓦwww.korean consulatesf.org.

Sri Lanka

Capital Colombo
Population 19 million
Languages Sinhala, Tamil and English are official languages
Currency Rupee (Rs)
Religion Buddhists are in the majority (70%), with Hindu (15%), Christian and Muslim minorities

Climate Tropical, with two distinct monsoons
Best time to visit Nov–April for the south and west coasts; Jan–April for the hills; May–Sept for the east coast
Minimum daily budget $10/£6

A small country, Sri Lanka nonetheless offers an enormous variety of quintessentially Asian experiences. The island is dotted with ruins from ancient Buddhist empires, including serene, gigantic Buddha figures, as well as dagobas, white-painted domed shrines ranging from just a few metres tall to immense, imposing structures; variations of those are found in India, Thailand, China and other Asian countries. Other architectural features worth keeping an eye out for are buildings dating from the Portuguese, Dutch and British colonial periods, which lasted from the first European arrival in 1505 through to Independence in 1948.

Sri Lanka also boasts glorious landscapes, with lovely beaches, cool rolling hills, mountains and huge tracts of rainforest, excellent for spotting wildlife. Many bird species like it here too, spending the winter on Sri Lanka's southern coasts before returning to temperate zones. Outside Colombo and Kandy – the main cities – the island has a rural feel, making it more manageable than chaotic India to the north.

Up until early 2002, when a ceasefire was agreed, Sri Lanka was plagued by a violent civil war between the Hindu Tamil minority and the Buddhist Sinhalese majority, which raged for more than twenty years. The disputed territories were essentially the whole of north and east Sri Lanka, and throughout the conflict these areas were too dangerous to visit. Visitors instead confined themselves to the south and the west of the island, although even here there remained some risk, with Colombo being targeted by bombers at various times. Although peace talks stalled in 2003, the peace has largely held, although violent incidents continue to be reported and the truce feels rather fragile.

Just as economic and tourist recovery looked set, huge swathes of coastal Sri Lanka were destroyed by the Asian tsunami of December 2004, and rebuilding from that disaster has been painfully slow. Check with embassies, newspapers, websites and travellers' newsgroups on the Internet to find out the current stuation around the island regarding security and progress of reconstruction when planning your itinerary; also ask local people, local authorities and your own foreign office or embassy once on the island, before venturing to the north or east.

Main attractions

- **Colombo** Though this is where everyone arrives, most visitors don't linger long in the capital. However, the National Museum and the Dutch Period Museum are worth a look, while the Raja Maha Vihara, 13km from the city centre, is the most visited Buddhist temple on the island, built on a site that Buddha himself is said to have visited. For retail therapy, there are some extremely stylish shops selling modern Asian chic gifts, homewares, soft furnishings and clothes, making the city an ideal last stop.

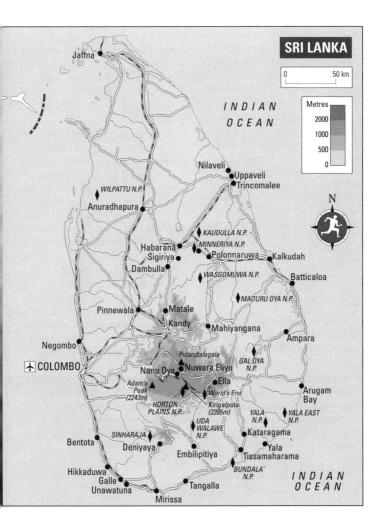

- **Adam's Peak (2224m)** The mountain is a place of pilgrimage for Muslims, Hindus and Buddhists, who believe that the metre-long foot-like imprint in a rock on the peak belongs to Adam, Shiva and the Buddha, respectively. The less devout can also make the three- to four-hour ascent (up a total of 4600 steps) from the village of Dalhousie to see the sunrise and marvel at the Shadow of the Peak a few minutes later, when the perfectly triangular silhouette of the mountain is distinctly visible on the countryside below. These are best seen under the clearer skies of January to April, which is also the height of the pilgrimage season, although trekking at other times of the year is perfectly possible.

- **Anuradhapura** The island's capital from the fourth century BC until the ninth century AD, Sri Lanka's holiest town has much of historical interest. The Ruwanwelisiya dagoba is over 50m tall and surrounded by a wall of carved elephants. The town is best known for the Sri Maha Bodhi tree, which draws pilgrims from throughout the Buddhist world; the tree is believed to have grown from a cutting – brought to the island well over two thousand years ago – taken from the original bo tree in India under which Buddha attained enlightenment.

- **Polonnaruwa** Set beside a huge artificial lake, Polonnaruwa was the medieval capital of the island, after the decline of Anuradhapura. The town is the site of numerous well-preserved chambers, palaces and temples spread over a huge area, many still boasting fine carvings and friezes. Best known are the sublime Buddhist images, the Gal Vihara, carved by an unknown artist out of a towering granite rock face; there are three main figures, shown standing, seated and reclining.

- **Pinnewala Elephant Orphanage** Elephants are a pervasive Sri Lankan image, whether painted or sculpted. Pinnawela offers a great chance to see live ones at close quarters; orphaned, abandoned or injured infant elephants are reared and trained here. Be certain to catch them during bathing time in the river.

- **Kandy** Situated on the hills surrounding a huge artificial lake and reachable by a scenic train ride from Colombo, Sri Lanka's cultural capital is a cool and picturesque place to hang out. It is also the home of one of the most venerated temples in Sri Lanka, the Dalada Maligawa or Temple of the Tooth – so named because it holds what's believed to be a tooth of the Buddha, rescued from his funeral pyre.

- **Sigiriya** Built on top of a massive 200-metre-high granite monolith, this fifth-century fortress stands sentinel over the surrounding plains. The stronghold was created by the murderous King Kassapa who, after killing his father to

Mean temperatures (°C) and rainfall (mm)

Average daily temperatures (maximum and minimum °C) and monthly rainfall (mm)

	Jan	Feb	Mar	Apr	May	June	July	Aug	Sept	Oct	Nov	Dec
Colombo												
max °C	30	31	31	31	31	29	29	29	29	29	29	29
min °C	22	22	23	24	26	25	25	25	25	24	23	22
rainfall mm	89	69	147	231	371	224	135	109	160	348	315	147

grab the throne, feared retribution from the rightful heir, his brother, and took refuge here. A sheltered overhang in the rock face contains well-preserved fresco paintings. Much of the climb is up a rather exposed staircase but the views from the top make it worth the effort.

● **South coast beaches** Many villages and resorts of the south coast's glorious beaches were destroyed by the Asian tsunami and restoration is proceeding slowly. It's difficult to predict precisely how the reconstructions will proceed, and although resorts further north such as Bentota and Hikkaduwa are better known, check out charming Mirissa, Tangalla and Unawatuna in the south if you can, they are the real gems.

Also recommended

● **Ella** A small, peaceful, attractive village set at around 1000m in the hills. It is cool but not cold and has some fabulous views down to the plains. There are plenty of local walks; the most energetic can climb nearby Ella Rock for even more spectacular views, and the train journey from Ella to Nanu Oya is one of the most picturesque in the country.

● **Sunrise over World's End** The highest plateau in Sri Lanka has a viewpoint over a one-thousand-metre drop, from where you can admire the clouds several hundred metres below.

● **Galle** Enclosed inside the ramparts of the old Dutch Fort, this port town retains much of its colonial ambience. It is possible to walk most of the way around the ramparts for great views across the town and out to sea, especially lovely at sunset.

● **Cricket** Sri Lankans are mad about the game, and there's often a foreign side on tour. Go to a match and experience the wild atmosphere and loud, exuberant crowd.

● **The flamingoes of Bundala National Park** The park is Sri Lanka's best area for bird-watching at any time of year, with thousands of flamingos crowding its lagoons and wetlands from January to April.

● **Yala National Park** Although its elephants are the main draw, you'll probably see more tourist jeeps in Sri Lanka's most popular park. You've also a chance of spotting leopards here, as well as deer, sloth bears, crocodiles, wild boar, jackals and around 130 species of bird, including the impressive hornbill.

● **Tea** Sri Lanka is the world's biggest tea exporter and in the upland areas around Nuwara Eliya the hillsides are covered with its brilliant green bushes. Visit one of the tea factories to learn about the intricate process that gets the leaves from the field to the pot.

Festivals

February *Navam Poya*. Celebrating Buddha's announcement of his impending death, this is one of the island's biggest festivals, taking place at Gangaramaya temple in Colombo, and featuring parades of dancers, drummers and elephants.

July/August *Esala Perahera*. Sri Lanka's most extravagant festival, honouring Buddha's sacred tooth relic from the Temple of the Tooth, takes place over ten days in Kandy. The great final procession includes fabulously bedecked elephants, accompanied by dancers and drummers.

July/August *Kataragama*. Fire-walking and self-mutilation are the most famous aspects of the annual celebration at Kataragama temple – sacred to Buddhists, Hindus and Muslims.

July/August *Vel.* Colombo's most important Hindu festival includes a procession of the chariot of Skanda, God of War, across the city.

Routes in and out

Although Sri Lanka is separated from India only by the narrow Palk Strait, there is no ferry route between the two countries and the construction of a bridge has been under discussion for decades. All arrival and departure is through the international airport at Colombo.

Sri Lanka online

Ari Withanage's Welcome to Sri Lanka – Ⓦwithanage.tripod.com Run by Ari, a Sri Lankan living just outside London, this excellent site gives a thorough introduction to all aspects of the island, with plenty of detail and fine pictures.

Arugam Bay – Ⓦwww.arugam.info This well-loved surf spot on the east coast was flattened by the Asian tsunami. This site is operated by the Hotel Association of Arugam bay and details the events, reconstruction and current practical details for visiting.

Infolanka – Ⓦwww.infolanka.com General umbrella site with links to articles and other sites on every aspect of Sri Lankan life, including religion, politics, travel, sport and cooking.

Sacred Sites of Sri Lanka – http://lankabhumi.org Serious and fascinating site about all aspects of the sacred places in Sri Lanka. There are some fabulous images and useful links: the ones to Adam's Peak and Sigiriya are especially fruitful.

WWW Virtual Library Sri Lanka – Ⓦwww.lankalibrary.com Excellent general site with a monster number of links to sites on Sri Lankan tourism, culture and religion, as well as up-to-the-minute news. There's also a good forum.

Books

Romesh Gunesekara *Reef.* Evocative, moody tale of a house boy, his mentor and their obsessions with cooking

△ Pinnewala Elephant Orphanage

and the underwater world, by one of Sri Lanka's most well-known and accomplished authors.

Michelle de Kretser *The Hamilton Case*. Set in the time around Independence, this historical thriller, excellent for period detail, follows the story of lawyer Sam Obeysekere, who gets involved in the murder of a British tea planter.

Michael Ondaatje *Running in the Family*. This is a memoir of the author's eccentric Burgher family during the first half of the twentieth century.

Films

Death on a Full Moon Day (*Pura Handa Kaluwara;* Prasana Vithnage, 1998). One of Sri Lanka's best-known directors tackles the war, with this tale of a blind father who refuses to believe that his soldier son is dead. See also his *Ira Madiyama* ("August Sun") which juxtaposes the stories of a Muslim refugee, a Sinhalese widow and a government soldier in the maelstrom of the war.

Mansion by the Lake (*Wekanda Walauwa*; Lester James Peries, 2002). Set in rural Sri Lanka in the 1980s, Sujata Rajasuriya and her daughter return from years in London to sell the family mansion. One of Sri Lanka's few directors to have made his name in the West returns to his usual themes of families as a microcosm of social, political and economic changes in the world outside.

A Mother Alone (*Duvata Mawaka Misa*; Sumitra Gunawardena, 1997). This film tells the story of Thushari, unmarried and pregnant, as she is shunted around the family to try to avert the shame of her situation; the film tellingly illustrates the lives of women in Sri Lankan society.

Saroja (Somaratne Dissanayake, 1999). This controversial story of a wounded Tamil Tiger fighter who takes refuge in a Sinhalese village, explores themes of reconciliation, friendship and humanity in the time of war.

Sri Lankan tourist offices

ⓦ **www.srilankatourism.org**
Australia 29 Lonsdale St, Braddon, ACT 2612 ☏6/2306 002, Ⓕ 6/2306 066.
Canada Contact the US office.
Ireland 59 Ranelagh Road, Dublin 6 ☏3/1496 9621, Ⓕ3/1496 5345.
New Zealand Contact the Australian office.
UK 26–27 Clareville House, Oxendon St, London, SW1Y 4EL ☏020/7930 2627, Ⓕ020/7930 9070.
USA 115 Inner Avenue #323, Edison, NJ 08820 ☏732/516-9800, Ⓕ732/452-0087.

Sri Lankan embassies and consulates

ⓦ **www.srilankatourism.org**
Australia 35 Empire Circuit, Forrest, Canberra, ACT 2603 ☏02/6239 7041, Ⓕ02/6239 6166.
Canada Suite 1204, 33 Laurier Ave W, Ottawa, Ontario K1P 1C1 ☏613/233-8449, Ⓕ613/238-8448.
New Zealand Contact the embassy in Canberra.
UK 13 Hyde Park Gardens, London W2 2LU ☏020/7262 1841, ⓦwww .slhclondon.org.
USA 2148 Wyoming Ave NW, Washington, DC 20008 ☏202/483-4026, ⓦwww.srilankaembassyusa.org.

Taiwan

Capital Taipei	**Climate** Subtropical, with a rainy
Population 21 million	season in May and June
Language Mandarin, Chinese	**Best time to visit** Good at any
dialects including Taiwanese and	time but avoid festivals, especially
Hakka, and ten tribal languages	Chinese New Year, as transport is
Currency New Taiwanese dollar	booked solid and hotel prices soar
(NT$)	at these times
Religion Buddhism, Daoism and	**Minimum daily budget** US$30/£20
Confucianism	

Taiwan has had a turbulent history, with Chinese dynasties and foreign powers seeking sovereignty over the island. Today its situation is ambiguous: at the end of the civil war on mainland China in 1949, with the communists set to win, the leader of the nationalist Kuomintang, Chiang Kai-shek, led an exodus of soldiers, merchants and scholars to Taiwan. They proclaimed the island the Republic of China, the name it retains today. China views Taiwan as a dissident province, while Taiwan has never declared independence from the mainland but views itself as the legitimate government of China. While relations have thawed to some extent, military intimidation by the mainland and a war of words between the two continue.

Taiwan today is home to some of the noisiest, most frantic cities in Asia, but also offers gorgeous mountain, coastal and inland scenery and a vibrant religious and cultural life. It's a startling mixture of a modern industrial nation at the cutting edge of computer technology and production, alongside age-old beliefs and practices, with literally thousands of atmospheric temples.

There are also plentiful opportunities to get out into the countryside, either to take it easy and admire the views along with the rest of the day-trippers, or to get off the beaten track and take advantage of opportunities for trekking and camping. While the mountain scenery is serene and tranquil, bear in mind that Taiwan is one of the most densely populated countries in the world – you'll be hard pushed to get away from everybody. And as you won't come across many other Western tourists or a backpacker circuit, you'll have ample opportunity to mingle with and meet local people.

Main attractions

● **Taipei** The capital is a congested place, with three million people in the city itself and another three million in the surrounding countryside. That said, it has plenty of attractions to detain you for a couple of days, including atmospheric temples, museums, historic monuments and teeming night markets. If you do nothing else here, visit the National Palace Museum, featuring the world's finest array of Chinese artefacts, moved here in 1948 by the Kuomintang; it's such a huge collection that only a tiny fraction is displayed at any one time.

Chien Kuo is one of the largest jade markets in the world, with more than nine hundred sellers. Also a must-see is

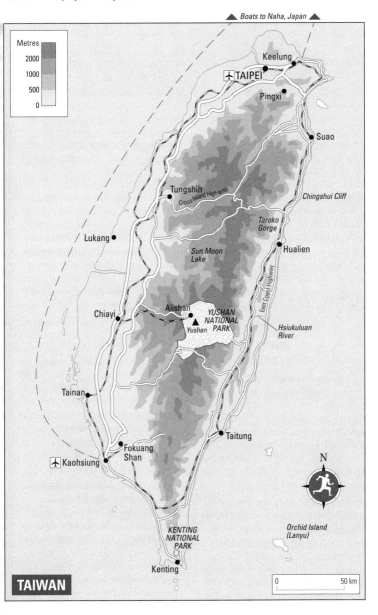

▲ Boats to Naha, Japan ▲

Metres
2000
1000
500
0

Keelung

✈ TAIPEI

Pingxi

Suao

Tungshih
Cross Island Highway

Chingshui Cliff

Taroko
Gorge

Lukang

Sun Moon
Lake

Hualien

East Coast Highway

Alishan

YUSHAN
NATIONAL
PARK

Chiayi

Yushan

Hsiukuluan
River

Tainan

Taitung

Fokuang
Shan

✈ Kaohsiung

N

KENTING
NATIONAL
PARK

Orchid Island
(Lanyu)

Kenting

TAIWAN

0   50 km

Mean temperatures (°C) and rainfall (mm)

Average daily temperatures (maximum and minimum °C) and monthly rainfall (mm)

	Jan	Feb	Mar	Apr	May	June	July	Aug	Sept	Oct	Nov	Dec
Taipei												
max °C	19	18	21	25	28	32	33	33	31	27	24	21
min °C	12	12	14	17	21	23	24	24	23	19	17	14
rainfall mm	86	135	178	170	231	290	231	305	244	122	66	71

Snake Alley, where fortune-tellers, tattoo parlours, fruit sellers and restaurants nestle alongside stalls where you can try a drink of snake blood and bile (and optional venom), removed from specimens freshly killed and skinned in front of you. This mind-boggling concoction is said to strengthen the eyes, spine and sexual vitality.

● **Taroko Gorge** On the east coast, the island's main tourist attraction features a thundering river, towering cliffs and plenty of excellent opportunities for camping and trekking. The most picturesque route to the gorge is via the 200-kilometre-long Cross-Island Highway from Tungshih, with fabulous scenery – tropical valleys, mountain panoramas and lakes – all along the way.

● **Kenting National Park** In the sunny, fertile lowlands of the far south of the island, this park, near the town of Kenting, has white beaches, forests, an attractive coastline, waterfalls, hot springs and plenty more to explore. On the beaches, there are plenty of watersports to try by day, and pubs, discos and karaoke bars to choose from at night.

● **Alishan** At 2190m, the best of the island's mountain resorts doesn't merely offer an escape from the lowland heat; it's a gorgeous spot, surrounded by cedar and pine forests, with the blossoming of the cherry trees a special feature in the spring. Among the numerous treks here, the obligatory excursion

is the one to the peak of 2489-metre Chu Shan (Celebration Mountain), where several thousand people jostle every morning for views of the sunrise. Some Westerners are disappointed by the frequently misty weather, but local people are just as happy whatever the conditions, believing that mountain mists contain a high density of *qi*, the "life force". The narrow-gauge steam train from Chiayi to Alishan is an especially picturesque route there, taking three and a half hours to climb up through the rolling hills, negotiating 50 tunnels and 77 bridges en route.

● **Tainan** Temples are the main reason to visit this city, said to contain around two hundred of them. The most famous is the Temple of the Jade Emperor, the oldest Daoist temple in the city, where a constant stream of visitors comes to pray in a highly atmospheric setting: every wall, ceiling and door is adorned with detailed carvings and frescos, and spirit mediums here are often involved in rituals in which they attempt to contact the dead on behalf of the living.

● **Taking the east coast highway from Suao to Taitung** In places, the road is carved out of cliffs which drop a sheer 1000m into the crashing surf below. The most dramatic part is between Suao and Hualien, which includes a section called Chingshui Cliff where the drops beside the road are especially vertiginous. About halfway between Hualien and Taitung, the Hsiukuluan River is Taiwan's most popular white-water rafting area.

Also recommended

- **Lukang** A major harbour from the seventeenth to twentieth centuries, this small west-coast town retains its tiny alleyways and historic atmosphere. In the centre of town, the Lungshan Temple, dating from the eighteenth century, has fantastically carved ceilings; it was dedicated to Kuanyin, the goddess of mercy, by Chinese settlers in thanks for their safe crossing from the mainland. The craftsmen here still produce furniture, fans, lanterns and incense using traditional techniques, and the Lukang Folk Art Museum is a good place to view fine, historic examples of their art.

- **Fokuang Shan** This modern temple/monastery complex in the rolling hills northeast of the city of Kaohsiung is the centre of Taiwanese Buddhist scholarship. There are four main temples, all magnificent and spacious, with the largest dedicated to Buddha; its walls are lined with 14,800 niches, each containing a tiny golden Buddha statue. At the other end of the scale, a 32-metre Buddha – the largest on the island – lies in the grounds, surrounded by life-sized statues of 480 Buddhist disciples.

- **Scaling Yushan** At 3997m this is the highest peak on the island, higher even than Mount Fuji. To reach the summit you'll need to spend two nights on the mountain, watching the sunrise from the top.

- **Sun Moon Lake** Set 750m up in the hills, this popular spot was created by damming the valley here for a hydroelectric scheme. The surrounding forests and bamboo groves contain many excellent treks.

- **Lanyu or Orchid Island** Just 45 square kilometres in size, this is home to over four hundred Yami people, the island's indigenous inhabitants, who still lead a seafaring lifestyle. Reached by ferry from Taitung, Lanyu has excellent coastal scenery and volcanic countryside, and is a great place to explore.

Festivals

February *Lantern Festival*. Nationwide celebration that varies from area to area (in Taipei and Kaohsiung it lasts several days) but reliably includes fireworks, paper lanterns, lion and dragon dances. It is especially picturesque in Pingxi, east of Taipei.

April/May *Birth of Matsu*. Matsu is the most popular goddess on the island (there are more than five hundred temples dedicated to her). A week of celebration includes a 280-kilometre pilgrimage from Tachia to Hsinkang Temple, parades, dragon and lion dances.

June *Dragon Boat Festival*. Nationwide exuberant and striking one-day festival, one of Taiwan's most important, in which fabulously decorated boats race in rememberance of the suicide of poet Chu Yuan.

Routes in and out

International airports serve Taipei and Kaohsiung. Ferry services operate into Kaohsiung and Keelung from Naha, Japan. There's no direct travel between mainland China and Taiwan; Hong Kong is a popular transit point.

Taiwan online

Atayal – Ⓦwww.atayal.org News, culture, language and history about the ten indigenous tribes of Taiwan

△ Temple dragon

who together number about 400,000 people.

Forums – ⓦ www.forumosa.com Forums about every imaginable aspect of Taiwanese life, including plenty of interest to visitors such as travel, driving, events and volunteering.

National Palace Museum – ⓦ www .npm.gov.tw Extensive and colourful site illustrating many of the treasures of this amazing museum – inspirational if you're thinking of a trip and some consolation if you'll never make it there. Especially useful now as it details current renovations.

Tainan – ⓦ http://taiwan.wcn.com .tw/en/tainan Excellent introduction to the city of Tainan, especially its temples and their significance. Find out where local people go to pray for a mate or to change the sex of their unborn child, and to communicate with the dead. It's also strong on local food – such as Coffin Cakes and Passing the Lean Months Noodles.

Travel in Taiwan – ⓦ www.sinica.edu .tw/tit A monthly travel magazine featuring heaps of information for visitors, with articles and excellent photos covering every area and every facet of the island – from serious history through to sights, shopping and dining.

Books

Eds: Ann C Carver and Sung-Sheng Yvonne Chang *Bamboo Shoots After Rain: Stories by Women Writers of Taiwan*. Ranging from the 1920s until modern times, this is a good introduction to the literature of a society in transition.

Hsien-Yung Pai *Crystal Boys*. This controversial story about a gay Taiwanese man was the first Taiwanese novel to tackle homosexuality. It offers keen insights into Asian family dynamics often inaccessible to Western readers.

Li Qiao *Wintry Night*. This is an abridged translation of the three-volume saga by one of Taiwan's most prolific authors, following the history of the Peng family of Chinese settlers from the 1890s through

World War II, alongside the history of the island from the nineteenth century.

Wang Chen-hi *Rose, Rose I Love You*. A social satire on the Taiwanese love of money, told in the distinctive voice of a pedantic teacher who is trying to teach English to a crowd of prostitutes so they can extract money from American GIs visiting the island for R&R from the Vietnam War.

Films

East Drink Man Woman (Ang Lee, 1994). Now a mainstream Hollwood director, this was one of the earliest Lee films to make an impression on Western audiences. It investigates the relationship between an ageing chef and his daughters via the Chinese obsession with food.

The Time to Live and the Time to Die (Hou Hsiao-hsien, 1985). Partly autobiographical story, by one of Taiwan's best-known directors, of childhood in a poor rural family set against a background of war, displacement and urbanization in the 1950s.

Vive L'Amour (Tsai Ming-liang, 1994). Prize-winning but ultimately bleak look at the lives of three isolated people in Taipei.

Yi Yi (Edward Yang, 2000). Arguably Yang's best film so far, this replays his constant theme of the problems of modern city life, this time looking at the middle-class Jian family as they struggle with the rush of time.

Taiwanese tourist offices

ⓦwww.tbroc.gov.tw
Australia Taipei Economic and Cultural Office, Suite 1904, Level 19, MLC Center, 19–29 Martin Place, Sydney, NSW 2000 ☎02/9231 6942, ⓦwww.taiwantourism.org.
Canada Contact the US office.
New Zealand Contact the Australian office.
UK Contact the Taipei Representative office below.
USA c/o Taipei Economic and Cultural Office, 4201 Wisconsin Ave NW, Washington, DC 20016-2137 ☎202/895-1800, ⓕ202/363 0999. Offices in Atlanta ☎404/870-9375; Boston ☎617/737-2050; Chicago ☎312/616-0100; Houston ☎713/626-7445; Kansas City ☎816/531-1298; Los Angeles ☎213/389-1215; Miami ☎305/443-8917; New York ☎212/557-5122; San Francisco ☎415/326-7680; and Seattle ☎206/441-4586.

Taiwanese embassies and consulates

ⓦwww.tbroc.gov.tw
Australia Taipei Economic and Cultural Office, Unit 8, 40 Blackall Street, Barton, Canberra, ACT 2600 ☎02/6120 2000, ⓕ02/6273 3228.
Canada Taipei Economic and Cultural Representative Office, World Exchange Plaza, 45 O'Connor Street Suite 1960, Ottawa, Ontario K1P 1A4 ☎613/231-5080, ⓕ613/231-7112. Offices in Toronto ☎416/369-9030; and Vancouver ☎604/689-4111.
New Zealand Contact the Australian office.
UK Taipei Representative, 50 Grosvenor Gdns, London SW1W OEB ☎020/7881 2650, ⓦwww.tro-taiwan.roc.org.uk. Offices in Edinburgh ☎131/220 6886, ☎http://dspacedial.pipex.com/troed.
US 1 East 42nd St, 4th Floor, New York 10017, ☎212/486-0088, ⓦwww.taipei.org.

Thailand

Capital Bangkok	**Climate** Tropical
Population 63 million	**Best time to go** November to
Language Thai	February (but March–Sept for
Currency Baht (B)	peninsular east coast)
Main religion Theravada Buddhism	**Minimum daily budget** $10/£5

The perfect place to start a cross-Asia trip, Thailand has a well-established tourist infrastructure, with good transport links, plenty of backpacker-oriented guesthouses and a thriving travellers' scene. Hard-core travellers dislike the place for those very reasons, considering it too easy, too popular, and over-explored – in short, not cool enough. But to most visitors it's simply a great holiday destination.

Bumming around on tropical beaches is the most popular tourist activity, with trekking in the northern hills a close second. Further south, swaths of intact rainforest have been conserved as national parks, offering a good chance of seeing monkeys, tropical birds and even elephants from the trails. Thailand also has plenty of cultural highlights, including well-preserved ruined cities from almost every major period in its history, the finest of which are the Hindu-Buddhist temples built by the ancient Khmers of Cambodia a thousand years ago. In contemporary Thailand, ninety percent of the population are Buddhists, so there are also plenty of working temples to explore.

Thai food is another highlight – pungently laced with chilli and delicately flavoured with lemongrass and coconut, it's also deliciously inexpensive. English is spoken by Thais working in the tourist industry, but not off the beaten track.

Main attractions

- **Bangkok** Most people spend a few days in the Thai capital, but many find the pollution, traffic congestion and chaotic street life extremely wearing. There's plenty to take you off the street, however, including the glittering Grand Palace compound and its beatific gigantic Reclining Buddha; the comprehensively stocked National Museum; the massive Chatuchak weekend market, with over eight thousand different stalls to peruse; and a happening nightlife that runs the full range from cutting-edge clubs to depressing strip joints.

- **Beaches** Thailand's beaches are among the world's best. You'll find the most developed and expensive resorts, and some of the finest sands, on the islands of Ko Samui and Phuket, while backpackers tend to head for the more budget-oriented Ko Pha Ngan, Ko Tao, Ko Lanta and Ko Mook. Krabi's Railay beaches are nothing short of stunning, Ko Samet makes an easy and economical break from Bangkok and Ko Chang is handy for travellers heading in or out of Cambodia.

- **Trekking** Unlike the organized treks in the Himalayas, Thailand's so-called

THAILAND

BURMA

Mae Sai
Chiang Saen
Houayxai
Chiang Khong
Chiang Rai
Louang Phabang

LAOS

Pai
Mae Hong Son
Chiang Mai ✈
Phayao
Nan

VIENTIANE

Mae Sariang
Phrae
Chiang Khan
Sang Khom
Nong Khai
Nakhon Phanom
Thakhek
Khammouan

Ping
Loei
Udon Thani
Ban Chiang
Sakon Nakhon
Savannakhet

Sukhothai
Phitsanulok
Khon Kaen
Mukdahan

Mae Sot
Kamphaeng Phet
Nan
Khon Kaen

Umphang
Yasothon
Ubon Ratchathani
Mun
Mekong

Three Pagodas Pass
Sangkhlaburi
Lopburi
Khorat
Phimai
Surin
Si Saket
Chong Mek
Pakxe

Kwai
Chao Phraya
Ayutthaya
Phanom Rung
Kap Choeng
Sa Ngam

Kanchanaburi
Nakhon Pathom
BANGKOK ✈
Sa Kaew
Aranyaprathet
Angkor

Phetchaburi
Pong Nam Ron
Poipet
Sisophon
Siem Reap
CAMBODIA

Pattaya
Ban Laem
Phsa Prom

Hua Hin
Rayong
Chanthaburi
Tonle Sap

Ko Samet
Trat

ANDAMAN SEA

Prachuap Khiri Khan
Ko Chang
Hat Lek
Koh Kong

PHNOM PENH

Sihanoukville

Chumphon
ANG THONG NATIONAL PARK
Ko Tao

Ranong
Ko Chang
Ko Pha Ngan

Ko Phayam
Ko Samui ✈

GULF OF THAILAND

VIETNAM

Ko Surin
Ko Similan
Khao Lak
KHAO SOK NATIONAL PARK
Surat Thani

Phang Nga
Krabi
Nakhon Si Thammarat

✈ Phuket
Ko Phi Phi
Ko Lanta
Ko Mook
Trang

THALE BAN NATIONAL PARK

KO TARUTAO NATIONAL MARINE PARK
Satun
Hat Yai

Langkawi
Kuala Perlis
Padang Besar
Alor Setar
Betong
Sungai Kolok
Kota Bharu

MALAYSIA

N

Metres
1000
500
0

0   100km

VIETNAM

Mekong

Mean temperatures (°C) and rainfall (mm)

Average daily temperatures (maximum and minimum °C) and monthly rainfall (mm)

	Jan	Feb	Mar	Apr	May	June	July	Aug	Sept	Oct	Nov	Dec
Bangkok												
max °C	32	33	34	35	34	33	32	32	32	31	31	31
min °C	20	22	24	25	25	24	24	24	24	24	22	20
rainfall mm	8	20	36	58	198	160	160	175	305	206	66	5
Chiang Mai												
max °C	29	32	34	36	34	32	31	31	31	31	30	28
min °C	13	14	17	22	23	23	23	23	23	21	19	15
rainfall mm	0	10	8	36	122	112	213	193	249	94	31	13
Surat Thani (peninsular east coast)												
max °C	30	33	34	35	34	32	32	32	31	30	28	32
min °C	20	20	22	24	25	25	25	25	25	25	23	23
rainfall mm	40	11	18	67	184	121	120	112	205	261	304	98
Phuket (peninsular west coast)												
max °C	32	33	33	33	32	31	30	31	30	30	30	31
min °C	24	24	24	26	25	25	25	25	24	24	24	24
rainfall mm	35	31	70	148	281	299	283	274	323	368	204	71

"hill-tribe treks" focus on the ethnic-minority villages that you walk to, rather than on the walking itself or the scenery. The hill tribes live way out in the sticks, but their villages are connected by tracks, so the hiking is not difficult. Most treks last two to four days and feature nights in the villages, as well as an elephant ride and some river rafting. The main trekking centres are the northern cities of Chiang Mai and Chiang Rai, but routes out of both are hugely oversubscribed, so it's better to start from Mae Hong Son, Pai, Kanchanaburi or Umphang instead, where trails are quieter and more rewarding.

● **Chiang Mai** Best known as the hub of the trekking industry, Thailand's second city is also an attractive and popular destination in its own right, famed for charming traditional temples, its hill-tribe museum, and delicious Burmese-style cuisine, which blends strong spices with sweet coconut cream (several places run cookery courses). Guesthouses are plentiful here, the night bazaar rates as one of the country's most rewarding shopping experiences, and many visitors prolong their stay to take a short course in Thai cookery or traditional massage.

● **The ruined former capitals of Sukhothai and Ayutthaya** Dating from the thirteenth century, Sukhothai is a beautiful example of thoughtful city planning enlivened by lakes and elegant statues of the Buddha. The 300-year-old temples and palaces of Ayutthaya display a refined mix of Hindu and Buddhist sculpture, and are fun to explore by bicycle. Both sets of ruins are now conserved as historical parks.

● **Kanchanaburi** Sited on the banks of the River Kwai, the town is most famous for its role as a POW camp in World

War II and for its bridge, whose destruction by the Allied Forces was immortalized in David Lean's movie. There are plenty of sobering World War II sights in the town, as well as a reasonable range of trekking, rafting and cycling options that make the most of the fine river scenery, plus some appealing rafthouse accommodation too.

Also recommended

● **Khao Sok National Park** Here you can sleep in a tree house under limestone karst, wake to the sound of hooting gibbons, and take an adventure tour via waterlogged caves and jungle trails to a lake.

● **The ancient Khmer temple of Phanom Rung** This exquisite pink sandstone complex was built in the tenth century as a blueprint for the Angkor temples across the border in Cambodia.

● **Thai massage** Enjoy a traditional at Bangkok's Wat Pho temple, then learn the techniques yourself at a course in Bangkok or Chiang Mai.

● **Snorkelling and diving off the remote Similan Islands** The turquoise water, powdery sand and banks of coral are regularly visited by sharks, rays and turtles.

● **The Mae Hong Song loop** Hire a motorbike and spend as many days as you can spare on the circular 600-kilometre route through the glorious upland scenery of the remote northwest.

● **The Southern Folklore Museum, near Songkhla** Featuring plenty of intriguing household objects and some reconstructed rural homes, this unusual museum also occupies a fabulous spot on a hillside overlooking nearby fishing villages.

● **Kayaking around the Krabi coastline** An exhilarating way of exploring the spectacularly craggy outcrops and remote uninhabited islands off the southwest coast.

● **Sang Khom** It's great to just chill out in this idyllic tree-shaded little town on the Mekong river, where you can hire bicycles to visit traditional local villages and mess about on the water in inner tubes and dugout canoes.

● **Pai** This laid-back north-Thai town has a distinct New Age air and is the perfect place to take some courses in alternative therapies, browse the art shops and arrange a trek.

● **Full-moon beach party** Join the hordes for the monthly full-moon parties on Ko Pha Ngan, an infamous backpackers' beach rave that attracts up to 30,000 clubbers.

Festivals

Ⓦ www.thailandgrandfestival.com
April 13–15 *Songkhran*. The Thai New Year is an excuse for a massive nationwide waterfight, with everyone dousing each other in the streets.
May *Bun Bang Fai (Yasothon Rocket Festival)*. Bawdy rain-making festival in Yasothon where beautifully crafted painted wooden rockets are paraded and fired.
October or November *Ngan Kin Jeh (Vegetarian Festival)* in Phuket and Trang. Chinese devotees celebrate their New Year by purifying themselves for nine days and then parading through town performing acts of self-mortification such as pushing skewers through their cheeks.
November *Loy Krathong*. Nationwide festival to honour the water spirits and celebrate the end of the rainy season. Baskets of flowers and lighted candles are floated on ponds, rivers, lakes, canals and seashores.

Routes in and out

Thailand's main international airport is in Bangkok, but some international flights also use the airports in Ko Samui and Phuket in the south and in Chiang Mai in the north. There are lots of buses linking major cities and tourist resorts in Thailand and Malaysia, and you can also travel between the two countries by train. Overland travel to Laos is also straightforward; the most popular border crossing is the Friendship Bridge which connects the Thai town of Nong Khai with Vientiane in Laos, but you can use four other crossings in the north and northeast. There are half a dozen

△ Monk collecting aims, Thonburi, Bangkok

legal overland routes in and out of Cambodia, of which the most used are from Aranyaphet to Poipet (for Siem Reap), and from Trat via Koh Kong to Sihanoukville (for Phnom Penh and the south).

Thailand online

Gor's World – ⓦwww.gorsworld.com Thai teenager Nattawud "Gor" Daoruang writes about drugs, teenage parenthood and other issues affecting his mates. Originally published as a regular column in the *Bangkok Post*.

Khao San Road – ⓦwww.khaosan road.com The "community website" for Southeast Asia's most notorious back-packers' ghetto gives a good taste of Thailand's travellers' scene, and includes guesthouse reviews, a forum and inter-views with local characters.

Thailand Blogs ⓦwww.thai-blogs .com Residents, expats and afficionados share their Thailand blogs.

Thailand Travel Forum ⓦtravelforum .org/thailand Active and well-admin-istered forum for travellers to Thailand; it gets lots of traffic and has a core of regular contributors.

Thai-UK ⓦwww.thai-uk.org Astute, wide-ranging site covering cultural, social and environmental issues and contacts for all would-be visitors to Thailand.

Books

Karen Connelly *Touch the Dragon* (Silkworm Books). The true story of a 17-year-old Canadian schoolgirl's one-year stay in a small town in northern Thailand; she spoke no Thai and was the only foreigner in town.

Alex Garland *The Beach*. Gripping cult thriller (made into a film in 1999) that uses a Thai setting to explore the way in which backpackers' ceaseless quest for

"undiscovered" utopias inevitably leads to them ruining the idyll.

Sandra Gregory with Michael Tierney *Forget You Had a Daughter*. The can-did and shocking account of a young British woman who was imprisoned in Bangkok's notorious Lard Yao prison after being caught trying to smuggle 89 grammes of heroin out of Thailand.

James O'Reilly and Larry Habegger (eds) *Travelers' Tales: Thailand*. Engrossing anthology of modern writings about Thailand, by Thailand experts, travel writers and first-time visitors.

Phra Peter Pannapadipo *Phra Farang: An English Monk in Thailand*. Behind the scenes in a Thai monastery: the frank, funny and illuminating account of a UK-born former businessman's life as a Thai monk.

Films

The Beach (Danny Boyle, 2000). The film of the cult thriller about the travel-lers' scene in Southeast Asia didn't go down well with everyone – not least Thai environmental groups, who accused the producers of damaging the island of Phi Phi Leh where some of it was shot.

Bridge on the River Kwai (David Lean, 1957). This classic movie wasn't actually made in Thailand and the story it tells is hugely embellished – but Allied POWs did build a Thailand–Burma railway in World War II and the site of the real Bridge, in Kanchanaburi, is much visited.

Iron Ladies (Youngyooth Thongkonthun, 2000). Warm-hearted, off-beat Thai comedy based on the often hilarious true-life adventures of a volleyball team from north Thailand that was made up of transsexuals and transvestites.

Tears of the Black Tiger (Wisit Sasanatieng, 2000). A gentle send-up of the Thai action films of the 1960s and 1970s, using exaggerated acting styles and comic-book colours to tell the story of handsome bandit Dum and his love for upper-class Rumpoey.

Thai tourist offices

Ⓦ**www.tourismthailand.org**
Australia and New Zealand 75/77 Pitt Street, Sydney 2000 ℡02/9247 7549 Ⓦwww.thailand.net.au.
UK and Ireland 3rd Floor, Brook House, 98–99 Jermyn Street, London SW1Y 6EE, ℡0870 900 2007, ℡020/7925 2511, Ⓦwww.thaismile.co.uk.
US and Canada ℡1-800-THAILAND; 61 Broadway, Suite 2810, New York, NY 10006 ℡212/432-0433, Ⓔinfo@tatny .com; 611 North Larchmont Blvd, 1st Floor, Los Angeles, CA 90004 ℡323/461-9814, Ⓔtatla@ix.netcom .com.

Thai embassies and consulates

Australia Ⓦthaisydney.idx.com .au. 111 Empire Circuit, Yarralumla,

Canberra ACT 2600 ℡02/6273 1149; plus a consulate in Sydney ℡02/9241 2542.
Canada Ⓦwww.magma.ca/~thaiott /mainpage.htm. 180 Island Park Drive, Ottawa, Ontario K1Y 0A2 ℡613/722-4444; plus a consulate in Vancouver ℡604/687-1143.
New Zealand 2 Cook St, Karori, Wellington ℡04/476 8618, Ⓦwww .thaiembassynz.org.nz.
UK and Ireland Ⓦwww.thaiconsul -uk.com. 29 Queens Gate, London SW7 5JB ℡09003 405456 or 020/7589 2944; plus consulates in Birmingham ℡0121/643 9481; Cardiff ℡0292/046577; Glasgow ℡0141/353 5090; Hull ℡01482/581668; and Liverpool ℡0151/255 0504.
US Ⓦwww.thaiembdc.org. 1024 Wisconsin Ave NW, Suite 401, Washington, DC 20007 ℡202/ 944-3600. Consulates in Chicago ℡312/664-3129; Los Angeles ℡323/962-9574, Ⓦwww.thai-la.net; and New York ℡212/754-1770.

Vietnam

Capital Hanoi	**Climate** Tropical
Population 83 million	**Best time to go** Late September–
Language Vietnamese	December, and March and April
Currency Dong (d)	**Minimum daily budget** $15/£8
Main religion Mahayana Buddhism	

Although Vietnam has recently enjoyed a bit of a tourist boom, the country features on relatively few mainstream itineraries and so still feels like an adventurous destination, particularly in comparison with Thailand and Malaysia. In addition, because of its long thin shape and its many useful overland border-points it's quite feasible to treat Vietnam as a transit destination on an overland trip between China and either Laos or Cambodia. Inevitably, the Vietnam War (which the Vietnamese refer to as the American War) of the 1960s and 1970s figures strongly in visitors' agendas. But when you've had your fill of crawling through guerrilla tunnels and posing beside downed helicopters, there are hill tribes, beaches and islands galore to check out, not to mention eleventh-century Hindu ruins, historic old towns, and 300-year-old Confucianist temples.

Starved of contact with the West after a decade and a half in the wilderness, the Vietnamese people are welcoming and full of fascinating stories; it's a bonus that English is widely understood. War sights aside, contemporary Vietnam is very much looking to the future, and although the economic boom of the 1990s was all too brief, this is not at all the browbeaten country you may have been expecting.

Though the public transport system is as slow as it is extensive, budget tour operators have taken up the slack and made it easier to travel between major attractions. The famous "Reunification Express" trains travel the country from top to bottom, taking a minimum of 34 hours to connect Ho Chi Minh City with Hanoi. Accommodation, however, is taking longer to improve – for every comfortable room in a quaint French colonial villa, there are five faceless cells in austere Soviet-style hotel blocks.

Main attractions

● **Hanoi** Vietnam's capital, in the north of the country, enjoys a relatively cool climate and is a surprisingly pleasant place to linger. Highlights include the historic Confucian-style Temple of Literature, the chaotically traditional alleys of the Old Quarter, and the rather macabre Ho Chi Minh Mausoleum, where the embalmed body of the great man is displayed in a glass box. The evocative Perfume Pagoda, a famous Buddhist cave temple on the Red River Delta, is also within daytripping distance.

● **Taking a boat tour round the dramatic Ha Long Bay** This is the best and most popular way to appreciate the beauty and drama of the bay, which is peppered with hundreds of bizarrely

Mean temperatures (°C) and rainfall (mm)

Average daily temperatures (maximum and minimum °C) and monthly rainfall (mm)

	Jan	Feb	Mar	Apr	May	June	July	Aug	Sept	Oct	Nov	Dec
Hanoi												
max °C	20	21	23	28	32	33	33	32	31	29	26	22
min °C	13	14	17	20	23	26	26	26	24	22	18	15
rainfall mm	18	28	38	81	196	239	323	343	254	99	43	20
Da Nang												
max °C	24	26	27	30	33	34	34	34	31	28	27	25
min °C	19	20	21	23	24	25	25	25	24	23	22	20
rainfall mm	102	31	12	18	47	42	99	117	447	530	221	209
Ho Chi Minh City												
max °C	32	33	34	35	33	32	31	31	31	31	31	31
min °C	21	22	23	24	24	24	24	24	23	23	23	22
rainfall mm	15	3	13	43	221	330	315	269	335	269	114	56

shaped limestone outcrops and yawning caves and is so spectacular it's listed as a World Heritage Site. The fishing island of Cat Ba makes the most interesting departure point.

- **Ho Chi Minh City** More famously known as Saigon, the former capital of South Vietnam is a hectic city, stuffed with venerable temples, classy restaurants and hundreds of bars. Most visitors make the "war sights" a priority, in particular the absorbing War Remnants and Ho Chi Minh City museums, and the former American Embassy.

- **The Mekong Delta** Southeast Asia's greatest river, the 4000-kilometre-long Mekong, rises on the Tibetan plateau and runs down through China, Laos, Thailand and Cambodia before reaching journey's end in Vietnam, where it fans out into dozens of smaller rivers to water the vast alluvial plains of the Mekong Delta. The scenes here are quintessential Southeast Asia: emerald rice paddies, fruit orchards, sugar-cane fields and coconut palms, tended by conical-hatted farmers and crisscrossed by waterways

that are chock-a-block with sampans and rowing boats. You can explore the area and its floating markets on day-trips from Ho Chi Minh City, or stay in one of the delta villages such as Can Tho, My Tho or Ben Tre.

- **Hué** During the nineteenth century, this aristocratic city reigned as Vietnam's capital, and today it boasts the finest traditional Sino-Vietnamese architecture, a legacy of the inspiration the Vietnamese emperors took from Confucianist China. The walled citadel still contains relics from the Imperial City, while a short boat ride up the city's Perfume River brings you to the seven imperial mausoleums, where each Nguyen-dynasty emperor designed himself an elegantly landscaped memorial of pagodas, pavilions and pleasure gardens. In complete contrast, Hué is also the most convenient departure point for day-trips to the infamously bleak stretch of land known as the DMZ, or Demilitarized Zone, 100km north of Hué on the Seventeenth Parallel, which served as the border between North and South Vietnam until reunification in 1975.

Hoi An This captivating historic port town is characterized by narrow streets and a clutch of beautifully preserved 200-year-old merchants' shophouses, some of which are still inhabited by family descendants and can be visited. It's also a famously good place to get silk outfits tailor-made at bargain prices. And if you're here on the night before the day of the full moon, in any month, you'll experience the highly atmospheric monthly Full-Moon Festival, when the town's electricity is temporarily switched off, the streets are illuminated by lanterns and there's traditional dance performed in the streets.

The Cu Chi tunnels near Ho Chi Minh City These are among the most visited sights from the American War. Scores of communist Viet Cong guerrillas lived for weeks on end in this 250-kilometre network of underground hideouts, attempting to evade capture by the American forces. Tunnel facilities included rudimentary subterranean hospitals, kitchens and classrooms, relics of which can still be seen today. Above ground, the place has become something of a war theme park now, with fake tripwires and a shooting gallery where visitors can play with M-16s and Kalashnikovs.

Also recommended

Beaches Vietnam may not be renowned for these, but the sands that ring remote little Phu Quoc island, close to the Cambodian border, are splendid. Other low-key beaches that are easier to get to and reasonably near Ho Chi Minh City include modest Long Hai, and the beautiful, and rather more up-market, Cape Mui Ne, near Phan Thiet. Though less laid-back, the more famous municipal beach in the city of Nha Trang has plenty of fans.

Trekking The region around the northern hill town of Sa Pa is inhabited by a variety of hill tribes and makes a rewarding destination for walkers. Most of the tribespeople arrived in the region about two hundred years ago, when persecution in their native China prompted a mass migration into the northern hills of Vietnam, Laos and, most famously, Thailand. Although some of the hill-tribe villages around Sa Pa are now firmly on the tourist route, many are not, so encounters up here can be more authentic than in over-packaged Thailand.

Meeting the "mad monk" of Da Lat Artist, Zen poet and Buddhist monk Vien Tuc welcomes visitors to his pagoda-cum-art gallery, Lam Ty Ni Pagoda, which houses thousands of his own abstract watercolours. Da Lat itself is a pleasant enough if rather self-consciously quaint hill-station town, surrounded by aromatic pine forests and enjoying a refreshingly cool climate.

Drinking freshly brewed bia hoi Pull up a stool and join the crowd round the barrel of *bia hoi* (draught beer) in one of the makeshift streetside joints in Hanoi or Ho Chi Minh City.

The Cham temples of My Son Dating back to the eleventh century, these evocative jungle-clad ruins of a group of Hindu temples still retain some carvings and statues despite the best efforts of countless American B52s.

Watching a water-puppet show The traditional art of storytelling using puppets that literally dance on water is exceptionally charming, despite being a very popular tourist attraction. Narratives are generally either folktales or legends and the puppeteers, hidden behind a screen, stand waist-deep in water to manipulate the wooden figures. The easiest place to catch a performance is in Hanoi.

Festivals

February *Water Puppet Festival*, Thay Pagoda, near Hanoi. A three-day extravaganza of water-puppet performances, organized as part of the Vietnamese New Year celebrations.

May or June *Tet Doan Ngo*. The summer solstice is marked across the country by parades and traditional dragon boat races.

Routes in and out

With Ho Chi Minh City and Hanoi both served by international flights, it's quite feasible – and very popular – to enter the country via one city and leave via the other. You can also enter (and depart) Vietnam overland – by train from China, departing from Beijing, Nanning or Kunming and arriving at Hanoi; by bus from Laos, via Lao Bao, to Dong Ha, via Cau Treo or Ban Nong Het to Vinh, and via Na Maew to Nam Xoi; by bus from Mukdahan in Thailand, via Savannakhet in Laos, to Dong Ha; by bus from Phnom Penh in Cambodia via Moc Bai to Ho Chi Minh City; and by boat and taxi from Phnom Penh to Chau Doc in the Mekong Delta.

Vietnam online

Hitchhiking Vietnam – Ⓦ**www .pbs.org/hitchhikingvietnam** Funny, straight-talking homepage that's a refreshing introduction to the country, with excerpts from the author's journal and photo album describing her seven-month trip around Vietnam plus quirky tips and recommendations for different places.

Jan Dodd's Vietnam – Ⓦ**www .jandodd.com** The homepage created by the co-author of the *Rough Guide to Vietnam* has guidebook updates and a list of her Vietnam top tens, plus an outstanding collection of links to all things Vietnamese.

Terra Galleria: Vietnam – Ⓦ**www .terragalleria.com/vietnam**

△ Ha Long Bay

A photographer's guide to the photo opportunities of Vietnam, with a stunning gallery of shots.

Things Asian – Ⓦ www.thingsasian .com Vietnam is the main focus of this pan-Asian site, with hundreds of well-written stories on all areas and aspects of travel in the country, plus a photo gallery and travel tips.

Books

Maria Coffey *Three Moons in Vietnam*. The touching, warm-hearted story of a British woman's journey around Vietnam with her husband, from Ho Chi Minh City to Ha Long Bay, travelling mostly by sampan and bicycle.

Duong Van Mai Elliott *The Sacred Willow: Four Generations in the Life of a Vietnamese Family*. The author illuminates the history of her country from the late nineteenth century to the end of the twentieth through the characters and experiences of her own extended family, among them a mandarin at the imperial court and an anti-French Viet Minh resistance fighter.

Bao Ninh *The Sorrow of War*. An award-winning modern classic that follows a very young North Vietnamese army captain through the American War and into the post-war years as he works as part of a team that searches for the bodies of lost comrades. Though the novel is fiction, the author was born in Hanoi and was one of the few from his North Vietnamese Army brigade who survived the war.

Tim O'Brien *Going After Cacciato*. What does war do to people? Novelist Tim O'Brien has made his name as an eloquent chronicler of the emotional, physical and moral effects of the American-Vietnam War on the people involved on both sides and the land it destroyed. All his books are moving and

thought-provoking; this one starts with the notion that one American soldier in Vietnam, Cacciato, would, all things considered, prefer to be in Paris than fighting in Vietnam; he sets out to walk the 8600 miles necessary to get there, pursued by the men in his squad.

Andrew X Pham *Catfish and Mandala: A Two-Wheeled Voyage through the Landscape and Memory of Vietnam*. A Vietnamese American whose family fled to the US when he was 10 returns – by bicycle – to the country of his birth. As he travels he ponders the questions of identity, cultural bonds and memory that fill his head, interweaving them with vivid descriptions of the Vietnam he experiences in the late 1990s.

Films

Apocalypse Now (Francis Ford Coppola, 1979). The most famous of all the films about the American-Vietnam War, this operatic, psychedelic extravaganza shows us the war from inside the heads of some of the American soldiers who fought it.

Cyclo (Tran Anh Hung, 1995). Dubbed by some critics the Vietnamese *Pulp Fiction*, this is a shockingly graphic thriller set in 1990s' Ho Chi Minh City that paints a recognizable portrait of modern-day city life. It follows a desperately poor young cycle-rickshaw driver as he gets drawn ever deeper into S&M prostitution, drug smuggling and gang warfare. Tran Anh Hung's other films have quite different tones: *The Scent of Green Papaya* (1993) is set in 1950s' and 60s' Saigon and follows a young woman from the country who comes to the city to work as a maid; and in *The Vertical Ray of the Sun* (2001), three sisters in Hanoi discuss their lives and loves as they prepare a special family meal.

Heaven and Earth (Oliver Stone, 1993). Based on the autobiography of Le Ly Hayslip, who grew up with the war, was tortured by the Viet Cong and eventually fled to Saigon. The film ends with Le Ly in rural USA, struggling to cope with life as the wife of a damaged and violent former GI.

Indochine (Régis Wargnier, 1991). Catherine Deneuve stars in this beautifully shot three-cornered 1930s' love-story set during the final years of French colonial rule in Indochina.

The Quiet American (Philip Noyce, 2002). Michael Caine stars as the jaded foreign correspondent in this brilliant adaptation of Graham Greene's famous novel about cross-cultural romance, geopolitics and misguided American interests in 1950s' Saigon.

Vietnamese tourist offices

Ⓦ**www.vietnamtourism.com**
No overseas offices; contact the visa section of your nearest embassy.

Vietnamese embassies and consulates

Australia and New Zealand Ⓦwww .au.vnembassy.org. 6 Timburra Crescent, O'Malley, Canberra, ACT 2606 ℡02/6290 1556. Consulate in Sydney ℡02/9327 2539.

Canada 226 Maclaren St, Ottawa, Ontario K2P OL6 ℡613/236-0772, ⒺVietnam@lstar.ca.

UK and Ireland 12 Victoria Rd, London W8 5RD ℡020/7937 1912, Ⓦwww .vietnamembassy.org.uk.

US 1233 20th St NW, Suite 400, Washington, DC 20037 ℡202/861-0737, Ⓦwww.vietnamembassy-usa.org. Consulate in San Francisco ℡415/922-1577, Ⓦwww.vietnamconsulate-sf.org.

First-Time Asia

The Big Adventure

1

Planning your route

Hopefully, the previous section has given you a taste of what's on offer in Asia. Now you have to decide which countries to head for, which ones to leave out, and what order to see them in. Later in this chapter you'll find some suggestions for popular and creative itineraries across Asia, and in Chapter Five there's a roundup of pan-Asia travel literature and other travel publications that should also be a good source of ideas. But first, here are some elementary issues to consider:

- Your first task is to decide on the length of your trip. If money is the main consideration, check out Chapter Four to find out how far your budget will stretch.
- Do some research into the climate. Is it the right time of year to go trekking/white-water rafting/snorkelling and diving? Will it be raining all the time, or too hot to enjoy yourself? See Chapter Three for advice on this.
- Make some preliminary investigations into different ticket options, and check out relevant visa requirements, described in Chapter Two.
- Think about the pace of your proposed trip. Are you going to be whizzing through places so fast that you won't have any real sense of where you are or what each country is like? Are you allowing yourself enough time and flexibility to add new places to your itinerary or

linger in spots that you like a lot? Cramming too many destinations into your schedule means that you'll see far too much of the worst bits of a country, namely its bus stations and airports.

● Is your itinerary nicely balanced? Will you get bored if you see nothing but beaches for the next few months? Might you start longing for some hill-walking after weeks of museums and temples?

A shared experience?

Now is also the time to think about who you want to go travelling with, or if indeed you want to share your trip with anyone at all. There are obvious pluses and minuses to both options. Travelling with one or more companions means you always have someone to chat to and plan things with; you can mull over your experiences together and share your enthusiasms and worries; and you may well feel braver about exploring and experimenting if you're with someone else. On a practical level, you will save money because double and triple rooms are better value and taxi expenses will be halved; and there'll always be someone to mind the bags while one of you looks for a hotel room or nips off to buy a mango in the market.

However, travel is a surprisingly stressful activity: the heat, the hassle and the sheer strangeness of things are bound to fray your nerves, and guess who's going to bear the brunt of your irritability? Expect to get on each other's nerves and to fall out every so often, and be prepared to split up during the trip – either for a few days because you've got different priorities, or for good because your differences seem to be insurmountable. Bearing this in mind, you and your prospective companions should take a long hard look at your friendship and try to imagine it under stress. Will one person be making all the plans and taking all the responsibilities, and will that annoy you? Do you have broadly the same expectations of the trip and share a similar attitude to mishaps and hassles? Does one of you have a lot more money, and will that cause tension?

If travel puts a strain on friendships, imagine what it does to relationships. A disconcerting number of romances crack during a long cross-Asia trip, but then perhaps they weren't meant to last anyway. If yours survives it, you will have been brought closer together and will have lots of great stories and photos to coo over for many years to come.

Going solo

Solo travel is a more extreme and intense experience. You have to face up to everything on your own, and find the motivation to move on, explore and be sociable all by yourself. There will be lonely times for sure, and scary ones, and you'll probably get tired of eating out on your own every night. But you will also be a lot more open to your surroundings and you'll make more effort to chat to new people – as indeed they will to you (twosomes often put people off because they seem self-contained). Some people find they're more alert and receptive on their own, and most single travellers write much more interesting letters, emails and journals simply because they're desperate to blurt out all their experiences. And, of course, you have no one to answer to but yourself, which means you can change your plans at a moment's notice or idle away your days without feeling guilty.

Finding a travel companion

If you're nervous about going on your own, but can't find anyone to accompany you, all is not lost. Travel magazines, university noticeboards, newspaper personal columns and Internet newsgroups and travel forums are full of advertisements from people looking for travelling companions (see Chapter Five for some leads). Most advertisers have specific itineraries in mind and will want to meet and discuss plans quite a few times; if you don't find an ad that fits your bill, why not place one yourself? Just be sure to use your common sense when meeting any stranger for the first time, however genuine they sound on the Net or on the phone: arrange to meet in a public place, and don't give them your address too early. Travelling with an unknown person will bring its share of unpleasant surprises, so you should definitely discuss ground rules before you go and perhaps even set off on a dummy trip – a weekend away, for example – before the big departure. But it can also be unexpectedly fun, and with any luck you'll have made a new friend by the trip's end.

Even if no one suitable turns up before you set off, you'll find it remarkably easy to hitch up with travel companions once you've actually arrived in Asia. The backpackers' scene is well established in major Asian towns, cities and beach resorts, and guesthouse noticeboards are usually thick with requests for travelmates. Bangkok's Khao San Road, Hang Bac in Hanoi, the Paharganj area of New Delhi, and Thamel and Freak Street in Kathmandu are all fruitful places to look.

Joining a tour

For some people, joining an organized tour is the most appealing introduction to Asia. This takes away a lot of the more daunting elements – like arranging local transport and accommodation yourself – and often means that you're accompanied by an expert whose in-depth knowledge of the country can really enhance your stay. Hundreds of tour operators offer trips to Asian destinations (see Directory, pp.412–414, for some recommendations) and the range of packages is phenomenal: there are short city breaks, week-long beach holidays, cultural tours, walking tours, adventure tours (kayaking, trekking, wildlife-spotting), off-the-beaten-track tours, tailor-made tours, language-learning tours and even culinary tours. Some tours whisk you around the highlights of two or even three countries in just a couple of weeks; others offer long, slow, overland journeys lasting anything up to six months. Most operators specialize in either upmarket or mid-market packages, but there are a few economy packages, featuring homestay accommodation and local transport, and the long overland ones are pretty basic, with participants sharing cooking chores and contributing to the food kitty.

One option worth considering if you're on your own or a bit apprehensive is to start your trip by joining an organized tour from home for a few weeks, then branch off by yourself when you've gained more confidence and Asia know-how; many tour operators are used to this and offer tour-only prices so that you can arrange your own flights. This is also fairly common practice on the youth-oriented overland tours (such as those run by Exodus, Dragoman and Explore Worldwide), and gives you a good grounding as well as the chance to meet possible onward travel companions.

A sponsored holiday

A potentially interesting way of joining a tour and exploring a country while contributing something useful is to participate in a fundraising activity holiday in aid of a charity. Many of the major-league charities organize one or more of these events every year; recent examples have included a fortnight's cycle ride from Hanoi to Ho Chi Minh City, a nine-day horse ride across the Mongolian plains, a nine-day trek along a section of the Great Wall of China, a climb up Malaysia's Mount Kinabalu followed by trekking through the jungles of Borneo, and a trek to Everest Base Camp in the Nepali Himalayas. For some expeditions, training in advance to get fit is part of the challenge, while for others the emphasis is more on having an energetic holiday and making some money for a good cause at the same time.

Each charity has a different way of organizing these events, but most ask for a minimum amount of sponsorship – which tends to be between £1500/$2700 and £3000/$5400 in the UK for a fortnight's trip. It's up to you how to get this money, though organizers usually offer advice and sometimes even practical help. Obviously some of your money is used to cover your expenses – these are holidays after all, with reasonable board and lodging provided, as well as time set aside for sightseeing where relevant – but not everyone is happy at the percentage of the fee which goes in the charity box, so check first before registering. In addition, some people feel uncomfortable that their friends, families and colleagues are effectively financing the trip – hence the increasing emphasis on the pre-trip challenge of getting fit, which shows that you're working for your sponsorship. Another thing to check is the amount of free time incorporated into the schedule: some trips are so tightly timetabled that there is no time to explore on your own.

If you have a favourite charity, contact them to see if they're planning any fundraising holidays. Otherwise, look for adverts in the travel sections of national newspapers, and in the travel magazines described in Chapter Five. The long-established organization Charity Challenge (☎020/8557 0000, ⊛www.charitychallenge.com) runs a dozen different fundraising adventure holiday programmes in Asia, most of them treks and mountain-bike rides, and has dozens of charities on its books, so you can choose which one to support, or add your own to the list. For information on working with a charity while you're in Asia, see the section on "Volunteer programmes", below.

Volunteer programmes and placements

Organizing a place on a volunteer programme is an increasingly popular way of anchoring a trip and giving it substance.

A different kind of trip

When I packed in my job, I decided to go travelling for a while, but I wasn't interested in just bumming around and wanted to try and get under the surface of things instead. Indian Volunteers for Community Service (IVCS) fitted the bill perfectly: a three-week visitors' programme at a small rural development project in northeastern India.

On our first day at the project, the ten new volunteers were all taken to the nearest town to buy traditional north Indian style dress: *salwaar kameez* for the girls and *pajama* for the boys. This was to make us feel and act like we weren't just tourists, and also to help us blend in better with the villagers of Amarpurkashi. Back at the village, we spent the next three weeks following an informal programme of yoga, Hindi lessons and cultural lectures in the morning, and rural development workshops in the afternoon. In between, we got involved with local projects like reorganizing the polytechnic's library and helping with the literacy campaign. And we helped out in the kitchens, and gave regular English lessons at the village school and the rural polytechnic. We also socialized with the villagers and were invited to join their festivities, including one which was held to honour the birth of a baby boy.

I couldn't have asked for a better introduction to India. Though there was quite a big group of us Westerners, we all got involved in community life and experienced things tourists rarely get to see and do. By the end of the three weeks I felt acclimatized, confident and eager to do some exploring, so I spent the next five months making informal visits to development projects in other parts of India, using contacts I'd made at Amarpurkashi.

Juliet Acock

Programmes can last anything from a week to six months, but the emphasis is always on participation in activities that contribute directly towards your host community; generally, you pay your expenses as well as donating your time and skills, though in some cases you'll be paid a local salary. The big attraction is the opportunity to get involved in local life at a deeper and potentially more fulfilling level than you would as a backpacker or on a fundraising adventure holiday. Typical volunteer programmes include coral surveying in the Philippines, teaching English in Nepal, and assisting in museums in China. Volunteer projects vary widely and while some are very rewarding, others can feel unsatisfying, even futile. To help choose the best one, ask lots of questions before signing up and try to contact some former volunteers – a service offered by many of the most reputable outfits.

To join a volunteer programme you need to contact the relevant organizations in your home country before you set off. Established organizers of short-term volunteer projects are listed in Directory on pp.415–417. For a more comprehensive roundup, see online resources such as the Year Out Group (ⓦwww.yearoutgroup.org), Travel Tree (ⓦwww.traveltree.co.uk),

Volunteer Abroad (@www.volunteerabroad.com), Action Without Borders (@www.idealist.org) and World Service Enquiry (@www.wse.org.uk), all of which have links to scores of volunteer-placement organizations as well as details of current vacancies in paid as well as unpaid jobs. The World Guide and Information Network to Voluntary Work in Nature Conservation produces a useful book called *Green Volunteers*, which contains information on 180 wildlife and environmental projects around the world; order it at @www.greenvol.com. The same publisher, Vacation Work (@www.vacationwork.co.uk), has an extensive catalogue of similar titles, including *The International Directory of Voluntary Work*. The organization Working Abroad (℡01273/711406, @www.workingabroad.com) will compile a detailed list of 20–100 projects that fulfil criteria you set, lasting one week to six months or more, in over 150 countries worldwide. All you do is fill in the online application form, giving preferred dates, type of project and countries of choice, and pay $52/£29.

A variation on the volunteer programme is the placement or internship, whereby you get the chance to work in, say, a local newspaper, radio station, clinic, school, law firm, animal welfare centre or hotel. These placements are generally aimed at students looking for work or study experience. You pay for the privilege but the fee includes board and lodging. In some cases you will be benefiting the community, in others you'll just be learning more about the job – and the country. For details of agents offering these placements check Travel Tree (@www.traveltree.co.uk) and see Directory pp.415–417.

You don't always need to set up your voluntary work in advance. Some local charities are happy to accept volunteers who walk in off the street and have no qualifications except a desire to help out for a few days; consult guidebooks and the Internet for details, or check the traveller-oriented collective Go MAD: Go Make a Difference @www.go-mad.org for leads.

At the other end of the spectrum, the big international voluntary organizations like VSO (@www.vso.org.uk), the Peace Corps (@www.peacecorps.gov) and Australian Volunteers International (@www.ozvol.org.au) employ people for longer periods (generally a minimum of two years) and require specific qualifications; these jobs are always paid. For information on finding other kinds of paid work in Asia, see p.241.

Taking the kids

Many package tours are child-friendly and offer good deals, but it's also increasingly common for independent travellers, including single parents, to take their kids to Asia. Children are considered a huge blessing in most parts of Asia and yours will be treated accordingly. Outside the main resorts you're unlikely to find child-oriented entertainments, but there's usually so much going on that this shouldn't be an insurmountable drawback. And there's always the beach. As with adult travellers, certain countries or regions make for a smoother initiation into Asia than others – notably Singapore, Hong Kong, Japan and Taiwan – while China, India, Nepal and Pakistan may be better tackled after some acclimatization. Most of Southeast Asia falls somewhere in between.

The chief worry is how to keep your child healthy, but if you follow the advice given in Chapter Twelve, there's every chance that the whole family will have a hassle-free trip. To canvass other travelling parents' opinions, post your queries on the Kids To Go forum at ⊛thorntree.lonelyplanet.com or the Travelling with Kids Forum at ⊛www.deabirkett.com/forum.htm.

Where to start?

You probably won't have much trouble deciding where to start your trip – there'll either be an obvious geographical option, or your travel agent will twist your arm with offers of significant discounts if you go with their recommendation.

For Europeans, the usual gateway cities are Kathmandu, Delhi or Bangkok. These are the nearest entry points to Asia and generally the cheapest places to fly to. Australians usually begin somewhere in Indonesia, or in Singapore. Flying to Asia from America is a more long-winded process as you're literally travelling to the other side of the planet. From the East Coast, it's faster and nearly always cheaper to go via London, Amsterdam or Frankfurt, and then on to Kathmandu, Delhi or Bangkok. If you're starting from the West Coast, the cheapest routes will probably be to Seoul, Taipei, Tokyo, Hong Kong or Singapore.

Saving money should not be the only consideration, though, and you'd be wise to think about the stress factor of your first days and nights in Asia:

- Start yourself off gently. Many travellers find the poverty, chaos and crowds of India, for example, a very tough introduction to Asia, so you might want to begin your cross-Asia trip somewhere calmer, like Malaysia or Bali.
- For the gentlest introduction to a new country, consider arranging international flights to towns other than the capital cities. You can fly from Europe directly to Chiang Mai in north Thailand, for example, which means that by the time you've worked your way down to Bangkok (or across to Vientiane) you'll be blasé about big noisy cities and will exude the confidence of an old Asia hand. Or you could make use of the burgeoning number of budget airlines operating within Asia and buy a Los Angeles–Singapore flight, say, making an immediate connection to Cambodia's Siem Reap, perhaps, or to Krabi in south Thailand. See Chapter Two for information on the different types of air tickets available.
- If you've had a long flight, you'll probably be worn out when you arrive, so plan an easy schedule for the first week. Two or three nights in a pre-booked hotel near your place of arrival will give you a chance to sleep and acclimatize; then you might want to chill out on a beach somewhere, or relax in a smaller town or resort. See Chapter Seven for more advice.

Across Asia by air

Most people choose to do their cross-Asia trip by air, simply because it's faster and easier than going overland. Travel agents sort out all the details for you and everything is booked in advance, which is reassuring for anxious relatives and one less headache for you. Advice on buying the best plane ticket for your trip is given in Chapter Two.

The best approach is to work out your ideal route before you have your final session with the travel agent, picking a few well-placed destinations that you're absolutely determined not to miss. Once you've got your core must-sees, be prepared to be flexible about the in-between bits, bearing in mind that some routes are a lot cheaper than others. If possible, leave some extra free time at strategic intervals so that you're able to be spontaneous and follow up other travellers' recommendations once you're on the ground.

Before making any firm decisions about your ticket, check out the section on overland routes within Asia beginning on p.167. There are all sorts of intriguing bus, train and ferry routes between countries in Asia, and this can save you a lot of money on your air ticket, as well as enhancing your adventure.

Fear of flying

Not everyone relishes the idea of travelling to the other side of the world in a pressurized metal box that careers along thirty thousand feet above sea level with no visible means of support. Fear of flying is a relatively common anxiety – apparently seriously affecting one in five adults – making overland travel a necessity rather than a choice for many people. But, while getting to Asia by land and sea can be a very enjoyable experience (see opposite), there are a number of courses and other resources to help those who would like to combat their dread of air travel. The self-help website ⊛www.anxieties .com has a comprehensive section on fear of flying, with advice, practical step-by-step programmes and plenty of comparative statistics to impress on you how safe air travel actually is. Several airlines, including British Airways and Virgin Atlantic, run regular therapy workshops which aim to help you deal with your fear by taking you through a simulated flight – some even culminate in a short real flight. In the UK, prices are £180–235 for a one-day course and there's a directory of them on ⊛www.airfraid.com. For workshops and self-help courses in the US, see the US section of ⊛www .airfraid.com, which also includes details about the multi-part fear-of-flying DVD courses designed by SOAR (☎1-800-FEAR FLY, ☎914-763-9603, ⊛www.fearofflying.com; $125–480). In Australia, Qantas-staffed weekend courses are run by Fearless Flyers (☎02/9522 8455, ⊛www.fearlessflyers .com.au; AU$850). The Qantas team has also produced a book, *The Fearless Flier's Handbook* by Debbie Seaman; other books on the subject include *The Easy Way to Enjoy Flying* by Allen Carr and *Flying Without Fear* by Duane Brown. For advice on how to enjoy your flight, see Chapter Seven.

Round-the-world classic: UK–India–Nepal–Thailand–Malaysia–Indonesia–(Australia)–UK

This is a classic first-time Asia itinerary for anyone making their way there from Europe, giving you the run of the best of South and Southeast Asia with the added option of rounding off your trip in Australia. The route can be done on a round-the-world ticket, a multi-stop ticket or even on an open-jaw return – see pp.201–205 for details on which ticket would be most suitable for you. For Australians, the same route applies, but in reverse, with the option of extending to Europe if you want.

The first port of call on many round-the-world trips is Delhi, chiefly because it's only ten hours' flying time from London. Although the Indian capital is not necessarily an easy opener for first-timers, it is well positioned for trips to Rajasthan and the Himalayas. But if you're going to head south to the beaches of Goa or Kerala, get an international flight to Mumbai instead. Kolkata is a more unusual alternative, but a useful one as you can get cheap routeings to Bangkok via Dhaka in Bangladesh. From any point in India you have the choice of flying or overlanding to Kathmandu (see p.170), but to continue to Bangkok you'll have to fly as it's currently impossible to cross Burma overland.

If you decide to leave out the Indian subcontinent altogether, your trip will begin in Bangkok. From there, you have a choice of flying in short hops through Thailand, Malaysia, Singapore and Indonesia, or making the long trek south overland. You may also want to factor in enough time to explore Laos, Cambodia and Vietnam from Thailand first, either overland or by local airlines. Travelling from Bangkok to Bali by bus, train and boat will save you heaps of money, but is obviously a lot more time-consuming. If you want to stop off for a while in all four countries en route then allow yourself at least two to three months for this part of the trip. There's a lot of ground to cover – Sumatra, for example, is the fourth largest island in the world – and the whole adventure becomes a real slog if you try to cram it all into three weeks.

In fact, the most popular route south from Bangkok is a combination of flying and overlanding. You can either weave a couple of flights into your round-the-world ticket before you go (for example, between Malaysia and Sumatra, and between Java and Bali), or buy flights in Asia as and when you get tired of long bus journeys. Bangkok is a good centre for cheap flights (visit ⓦwww.statravel.co.th for a list of sample fares); there's a growing number of budget inter-Asia airlines (ⓦwww.airasia.com, ⓦwww.jetstarasia.com, ⓦwww.fly12go.com, ⓦbangkokair.com) and internal flights within Indonesia are both inexpensive and extensive. Long-distance overnight trains and buses cover the Thai–Malaysian–Singapore peninsula, and you can easily island-hop all the way from Malaysia to Bali and even on to East Timor if you have the time.

Overland routes into Asia from Europe and Australia

For some travellers, the process of getting to Asia is part of the whole adventure. However, time is the major factor here, and the expense

Delhi to London on a motorbike

After six months exploring India on an elderly Enfield Bullet, bought in Delhi for £600, I thought the bike would make a good souvenir. Shipping it was an option, but somehow riding the 10,000-odd miles home across Asia seemed a lot more interesting . . .

My route was a fairly standard one, taking me through Pakistan (with a side-trip up the Karakoram Highway into the northern hills), and then on to Iran and Turkey. Over the next five months, I rode through some of the most stunning and least-touristed areas of Asia, beneath soaring mountains, through barren deserts and across fertile plains. All the way along, people were exceptionally hospitable – there was always someone around to help me decipher squiggly road signs, direct me to a mechanic or, frequently, invite me home to stay with the family.

The gradual transition from East to West was fascinating: the culture, climate and terrain changed imperceptibly day by day. On top of that, there was something immensely satisfying about tracing a line on the map across two continents and actually following it on the ground.

Nicki McCormick

may be off-putting too – though trains, buses and boats are generally cheaper than flights, you will have spent a fair bit on accommodation and food before you even arrive in Asia.

The overland routes listed below are just a handful of the possible options. Though we've described them as routes *in to* Asia, they're quite feasible when done in reverse. It's almost, but not quite, possible to travel all the way from Australia to Britain (and back) without resorting to an aeroplane. The only hiatus comes when you need to cross the sea between northern Australia and East Timor. Unless you cadge a ride on a yacht or a cargo boat, you'll have to get an Airnorth flight (Ⓦwww.airnorth.com.au) from Darwin to Dili in East Timor, after which you can island-hop all the way to Singapore. In reality, most Australians choose the easy option and fly straight into Bali, beginning their journeys from there.

Some people choose to travel overland to Asia under their own steam, either in a car or on a motorbike, typically along the route blazed by the hippie travellers of the 1960s and 70s. Though it is also possible to buy a vehicle in Asia and travel back home with your own wheels, this option entails even more paperwork; the bureaucracy involved in riding a motorbike back from India, for example, is so overwhelming that some travellers give up before they even get started.

Once in Asia you have the option of continuing your travels by road, rail and river (see "Overland routes within Asia", p.170), or you can buy a series of air tickets as you go.

The Trans-Siberian Railway

The Trans-Siberian Railway is *the* classic overland route into Asia, but it's nowhere near as cheap as flying one-way to Beijing. All its trains begin in Moscow and travel east to Irkutsk, beyond which the line divides into three: the Trans-Mongolian route branches off to Beijing via Ulaanbaatar, the Trans-Manchurian route also goes to Beijing, but via Harbin, while the Trans-Siberian proper goes to Vladivostok via Khabarovsk. Taking the Trans-Mongolian route from Moscow to Beijing means spending six days on the train, while the Trans-Manchurian route from Moscow to Beijing takes seven days. If you are patient, have lots of time and have paid meticulous attention to visa requirements, you can then continue by train from Beijing to Hanoi in Vietnam (2 days). If you choose the Trans-Siberian route from Moscow you'll end up in Vladivostok (7 days), from where there are more or less weekly ferries to Fushiki in Japan (@www.bisintour.com; 40hr).

Standard Trans-Siberian tickets for any of the three routes are direct and do not permit stops or side-trips. The most economical way of buying a non-stop ticket in advance is online through a Russian travel agent such as Way To Russia (@waytorussia.trainline.ru); for Moscow–Beijing they charge $480/£260 first class, $310/£170 second class, and for Moscow–Vladivostock it's $700/£380 or $390/£210. A rail ticket from London to Moscow will cost you about $380/£200. For the direct westbound Beijing–Moscow route, booking through the Chinese travel agency CITS (@www.cits.net) will cost you around $400/£220 first class or $250/£135 second class. If you want to add in stops and side trips you'll need to go through a specialist tour operator, who can also arrange all the visas and other paperwork. These Trans-Siberian tours are quite pricey, not least because stopping tickets cost a lot more than non-stop ones. Sundowners travel agency offer budget Trans-Siberia packages for 18–35-year-olds on their Vodka Train tour (@www.vodkatrain.com; from $1520/£880).

For a full rundown of everything you need to know about visas, life on the train and ideas for stopoffs, see the *Trans-Siberian Handbook,* published by Trailblazer, and the exceptionally detailed The Man in Seat Sixty-One website at @www.seat61.com/Trans-Siberian.htm.

The hippie trail: from Europe to Kathmandu via Turkey, Iran, Pakistan and India

In the flower-power days of the 1960s and 70s, the most popular route for adventurous, spiritually curious, budget travellers was to meander slowly overland from Istanbul to Kathmandu, taking in Iran, Afghanistan, Pakistan and India along the way. The route came to be known as the hippie trail and, almost a half a century later, it's still a fascinating way of travelling between Europe and Asia. These days, international politics permitting, the most common way to do this route is by car or motorbike, though it's also possible by public transport or with an organized tour.

With your own vehicle, if you put your foot down and ignore the temptations of the countries en route, you can reach Delhi from London in 21 days. However, doing it this way obviously involves some serious preparation, both for yourself and your vehicle. The paperwork is the biggest headache – visas need to be sorted out well in advance of your departure date, especially for Iran, and you will also need a special document for your vehicle known as a *carnet de passage*. Bikers should check out Trailblazer's *The Adventure Motorcycling Handbook*, which contains full details of all these requirements, and the forum at ®www.adventure-motorcycling .com; car drivers and travellers intending to use public transport should consult Lonely Planet's *Istanbul to Kathmandu*.

Some tour operators (such as Dragoman and Exodus; see Directory, p.413) organize group overland trips along these routes in converted lorries. The trips take from four to thirty weeks, the age range is generally between 18 and 40, and the all-inclusive cost is quite reasonable. If you're nervous about setting off for Asia on your own, then this could be a good way to start.

Overland routes within Asia

Before fixing your ticket routeing, think about spicing up your flight itinerary with some overland routes in between. It's a great feeling to watch from a train window as one country slowly metamorphoses into another – far more satisfying than whizzing over international borders at thirty thousand feet – and in nearly every case it will be a lot cheaper than flying. Sometimes it's also quicker and more convenient than backtracking to the airport in the capital city. Overlanding under your own steam, especially by bicycle can also be an exhilarating way to travel; see box above for more.

△ Kathmandu Valley, Nepal

Having the right paperwork is essential for overland routes, as most countries demand that you specify the exact land border when applying – see Chapter Two for more advice on this, and be sure to check out the viability of your proposed overland route before making any firm flight bookings. You'll find a detailed list of the current designated border crossings in Asia on pp.174–176, and there's more detail in the individual country profiles on pp.19–153.

Southeast Asia: Thailand–Malaysia–Singapore–Indonesia–East Timor

By far the most popular overland route within Asia is the trip down from Thailand into Malaysia. Having lingered on the coasts and islands of southern Thailand (Ko Samui, Ko Pha Ngan, Krabi and Ko Lanta to name just a few), you can cross into Malaysia quite effortlessly by train, bus or minibus: nearly all major towns and resorts between Bangkok and Kuala Lumpur run long-distance cross-border transport. Not surprisingly, Bangkok–Kuala Lumpur is a common "surface sector" leg on round-the-world, Circle-Asia and open-jaw tickets (see Chapter Two). Some people round off this overland route with a few days on the island of Singapore, which is connected to southern Malaysia by a causeway.

A relatively popular extension to the Thailand–Malaysia route is to continue on into Indonesia by sea. There are frequent ferries and speedboats from various ports in Malaysia to Sumatra, and from Johor Bahru and Singapore to Indonesia's Riau archipelago. Most of these ferries take just a few hours to travel between Malaysia/Singapore and Indonesia. Ferries connect each Indonesian island with its neighbour, and when you finally arrive in West Timor you can get a bus across the border into independent East Timor.

Indochina: Thailand–Laos–Vietnam–Cambodia–Thailand

The overland trail from Thailand across Indochina is becoming increasingly well travelled, and makes an interesting circular route that can be done without ever taking to the air. Bear in mind, however, that road transport in Laos and Cambodia is very slow and can be exhaustingly uncomfortable. Cycling between countries is also a tempting option in this part of Southeast Asia: see p.171 and p.334 for more information.

There are currently five crossings between northeast Thailand and Laos, the easiest and most popular of which connects Nong Khai and Vientiane. Laos has four gateways into Vietnam, all of them served by buses. Laos and Cambodia are connected via a boat service that runs from the Mekong River island of Voen Kham (south of Pakxe) to Stung Treng in northern Cambodia. You can also enter Cambodia via the Mekong from Vietnam, travelling from Chau Doc in the Mekong Delta to Phnom Penh; in addition, Vietnam runs a useful cross-border bus service from Ho Chi Minh City to Phnom Penh via Moc Bai. You can overland between Cambodia and Thailand at half a dozen points, of which the most commonly used are between Poipet (connected by bus to Siem Reap/Angkor) and Aranyapathet (a six-hour train journey from Bangkok), and via Koh Kong, for Sihanoukville and Trat (east Thailand).

Overland from China to Thailand via Indochina

As China has useful land borders with both Laos and Vietnam, the Indochina circuit described above can easily be adapted into a smooth overland link between China and Thailand, and makes it feasible to do the entire journey from London to Hanoi by train. It's also increasingly popular to travel between China, Vietnam, Cambodia, Laos and Thailand by bicycle: see the box on p.171 for some useful cycling resources.

The Beijing–Nanning–Hanoi train enters Vietnam at Dong Dang, where there's also a road crossing. Trains from Kunming in China's southwestern Yunnan province cross the border further west and terminate at Hanoi. If you're on a motorbike or bicycle, you can also follow a scenic coastal route that runs via the road border at Dongxing/Moc Bai to Haiphong. Once in Vietnam, you can choose to travel to Laos or Cambodia, as outlined above.

The China-Laos border is at Mo Han/Boten, with bus connections from Kunming to Vientiane and Jinghong to Oudomxai or Louang Namtha. From Laos you can head east into Vietnam, west into Thailand or south into Cambodia.

By bus from India to Nepal

Overlanding between India and Nepal is straightforward and popular, and a useful surface sector in Circle Asia and open-jaw tickets

Border crossings and international ferries

All the border crossings listed below are served by public transport. Burma and Sri Lanka are currently the only two countries that are inaccessible to overlanders. Except where stated, all the following border crossings are currently accessible from both sides.

Indian subcontinent

Pakistan–China By bus along the Karakoram Highway from Sust (Pakistan) to Tashkurgan (China).

India–Pakistan Bus or train from Amritsar to Lahore via Attari and Wagha.

India–China No overland crossing allowed.

India–Bangladesh From Kolkata via Haridaspur and Benapole to Dhaka by train, rickshaw and bus; from Darjeeling via Haldibari to Chilahati by train; from Shillong via Dawki/Tarnabil to Sylhet by bus. Also, from West Bengal: between Burimari and Patgram; Balurghat and Hili; and Lalgola and Godagari; plus from Agartala in Tripura to Akhaura.

India–Sri Lanka Owing to the unrest in Sri Lanka, the ferry service between the two countries is suspended indefinitely.

India–Nepal Several crossings convenient for foreigners, including: by bus from Delhi, Varanasi or Gorakhpur via Sonauli and Bhairawa to Mahendra Nagar, Pokhara or Kathmandu; by bus from Bodh Gaya, Kolkata or Patna via Raxaul and Birganj to Pokhara or Kathmandu; and by bus and/or train from Siliguri, Darjeeling or Kolkata via Kakarbitta to Pokhara or Kathmandu.

Bhutan–India By road from Thimpu via Phuntsoling to Siliguri or Darjeeling; and by road via Samdrup Jongkhar to Assam district (this route is not permissible in reverse).

Nepal–China (Tibet) Currently not allowed for independent travellers on public transport (though it is permitted in the other direction). However, foreigners who have booked inclusive tours of Lhasa (these can be arranged in Kathmandu) are allowed to cross here; the tour companies organize the paperwork.

Southeast Asia

Thailand–Malaysia and Singapore By direct train from Bangkok to: Penang, Kuala Lumpur via Hat Yai, or Singapore via Penang. By bus or share-taxi from Hat Yai to Penang or Singapore. By share-taxi from Betong to Butterworth via Keroh; by road from Ban Taba to Kota Bharu. By ferry from Satun to Kuala Perlis and Langkawi.

Malaysia–Singapore By bus, train or ferry.

Malaysia and Singapore–Indonesia By ferry or speedboat from Penang to Medan in northern Sumatra; from Melaka to Dumai in northern Sumatra; from Kuala Lumpur, Johor Bahru or Singapore to Batam, Bintan and Karimun islands (in Indonesia's Riau archipelago). By bus from Kuching

(Sarawak) via Entikong to Pontianak (Kalimantan). By ferry from Tawau (Sabah) to Pulau Nunukan in northeastern Kalimantan.

Indonesia (West Timor)–East Timor By bus from Kupang to Dili via Batugede. By road into Oekusi via Oesilo.

Philippines–Indonesia There are international ferry routes between General Santos and Bitung in northern Sulawesi, but some are served by cargo boats (many of them unlicensed and overloaded) and are considered unsafe due to pirate attacks in local waters.

Indochina

Thailand–Laos By bus from Nong Khai to Vientiane; and from Chong Mek via Ban Mai Sing Amphon to Pakxe. By ferry across the Mekong River from Chiang Khong via Houayxai to Louang Phabang; from Nakhon Phanom via Thakhek to Vientiane; and from Mukdahan to Savannakhet.

Thailand–Cambodia By bus and boat or share-taxi from Trat to Sihanoukville and Phnom Penh, via Ban Hat Lek and Koh Kong. By bus and train from Aranyaprathet to Sisophon and Siem Reap, via Poipet. By bus from Surin via Kap Choeng/O'Smach to Anlong Veng. Via Sa Ngam near Si Saket province to Choam. By chartered minibus from Pong Nam Ron to Ban Laem or Phsa Prom for Pailin.

Cambodia–Laos By boat and bus from Stung Treng to Don Khong and Pakxe via Voen Kham.

Laos–Vietnam By bus from Savannakhet and Xepon to Hué or Hanoi, via Lao Bao and Dong Ha. By bus from Lak Xao to Vinh, via Kaew Nua and Cau Treo. Via Ban Nong Het to Vinh, and via Na Maew to Nam Xoi.

Vietnam–Cambodia By bus and share-taxi from Ho Chi Minh City via Moc Bai and Bavet to Phnom Penh. By taxi, boat and bus from Chau Doc to Phnom Penh via K'am Samnar.

Vietnam–China By bus or rail from Hanoi via Dong Dang and Pingxiang to Nanning; by bus or rail from Hanoi via Lao Cai and Hekou to Kunming in Yunnan; with your own transport from Haiphong to Nanning (Guangxi) via Mong Cai and Dongxing.

Laos–China By bus from Vientiane to Kunming (Yunnan) via Boten/Mo Han; by bus from Oudomxai and Louang Namtha via Boten/Mo Han to Jinghong (Yunnan); by bus and boat from Louang Phabang via Boten to Mo Han (Yunnan).

China, Mongolia and Japan

China–Mongolia By train (Trans-Mongolian Express) or bus from Beijing or Hohhot to Ulaanbaatar via Erlianhot and Zamyn Uud.

China–India No overland crossing allowed.

China–Pakistan By bus along the Karakoram Highway from Tashkurgan (China) to Sust (Pakistan).

China (Tibet)–Nepal Informal shared jeeps via Zhangmu to Kathmandu, but not allowed going from Nepal into Tibet unless on a tour.

China–Laos By bus from Kunming (Yunnan) to Vientiane via Mo Han/Boten; by bus from Jinghong (Yunnan) to Oudomxai or Louang Namtha via Mo Han/Boten.

China–Vietnam By bus or rail from Nanning (Guangxi) via Pingxiang and Dong Dang to Hanoi; by bus or rail from Kunming in Yunnan via Hekou and Lao Cai to Hanoi; with your own transport from Nanning via Dongxing (Guangxi) and Mong Cai to Haiphong.

China–South Korea By ferry to Incheon (near Seoul) from Tianjin (near Beijing), Qingdao and Weihai (both in Shandong), and Dalian and Dandong (both in Liaoning).

China–Taiwan None.

Taiwan–Japan By ferry from Keelung to Naha in Okinawa.

China–Japan By ferry from Shanghai to Osaka and Kobe, from Tianjin (near Beijing) to Kobe, and from Qingdao to Shimonoseki.

Japan–South Korea By ferry and hydrofoil from Shimonoseki and Fukuoka to Busan.

(see Chapter Two). The easiest approaches are from Patna and Gorakhpur, which between them have useful train services to and from Delhi, Varanasi, Darjeeling, Gaya and Kolkata. Patna runs buses to Kathmandu via the Nepali border at Raxaul, and Gorakhpur runs buses to another border point, Sonauli, where you can get connections to Pokhara and Kathmandu. The seventeen-hour journey from the Kakarbitta border crossing to Kathmandu is more of a slog, but Kakarbitta is very handy for Darjeeling, and close to Silgiuri, which has good rail connections with Kolkata and Delhi.

India to China via Pakistan and the Karakoram Highway

This unusual trans-Asia route is longer and more challenging than the classic version through India and Southeast Asia, as travel is relatively difficult in Pakistan and China, and travellers quite rare. For many people, this is part of the route's appeal. Regional politics permitting, the Pakistan–China section can be woven into all sorts of Asian and round-the-world itineraries. It can feature as the middle section of a major overland trip from Europe to Indonesia, following on nicely from the hippie trail to Pakistan (see p.170). It feeds easily into the China–Indochina route described above, becoming the meaty preamble to a more light-hearted Southeast Asian trip: the route from Thailand, through Malaysia, to Indonesia (see p.172) will almost certainly seem like a picnic after the bureaucracies of north Asia. Or you can treat it as the surface sector of an open-jaw return or a Circle Asia flight (described in Chapter Two), buying a plane ticket that flies you into Delhi and then takes you out of Bangkok or Singapore a few months later, giving you the option of buying some internal flights en route if necessary.

Riding high

My love for long-distance pushbiking came about step by step, and the first step was spending three months camping and cycling in Holland. There's a kind of rhythm to camping and cycling: up with the sun, cooking your own food on flame-throwing MSR camp stoves and scoping out friendly houses to camp next to. All stuff which comes in handy everywhere in the world. The first Himalaya trip came from being in a bike accident that broke my arm in three places and put me in plaster and physio for four months. Rotting away, bikeless, in London, I began cooking up cool routes for when I had two arms again. I bought a return ticket to India, which I changed to the maximum six months after about a fortnight in the Indian Himalaya. Still with my right wrist in a support splint, I rode for the first month with a Canadian who could help carry the bike over landslides and up hotel stairs. After that first month, I was strong enough to ride and carry my bike everywhere, and happy riding alone in north India. Since then, I haven't really looked back and am now on a two-year bike trip to travel the length of the Himalaya, as described in ⓦ www .himalayabybicycle.com.

I'm not a sporty person (a school report once read "We think that Laura could enjoy PE, but we've never seen her doing any"). The cycle trips aren't about sport – it's more a way of travelling that is totally independent, and brilliantly simple: just get on the bike and ride! Buses leach energy, but travelling by bike makes you look after yourself and keeps you strong and healthy. You take in one hundred percent of what's going on around you – there's no chance to fall asleep and miss it all.

The hardest part is always leaving. I'll have the idea for the trip, tell my family about it, and then privately wonder why I want to head off for places like Pakistan by myself, on a bicycle... But the minute I sniff a new country in my nostrils, the change of heat, the light... I'm pulled in straight away.

Laura Stone

Delhi is the obvious entry point to India if you're heading up to Pakistan, but it may be worth flying into one of the regional airports instead, such as Chennai or Kolkata, if you want to explore southern or eastern parts of India first. You can either cross into Pakistan overland (via Amritsar) or fly into Hyderabad from Mumbai or Kolkata, or into Lahore and Islamabad from Delhi.

From Pakistan you can take a bus into China via the spectacular Karakoram Highway, which starts in Rawalpindi and goes via Gilgit to Kashgar in far northwest China. This should take about four days but is only feasible from May to October when the Karakoram Highway is not snowbound. This route is also Asia's most famous long-distance cycle route, taking around six weeks to complete in either direction: see the box on p.171 for more info. Useful resources for all Karakoram travellers include Lonely Planet's *Pakistan and the Karakoram Highway*, and there's also the cyclist-oriented website The Karakoram Highway and Beyond (⊛home.hkstar.com/~roz/Index.htm).

The direct overland route from Kashgar to Ali in western Tibet is closed to foreigners, so if you want to make a side-trip into Tibet you'll have to head east from Kashgar to Golmud and then southwest to Lhasa: from 2007 the Golmud-Lhasa leg should be possible by train, on the long-awaited Qinghai–Tibet railway, most of which travels at an altitude of over 4000m. From Lhasa you can fly east to Chengdu, which has good transport connections with Kunming as well as the main cities of eastern China.

By sea from China to South Korea and Japan

If you're in eastern China, it's quite possible and inexpensive, if time-consuming, to take a boat across to South Korea and then continue by ferry to Japan; or you could take a direct boat from China to Japan. Once you've seen your fill of Japan you could take the ferry from Kobe or Osaka across to Shanghai, take a train to Beijing and make the long haul back to Europe on the Trans-Siberian Railway (see p.169). The route works equally well in reverse. There's also a ferry service between the Japanese port of Fushiki and Vladivostok, at the end of the Trans-Siberian line.

There are regular boats to Incheon near Seoul from Tianjin (near Beijing), Qingdao and Weihai (both in Shandong), and Dalian and Dandong (both in Liaoning). The Weihai connection is the shortest, at fourteen hours. Hydrofoils and ferries to Japan run daily from Busan in southern South Korea to Fukuoka (3hr) and Shimonoseki (9hr). To travel between China and Japan by boat takes around 48 hours; services run once a week from Shanghai, alternately to Kobe or Osaka.

Themes for travel

Rather than base your trip round tourist sights and famous land-scapes, you might consider planning your route around specific activities instead. We've selected some popular highlights below. You'll find specialist guidebooks covering some of these themes, though any decent travel guide should have at least a few pointers on a country's most interesting activities.

Trekking and hiking

There's plenty of scope for interesting treks and hikes in Asia, and you don't necessarily have to be an experienced walker to enjoy them. In Asia, you'll find the word "trek" used to refer to a long-distance walk, where you will spend the night or several nights en route. "Hike" generally means a walk taking a day or less.

In many cases you can do hikes and treks unassisted, so long as you have a decent route map and are dressed for the occasion. But in some places you'd be foolhardy to go without a guide: jungles, for example, are notoriously hard to navigate, even if you do possess a map, and high mountain passes are usually best negotiated with the help of a local expert. For long, arduous treks you'll probably need to hire a porter as well, to help carry tents and food. Travellers often join forces to arrange cheaper group treks, and in the more established places tour operators organize daily group treks along standard routes.

Don't forget to check on the climate (mid-June to late September, for example, is hopeless for trekking in the Himalayas), and remember to pack suitable clothes and footwear (see Chapter Six for specific advice). Here's a selective roundup of hikes and treks to whet your appetite:

- **Bhutan** Masses of hiking and trekking potential, from short, scenic walks along river valleys or up mountainsides to visit temples and monasteries, to the 24-day Lunana Snowman Trek across half of the country.
- **China** Highlights include the one- to three-day trek through the alpine scenery of Sichuan to the spectacular tongue of ice known as Hailuo Guo Glacier; hiking in the hills around Xinjiang's Tian Chi (Heaven Lake), surrounded by snowy peaks and pine forests and staying in Kazakh nomads' tents; and the two-day trek through Tiger

Leaping Gorge in Yunnan, the world's deepest canyon. Much more arduous, but popular nonetheless, is the three-day circumnavigation of Tibet's sacred Mount Kailash, stopping at monasteries en route.

- **India** There are challenging Himalayan treks of two to twelve days through forests and valleys, alongside mountain streams, past remote villages, and over sometimes snowy passes, with constant Himalayan views on all sides. The less difficult routes start from Dharamsala; the more strenuous ones – through the Zanskar and Ladakh regions – begin in Leh. See *Trekking in Ladakh* (Trailblazer) for a comprehensive account of what's entailed.

- **Indonesia** There are plenty of one-day volcano hikes, including the sunrise walk up Java's awesome Mount Bromo and the hike up Keli Mutu on Flores to see its famous three-coloured crater lakes. West Papua's Baliem Valley offers scores of flatter trails to follow, taking you through cultivated land to interesting Dani villages. One of the most popular of the longer treks takes you up to Gunung Rinjani's crater rim on Lombok, a two- to four-day expedition that can also include the crater lake and, for the very fit, the summit. Another highlight is the six-day route through Gunung Leuser National Park in north Sumatra, from Ketambe to the orang-utan sanctuary in Bukit Lawang.

- **Malaysia** Almost everyone who makes it across to Sabah on the East Malaysian island of Borneo attempts the two-day hike to the summit of Mount Kinabalu (4101m). Neighbouring Sarawak offers some strenuous day-hikes in Gunung Mulu National Park, through rainforest to the razor-sharp fifty-metre-high limestone pinnacles, plus exploring parts of the largest cave system in the world, while the Bario Loop is a tougher five-day experience in the jungle of the Kelabit highlands near the Kalimantan border, with nights spent at longhouses en route. On Peninsular Malaysia, the biggest draw is Taman Negara National Park, which has a good selection of one- to four-day trails through the rainforest, some of them taking in observation hides en route.

- **Nepal** The Nepal Himalayas are the most popular area in Asia for trekking; there are literally scores of possible options (see p.99 for an overview). Independent trekking is quite feasible (though check the current security situation first), but guides, porters and organized tours are also available from Kathmandu and Pokhara. For detailed practical info, consult the relevant trekking guides published by Trailblazer, such as *Trekking in the Everest Region* and *Trekking in the Annapurna Region*.

- **Pakistan** In the north of the country, where the Himalayas, Karakoram and Hindu Kush mountain ranges collide, you'll find some of the best, and least crowded, trekking in the world. The trekking centres of Shigar near Skardu, Gilgit and Chitral all offer treks that last from one day to several weeks, with the chance to take in glaciers and 5500-metre passes.

- **Philippines** Highlights include the steep four-day ascent and descent into sacred Mount Banahaw's thickly forested crater, in Quezon National Park; the picturesque day-long hike through sculptured rice-paddy valleys to the traditional village of Batad in Ifugao; and the trek up to the impressive crate lake on eerie, volcanic Mount Pinatubo.

- **South Korea** This country has seventeen national parks, nearly all of them offering scores of well-maintained trails. One of the best is Seorak-San National Park, whose tracks run via craggy peaks and forested slopes, taking in waterfalls, Zen temples and mineral springs along the way. Other good ones are Jiri-san, which has long trails through the mountains, and the wooded valleys of Songni-san, where you'll come across lots of important temples and hermitages while hiking.

- **Sri Lanka** The night-time trek up Adam's Peak in time for the sunrise is one of the highlights of the country.

Trekking in Tibet

Choosing to trek into the Kailash region of Tibet, I ruled out venturing near the city in order to avoid fellow "travellers". We saw no one for days, with the exception of sheep, yaks and a few nomads. Not even a trace of civilization. An unforgiving wind swept across the plateau, and there were no trees, just low bushes, random rocks, high mountains and rolling hills. I had known what to expect: I knew the population was sparse, and that we would see no one until we reached Mount Kailash, but the desolate and almost Martian landscape made me long all the more for people.

The rivers we crossed were too cold for bathing, and plumbing was nonexistent. Thinking I was an eco-traveller, I carried plastic bags in which to dispose of my toilet paper. But I soon realized that trash and human waste were not confined to the towns. There was garbage scattered across the land, in the middle of nowhere, like it belonged there. Perhaps it had been dropped by pilgrims on their way to Kailash, or by Western tour groups from the windows of their Land Cruisers.

When we finally arrived at Mount Kailash, the sacred home of the Hindu god Shiva, and the centre of the Buddhist universe, happy pilgrims appeared. Finally, people! Pilgrims older than my deceased grandparents had walked 56 kilometres in a single day – at altitudes of over 4500 metres. I was amazed. It took me three days to circumambulate the mountain, following a well-trodden path round the holy peak. Devout pilgrims prostrated themselves as they walked through incoming blizzards. One Hindu pilgrim had walked all the way from Delhi in India. He'd begun his journey two months earlier and had hitched rides, slept out in the open and crossed the Himalayas barefoot. In contrast, I wore heavy winter gear, walked no more than ten steps before having to gasp for breath, and slept inside a tent, wrapped in a down sleeping bag.

Karen Christine Lefere

- **Taiwan** Several good trails in the central mountain ranges, especially around Sun Moon Lake, from Alishan to view the sunrise from the peak of 2490-metre Chu Shan, and the two-night trek up Yushan, which at 3952m is the highest mountain in East Asia.
- **Thailand** A huge percentage of visitors to Thailand go jungle-trekking in the northern hills around Chiang Mai, Chiang Rai and Pai, mainly to see hill-tribe villages but also for elephant rides and white-water rafting. There's more remote and less commercial trekking from Kanchanaburi and Umphang, or head for the steamy southern jungles of Khao Sok National Park.

Wildlife spotting

Asia is home to some of the most unusual animals in the world, including the tigers and elephants of India and Indonesia, the snow leopard of northern Nepal, the yaks of the Himalayas and Tibetan plateau, and the orang-utans of Kalimantan, Sumatra and Sarawak, not to mention scores of extraordinary birds. Many of these creatures are now endangered, as the pressure from an expanding human population and the continued trade in rare species threatens their existence, so you're unlikely to happen across many of them on a random hike in the mountains or the jungle. However, Asia has a fair number of national parks where rare fauna and flora are, at least in theory, protected from poachers, and many of these places are accessible to tourists.

The places listed below are the cream of the crop, highlighted because you have a good chance of seeing wildlife there and can travel independently without much trouble. You'll need to be careful about the timing of your visit to any national park, as birds and animals tend to be more social and therefore easier to spot at certain times of the year. Consult relevant guidebooks for advice on this, or consider taking a specialist wildlife tour with one of the operators listed on pp.412–414. For bird guides to Asia, John MacKinnon's *Field Guide to the Birds of Borneo, Sumatra, Java and Bali* is a classic, and *Where to Watch Birds in Asia* is also recommended.

- **Bangladesh** An exceptionally rewarding country for bird-watching, Bangladesh is home to many species that are otherwise only found in either India or Southeast Asia, and is also a major wintering ground for migrant birds. The mangrove swamps and coastal wetlands of the Sunderbans are good places to spot cranes and golden eagles (and there's a very remote possibility of seeing a Bengal tiger here, too).

The Madhupur Forest Reserve is renowned for its brown wood owl and the dusky owl, and you'll see rhesus monkeys and langurs here as well. Several species of pochards and teals visit the Sunamganj wetlands in Sylhet, as do crakes and various fishing eagles.

- **Bhutan** The snow leopard is the most elusive of Himalayan creatures but you do have a chance of seeing one here, especially on the longer treks away from population centres. And there's always the yeti to think about while you're waiting.
- **India** The tiger population is famously in decline in India, but you've a reasonable chance of spotting one at Kanha Tiger Reserve and in Bandhavgarh and Ranthambore national parks. Wild elephants are a little more common, and best looked for in the Periyar Wildlife Sanctuary and Corbett National Park. Kaladeo National Park is one of the most famous bird reserves in the world, with huge breeding colonies of cranes, storks, flamingoes and ibis, and the winter population of cranes in the desert village of Keechen is a similarly impressive sight.
- **Indonesia** Highlights on Sumatra include the Bukit Lawang orang-utan sanctuary, and the hornbills, Argus pheasants and numerous other birds of Kerinci-Seblat National Park. On Komodo, everyone goes to gawp at the enormous and ferocious monitor lizards known as Komodo dragons; while West Papua is famous for its spectacular birdlife, including birds of paradise (best seen in Pulau Yapen), and innumerable cockatoos, parrots and cassowaries that can be spotted almost anywhere, along with heaps of gorgeously coloured butterflies.
- **Malaysia** There are common sightings of gibbons, macaques and monitor lizards in the easily accessible Taman Negara national park on the peninsula. In Sabah, the big draws are the Sepilok Orang-utan sanctuary, the flowers of Sabah's Mount Kinabalu – including a thousand species of orchid, 26 types of rhododendron, and various bizarre insect-eating pitcher plants – and the chance of seeing the proboscis monkey, found only in Borneo and most likely spotted along Sabah's Kinabatangan river. Gunung Mulu National Park in Sarawak is renowned for its phenomenal birdlife, which includes eight species of hornbill.
- **Nepal** Trekkers rarely see any interesting mammals in the mountains; it's much more rewarding to head for the plains of the Tarai, where there's a good chance of spotting rhinos, monkeys and possibly bears at the popular Chitwan National Park. Langurs and wild pig are frequently sighted in Bardia National Park, where you also have a reasonable chance of encountering a rhino, a tiger, or even a Gangetic dolphin. Swamp deer, crocodiles and awesome birdlife, including

heaps of cranes, cormorants and eagles, are good enough reasons to visit Sukla Phanta Wildlife Reserve.

- **Sri Lanka** Bundala National Park is famously rewarding for bird-watching, and is especially known for flamingoes. There's a reasonable chance of spotting wild elephants in Yala National Park, but Pinnewala Elephant Orphanage is the place to see dozens of them at extremely close quarters.

Diving

Internationally certified scuba-diving courses are cheaper in Asia than in most other parts of the world and, once you've done your training, the potential for underwater exploration is phenomenal. The reef life is as diverse, prolific and fascinating as anywhere on the planet, and as the water tends to be bath temperature you won't always need a full wetsuit. You will find reputable dive schools in all the major resorts listed below, and the same places also organize dive trips and rent out equipment. The worldwide Professional Association of Diving Instructors, or PADI, keeps an up-to-date list of PADI-approved dive centres around the world, which can be viewed at ⓦwww.padi.com; the same is true of the National Association of Underwater Instructors, at ⓦwww.naui.org. In Thailand, you should expect to pay $200–380/£100–200 for the four-day open-water PADI course. In the Philippines, dive excursions to local reefs cost from $20/£10, including equipment and one tank, or from $1200/£600 for a week's all-inclusive live-aboard dive package to the more remote and exceptional reefs.

Though you can dive year-round in Asia, some seas become too rough and visibility drops during the rainy season (see Chapter Three), so check with a specialist diving guidebook before fixing your trip. There are a number of recommended diving guides, all of which describe and illustrate the marine life as well as detailing the best dive sites. Periplus has the widest coverage with a guide to diving in the whole of Southeast Asia, plus individual diving guides to Indonesia, Thailand, Malaysia and the Philippines. Lonely Planet does specialist dive guides to Thailand, Bali and Lombok, and the Philippines, and the Globetrotter Dive Guides series published by New Holland covers Malaysia and Indonesia. The online version of the divers' magazine *Asian Diver,* ⓦwww.asiandiver.com, is another good source of information, and includes travellers' reports and a forum.

- Still way off most beaten tracks, tiny **East Timor** offers spectacular, world-class diving without the crowds. As well as several impressive wall dives, especially near Tutuala, there are plenty of chances to swim with manta rays, sharks, turtles and dugongs.
- Boasting warm, clear waters and a breathtakingly diverse marine life, **Indonesia** offers masses of quality dive sites. The most accessible of these are found off north and west Bali; off the Gili islands in Lombok; and in Sulawesi at the Bunaken-Manado Tua Marine Park. Flores is also becoming an increasingly popular diving destination and there's great diving at the more remote Pulau Derawan, off northeastern Kalimantan. If you've got plenty of money, live-aboard charters open up areas off Maluku and West Papua.
- **Malaysia**'s best diving facilities are centred on Pulau Tioman, but there are lots more dive centres on other east-coast islands, including Pulau Perhentian, Pulau Redang and Pulau Kapas. Aficionados head for Pulau Sipadan off Sabah, though check the security situation there first.
- The thousands of islands that make up the **Philippines** archipelago are ringed by over four thousand square kilometres of reef which, not surprisingly, makes the country one of Asia's most important diving destinations. The main dive centres are at Moaboal, Puerto Galera and Boracay, but the cream of the reefs are off the Palawan Islands and Occidental Mindoro, and there are exciting shipwreck dives off Busuangra.
- **Sri Lanka** is encircled by potentially rewarding reefs but the volatile political situation and the 2004 tsunami have made diving an uncertain activity for the moment, so you'll need to check Internet travel forums for the current situation.
- In **Thailand** there are numerous dive centres at the resorts on Phuket and in Pattaya and Krabi, but the best reefs are around the outlying islands, particularly Ko Similan, Ko Surin and Ko Tao.

Chasing the adrenaline rush

For most people, a bus trip on the Trans-Sumatran Highway, a few hours in a tiny, overladen ferry boat in heaving seas, or a few minutes aboard some of the domestic airlines, generate quite enough excitement. But there are all sorts of other ways to spice up your trip, some of which are listed below. For more inspiration, and tales from the hot seat, have a look at the online version of the Hong-Kong-based

△ Rock-climbing in Krabi, South Thailand

magazine *Action Asia,* ⓦwww.actionasia.com, which covers everything from mountaineering to windsurfing in Asia. If you're planning to do any of the following adventure sports, be sure to advise your insurance company before buying your policy.

- **Kayaking** Paddle your own canoe through mangrove swamps, jungle rivers and island caves in south Thailand, north Vietnam and the Philippines.
- **Marathon-running** Take your mind off the pain of a 26-mile run by enjoying some of the finest scenery on the planet. In China, the Great Wall Marathon (ⓦwww.great-wall-marathon.com) includes a seven-kilometre stretch on the Great Wall itself, plus around 3700

steps; it's held at the end of May. The Himalayan 100-mile Stage Race (🌐www.himalayan.com) takes you past four of the world's five highest mountains (including Mount Everest), is organized in five daily stages and is open to runners and walkers; it's held in late October and begins from Darjeeling in India.

- **Mountaineering** While most travellers go to Nepal to trek, the country is also the world's centre for serious mountaineering expeditions, as is the entire length of the Himalayas. The colossal Karakoram peaks of Nanga Parbat (8126m) and K2 (8900m) are both tackled from inside Pakistan. And at 5030m, Puncak Jaya in West Papua (Indonesia) is the highest peak in Southeast Asia and one of only three snowcapped equatorial mountains in the world.

- **Rock-climbing** The limestone karst that peppers the Krabi coastline of southern Thailand and Ha Long Bay in north Vietnam is crying out to be scaled. There are even more karst routes around Yangshuo in southern China. Rock-climbing's also a popular sport in South Korea, too, particularly in Bukhan-san National Park, which is nicknamed "little Yosemite" because of its myriad perpendicular cliff faces. And in Laos, there's a recently developed set of bolted routes at Ban Pak Ou, near Louang Phabang.

- **Skiing, heli-skiing and snowboarding** in the Indian Himalayas. Take a very expensive helicopter flight out of Manali, then do spectacular runs from around 4000m. Or set your sights and your wallet even higher for heli-ski trips in the Annapurna and Everest areas of the Nepali Himalayas. There are less dramatic, and less costly, opportunities for skiing and snowboarding in mountainous South Korea, in northeast China's Heliongjiang province, and in the Japan Alps.

- **Surfing** along the southern and western side of the Indonesian archipelago. The best facilities are in Bali but there are also top breaks off Sumatra, Lombok and Sumbawa, plus the world-famous G-Land breaks off the eastern end of Java. See *Indo Surf and Lingo* (🌐www.indosurf.com.au) for more detail. In Sri Lanka there are surf centres in Hikkaduwa and Midigama and, in the Philippines, Luzon gets reliable waves, as does Siargao Island off Mindanao. Wanna Surf (🌐www.wannasurf.com) describes and rates breaks all over Asia, from Indonesia to China, and *Surfer* magazine's website (🌐www.surfermag.com) carries surf news and tips for Asia and elsewhere and sells online surf reports on all the major Asian breaks.

- **White-water rafting** In Nepal, you can race down choppy Himalayan rivers, through wooded canyons and jungle, past villages and beaches. It's less popular in the Indian Himalayas, but the scenery's almost as good – particularly around Leh, Manali and Rishikesh. And, in

Pakistan, there's some spectacular rafting around Gilgit. Alternatively, try the rivers of west Thailand, around Umphang; or the Chico, Cagayan and Bombongan rivers on Luzon in the Philippines.

Spiritual quests

Westerners have been going to Asia on spiritual quests for decades, so there are heaps of foreigner-oriented courses to choose from. They're generally inexpensive and last from a few days to several weeks; most are residential. The usual procedure is to enrol on the spot for the next available course, so, unless you're very short of time, there's generally no need to book a place before you leave home.

Don't be put off by the fact that these courses are designed for visiting foreigners: the truly authentic programmes last for months (if not years), are conducted in the local language, and would be far too rigorous for first-timers. In most cases, the foreigners' courses are quite demanding enough: the daily programme generally starts around 5am; the food is healthy but hardly indulgent; sex, drugs and drink are all forbidden for the duration; and some course leaders ask you to stay silent for most of the day. With any luck you'll come away in a calmer and healthier state of mind and body and may also have learnt a bit more about the Asian way of looking at the world. It's quite feasible to practise your newly acquired yoga or meditation skills on your travels, especially if you're staying near a beach. We've selected a few of the most popular centres for yoga and meditation instruction, but there are plenty more: have a look at ⓦwww.buddhanet.net/asia.htm, which is an extensive directory of Asian Buddhist centres catering for foreign students, and ⓦwww .dhamma.org, which lists forthcoming Vipassana meditation courses worldwide.

- **India** is the spiritual heartland of much of Asia and the most popular place for travellers pursuing spiritual interests. Established centres for yoga and meditation courses include Rishikesh (ⓦwww .yogaholidays.net/magazine/Rishikesh.htm) – famous as the place where the Beatles met the Maharishi – and Dharamsala, home-in-exile of the Tibetan Buddhist leader the Dalai Lama, and hundreds of his compatriots. The holy city of Varanasi is another good place to find yoga and meditation gurus. Among India's countless yoga centres (known as ashrams) some of the most popular with travellers are the Root Institute in Bodh Gaya, scene of Buddha's enlightenment (ⓦrootinstitute.com); the Sivananda ashram in Kerala (ⓦwww.sivananda.org/neyyardam); and Sri Pattabhi Jois' Ashtanga Yoga Research Institute in Mysore (ⓦwww.ayri.org). For some more options, see ⓦindia.yoganet.org.

- **Japan** is the home of Zen Buddhism, and Kyoto the best place to find introductory Zen retreats catering for foreigners. Many temples across the country host half-day meditation sessions and overnight stays for foreigners: see ⓦwww.sotozen-net.or.jp/kokusai/list.htm for a detailed list.

- Like India, **Nepal** also attracts a large number of travellers looking for yoga and meditation courses, most of whom end up at Tibetan-Buddhist ashrams in the Kathmandu Valley. One of the most famous is Kopan Monastery (ⓦwww.kopan-monastery.com), which holds 7–30-day international courses throughout the year. See ⓦwww.fpmt.org/centers/nepal.asp for further leads.

- In **Thailand**, the most popular meditation course is the ten-day Vipassana programme held every month at Wat Suan Mokkh in Surat Thani (ⓦwww.suanmokkh.org). Other options include ten-day retreats on Ko Pha Ngan (ⓦwww.watkowtahm.org) and five- and ten-day course courses just outside Chiang Mai (ⓦwww.sivalicentre.com).

- Zen (Son) Buddhism is widely practised in **South Korea** and the Korean Tourist Board (ⓦenglish.tour2korea.com) carries information and links for the temples whose retreats – lasting from two days to three months – are open to international students. Several temples in Seoul also run half-day meditation courses.

Learning a new skill

With all that time on your hands, why not learn a new skill while you're in Asia? The places listed below are renowned on the backpacker circuit for their short, traveller-oriented courses, where you might learn batik painting in a couple of days, or the fundamentals of Mandarin in a couple of weeks. None of these courses require any special aptitude or prior knowledge, and most are informal and relatively superficial, but they're a fun way to get a little further under the skin of a country or a region. Backpackers' guidebooks usually carry details about course durations and prices, but you rarely need to book a place in advance, as most people just turn up in the town and find out what the schedule is.

- **Arts and crafts** Design yourself a T-shirt or paint your own wall-hanging in Indonesia by taking a short course in batik design and dyeing in Yogyakarta (on Java) or Ubud (Bali). You can also learn batik making at Cherating and Kota Bharu in Malaysia. In Kyoto, the Japanese cultural capital, you can take workshops in various traditional arts, including woodblock printing, textile dyeing, calligraphy and ikebana flower arranging.

- **Cookery** Is the best way to understand a nation through its cuisine? Find out on a cookery course, outlined in "Food" opposite.

- **Diving** There are plenty of dive schools in Indonesia, Malaysia, Thailand and the Philippines, as well as in East Timor, where you can do one-day introductory courses as well as internationally approved certificate courses. See p.184 for more advice.

- **Language** All Asian capitals have language institutes catering for foreign students and interested tourists; contact tourist offices and/or embassies in your own country for details, and see the list of Specialist Tour Operators on pp.412–414 for language-learning holidays.

- **Martial arts** In China, home of kung fu and producer of a thousand of martial-arts movies, you can do kung fu courses in the travellers' centre of Dali (Yunnan), and in Beijing or, if you're really serious, you can take a minimum two months' course at the world-famous Shaolin Si Buddhist temple in Henan (🌐www.shaolins.com), where the kung fu cult was born hundreds of years ago; see their DVD *Shaolin: Wheel of Life* for inspiration. Korea is the spiritual home of taekwondo, and you can take various courses in Seoul (🌐english.tour2korea.com), plus there's an annual martial arts festival in Chungju, where modern taekwondo originated. In Thailand, tourists are welcome to train at certain Thai boxing camps in Chiang Mai and Bangkok (🌐www.tourismthailand.org).

- **Massage** Become a hit with fellow travellers by learning the basics of traditional Thai massage in Chiang Mai (🌐www.thaimassageschool.ac.th) or Bangkok (🌐www.watphomassage.com). Or do an introductory Japanese shiatsu massage course in Tokyo or Kyoto.

- **Music and dance** You'll get a lot more out of watching cultural performances if you've tried a few steps or banged out a few tunes yourself. You can learn to play the sitar and other classical Indian instruments in Varanasi and Udaipur, and beginners' courses in Indonesian dance and gamelan instruments are held regularly in Ubud and Yogyakarta.

- **Yoga and meditation** Open up your mind, and loosen up your limbs – a huge variety of yoga and meditation courses are held in India and Nepal; see "Spiritual quests", p.188.

Food

What could be better than slurping a bowl of *tom yam* soup in a Thai night market or tucking in to an Indian *thali* in a Delhi canteen? Once tasted, the real thing, eaten on location, is rarely forgotten – and chances are food will become a bit of a travel obsession. Asia is home to two of the world's greatest cuisines – Indian and Chinese – (three if you count Thai), as well as some of the weirdest and most unpalatable dishes you could ever want to be offered (Mongolian sheep's eye anyone?). Searching out special local foodstalls and restaurants is a great way to get off the beaten track when you're travelling, and eating at them can make you feel more adventurous than any jungle trekker – as you'll discover when you're given a bowl of rancid yak-butter tea in Tibet, for example, or a deep-fried Cambodian tarantula. Just be sure to follow the food hygiene advice in Chapter Twelve, and check out the dining-etiquette tips in Chapter Eight. Another good way to expand your culinary horizons is to have a go at cooking local dishes yourself, and there are chances to do that on cookery courses in an increasing number of travellers' centres across Asia.

For a spot of gourmet tourism inspiration, check out *Ant Egg Soup: The Adventures of a Food Tourist in Laos* by Natacha Du Pont De Bie, and Anthony Bourdain's *A Cook's Tour*, which describes his encounters with extreme cuisine in Japan, Vietnam and Cambodia. Also recommended is Lonely Planet's series of pocket *World Food* books, covering the food culture of India, Hong Kong, Indonesia, Japan, Malaysia and Singapore, Thailand, and Vietnam, and featuring recipes, menu readers and restaurant tips as well.

- **China** China boasts an enormously diverse and complex cuisine with meals and even individual dishes carefully constructed to achieve a balance in flavours, taste, texture and colour. This can be hard to appreciate if you eat alone and can only sample a couple of dishes. Regional cuisines are very distinctive, with *dim sum* the trademark Cantonese style, and rich, chilli-hot dishes the speciality of Sichuan food. You get the best of everything in Hong Kong's canteens and street stalls. If you want to learn how to make southern Chinese food, head for the travellers' centre of Yangshuo, near Guilin (ⓦwww .yangshuocookingschool.com).
- **India** Indian food has a justifiably high reputation the world over but it is the sheer variety and number of regional specialities that

takes most visitors by surprise, from the tandoori cuisine of the north, where breads and meats are baked in traditional clay ovens, through to the coconut-laced, lightly spiced dosa pancakes of the south. India is also heaven for vegetarians as pretty much every eatery offers both "Veg" and "Non-veg" menus.

- **Japan** Raw fish sashimi is the iconic dish here, and it's famously pricey, but Japan is also the home of the enjoyable budget alternative, the conveyor-belt sushi restaurant and, as elsewhere in Asia, noodle soup is a cheap and ubiquitous belly-filler. Many restaurants display plastic models of their main dishes in the window, which makes it easier to know what you're getting.

- **Thailand** *Pat thai* fried noodles is everyone's favourite, and you can't go far wrong with the northeastern speciality of fried chicken with sticky rice, but mostly the flavours of Thai cuisine are more subtle and sophisticated – stir-fries and curries laced with lemongrass, ginger and coriander and often fired up with chilli. The best and cheapest places to sample authentic Thai dishes are the night markets that sizzle through the night in every town. There are plenty of Thai cookery courses in Chiang Mai (⊛www.thaicookeryschool.com) and Bangkok (⊛www.thaihouse.com; ⊛www.maykaidee.com).

- **Vietnam** The national dish is *pho*, a fragrant but hearty noodle soup that's flavoured with cinnamon and handfuls of fresh herbs and is usually eaten for breakfast. It's a street food, brewed up by itinerant cooks on street corners and eaten on stools alongside and you can find it anywhere, but most famously in Hanoi. Rice-flour spring rolls, *nem*, are the other classic dish, filled with vermicelli and minced shrimp and served with fresh mint and coriander. Learn to cook them both in Hanoi or Ho Chi Minh City (⊛www.expat-services.com).

Visas, tickets and insurance

O nly a very few countries in Asia actually refuse entry to independent travellers (the Himalayan kingdom of Bhutan, for example), but in many cases you can only enter via certain air- and seaports if you've obtained a visa in advance; in a few cases you're not allowed to enter by land borders at all. With this in mind, it's essential to start researching the visa situation for all your intended destinations as early as possible – before you pay for your air ticket, and before it's too late to get all the paperwork done.

Though you need to find out about the visa requirements for all your intended destinations before buying your ticket, you shouldn't actually apply for your visas until you've got firm bookings for your tickets, as most visa applications ask for your arrival and departure dates.

Visas and borders

Lots of Asian countries are crying out for tourists to come and visit, so they make visas easy to obtain and often issue them free of charge as well. Thailand, for example, grants visitors thirty-day tourist visas on arrival at major airports and land-borders. All you need do in

Visa requirements

The following table indicates whether you need to buy a visa before you arrive. It's meant as a planning aid only and applies to entry via the most popular gateways. As rules change quite often, you should double-check by calling the relevant embassies. In the countries that let you in without an advance visa, the number of days you're allowed to stay is given in brackets; you may be able to get a longer visa by applying in your home country before you leave. Some countries charge for visas on arrival, payable at immigration.

	EU	US/Can	Aus/NZ
Bangladesh	*no (15 days)	no (15 days)	no (15 days)
Bhutan	yes	yes	yes
Brunei	no (UK: 30 days; most EU: 14 days)	no (US: 90 days; Can:14 days)	no (Aus:14 days; NZ: 30 days)
Cambodia	†no (30 days)	no (30 days)	no (30 days)
China	yes	yes	yes
East Timor	no (30 days; Portugal: 90 days)	no (30 days)	no (30 days)
Hong Kong	no (90 days; most EU: 90 days)	no (90 days)	no (UK: 180 days)
India	yes	yes	yes
Indonesia	no (30 days)	no (30 days)	no (30 days)
Japan	no (UK: 6 months; most EU: 3 months)	no (90 days)	no (90 days)
Laos‡	no (15 days)	no (15 days)	no (15 days)
Malaysia	no (3 months)	no (3 months)	no (3 months)
Mongolia	yes	no (US: 3 months) yes (Can)	yes
Nepal	no (60 days)	no (60 days)	no (60 days)
Pakistan	yes	yes	yes
Philippines	no (21 days)	no (21 days)	no (21 days)
Singapore	no (30 days)	no (30 days)	no (30 days)
South Korea	no (US: 30 days; Can: 6 months)	no (90 days)	no (3 months)
Sri Lanka	no (30 days)	no (30 days)	no (30 days)
Taiwan	no (30 days)	no (30 days)	no (30 days)
Thailand	no (30 days)	no (30 days)	no (30 days)
Vietnam	yes	yes	yes

* Anyone intending to arrive by land should get a visa in advance.

† Anyone intending to arrive by land from Vietnam or Laos should get a visa in advance.

‡ If entering anywhere other than Wattay Airport in Vientiane, Louang Phabang Airport or the Thai–Laos land borders, get a visa in advance.

△ Border-control guard, Hanoi, Vietnam

such situations is show the immigration officials that your passport is valid for at least another six months and that you have a ticket out of the country (sometimes, you need only show you've got enough money to buy an onward ticket). However, if you want to enter the country through a less frequented route or stay longer than the statutory period granted upon arrival, you'll probably need to apply for a visa before you travel (though in some countries you can apply for an extension while there). Rules change all the time, especially in countries where the political climate is volatile, and often vary according to nationality because of specific reciprocal agreements. The table opposite gives a broad outline of visa requirements in Asia, but you should confirm details with the relevant embassies (see pp.19–153).

Land borders are especially unpredictable – at the time of writing it was illegal to travel overland between China and India. And while travellers can currently cross into Nepal from Tibet without difficulty, they cannot travel independently into Tibet from Nepal. You should also bear in mind that despite the very long border, there's only one crossing between India and Pakistan (between Wagah on the Pakistani side, east of Lahore, and Attari, west of Amritsar on the Indian side) and that to travel overland between Vietnam and Cambodia, Cambodia and Laos, and Laos and Vietnam, you need to arrange visas in advance. Details of overland border crossings are given in Chapter One.

On the whole, if you do need a visa, it's best to apply for one in your home country, with a couple of provisos: most countries require you to start using your visa within a specified time, usually within three or six months of it being issued, which is clearly hopeless if you'll be hitting India seven months after, say, leaving Australia. In such cases you'll have to get that visa from the relevant embassy somewhere en route. Also, not every nation has an embassy or consulate in every country (Laos, for example, has no representatives in the UK), which means you either have to arrange your visa through an agency or, if feasible, get your visa in Asia – in Bangkok, for example. Sometimes visas are *easier* to get en route: visas for China are simplest to obtain in Hong Kong (though these are then valid from the date of issue and not from date of entry); and Lao visas are quicker to get in Bangkok as all visa applications have to be sent to Laos

Déjà vu on the Karakoram Highway

We reached the front of the queue and I handed the Pakistani officer our passports, open at the Chinese visa. He glanced casually at the first, then a little more deliberately at the second and finally scrutinized the pair together, side by side. Then he raised his head abruptly and peered over the lectern.

"What is this? These have not been signed! They must be signed, you cannot use them!" he barked.

"What? Surely not!" I protested. "Where?"

"There! Can't you read?"

"Well, actually, no," I admitted. "Not Chinese. Look, it's just an administrative error. These are genuine visas, they'll see that."

But it was no good, he was adamant the Chinese would not let us enter, and therefore he could not let us leave Pakistan.

"You'll have to go back to Islamabad and get them signed. Next!"

Slightly bewildered, I sat down and tried to come to terms with the appalling prospect of going all the way back. We had just spent three weeks exploring the Karakoram Highway and now we had to retrace our steps. In the end it took us four days and a catalogue of hassles, including an unpredicted holiday at the Chinese embassy, a bus breakdown, a randy fellow passenger and an awful lot of déjà vu.

Neil Poulter

for approval – considerably speedier when done from Thailand (it takes less than a week) than from Europe (about two months). On the other hand, getting an Indian visa is ridiculously bureaucratic in Nepal and much better done elsewhere.

Even when you have your visa, this doesn't necessarily give you *carte blanche* to roam wherever you wish. In some countries (like China, India, Laos, Malaysia and Vietnam) you also need special permits to visit remote or politically sensitive areas; trekking in parts of both Nepal and Pakistan is subject to restrictions; and many countries have areas where foreigners are not permitted at all – some parts of Tibet and border areas of India, for example. Permits for trekking and for visiting restricted areas are usually issued in the relevant country, but it's always worth checking with embassies before you go and maybe applying in advance. For example, Restricted Area Permits for the Indian northeastern hill states of Manipur, Mizoram, Nagaland and Arunchal Pradesh can be applied for in Delhi and Kolkata, or at Indian embassies and high commissions overseas.

Applying for a visa

Even in the most efficient embassies, applying for a visa is a time-consuming procedure – queues may stretch down the hallway, and most embassies and consulates keep unhelpfully short hours. Many embassy websites (see County Profiles, pp.19–153) now have visa application forms available to download and should also carry details of application requirements (photos and documentation needed, and whether you can pay by cash, cheque or credit card) as well as opening hours. Take national holidays into consideration, both yours and theirs – not only do embassies close on these days, but queues are twice as long on the days before and after. The same advice applies when picking up your visa. Finally, get to the embassy as close to opening time as possible, and take a good book.

If you've got plenty of time before your departure, it's easier to apply by post, though this might not be feasible if you've got several different visas to collect. Alternatively, you could use the specialist visa service offered by major travel agents (see Directory, p.411, for a list of these). Expect to pay around $40 in the US, £20 in the UK or A$30 in Australia for the service, in addition to the fee charged by the embassy. Here are a few more points to remember when applying for visas:

- Be as accurate as you can about the date of your arrival in the country, as some embassies – eg Vietnam's – issue visas with exact dates on them; if you can't be certain, delay applying for a visa until later.
- Consider applying for a multiple-entry visa rather than a single-entry one. This gives you increased flexibility (enabling you to make a side-trip into Nepal from India, for example), and is especially useful if there's any possibility that you might be leaving a country and then going back there later (to catch a plane for example).
- In some countries, the authorities regard writers and journalists with suspicion, so it's advisable to be vague about these occupations on the visa form (they're unlikely to check).
- Some countries are hostile to passport-holders of particular nations. Islamic countries, for example, often refuse entry to Israeli passport-holders; this is true of Bangladesh, Indonesia and Malaysia. Check with embassies for details.
- If you know that the statutory amount of time on a tourist visa is just not long enough for your trip, you could try applying for a special student or business visa. Sometimes it's enough to have a written invitation from someone in the host country; alternatively, try signing up with a language school or a meditation centre and getting a letter from the principal.
- When collecting your visa, check that all the details are correct, and that, if necessary, it has been signed.

Extending your stay

Some countries offer a way of extending your visa once you're there; check websites and the embassy in your home country for details. In Thailand, for example, you can go to any of the provincial immigration offices around the country and get a thirty-day extension for about $50/£30; in Nepal you can apply for three consecutive 30-day extensions on top of your original 60 days, giving you up to 150 days in the country. Most extensions require two or three passport photos, and it always helps if you're dressed smartly when applying. In some countries, certain types of visa are absolutely non-extendable: Indian tourist visas for example.

All is not lost if you can't get a long enough visa. If you're planning to overstay by a few days, then – in some countries – you may as well just put aside some money for the fine that you'll be landed with when you fly out; in Cambodia it's around $5/£3 per day. In other countries, however, this is definitely not a great idea – China and Vietnam charge $50/£35 a day, sometimes more, for overstaying, and Indonesia threatens anyone who overstays by more than sixty days with either a five-year prison sentence or a fine of $25,000.

Alternatively, you can do what numerous long-staying travellers do: cross the nearest border to get a new tourist visa and come back in again. In some places this is simple: in Indonesia, for example, you can either fly to Singapore, or take the two-hour boat ride there from Batam Island and then back again. In Thailand you can simply walk into Laos or Burma and back; if you're in southern Malaysia you can zip across to Singapore; while from Japan the cheapest exit is by boat to South Korea. Always ask other travellers for advice on the best exit strategy, however, as immigration policies are changeable and there are occasional clampdowns to try and deter travellers from using this option instead of applying for a work visa for example.

Buying a ticket

The travel industry is a hugely competitive business, so it pays to shop around when looking for the best fare. It's unusual for travellers to buy air tickets direct from the major airlines – only business travellers can afford the standard airline fares; you'll probably be buying from a travel agent who, through dealing in limited blocks of seats that the airline doesn't think it can sell at full price, is able to offer discounts on air tickets. The Internet is also a fertile source of cheap flights: see the Directory, p.411 for addresses and websites of recommended agents.

When you've worked out an itinerary, call up one of the major discount travel agents or, better still, go and see them, and ask the travel consultant's advice. Staff at these places are usually well travelled themselves; they know what they're talking about and generally aren't out to rip you off. Youth- and student-oriented travel agents give significant discounts to travellers who are under 26, and some places extend their deals to anyone under 35; student-card holders of any age are often entitled to cut-price deals as well.

In the UK and Australia, always check that the travel agent you're dealing with is bonded with one of the big travel associations – such as ATOL (®www.atoldata.org.uk) or ABTA (®www.abtanet.com) in the UK, or AFTA (®www.afta.com.au) in Australia – before you give them any money. If they are bonded you will be refunded if the agent goes bust before you fly out; if not you will lose your money and your ticket. There's no comparable organization in the US – here, and also in the UK and Australia, paying for your ticket by credit card is an alternative way to protect yourself against unreliable bucket shops, as the credit-card company is obliged to reimburse you if the agent doesn't; this does not extend to Visa debit-card holders.

Some Eastern and Central European airlines offer very cheap fares to Asia, but have notoriously poor efficiency (and, in some cases, safety) records and many major travel agents refuse to sell their flights. If you're looking for a rock-bottom fare and willing to take the chance, it may be worth contacting these airlines directly; alternatively, look through the classified ads for a travel agent that sells their flights.

How to save money on your flight

- Do some serious surfing.
- Ring round half a dozen travel agents. Some travel agents have special discount arrangements with particular airlines, so check the price of the exact same flight with several different agents.
- Investigate several different types of ticket (see pp.201–206), even if you already think you know what you want.
- Book early. The best deals will be snapped up fast, leaving latecomers with the expensive flights. If you want to fly from Europe to India at Christmastime, for example, you should book your ticket by September to ensure a reasonable fare. And if you're heading from the US to Nepal for the popular October to November trekking season, you need to make your reservations around June.
- Be as flexible as possible about your departure date. Airlines have high, low and shoulder seasons and prices vary accordingly, so you can sometimes make a significant saving by altering your schedule by a week or two. As a general guide, high season for flights to Asia covers the busiest holiday periods, namely mid-December to mid-January, and July to mid-September; shoulder season wraps around the peak winter season, usually from November to February (when most parts of Asia are enjoying their pleasantest weather); and the remaining months are low season.
- Be equally flexible about your routeing. It's generally more expensive to fly into less popular regional airports – such as Chennai in India rather than Mumbai or Delhi – simply because demand is low and competition slack. Perhaps an inexpensive overland connection (from Mumbai, for example) would do just as well, especially if it saves you

$150/£90 or more. On the other hand, spending your first night in Chennai will be less stressful than kicking off with Mumbai, so the extra cost might be worth every penny.

Which ticket?

Most discounted flights have restrictions on them, which your travel agent should explain. For example, once you've paid for your ticket, you probably won't be able to cancel it and may not be able to change your initial departure date (though return dates and the onward segments of round-the-world tickets are nearly always flexible). Most holiday insurance policies (see p.207) cover unavoidable cancellations and delayed departures. Many discounted tickets also have time restrictions on them, with a minimum stay of seven days and a maximum of thirty or ninety days, though this varies according to the airline.

Sometimes it's worth paying a little extra for your international flight to qualify for special perks. Some airlines offer good deals on domestic flights if you fly in and out of the country on the national carrier. Malaysian Airlines, for example, sells an inexpensive pass entitling you to five internal flights if you fly to Malaysia with them. Similarly the ASEAN pass is a good deal for flights between Asian countries, but you do need to arrive in Asia with one of the participating airlines (see p.315). And, while the ANA Visit Japan Fare pass ($100 for any domestic flight) doesn't need to be bought in conjunction with an international ANA flight it does need to be bought before arriving in Japan. For a comprehensive round-up of available air passes see ⓦwww.airtimetable.com/airpass_asia.htm and for advice see Chapter Ten.

One-way tickets

One-way tickets always work out more expensive than a return flight, so this is only a viable option if you're unsure when or how you'll be returning. On the plus side, one-way tickets are adventurous and liberating; overland transport in Asia is temptingly inexpensive, and airline tickets bought in Asia are good value, particularly in Bangkok, Kolkata, Delhi and Singapore.

However, buying a one-way ticket can create problems with getting visas, as most countries require proof that you are actually going to move on to another country within a reasonable time limit. In many cases, you will need to show evidence of onward or return travel plans, either when applying for a visa in your home country, or at the border when getting a visa on the spot. The easiest way to bypass this is to decide on an overland route out of the country and make sure you have the details and proof of sufficient funds when asked. Of course, this only works if the route you have in mind is a legal way of exiting the country so verify this with travel agents, embassies and guidebooks first. Some travellers get round all this by buying the cheapest return flight available and then getting a refund for the unused return sector, but read the small print before going for this option – certain tickets may not be refundable and, even if they are, you'll only be able to collect the refund from the office that issued the ticket.

Open-jaw returns

Open-jaw tickets allow you to choose different airports for your arrival and departure, which means you can minimize backtracking during your trip. One example would be to fly from London into Delhi and then fly from Mumbai back to London, making your own way overland between Delhi and Mumbai. On some airlines, it's possible to buy an open-jaw that flies you into one country (eg Thailand) and out of another (say, Singapore), leaving you a fairly lengthy overland sector to organize yourself. Open-jaw prices are generally calculated by halving the return fares to each destination and then adding the two figures together.

Stopover returns

If you're only visiting one or two countries in Asia, then buying a return ticket with a stopover option will probably be your best deal, particularly as most stopovers are offered free of charge. Flying from

Sydney to Delhi, for example, you could stop over in Singapore, Kuala Lumpur, Bangkok or Kathmandu, depending on which airline you use; flying London–Kathmandu, you could stop in Karachi or Delhi. Most airlines allow you to stop over for up to three months, and you can usually choose whether you stop off on the way out or on the way back; you may even be allowed to do both. Don't forget to find out whether you need a visa for your stopover destination.

Round-the-world and other multi-stop tickets

The next step up from a stopover return is a multi-stop ticket, most popularly a round-the-world (RTW) ticket that, for Europeans, takes you out to Australia/New Zealand via various Asian cities and back home again via North America. More restricted versions of RTW tickets include Circle Asia and Circle Pacific tickets. The best value RTW tickets are those designed by the main airline alliance groups such as Star Alliance and Oneworld Alliance, and those designed by travel agents using the cheapest flights currently on offer.

The cheapest way to get the most out of almost any RTW ticket is to include one or more "surface sectors" – sections of the journey not included in your ticket, therefore requiring you to make your own way by land, sea or locally purchased flight. The easiest and most popular international surface sector in Asia is from Bangkok to Kuala Lumpur or Singapore (or vice versa), which can be travelled as you please, either slowly, with several stops on the way, or in one swoop by overnight train, bus or local flight that you organize from Bangkok. Overland trips between Delhi and Kathmandu are another favourite surface option. Do look carefully at the possible surface sectors as not all of them are covered by as many transport options as Bangkok–Singapore; because of Burmese border restrictions, for example, any Bangkok–Delhi surface sector will either involve a very long journey via Tibet and Nepal or will require you doing the surface sector on a locally purchased international flight.

Airline alliance RTWs

Star Alliance (⊛www.star-alliance.com) is a network of sixteen airlines, including Air Canada, Air New Zealand, All Nippon Airlines, bmi, Lufthansa, Singapore Airlines, Thai Airways and United. Oneworld Alliance (⊛www.oneworldalliance.com) comprises eight airlines, including Aer Lingus, BA, Cathay and Qantas, and their affiliates. Both alliances offer competitively priced, but differently organized RTW programmes. Some restrictions apply to both: journeys must be in a continuous east- or westbound direction, with no unavoidable backtracking outside specified regions, must last between ten days and one year, and must end where they began.

For RTW routes that include India and Nepal, Star Alliance is the better option. Their RTW ticket allows up to fifteen free stops around the world and the price depends on the mileage of your total route: 29,000 miles will set you back £1399/US$3800/A$2799; 34,000 miles costs £1749/US$4400/A$3299; and 39,000 miles £1849/US$5150/A$3879.

The Oneworld Explorer RTW pricing system is based on a six-zone system, with low- and peak-season rates applicable from certain regions. All Oneworld RTWs that include Europe, the Far East and Australia count as a four-zone ticket and cost from £1319 or A$3239; from North America you're looking at a five-zone ticket for US$4600.

Another option that's especially good for Southeast Asia is the Great Escapade fare (⊛www.thegreatescapade.com//the_great _escapade.html), a joint venture by Air New Zealand, Virgin Atlantic, Singapore Airlines and Silk Air that permits unlimited stops. Their RTW fare is based on mileage and seasons, starting at £860/ US$2999/A$2639 for the first 29,000 miles, plus an extra £71/ US$150/A$150 for an extra 1500 miles, £143/US$250/A$250 for 3000miles and £214/US$300/A$300 for another 4500miles.

Travel agents' RTWs

Off-the peg RTWs are usually put together by a travel agent using the current best deals offered by two or three airlines. The main budget travel agents (see the Directory for a list) usually have half a dozen ready-to-go RTWs, which will be the cheapest available at the time, but these can always be adapted, at varying cost, to suit individual preferences. As internal and short-hop flights are generally cheaper to buy inside Asia than out, and given the dramatic expansion of budget airlines within Asia (see ⊛www.leisuretraveler.net /discount-airline-locator.asp for a list and links), you may find it more economical to buy a skeleton RTW with long surface sectors and then add whatever extra flights you need once you've got there.

Once you've decided on your key RTW cities and paid for your ticket, you can't alter the route, but you can usually change the dates of component flights free of charge. The cheapest deals generally see you setting off between late April and mid-June, while the priciest time to begin your trip is in the pre-Christmas fortnight.

A few sample travel agents' off-the-peg RTWs (low season, excluding taxes):

- Under £800: London–Brunei–Singapore surface to Bangkok–Perth surface to Brisbane–Colombo–Delhi–London.
- Under £1300: London–Delhi surface to Kathmandu–Bangkok surface to Ho Chi Minh City–Singapore–Penang–Brisbane overland to Sydney–Auckland–Fiji–Los Angeles–Seattle–New York–London.
- Under US$1800: New York–Bali surface to Bangkok–Cairo–Athens surface to London–New York.
- Under US$2300: Los Angeles–Manila–Hong Kong surface to Kunming–Chiang Mai surface to Bangkok–Mumbai surface to Delhi–Paris–London–Los Angeles.
- Under C$3800: Toronto–Los Angeles–Fiji–Sydney–Singapore surface to Bangkok–Hong Kong–Taipei–New York–Toronto.
- Under A$2200 or NZ$3200 Sydney/Darwin/Perth/Auckland–Bangkok–Kathmandu surface to Delhi–Colombo–London–Montreal–New York–Los Angeles–Sydney/Darwin/Perth/Auckland

Charters and courier flights

Charter flights to major holiday resorts (such as Goa and Phuket) are sometimes cheaper than discounted fares on scheduled flights. Charters are sold through high-street travel agents and sometimes include accommodation as well (you're under no obligation to use the accommodation for any or all of the time if you want to move on), but you're generally limited to a two-week trip – a month at most. Some package-tour operators also offer good last-minute discounts on any plane seats left unsold in the last week or ten days before departure. These are advertised in travel agent windows, in newspapers, on the Internet and, in the UK, on ITV's Teletext service.

One other way to get a really cheap flight is to become a courier. A few courier companies offer heavily discounted international flights to travellers willing to accompany documents and/or freight to the destination for them. There's nothing dubious about these companies or their goods: it's just cheaper for them to subsidize a traveller's fare than send one of their own employees. Courier deals are advertised in the press and sold through special agents such as the International Association of Air Travel Couriers (🌐www.courier .org) and, in the US, Air Courier Association (☎1-800/339-7556, 🌐www.aircourier.org); you'll usually need to pay a nominal joining fee to qualify.

Courier flights are only available to certain destinations (chiefly Bangkok, Hong Kong, Manila, Seoul, Shanghai and Tokyo), but can be up to fifty percent cheaper than advertised rates (eg New York to Bangkok return for $300 and London to Tokyo return for £275). Most have considerable restrictions attached: you will probably have to come back within a month, and might only be allowed to take carry-on luggage with you, as some courier companies use your luggage allowance themselves. Usually only one courier is needed per flight, which makes things more complex if you want to travel with a friend or in a group.

Booking your ticket

To make your arrival as hassle-free as possible, try to book a flight that touches down in daylight, remembering that it could take up to two hours to get through immigration and collect your baggage and that the sun sets around 6pm in South and Southeast Asia. This will give you plenty of time to sort out your ride into the city and get to your accommodation before it's dark. Though things do not necessarily grind to a halt as soon as the sun sets, everything becomes more difficult – and unnerving – after dark. Not only is it safer to arrive during daylight, but the airport tourist information desk and cash exchange booths may not be open 24 hours a day. For more advice on planning your arrival, see Chapter Seven.

For long-haul flights and RTW tickets, it's nearly always acceptable to make provisional bookings on a ticket, though many travel agents ask for a small deposit – transferable but non-refundable – to deter time-wasters. You can always just grill the staff for information and then think about it for a few days. Full payment on long-haul tickets is usually only due six weeks before departure.

Remember that ticket prices fluctuate according to the time of year (see p.200); it's always worth checking with your travel agent whether you could save money by going a week earlier or later than planned. Other things to ask your travel agent include:

- Seat reservations. Some airlines let you book your actual seat (window/aisle) when buying your ticket.
- Ordering special food for the flight. All international airlines cater for a range of special diets (such as vegetarian, kosher and diabetic), but these must be ordered in advance, either through your travel agent or by calling the airline yourself.
- Reserving a room at your destination. Most travel agents can book mid-range hotels for you (from about $25/£16 a double in Bangkok, for example). Though more expensive than doing it yourself when you get there, this is a good idea for your first couple of nights in Asia as it's one less thing to worry about when you arrive (for more details, see Chapter Seven). Some agents even throw in several free nights with flights on particular airlines; this is known as an inclusive tour (IT).
- Travel insurance. Many travel agents offer their own travel insurance to customers (see below for advice on insurance).
- Visa service. Major travel agents will get visas for you – especially useful if you're in a hurry, though it's much cheaper to obtain them yourself.
- Vaccinations. The biggest travel agents have on-site health centres where you can get your jabs and buy first-aid kits and malaria pills (see Chapter Twelve for travel health advice). Though not cheap, these centres give reliable advice and will sometimes see patients without an appointment.
- First-class lounge facilities/arrangements. With many airlines you can pay to use the first-class lounge (usually $10–20/£7–15), with free coffee, newspapers, comfortable chairs and sometimes even showers, even if you are travelling economy – invaluable if you have transfers or get delayed.

Insurance

Whatever the length of your trip to Asia and your itinerary you'll need to arrange travel insurance – covering medical treatment and your personal possessions. Medical insurance is vital in case you get seriously ill or are involved in an accident. It will mean that you can afford to get the best care, which in some places will only be available in expensive private hospitals; you will also be entitled to free medical evacuation to your home country if necessary. Some policies aimed at backpackers exclude baggage cover to keep costs down, but we would advise you to consider this carefully. You may only be taking your tattiest clothes with you, but the cost of replacing everything, including rucksack and perhaps sleeping bag and camera, can be very high.

- Many major travel agents sell travel insurance but to get the best deal compare their prices with others before committing. Online providers to get you started include ⓦwww.columbusdirect.com, ⓦwww.roughguidesinsurance.com, ⓦwww.statravel.com and ⓦwww.trailfinders.com, and there's a comparison feature at ⓦwww .insuremytrip.com. One year's basic worldwide backpacker insurance can cost as little as £200 without baggage cover, or up to £400 with baggage cover and fewer exclusions. Although some credit cards advertise travel insurance as part of their package, there are usually conditions attached – you must book the holiday using your card, and it is extremely unlikely that overall cover will be adequate.
- Don't buy until you have fixed your dates of travel and your itinerary, but do buy as soon as you've paid for your ticket, as your policy may entitle you to compensation if you then need to cancel your trip due to emergency circumstances (illness, death in the family, civil war at your destination).
- If you are planning several trips over the space of a year, consider an annual policy, which usually works out cheaper than buying insurance separately for each trip. Check the maximum allowable length for each trip and the total maximum travelling time allowed. These policies are not suitable for those going on one year-long trip.
- For lengthy trips, head for travel insurers who specialize in longer deals (student insurance companies are worth checking even if you're not a student). You don't want to buy a policy from a company specializing in shorter trips and then pay to add on each week or month – it'll be more expensive.
- Check whether you can add on time once you are travelling or reclaim money for unused time.
- Some insurance companies will allow travel companions or home-sharers to buy a policy for a couple, rather than two separate policies.
- What activities does your potential choice of insurance company classify as "hazardous pursuits"? These are usually excluded from cover and include bungy-jumping, paragliding, scuba diving and skiing, but some companies put riding a bicycle or trekking in remote areas under this heading. Paying a surcharge may get you cover for

activities you want to pursue, or you may have to find another insurer, but either way you should think about all the exciting things you may do on your trip and buy your insurance accordingly.

- Make sure you note any limits on the value to which your possessions are covered. Most policies have single-item limits that don't cover camcorders or expensive cameras. It may be easier to add these items to an existing household insurance policy under an "all risks" clause that covers the item outside the home. Laptops are notoriously hard to insure, but try ⊛www.statravel.com.

- Check how high the "excess" – the amount you have to pay on each insurance claim – is before you buy your policy. If, for example, the medical bill you paid in Thailand comes to $90/£55 and the excess on the policy is $50/£30, you'll only get $40/£25 back from your insurer.

- Make sure there is a 24-hour emergency medical line in case of accident or illness and take the number with you.

- Familiarize yourself with the claims process: in cases of theft, for example, you must get a police report to submit when making a claim.

- Any claims won't usually get settled until you get home, so it is wise to have emergency funds – a credit card is the easiest – to cope with reimbursement costs on the spot.

- If you have particular circumstances (you might be over a certain age or have a medical condition, for instance), some insurers may be hesitant about covering you, so start your research early. The chances are that you will find a company who will offer cover, but it may take some time to track them down.

3

When to go

If you've got no constraints on the timing of your trip to Asia, make good weather your priority. Contrary to the tourist-brochure image, the Asian climate is not all summery days and balmy nights – sometimes it's too hot even to venture outside the door, while in certain regions you might get nonstop rain for a week or more, or even snow in the mountains. But with careful planning it's possible to organize an extended itinerary that follows the best of the weather across the continent – "best" here means least extreme, because that's when travel is generally easiest and most comfortable; see the box on p.215 for a list of the best times to visit each country, and country profiles on pp.19–153 for individual climate charts. On the other hand, don't let the prospect of very hot or very wet weather deter you altogether – just be prepared for travel arrangements to be less reliable and for tempers to get more easily frayed.

There is no single time of year when the whole of Asia is out of bounds because of inclement weather, but in the main the northern hemisphere's winter (November to February) is considered to be the pleasantest time to visit the region and is therefore classified as peak season. Prices are at their highest during this period, for everything from international airline tickets to accommodation; the best-value hotels get fully booked and many places are uncomfortably crowded.

The weather is only one factor, of course. You might want to time your visit around a specific event instead – the blooming of

Extreme measures

Travelling in extreme heat or cold can affect your budget as well as your state of mind and body. Most air-conditioned rooms cost at least a third more than fan-cooled ones, but sometimes that's a price worth paying when temperatures and humidity levels are unbearably high. If your finances won't stretch that far, take refuge in cafés and fast-food joints that can afford their own cooling systems; big supermarkets and modern shopping malls serve the same purpose. At night, try wrapping yourself in a wet sarong or sheet when you go to bed – that should keep you cool for long enough to get to sleep. Though air-con trains and buses are generally overrated (it's usually much more refreshing to throw open the window instead), taxis, whether air-conditioned or not, can be a real boon in the sweltering midday heat, so that's another expense to consider.

Conversely, you may be glad of heating in certain highland areas; again you will have to pay extra for this, though you might be able to get by with renting extra blankets and ensuring the showers have hot water. A cautionary note on primitive heating systems: it's essential that you check both your bedroom and the bathroom for decent air vents before using any gas- or coal-fired heater, as toxic fumes from these fires can and do kill.

the metre-wide rafflesia, the world's largest flower, which blossoms in Sumatra, Java and Malaysia in August or September; the mango season in India (April–August) is well worth a detour, as are many of the major Asian festivals, detailed on pp.220–222. Or perhaps you want to be certain to catch the notorious full-moon party, held every month on the Thai island of Ko Pha Ngan. More prosaically, if you're hoping to pay for your trip by finding a job at the end of it – in either Europe or Australia – remember that timing is important here too. In Europe, May to September is the best time to find work in pubs, on building sites and on fruit farms; in Australia there's fruit and veg picking from November to April in the south, and from May to November in the far north, while in coastal Queensland there's work available all year round.

The climates of Asia

Wherever you are in the world, the local climate is determined by latitude, altitude and continental position (distance from the sea), plus an assortment of microclimates. Within Asia, the two annual monsoons (seasonal winds) also play a crucial part.

The further a place is from the equator, the more defined its seasonal differences: northern Japan, for example, which shares roughly the same latitude as southern France or Quebec, has four distinct seasons. Summertime temperatures in Sapporo average 24°C, while winter ones average 2°C. As a general rule, this makes the northern hemisphere's spring and autumn the mildest and most pleasant time to visit the temperate regions of north Asia such as Japan, South Korea, China, northern India, Nepal and Bhutan. Spring and autumn are also the seasons for trekking in the Himalayas. Summer in north Asia varies from the pleasingly warm to the stiflingly hot (air pollution and smog make cities like Shanghai and Xian almost unbearable from June to September), and winter days can get very cold, though skies are often invigoratingly blue.

As you move further south towards the equator, the weather gets warmer and the seasons become less distinct. By the time you cross the Tropic of Cancer – a line of latitude that runs just north of Vietnam and 450km south of Delhi – and enter the tropics (the zone that straddles the distance either side of the equator from the Tropic of Cancer in the north to the Tropic of Capricorn in the south), there is precious little change in temperature at any time of year: Kuala Lumpur averages 31°C in December and 33°C in May.

Instead, seasons in the tropics are defined by the amount of rainfall and, to some extent, by the relative humidity. So you get a "cool" season (comparatively low humidity and little rain), a hot season (high humidity and little rain) and a rainy season (high humidity and lots of rain). These are only loose classifications, however, and are explained in more detail later below (for deeper meteorological insight, consult *The Rough Guide to Weather*). Humidity also intensifies the closer you get to the equator, making central Sumatra and central Kalimantan, for example, sticky and sultry all year round, while northern Thailand and northern Vietnam, which both lie close to the Tropic of Cancer, only get really humid just before the monsoon arrives.

Monsoons: tropical Asia

Though the temperature may not affect the timing of your trip to tropical Asia, you will probably want to avoid travelling there during the wet season. Wet seasons are relatively predictable in Asia, as the rains are brought to the continent by seasonal winds, known as monsoons, which follow a particular timetable and itinerary. Asia is hit by two monsoons a year, one bringing mostly wet weather (May–Oct), the other mainly dry weather (Nov–April). Monsoons are capricious, however, and although local lore has it that they should arrive in each place on the exact same date every year, they often turn up several days or even weeks late. Worse still, they can bypass whole areas altogether, leaving the farmers battling against drought for years.

May to October: wet-season travel

The southwest monsoon arrives in west-coast regions of Asia at around the end of May and brings rainfall daily to most of Asia (excepting certain east-coast areas, explained below) by mid-July. From then on you can expect overcast skies and regular downpours across the region till October or November. To get an idea of just how wet Asia can be during the rainy season, compare London's wettest month (64mm), or New York's (109mm), or Sydney's (135mm), with Bangkok, which gets an average of 305mm of rain every September.

This, then, is overall the worst time to travel in tropical Asia. Quite apart from getting soaked whenever you leave your hotel, you'll be uncomfortably sticky in any rainproof gear (use an umbrella instead) and may also have to ward off leeches, malarial mosquitoes and other wet-weather bugs. Diseases like Japanese encephalitis spread faster in these conditions, too (but are mainly confined to rural areas; see p.355), and you'll be more prone to fungal infections and unhealthy skin.

Diving will be a complete waste of time as visibility will be minimal, surfing will likely be out of the question, and beaches often languish under the garbage washed up by the storms. Some islands, such as Thailand's Ko Similan, are impossible to get to at this time, while other regions may be inaccessible because the roads have turned to mud.

Fierce tropical winds are also more frequent during the rainy season. Known as typhoons in the western Pacific and cyclones in the Bay of Bengal, these hurricanes hit certain parts of Asia, notably the Philippines, Bangladesh and southeast China, at speeds of over 120km per hour, leaving a trail of flattened crops, battered houses and an inevitable toll of human casualties as well. Typhoons can be especially dangerous on the coastal plains where tidal waves cause additional destruction, so you should always heed local advice about places to avoid during a typhoon. As forecasters usually predict typhoons a few days in advance, you should have plenty of time to prepare and protect yourself (see p.393 for more typhoon advice).

However, rain needn't put a damper on *all* Southeast Asian itineraries. In some places (like west-coast Peninsular Malaysia) downpours are limited to just a couple of hours every day for two or three months during the wet season, and these storms are often so regular they arrive at the same time every afternoon. Waterfalls spring back to life, rice paddies flood picturesquely, and this is often the best time of year for flowers.

The rainy season is generally low season for the tourist industry, and this can have many advantages, including discounted accommodation and more chance to spend time with local people. Note that, despite the weather, some airlines and swanky hotels treat July and August as a special peak season, because this is the time the northern hemisphere takes its summer holidays.

For travellers, east-coast beaches and islands that are not affected by the southwest monsoons come into their own during this time – that makes May to October peak season for Ko Samui, Ko Pha Ngan and Ko Tao in Thailand, and the best time to head for east-coast Sri Lanka; east-coast Malaysia is at its best between March and July. Off season for these coasts and islands is between November and April, during the northeast monsoon.

The end of the rainy season is another good reason for a party, particularly in Cambodia, where traditional boat races are held on the swollen rivers of Phnom Penh and around Angkor, and in Laos, where elegant longboats race up the Mekong River in an attempt to lure the water spirits back from the paddyfields.

November to February: the best time to go

The wind direction is reversed during the northern winter when the land cools down, so the northeast monsoon brings drier, less humid, slightly cooler weather to most of tropical Asia (east-coast areas excepted) between November and February. This is the best time overall to travel in tropical Asia.

In December, you can expect maximum daytime temperatures of 31°C in Bangkok, 23°C in Delhi, 30°C in Manila, and 28°C

The best time to visit . . .

What follows is a very broad guide to the best season for travelling, assuming you want the weather to be as dry and mild as possible. Mildness is a relative concept: a mild maximum daytime temperature in Jakarta is 31°C, in Ho Chi Minh City it's 27°C and in Kathmandu it's 26°C. The summary below is meant only as an introduction to help with general route-planning and preparation; for fuller details, refer to individual country profiles on p.19–153, and check your guidebooks or with tourist offices. The BBC weather centre website (⊛ www.bbc.co.uk/weather/world) carries a list of average monthly weather conditions in major cities worldwide, or see ⊛ www.wmo.ch/web-en/member.html to find links to national weather services around the world.

Bangladesh: Oct–Feb.

Bhutan: Oct–Nov; Feb–April.

Brunei: Feb–Aug.

Cambodia: Nov–March.

China: March–May; Sept–Nov; Hong Kong: Sept–Dec; Tibet: April–Oct.

East Timor: May–Nov.

India: Oct–March (except in the southeast); April–Sept (Himalayas and the southeast).

Indonesia: May–Oct (except north Sumatra and Maluku); Nov–April north Sumatra and Maluku).

Japan: March–May; Sept–Nov.

Laos: Nov–March.

Malaysia: March–July (peninsular east coast, Sabah & Sarawak); Dec–Feb (for peninsular west coast).

Mongolia: June–Sept.

Nepal: Oct & Nov; Feb–April.

Pakistan: Nov–March (for the south); April–Oct (for the north, with trekking best from June–Sept).

Philippines: Nov–Feb (except stretches of southeast coasts); March & April (for southeast coasts).

Singapore: Nov–Jan is cooler, but Feb–Oct is drier.

South Korea: April–June; Sept–Nov.

Sri Lanka: Nov–April (south and west coasts); May–Sept (east coast).

Taiwan: Nov–April.

Thailand: Nov–Feb (except peninsular east coast); March–Sept (for peninsular east coast).

Vietnam: Sept–Dec; March & April.

in Vientiane. Unfortunately, prices are at their highest during this period, peaking over Christmas and New Year, and the classier hotels add a peak-season supplement to their already inflated rates.

The main exceptions to the above pattern are the east-coast regions of Vietnam, peninsular Thailand, peninsular Malaysia, and Sri Lanka, and the southeastern region of India. Due to various complicated factors, the most obvious of which is their east-coast location, these areas get rain when the rest of tropical Asia is having its driest period, but stay dry during the southwest monsoon. Islands off these coasts are all best avoided between November and February, when boat connections are sporadic, beaches awash with flotsam and waves too high for a relaxed dip. Diving is unrewarding too, because the water gets quite cloudy. Eastern Malaysia (Sabah and Sarawak) is also subject to the northeast monsoon and some roads become impassable during this time.

Much of Indonesia, however, gets the worst (or best) of both monsoons, attracting the west-coast rains from May to October, and the east-coast rains from November to February. In some parts of the archipelago – like equatorial Sumatra – barely a week goes by without a shower or two, while the islands that lie relatively far south of the equator, like Sumba, experience an annual dry season that usually runs from April to October. Nearby East Timor also enjoys a relatively dry season from May through October.

February to May: the heat is on

By February, the heat is starting to build up right across the plains of tropical Asia, reaching a crescendo in May. During this month, Bangkok temperatures peak at 34°C in the shade, and it's 41°C in Delhi, 34°C in Manila, and 32°C in Vientiane. Though travel is perfectly possible during the hot season, it can be hard work, not least because the humidity is so high that it saps your energy and can make you loath to leave the air-conditioning between 10am and 3pm. Heat exhaustion is more likely too (see p.361).

The weeks before the rains break are a notoriously tense time in tropical Asia: tempers are short, people are more likely to resort to violence, and the suicide rate goes up. Depleted water supplies mean many rural households struggle to keep their crops and livestock alive, and electricity in towns and villages is often rationed because there simply isn't enough water to run the hydroelectricity plants all day long. It's especially important to take a torch if travelling at this time of year, as budget hotels rarely have their own generators.

Many Asian cultures believe the rains are controlled by gods or spirits, so the end of the hot season is a good time to catch rain-making festivals. The people of Laos and northeast Thailand traditionally regard rain as the fruit of heavenly lovemaking, so in mid-May they hold an exuberant rocket-firing festival to encourage the gods to get on with it.

Places to avoid at all costs during the hot season include the Pakistani region of Baluchistan which, by the end of May, becomes one of the hottest places in the world, with peak daytime temperatures averaging 46°C; you won't get much relief across the border in India at this time, either, where the Rajasthani town of Jaisalmer swelters in the low forties throughout May and June.

Altitude: the Himalayas

Temperatures plummet by 6.5°C for every 1000m you gain in altitude, so the higher you go the colder the air becomes – worth bearing in mind when you're sweltering on the tropical plains (see box below for suggested upland getaways).

The Himalayas are Asia's major mountain range and, though the climate here is much cooler than on the lowlands, it too is affected

---

If you can't stand the heat . . . get out of the city

When the mid-morning mercury hits 35°C and the humidity averages ninety percent, it's time to think about cooling yourself down. If you can't get to the seaside, consider heading up into the hills instead.

During the Raj era, the colonial Brits decamped en masse every summer to the Indian hill stations of Shimla, Ooty, Darjeeling and Kodaikanal, and these old-fashioned resort towns are still pleasant places to visit, many of them reached by quaint steam trains that trundle up through tea plantations to the refreshing forested hills. Further south, in Sri Lanka, the hill resort of Kandy (488m) makes a lovely cool lakeside retreat from the roasting plains, and for a full-on chill-out you can continue up to the former colonial outpost of Nuwara Eliya (1890m), at its best in March and April. In Malaysia, hot-season temperatures up on the Cameron Highlands are a good 10°C cooler than down in the sweltering capital. Other popular upland getaways include the hills around Chiang Mai in northern Thailand, the Bolaven Plateau in Laos, Da Lat in south Vietnam, Sylhet in Bangladesh, Baguio in the Philippines, and the volcanic highlands around Berastagi in North Sumatra.

---

by the southwest monsoon. The torrential rain that drenches the Punjab from June to August falls as several metres of snow in the Everest region – making this an unpredictable and potentially dangerous time to go trekking. At lower elevations, the rains can cause landslides on mountain roads during this time, so it's as well to keep travel plans flexible or to avoid the region altogether. The exceptions to this rule are the dry mountain areas of Ladakh and north Pakistan, where summer is the best time to go trekking.

The snow is heaviest, however, during the cold winter months, and mountain passes above 4000m are usually blocked between December and April, with the snow line descending to around 2500m during this period. October and November are therefore the most popular months for trekking in Nepal and northern India: skies are clear and daytime temperatures fairly warm, especially in the sun (nights are always cold in the mountains). Lower-level trekking is also popular from February to mid-April.

Throughout Asia, mountain areas become inaccessible to vehicles as well as trekkers and mountaineers during the winter months. Heavy snowfall makes the 5000-metre-high trans-Himalayan Manali–Leh Highway impassable between November and April (although the road is officially shut between September 15 and June 15, public buses plough on until the last possible moment). And the similarly dramatic link between Pakistan and China, known as the Karakoram Highway because it crosses a 5575-metre-high pass in the Karakoram Mountains (the range containing the famous K2 peak), is also closed between November and April.

If you're not trekking or driving at very high elevations, however, the northern winter is a lovely time to admire the snowcapped peaks from a warmer vantage point in the Himalayan foothills and valleys. Though days are brisk and nights extremely cold, the air is crisp and fresh in this season, the skies are a brilliant clear blue and the mountains at their most spectacular. So long as you're kitted out with the right gear, this can be an exhilarating – and peaceful – time to be in northern India, Nepal, South Korea and northern Japan.

Continental position: deserts and plateaus

A region's continental position also has a huge effect on its weather. Places far from the sea tend to have extreme climates, with very hot, dry summers, very cold winters, and precious little rain at any time of the year. The high Tibetan plateau, northwestern China and Mongolia, for example, get negligible rain, choking summer dust storms and bitterly cold winters – temperatures in Ürümqi, in Xinjiang province, northwest China, never rise above minus 1°C between November and March, sinking to minus 22°C during the daytime in January. In July, however, temperatures average 28°C. Rajasthan, in the Thar desert in northwestern India, experiences a less extreme version of the same climate, so expect some cold nights here in the middle of winter and avoid high summer if you can.

Special events and local holidays

Many festivals and annual events are well worth planning your itinerary around – or even changing your schedule for. Religious festivals can be especially fun, many of them celebrated with street parades, food fairs (Thailand), dance performances (India), shadow-puppet plays (Indonesia) and masked dances (Bhutan and Ladakh), which tourists are usually welcome to attend (though you should ask locally first). As Buddhists and Hindus operate on a lunar calendar, as opposed to the Western Gregorian one, these festivals occur on different dates every year,

Soaking up the atmosphere, Indian style

It was Holi, the first day of spring, and the townspeople of Puri in east India were celebrating the day in traditional style, by taking to the streets with pails of water and armfuls of paint bombs, and chucking them at passersby. The owner of the guesthouse advised us not to go out until after midday, when the water-throwing had to stop. Foreigners were popular targets, he said, and it would not be a pleasant experience. But we had to go out, to buy tickets from the train station. From the safety of our rickshaw seat, we watched as people on the streets got sprayed, but we stayed fairly dry. Then the rickshaw driver turned down an alleyway and stopped, and the ambush began. A group of young guys rushed towards us, pelting us from all angles with buckets of water and handfuls of paint, which they rubbed into our faces and hair. It was pretty scary, and we got soaked. Our camera was sodden, I had paint in my eyes, and my clothes were stained for ever. Mission accomplished, they backed off and we drove on.

At the train station we stood soggily in the statutory queue. Just as we reached the sales counter, the ticket man's face dropped and we looked round to see another gang of water guerrillas bursting through the doors. This time everyone got soaked, not just the tourists, and files and papers were reduced to mush. Excitement over, the salesman proceeded with his form-filling, and we came away with our tickets.

Jo Mead

but tourist offices will be able to give you precise details. See individual country summaries, pp.19–153, for a guide to each country's most interesting festivals.

The biggest festivals can draw huge local crowds as well, so be prepared for packed trains and buses and overbooked hotels. If possible, reserve transport and accommodation well in advance and expect to shell out up to double the normal price for food and lodging. Occasionally, the volume and exuberance of festival crowds can become quite scary, and so may be best avoided – the water- and paint-throwing festival of Holi, which is celebrated throughout India and Nepal every February or March, is a typical example.

National public holidays tend to be more stuffy occasions, especially the ones commemorating political victories or rulers' birthdays, and are usually marked by military parades and speeches, if at all. Most businesses close on these days, as do markets and restaurants, though popular sights – particularly waterfalls, temples and public parks – will be chock-a-block with local people on their day off.

Good days . . .

We've chosen some of our favourite festivals below, but any guidebook will offer heaps more and ⓦwww.whatsonwhen.com reviews dozens of small- and large-scale celebrations in Asia and the rest of the world and give dates for the coming year.

- **Ice Lantern Festival in Harbin, northeast China** From January 5 to February 5, when temperatures sink to a chilly minus 30°C, the excess snow and ice in Harbin's Zhaolin Park is carved into extraordinary sculptures and even replica buildings such as life-size Chinese temples.
- **Ati-Atihan harvest pageants, Kalibo, the Philippines** This small town hosts a huge Mardi Gras-style extravaganza in mid-January. The streets are packed with people in outrageous costumes, there are days and days of excessive drinking and everyone joins in the dancing.
- **Thaipusam Hindu festival of ritual body-piercing, Singapore and Malaysia** To do penance for past sins and honour the deity Lord Subramaniam, the Hindu communities of Singapore and Kuala Lumpur hold an annual festival of self-flagellation and body transcendence in which devotees pierce their skin with an array of sharp objects, including tridents and steel arches. They process through the streets to the main Hindu shrine (in KL, at the Batu Caves on the

outskirts of the city), watched by vast crowds of spectators. Held at full moon in either January or February.

- **Buddhist New Year in Thailand, Laos and Cambodia** The Buddhist countries of Southeast Asia celebrate New Year in mid-April with nationwide public water fights – once symbolic of a purification ritual, but now more of an excuse for clowning about and drenching total strangers. The most-organized people circulate town in pick-up trucks fitted with hosepipes and water cannons, while others limit themselves to more genteel sprinkling. Any passersby, tourists included, will get a soaking, though it's quite refreshing at this time of year, April being the hottest month of the hottest season. The most exuberant New Year celebrations are held in Chiang Mai (Thailand) and Louang Phabang (Laos).

- **Cherry blossom picnics and maple-leaf viewing, Japan** Cherry blossom season begins when the first flowers appear in spring in Okinawa, the southernmost island of the Japanese archipelago, and for the next few weeks national TV broadcasts a nightly *sakura* forecast, showing how far the pink wave has progressed up the country. When the main island of Honshu turns pink (towards the end of April), the parks are packed with blossom-viewing picnic parties. Friends and families settle under the trees, getting drunk on saké, belting out karaoke songs and composing maudlin haiku poems about the fragile petals. Seven months later, the ancient capital of Kyoto flames a brilliant red for the last couple of weeks in November, when the maple trees light up the hillsides in spectacular displays. This is also your one chance to sample the bizarre local delicacy known as *momiji tempura* – fallen maple leaves fried in batter.

- **Spring fair in Dali, China** For five days every April or May, thousands of people from all over Yunnan converge

The Pushkar Camel Fair

Pushkar was hosting its annual fair, a combination of religious festival and huge camel market, with over fifty thousand animals brought in from all over Rajasthan. The streets were heaving with pilgrims, traders and tourists, and the bazaar spilled over into a labyrinth of dim, twisting alleys – market stalls a blaze of colour, the air thick with spices, dust and sweat. A sea of makeshift tents, camels and assorted livestock stretched far out across the plain. Tall, regal men dressed in waistcoats and long, baggy loincloths wandered among the animals, inspecting, discussing, bargaining. Turbans formed bobbing multicoloured dots among the ochre-brown mass, and even the camels were decorated with vibrant bridles of twisted cord, tasselled and beaded. Most animals stood or lay quietly ruminating, surveying their surroundings disdainfully, but every now and then a screeching and a swirl of dust would signify a runaway, pursued by groups of stick-wielding men.

Nicki McCormick

on Dali for horse-trading, wrestling matches, racing contests, dancing and singing.

- **Gawai Dayak harvest festival, Sarawak, East Malaysia** Parties in the traditional Iban longhouses are always riotous, but the biggest celebration of the year happens in June to mark the end of the rice harvest. Expect all-night drinking and heaps of food, plus lots of jokes, pranks and party games.

- **Naadam festival of traditional sports, Ulaanbaatar, Mongolia** Mongolian tribespeople show off their sporting prowess in horseriding (some of it bareback), archery and wrestling during a hugely popular and fiercely competitive three-day extravaganza held in nearly every town and village in mid-July.

- **Esala Perahera historical pageant, Kandy, Sri Lanka** For ten nights every July or August, extravagant torch-lit processions of costumed dancers, drummers and elephants in full regalia parade through the streets of Kandy in what's thought to be one of the oldest historical pageants in the world.

- **Pushkar camel fair, northwest India** For three days in late October or early November all roads seem to lead to Pushkar in Rajasthan, as crowds of 200,000 descend on this tiny desert town for India's biggest camel fair. Camels are paraded, raced and entered for competitions and the place brims over with market stalls and street entertainers. At night, visitors are housed in a specially erected tent city where huge marquees are equipped with camp beds and bush toilets.

△ Pushkar camel fair, India

. . . and bad days

Though the tourist industry never grinds to a complete standstill, there are certain public and religious holidays when you'll be hard-pressed to find hotels and restaurants open for business. In Bali, for example, the Hindu New Year, Nyepi, is celebrated in March or April with a day of complete silence and inactivity – shopkeepers are actually fined if they trade on that day, tourists are requested to stay within hotel grounds, and even the airport is closed for 24 hours.

Nor is it a great idea to land in China or Taiwan during the three-day Chinese New Year celebrations (in late January or early February) as everything will be closed, and you'll be unlikely to find a hotel room anywhere. The same is true of any town or city with a majority Chinese community – Singapore is an obvious example, but the hotels and restaurants in many Thai and Malaysian cities are also run by ethnic Chinese. If you want to be in one of these places for Chinese New Year (the firework displays can be unforgettable), then get to the city a couple of days early so you can stake your claim on a room and stock up on food. The same advice applies if you're in Sri Lanka over the Sinhalese New Year in mid-April, when lots of hotels and restaurants close down for a whole week.

Similarly, you might want to think twice about visiting an Islamic country during Ramadan, a month-long period of abstinence that falls during the ninth Muslim month (starting around September 24 in 2006, September 13 in 2007 and September 2 in 2008), when practising Muslims do without food, water and tobacco during daylight hours. This makes for a very stressed-out population, particularly by the third and fourth week, so you may not get the hospitality you were hoping for, especially in the more orthodox communities such as in Sumatra and Kalimantan. Many restaurants stay shut during the daytime throughout Ramadan, and in parts of Indonesia and Pakistan local bus services are less frequent during this month, too. If you are in Indonesia, Pakistan, Bangladesh, India, Malaysia or southern Thailand during Ramadan, be sensitive to your hosts and don't flaunt your food, drinks and cigarettes in front of them. On the plus side, as soon as darkness falls everyone heads out to make the most of their evening meal; there are some great night markets during Ramadan, and a general feeling of celebration every time the fast is broken.

Steer clear of big cities in the immediate run-up to elections, too, particularly in India and Bangladesh, where rallies can turn nasty and curfews may be imposed on and around polling day. It's not unknown for election results to be greeted with riots, so consider heading for safe havens in the hills or by the sea, instead of sticking around in the urban centres.

4

How much will it cost?

Budgeting is boring, but spending a bit of time thinking on it before you go will leave you more energy to enjoy Asia once you're there, rather than worrying about survival. Carefree and exotic as it may sound, there is actually nothing at all romantic about jetting off to the furthest place you can think of and realizing when you get there that you can't afford to eat or drink or sleep in a decent bed, that you've got a ticket that won't let you return home early, and you have to spend the first week investigating how you can get money wired to you. If you are seriously strapped for cash, it's worth planning a shorter trip – we guarantee you'll have a better time than if you embark on a longer, penny-pinching haul. This chapter will help you calculate your costs, give you ideas for making your cash go further and provide practical advice on how to take your money with you.

However carefully you work out your budget, though, there are bound to be unexpected expenses along the way, so try to take more money than you think you'll need. Global incidents such as war and the collapse of stock markets can cause serious currency fluctuations, wrecking your conversion calculations, while the insatiable urge to ship a divine granite elephant home from Bali or the pressing necessity for a white-water rafting trip down the Sun Kosi in Nepal will throw inflexible finances into chaos.

Exchange rates and currency fluctuations

For an idea of how much your money will be worth once you're on the road, you can check conversion rates for the most popular destinations in the financial pages of newspapers, at the exchange counter of your local bank, or using websites such as ⓦwww.oanda.com.

Economic conditions in Asia can change and change fast so it's worth keeping an eye on currency fluctuations prior to your departure. Inflation in Asian countries can be equally volatile and anyone operating on a shoestring budget with no room for manouevre can find themselves in serious trouble if prices rocket – for example, at the time of writing, annual inflation in many parts of the continent was around ten percent. If, however, inflation shoots up to 85 percent as it did in Laos a few years ago, it will send any pre-departure calculations haywire.

Exchange rates

The following exchange rates were correct as of the end of 2005. Rates given are for 1 US dollar/pound sterling/Euro.

Bangladesh (Taka): 65/116/78
Bhutan (Ngultrum): 44/78/53
Brunei (Brunei dollar):
  1.72/3.03/2.05
Cambodia (Riel): 4262/7503/5082
China (Yuan renminbi):
  8.1/14.2/9.6
India (Indian rupee): 44/78/53
Indonesia (Rupiah):
  10,204/17,964/12,168
Japan (Yen): 114/201/136
Laos (Kip): 10,842/19,087/12,929
Malaysia (Ringgit): 3.7/6.6/4.5

Mongolia (Tugrik): 1120/1972/1336
Nepal (Nepalese rupee): 73/128/87
Pakistan (Pakistan rupee):
  59/105/71
Philippines (Peso): 56/98/66
Singapore (Singapore dollar):
  1.7/2.9/2.0
Sri Lanka (Sri Lanka rupee):
  101/178/121
Taiwan (Taiwan dollar): 33/58/39
Thailand (Baht): 41/72/49
Vietnam (Dong):
  15,900/27,992/18,961

Budgeting

One thing to remember is that generalizations are dangerous. "Oh, Asia's cheap", you'll hear again and again. It is true that, compared with the major expense of your plane ticket, prices in Asia can seem cheap. But while you can find a basic beach hut in Goa or on the islands off the southeast coast of Thailand for about $5/£3 a night, you'll be paying at least $10/£6 for a bed in Singapore and $20/£12 in Hong Kong, while in Tokyo anything less than $24/£14 is very rare indeed. You'll find both extremes across the continent, for example a night in the *Raffles Hotel* in Singapore will cost you over \$400/£230, which buys almost three months' accommodation in parts of Indonesia; in India, a twelve-hour train trip can cost as little as \$5/£3 second-class and a cup of tea beside the road is just a few cents, but it's equally possible to spend \$200/£115 a night staying in luxury hotels in the big cities, or \$285/£164 flying between Delhi and Chennai. And while the Japan National Tourist Office does its utmost to entice you there, giving information on economical accommodation, food and travel in all its brochures, the truth is that you can manage in Japan on a New York or London budget – but not on a Bangkok one.

How much you spend naturally depends on the sort of holiday you want to have. While rock-bottom accommodation, local transport and food from simple roadside stalls in India, Cambodia, Vietnam or Laos is likely to set you back about \$10–15/£8–10 daily, once you start considering a bit more comfort, a few beers, better-quality food and the occasional minibus tour, then \$25–30/£14–20 is more realistic. It's relatively easy to sit at home and swear you'll manage without air-conditioning, bathe in cold water and love it, and never want a private toilet, but after a week in 45°C heat and ninety-percent humidity, a few cold showers at 3000m, or three days with chronic diarrhoea, your priorities will certainly alter.

Bear in mind that there are also plenty of potential costs outside your daily living expenses and these can quickly add up. Cambodia

△ Money changer

Sample budgets

Here is a rough indication of minimum daily costs in all the countries we cover. If you are planning internal flights or adventure activities, you'll need to add these on top:

Top-end countries will cost you $40/£23 a day upwards:

Bhutan	Japan
Brunei	Mongolia
China	

Mid-range countries should be manageable on a budget of $20–40/£11–23:

China	South Korea
East Timor	Taiwan
Singapore	

The **cheapest** countries can be coped with on under $20/£13 a day:

Bangladesh	Nepal
Cambodia	Pakistan
India	Philippines
Indonesia	Sri Lanka
Laos	Thailand
Malaysia	Vietnam

Three months in India

While it's possible to manage on around $10–11/£5–6 a day in India, this would mean staying in the cheapest hotels, eating only rice and dhal and

is generally very cheap for foreign visitors, yet the current admission charge to Angkor Wat is $23 per day, $43 for three days and $63 for a week. Recent price hikes at historic monuments in India mean that entrance to the Taj Mahal for foreigners now stands at Rs 750 ($17/£10). Postage and Internet costs are other potential budget busters. You need to reckon on US$0.40 to US$0.70 (23–40p) to send postcards from Asia, on top of the cost of the card itself. Internet access in tourist centres in Thailand and most other parts of the continent is about B60 an hour ($1.50/£1). Taken individually none of these expenses will break the bank but are worth taking into account in your calculations, especially for longer trips where money is very tight.

Even if you plan to have the budget holiday to beat all budget holidays, it makes sense to plan for the occasional splurge. Most travelling second class on all train journeys. If you bump up your luxury quotient, have a room with your own bathroom, vary your diet slightly and throw in a few first-class train journeys, then you're looking at $20–25/£11–14 a day, $140–175/£80–100 a week. Go further up the scale – book into mid-range hotels, eat in moderately priced restaurants and rent a car and driver for a few excursions – and a better estimate is around $35/£20 a day, $245/£140 a week. To travel reasonably but realistically, we recommend reckoning on covering around half the trip at the lowest rate – say six weeks at $70/£40 – four weeks at the middle rate – at $175/£100 – and then three weeks at the top-range above, giving a much more realistic rounded-up total of about $1855/£1060.

A three-month trip through Thailand, Malaysia and Indonesia

To spend a month in each country, you'd need about $1000/£550 if you work out your costs using a minimum daily budget of $10/£5 for Thailand and Indonesia, and $15/£8 a day for Malaysia. However, long-distance travel costs increase this figure significantly, especially if you fly, as does white-water rafting, clothes shopping and/or bar-hopping in Bali. Allowing for half the trip at the basic rate, and the other half at double this, (a total of $1530/£750) means you can afford some more comfortable accommodation and travel plus a few meals in pricier restaurants. However you'll need to double this again ($3000/£1600) if you intend to explore the entire Indonesian archipelago by plane or indulge in some serious adventure sports or hardcore shopping.

first-time visitors to Asia aim for a low weekly budget as far as living costs are concerned, but allow themselves the occasional treat such as a few nights in air-conditioned accommodation, some hot water every so often or perhaps a couple of local flights.

Generalizations about individual countries can be misleading, as some Asian countries are so vast that you'll find different price zones in different parts of the country. Everywhere in mainland China, budget travellers can manage on $16/£10 a day for food and travel, though, accommodation costs vary enormously: in Western Sichuan there are beds to be had for as little as $5/£3 a night, whereas in the east coast cities you'll be hard pushed to find one for less than $35/£20 a night. In Thailand, it's more a question of supply and demand: unappealing bungalows on the overcrowded Railay beaches near Krabi, for example, rarely charge less than $10/£6 a night, while much more inviting beach huts on nearby Ko Jum go for half that.

It's worth bearing in mind that throughout Asia prices can escalate sharply in peak season, with hotel rooms as much as doubling in price. Peak seasons vary locally, but Christmas and New Year are popular pretty much everywhere. On Bali, June to September – coinciding with the European holiday season – is very busy, whereas in Nepal, it's October and November that see a tourist rush to take advantage of the ideal trekking weather.

Saving money before you go

Some of the biggest savings you'll be able to make are those before you go. The best flight deals sell out early and you'll find that certain routes, eg to Goa for Christmas and New Year, are booked solid several months in advance. If you're rushing to fit visas, vaccinations and shopping into a few hectic weeks, you'll have to make hurried decisions and may end up paying to cut corners. The following tips can help:

- Shop around for your flight tickets and plan your itinerary with your budget in mind. You may well be better off visiting a few places in one region than racing across the continent – even in Asia the cost of train/ferry/internal-flight tickets adds up. A free stopover in Tokyo may seem like a good idea, but can you afford several days of high city prices? Taking a cheaper ticket that leaves you to travel from Bangkok to Singapore overland can sound appealing, but make sure you budget for the train or bus fare and the extra days on the road.
- Although there are plenty of visa services that will arrange visas for you (your travel agent may even offer to do this), it is always cheaper to do it yourself. However, you will need to allow plenty of time, especially if you are applying by post. See Chapter Two for more on visas.
- For certain countries, you'll need an armful of inoculations (see Chapter Eleven). Travel clinics provide excellent specialist information and are a time-saving and hassle-free way to get all your jabs. However, many injections are cheaper – even free – from your own doctor.
- If you're booking your first couple of nights' hotel accommodation before you leave home (see Chapter Seven), contact a few hotels directly and compare their prices with those on offer through your

travel agent. Also check online accommodation booking agents (listed on p.417) for good deals.

- By all means shop around for a good deal, but do *not* skimp on your insurance. Knowing that your medical costs and replacement gear will be paid for doesn't make a disaster OK, but it certainly makes it a whole lot more bearable. Don't consider going without insurance, lying about where you're heading or what you're intending to do, or underestimating the value of your stuff to get cheaper premiums – it isn't worth it. You could end up with tens of thousands of dollars of medical bills if you tell the insurance company you are going to Europe but end up being airlifted out of West Papua, or insist you are not taking part in any hazardous sports, but are injured white-water rafting in the Himalayas. Similarly, don't expect to be able to claim the full amount for your $200 camera if you tell the insurance company it's only worth $50. For more on insurance, see p.207.

Be economical

Don't assume you have to take everything with you from home. Some equipment that will be essential for your trip (see Chapter Six), such as lightweight clothes, insect repellent and mosquito nets, is cheaper once you are in Asia. Sarongs, those all-purpose coveralls, are cheap across the continent, as are Tiger Balm (a local ointment – useful to soothe insect bites), soap, shampoo, stationery, mosquito coils and detergent. However, sun block, tampons and deodorant are pricey throughout Asia, and hair conditioner can be expensive and difficult to find outside tourist areas.

One item to consider taking if you're going on a long trip is a water purifier (see p.363). The price of bottled water, particularly in tourist resorts, can be surprisingly high and could use up a substantial part of your budget over a long period.

Nothing you bring from home has to be sparklingly new – it certainly won't be after a few weeks on the road. Trekking equipment shops often have a board advertising secondhand gear, and outdoor sports magazines usually include a classified ads section. Try local thrift and charity shops for cheap cotton clothes, rucksacks, waterproofs and even boots, though do check the merchandise carefully – you don't want a pack with holes, broken zips and detached straps. Look for good value and don't get carried away by cheap prices (see Chapter 6 for advice).

Spending wisely while you're there

While many of the major savings can be made before you even leave home, there are plenty of ways to save money on the road. These tips may be handy:

- Take your International Student Identity Card (ISIC) if you have one. The response to this is variable – in some places it'll simply get a bemused look, but in others it can get you reduced entrance fees to museums and performances.
- Eat as local people do. Western food and drink cost much more than local food throughout Asia.
- You'll save money by eating in groups of two or more – many restaurant dishes come in family-sized portions, especially in China, Hong Kong, Singapore and Thailand, the idea being that diners share several dishes.

It's not fair?

Don't be too distressed if you see local people being charged less than you are – in several Asian countries there is an official two-tier pricing system in operation with foreigners paying more than local people for certain things. In China this applies to plane tickets and entry charges for museums and famous sights, while some hotels slap a foreigner's surcharge onto their prices. In Thailand, India and Sri Lanka, foreigners are charged more than local people for entry to all national museums and historic places (and in Thailand to all national parks, too), although this is gradually being phased out in Vietnam. For example, a foreigner pays Rs750 to enter the Taj Mahal, an Indian Rs20.

The reasoning behind all this is simple: foreigners can afford to pay more, therefore they should be charged more. It's a philosophy you will encounter time and again throughout Asia, from the woman selling mangoes in the market to the national airline company. Some travellers feel it's a fair cop, others fume against it at every turn. There is usually little you can do in official situations, except pay up. However, when dealing with local people, try to find out a fair price from those around you and endeavour not to pay too much more). If foreigners consistently pay way over the top for something, there is a danger is that prices will also rise for local people or that traders will prefer to provide services to foreigners. Accept that you'll end up paying somewhat over the odds on many occasions, but try not to get totally obsessed about it and feel you are constantly being "ripped off"– especially when the amount involved may be just a few pennies.

- Take advantage of the thriving secondhand market among travellers on the road – you can sell or swap items of equipment or guidebooks rather than buying them new. Many travellers' hotels and restaurants have noticeboards advertising goods for sale or swap.
- Hone your bargaining skills (see below) so that you don't pay over the odds for goods and services.

Bargaining

This is an aspect of Asian life that is very alien to visitors from the West. Some people take to it like ducks to water; others find it hard to cope with, no matter how long they stay on the continent.

It's important to remember that bargaining over the price of something is as much a ritual of social interaction as it is about saving money. Essentially it means that, with a few exceptions, the price of anything on offer is open to negotiation. However, if you offer a price and it is accepted, you are morally bound to go ahead with the purchase – so don't haggle if you haven't made up your mind whether or not you really want the item. It's perfectly acceptable, though, to wander around a market asking the prices just to get some idea of the starting figures.

Special price for you, madam

You might like the look of a pair of trousers in an Indian market. You enquire the price, the vendor asks five hundred rupees. You shake your head regretfully and offer two hundred (somewhere in the region of a third or a half the initial asking price is a good starting figure in India). He or she throws their hands up in horror – they have a family to support, how can you expect them to make a living when you are taking the profit out of their business and the rice out of the mouths of their starving offspring, and how about four hundred? You nod sympathetically, but you notice a tiny fault in the material, can't really see your way to paying that much, but could perhaps go as high as three hundred. The fault is nothing; here, he has another pair that are perfect, three-eighty? Ah, but you have seen some similar ones at a better price down the road, what about three-fifty? He agrees, smiles, this is a special price for you, madam – the transaction is done. All this may well have taken place over five minutes, an hour or even a week! However, it's always accompanied by smiles, gentle voices and good humour. Even if you can't reach an agreement, and often you can't, you can shake your head and walk away. This in itself can be a useful ploy in the process – many a bargain has been struck halfway down the street.

If you're really into bargain-hunting, it can be worthwhile doing your shopping early in the day. In parts of Indonesia, for example, vendors believe that a good early sale establishes their fortune in trading for the rest of the day, so start bargaining at lower "morning prices".

Fixed prices and discounts

The real difficulty in Asia is knowing when and when not to bargain. Basically, prices are fixed (non-negotiable) in restaurants; in supermarkets and department stores; on official public transport with tickets; in metered taxis; and in museums, parks or temples. Even in shops with prices labelled, such as CD and tape shops, you may be able to negotiate a better rate for purchases of ten or more or get a free tape thrown in.

As you move upmarket, the jargon changes slightly. So, for example, in a small guesthouse in Vietnam you might simply enquire whether they can let you have the room they offered you at 100,000 dong for 80,000 dong, whereas in a luxury hotel you could enquire about the availability of discounts, perhaps producing a business card for extra effect. You are far more likely to get discounts on accommodation during the low season than when the place is packed out. However, it's always worth bargaining if you're staying longer than a couple of nights as many places do good weekly and monthly rates.

Indulging yourself

It's worth bearing in mind that cheapness isn't everything. Asia is probably the best chance most people have of affording some five-star luxury – so why not make the most of the opportunity to join the jet set for at least a few days? For example, the slap-up tiffin lunch at the legendary *Raffles Hotel* in Singapore costs around $20/£11 and a night in the *Lake Palace Hotel* in Udaipur, one of the world's most spectacular hotels – it's an ex-maharajah's palace on an island in the middle of a lake – will set you back $230/£135. You can see Malaysia, Cambodia, Sri Lanka or India in style, with your own car and driver for the day, for $30/£20, or have a tailor-made silk suit run up in Bangkok for around $160/£100.

Whenever it's a toss-up between spending a bit of extra cash and putting your own safety at risk, you should always part with the cash.

How to take your money

However short your trip, *never* simply take a huge wodge of cash hidden about your person. You want flexibility and easy access to your money, but you also need security against loss and theft, and ideally some kind of backup or emergency funds. The best solution is to travel with a combination of cash, travellers' cheques and credit/debit cards. In case the exchange counter at the airport you're flying into is closed or out of cash when you touch down, it's a good idea to change a small amount of cash into the currency of your first Asian landfall before you leave home. However, there are cases where this isn't possible: for example, you cannot buy Indian rupees or Vietnamese dong abroad; and some other currencies are partially restricted, so you can only change very small amounts abroad at an appalling rate.

Cash

The US dollar is the hard currency of choice throughout Asia, as long as the notes are clean, new issue (rather than older) and in good (ideally almost pristine) condition. Even little hotels in the back of beyond may be willing to change a few dollars into local currency if you get caught short, but they're unlikely to look at any other form of foreign currency. Many businesses, big and small, across Asia will happily accept dollars instead of local currency. Always take small denominations ($1 and $5), as smaller businesses are unlikely to keep large cash reserves, and avoid $100 notes which can be hard to exchange as they are viewed with suspicion because of fake bills in circulation. The advantage of cash is that it's usually exchangeable even if you lose your passport. The big disadvantage is its vulnerability – if stolen, cash is untraceable and most insurance policies expressly exclude the theft of cash from their cover.

Travellers' cheques

Still an essential part of travelling in Asia, travellers' cheques are issued in a variety of currencies, usually at 1–1.5 percent commission, which is essentially the price you pay for peace of mind. However, you do need to be careful about whose cheques you carry. Whatever the other companies say, American Express is the most widely accepted brand in Asia. However, every now and again there is a localized scare about fraud involving one brand or another, and if you are relying totally on travellers' cheques you should think about taking cheques from two or more companies.

Although travellers' cheques in most major currencies are happily accepted at moneychangers and banks in tourist centres, get a bit off the beaten track and you'll find that only US-dollar cheques are acceptable. It pays to do some research before heading too far off into the wilderness, as in the remotest regions – in parts of Indonesia, Laos, Cambodia and Vietnam, for example – travellers' cheques aren't always exchangeable.

Travellers' cheques need careful handling. You must record the numbers of the cheques and tick them off on your list as you use them. Keep this record separate from the travellers' cheques themselves, because if the cheques are stolen or lost you must be able to report the missing numbers to the company. Also keep the emergency telephone number separate from the cheques – directory enquiries in a foreign language when you're upset isn't much fun. In general, travellers' cheques will be replaced at the company's nearest representative within a day or two, provided you have the missing numbers, information about the date and place of purchase, and some form of ID. However, if you're exploring the river systems of southern Sarawak in a longboat, the nearest Amex office could be a long trip away. You'll be very glad of a $50 or $100 emergency stash kept somewhere separate from your main money supply should the worst happen.

You always need your passport as identification to change travellers' cheques, so if your passport gets stolen, your travellers' cheques are useless. In addition, some banks, in an attempt to avoid fraud, insist that you also show them the receipt from the original purchase of the travellers' cheques – it has "Agreement to purchase" written on the back.

Credit cards

The extent to which credit cards are acceptable as payment varies hugely across the continent. Though most top-class hotels, restaurants and shops are happy to accept them (and you often get a very favourable rate of exchange when the bill comes in), they're not much use in establishments at the budget end of the market.

Credit cards are particularly useful for major outlays such as internal flights, the occasional hotel or restaurant splurge, or for very large souvenirs and the cost of shipping them home. They can also be useful when booking and pre-paying for a hotel room over the phone or fax (very handy at peak times of the year), though only at mid-range and top-end places.

Even if you don't plan on using it, a credit card is also a great emergency stand-by, since you can use it to obtain cash advances. Visa and MasterCard are the most widely accepted throughout Asia, both at banks and moneychangers; you can also use their cards to withdraw cash at ATMs (cash dispensers) once you are on the road – check the websites ⓦwww.visa.com and ⓦwww.mastercard.com for the locations of machines accepting their cards. There are machines accepting Visa cards in all the countries covered by this book, with the exception of Bhutan, Cambodia, Laos and East Timor, although you shouldn't expect them on every street corner. Networks are expanding all the time, so check close to your time of travel.

American Express offices provide a free personal cheque cashing service for Amex cardholders; access the locations of their offices worldwide on ⓦwww.americanexpress.com.

Whichever card you take, make sure you carry the emergency phone number with you to report theft of the card, and *never* let the card out of your possession, even stored in a so-called safe while you're away trekking for a few days (see p.390). Bear in mind that, if the card does get lost, getting a replacement sent out to you is likely to take at least four days, and that you'll need someone at home to organize paying your credit-card bill if it's going to reach home before you do.

Debit cards

Debit cards that are part of the Cirrus, Maestro and Visa networks can be used in ATMs worldwide. Just key in your PIN (personal identification number) and the system immediately accesses your bank account back home and can then flash messages to you in your own language. Needless to say, you have to have the funds in your account at home to support the withdrawal, and all the security warnings about credit cards also apply to debit cards. Using ATMs is an extremely convenient way of handling your money if you're sticking to major towns and resorts in countries that offer this service.

However, it is worth checking out the cost of using your card abroad with your bank; even though you get the relevant bank's official exchange rate (usually quite good), you will inevitably be charged an additional "handling fee" by your home bank on each transaction. This can be around two percent, or it might be a flat fee. The fee is particularly irksome when the ATM you're using has an unhelpfully low maximum withdrawal amount (£40 in some cases), so you end up having to pay three lots of handling fees if you want to withdraw £100.

The MasterCard website (@www.mastercard.com) contains lists, organized by country and town, of ATMs that accept Cirrus and Maestro – they are currently in all countries covered by this book except Bhutan, Cambodia, East Timor, Laos and Mongolia; @www .visa.com does the same for debit cards with the Visa logo, which can be used in Mongolia. Networks are expanding, but don't expect to find ATMs in the more rural areas.

It's also worth remembering that in Asia many ATMs operate differently from those you may be used to. Some machines give out the money first and then return the card – keep your wits about you, as it's easy to walk away without the card.

American Express' Travelers Cheque Card

The relatively new American Express' Travelers Cheque Card (see @www.americanexpress.com), which acts as a combination of travellers' cheques and plastic, may well be worth investigating – it's a pre-paid card that you can use like a debit card in ATMs, hotels and other businesses, topping it up as and when you wish.

Changing money

Whenever you change money you should check the exchange rate being offered and the commission charged on the transaction. Just as rates vary from bank to bank, so can the commission on the deal. In some cases you'll need to do your sums to decide on the best place to go. For example, £100 of Thai baht at B73 to the pound with a one percent commission fee is a better deal than a rate of B72 to the pound with no commission. One disadvantage of travellers' cheques is that you pay commission when you buy them and then usually end up paying again to cash them. However, the same applies to a cash advance obtained with a credit card: you'll be charged commission when you get the money, but it also attracts a 1–1.5 percent cash transaction fee on your bill.

Wherever and however you change money, at banks, moneychangers or hotels, shop around carefully, and do keep your exchange certificates. This is your proof that you changed the money legally and in many countries it's vital if you want to change unspent local currency when you leave the country, or want to pay for tourist tickets – for example, on Indian railways or for internal flights in China – with local currency.

Follow a few sensible precautions when changing your hard currency into local money and you'll be a few baht, rupiah or dong better off:

- In some countries there is a black market offering better rates than the banks or official moneychangers for hard currency. However, bear in mind that the local police or security forces often "sting" foreigners in this way: they set up the deal and then either arrest you for black-market trading or extract a bribe to avoid criminal proceedings. There is also a risk you'll get caught up in a crackdown on local operators, become the victim of sleight-of-hand tricks or receive counterfeit notes – kotong gangs in Manila are notorious for ripping tourists off; by the time you realise you've got far less cash than you were promised, they are long gone. The black market probably isn't worth it – especially as the difference between the official and unofficial rate is usually ridiculously small.
- The best rates are usually found in travellers' centres, such as Thamel in Kathmandu or Khao San Road in Bangkok, where there's plenty of competition.
- Don't be unduly suspicious of moneychangers. They are licensed by the local authorities, offer competitive and often better rates than the banks, have more flexible opening hours and often require less paperwork than banks. The last resort is to change money at hotels, where rates are usually the poorest.
- If you are passing through a country more than once, don't get rid of all your local currency until you leave for the final time, as you'll only have to get more each time you come back.
- Always get rid of coins before you leave a country though, as they are not exchangeable outside.
- At border crossings the chances are that rates will be poor. Change only what you need until you can get to a more competitive dealer.
- Always count your notes before you leave the cash desk, however long and tedious the process. Once you've left the desk it's almost

impossible to do anything about it. There are plenty of scams in operation: one involves folding notes in two so that you actually get half as much as appears to be being counted out; another is distracting you while counting out the money.

● Make sure you never run down to your last few cents before you change money.

Running out of money?

It is possible to get money wired out to you from home – especially useful in an emergency. However, hefty fees are charged for this. The most straightforward and expensive method is to use Moneygram (ⓦwww.moneygram.com) or Western Union (ⓦwww.westernunion .com), which transfer money to their overseas offices in a matter of minutes. This needs to be initiated by someone at home. Currently Western Union has the best coverage in Asia, with agents in all the countries covered in this book. Both companies charge between ten and thirty percent depending on the amount sent, with small amounts attracting a larger percentage charge.

An alternative is to get money wired to a local bank for you to collect. The efficiency and speed of the service varies across the continent; it's easier if someone in your home country can make the arrangements. Not surprisingly, it is relatively straightforward to transfer money to banks in Hong Kong (even so, it can take the best part of a day to arrange), but more time-consuming and haphazard to banks in Nepal and India, while in China it can take weeks. If you

Managing your bank account

If you use Internet banking at home it's tempting to imagine that you'll just carry on as usual while you are away. That's fine if you are travelling with your own laptop, but it's a bad idea if you'll be using Internet cafés to access your bank account. You have no way of knowing what spyware may be lurking on the computer (so that all your keystrokes are stored in the computer's memory for later retrieval), or whether the machines are networked in such a way that whatever you are doing can be snooped on from another machine. There are ways of adjusting the settings of any computer to safeguard you against this but the safest advice is not to use Internet cafés for Internet banking, but to instead make alternative access arrangements before you leave home or entrust a family member at home to access the account for you.

think you might need this service, have a chat with your home bank before you leave. You'll need to find a bank in the country you're visiting that has an agreement with the bank from which you wish to transfer funds, and you'll need your passport as ID to collect the money once it has arrived. Most banks charge a flat fee for transfers, which makes it more economical to send larger sums. Expect to pay $45/£25 per transaction.

Earning money while you're away

There are ways of profiting from your trip. No, we're not talking drug-running or importing gems from Thailand; however, it may be possible to supplement your money supply with a temporary job of some sort while you're away, or to sell the story of your journey and/or photos of your trip when you get back. It's worth looking into these options before you leave home because a bit of planning is required.

Discretion is the order of the day here, as many tourist visas expressly prohibit employment. Depending on the job, and the employer, you might get away with working on your tourist visa for a month or two; to work any longer entails regular "visa runs" across the nearest border. For official employment you'll need a working visa; contact the relevant embassy about this (see the country profiles for addresses). Information on doing unpaid, short-term voluntary work in Asia is given on p.161.

Before you travel, have a look at the Asian sections in *Work Your Way Around the World* (Vacation Work Publications) by Susan Griffith or

GI blues

The plan was to travel from London to Perth – I had $400. I sold my camera in Delhi, but by the time I got to Bangkok I was broke. Somehow I had to get to Bali. I wasn't particularly worried about it; something would turn up. And it did – I landed a role in a movie called *Saigon*. The screen test required a crew-cut as I was to be a GI, and I got one by marching around and saluting a bemused Thai hairdresser and saying loudly in English, "Shorter, shorter".

Heading to Lop Buri, however, where some evacuation scenes were to be filmed, I was singled out. I'd been surviving on $5 a day in India and it showed. The hard-as-nails American drill sergeant took one look at me and said, "Get him out of uniform." As I sloped off in scrawny shame, he called out, "You can play a civilian, son." Still, I was officially a GI (I had the haircut to prove it), and when the GIs went on strike for higher wages I got a rise too.

Chris Taylor

The Directory of Jobs and Careers Abroad (Vacation Work Publications) by Deborah Penrith. Once you start travelling, look for adverts in English-language newspapers and on noticeboards in travellers' areas; also talk to other travellers or approach potential employers directly.

In Japan, many young Western women get work as hostesses in bars where they entertain male customers. While there is nothing inherently seedy about most of these places ("hostess" is not a euphemism for "prostitute"), drunken fumblings are not unknown, and the same risks apply as in any situation where you might find yourself alone with a relative stranger. If you're considering this sort of work, be sure to sound out other Western women already employed in this way before you sign on.

Teaching English

One of the more common jobs is teaching English; Asia is swarming with people learning the language who yearn for a native speaker with whom to hone their skills. Most employment for foreigners is in private language schools, found in every city and catering for the full range of pupils, from beginners to pre-university students; the best pay is to be found in Japan and Taiwan. Classrooms are often small and the hours antisocial, as many students want classes in the evening or at weekends, but students are invariably eager, especially when they have a native speaker as a teacher, and the work is a good stepping stone to employment as a private tutor or better-paid jobs in the more established schools or universities.

You will find a TEFL (Teaching English as a Foreign Language) qualification very useful everywhere in Asia and it will give you access to better rates of pay. The most basic qualification is the Cambridge Certificate in English Language Teaching to Adults (CELTA), which is designed for those with no previous teaching experience, takes four or five weeks' full-time study (it is also available part-time) and is recognized throughout the English-teaching world. Courses are widely available in the UK and cost around £750–1200, but are well worth it if you are seriously contemplating teaching while you're away. The University of Cambridge (@www .cambridgeesol.org) publishes a list of 286 centres in 54 countries where CELTA is on offer. In the US the full-time CELTA course costs around US$2300–2600, in Canada C$2300–2500, in Australia

A\$2300–2700 and in New Zealand NZ\$3000. Part-time courses vary in length from a few months to a year but are generally cheaper. There are also centres in Bangladesh, Brunei, China, Hong Kong, India, Indonesia, Japan, South Korea, Malaysia, Pakistan, Singapore, Sri Lanka and Thailand where you can take the course once you are in Asia. This can be a pretty economical option: in Bangkok the CELTA course costs around \$1400/£948 (see Ⓦwww.eccthai.com or Ⓦwww.eliteinstitute.com).

For details of the profession, the different courses available and how to find work abroad, look at *Teaching English Abroad* by Susan Griffiths (Vacation Work Publications, Ⓦwww.vacationwork .co.uk). Websites such as Ⓦwww.teachermania.com, Ⓦwww.tefl .net, Ⓦwww.tefl.com, Ⓦwww.aaoefl.co.uk and Ⓦwww.esl-lounge .com advertise jobs at language schools all over the world, including a good selection in China, India, Indonesia, Japan, South Korea, Taiwan, Thailand and Vietnam. When you travel, don't forget to take photocopies of your qualifications and references from previous employers with you.

Working as a diving instructor

There is a good living to be made in Asia as a diving instructor especially as – rightly or wrongly – many novice divers prefer to be taught by a Westerner rather than a local person. Diving is especially popular in Indonesia, Malaysia, the Philippines and Thailand, and this is where most opportunities are to be found.

To become an instructor, you need relevant experience and certificates from one of the internationally accredited dive organizations. Alternatively, many travellers get the diving bug while they are overseas and quite a few end up taking all the necessary courses while they are on the road. For information about the training necessary for PADI qualifications, which are accepted throughout Asia, take a look at Ⓦwww.padi.com, which also gives the locations of diving centres and resorts.

5

Guidebooks and other resources

Once you've planned a skeleton route, you can enjoy filling in some of the detail by scouring guidebooks and tourist brochures, reading travelogues and talking to old Asia hands. Check out some of the millions of travel-related sites on the Internet (see the online sections in the County Profiles, pp.19–153, and Directory, p.249, for some good websites to start you off) and contact relevant tourist offices and embassies. And try asking your travel agent for first-hand recommendations – the bigger student-oriented travel agents advertise the fact that their consultants have been all over the world, and advising prospective travellers is part of their job.

Guidebooks

In an alien culture where you can neither speak the language nor read the signposts, a guidebook will be a real comfort to you in the first few days. You don't have to use it slavishly, but a good guidebook can make all the difference to your trip by showing you what to leave out of your itinerary and what to include. Don't buy your guidebook at the last minute, however, as it will also contain crucial advice on travel preparation, including what visas you'll need, which inoculations to organize, and what gear to take along. See the Directory, p.421, for a list of recommended travel bookstores.

On the other hand, you could waste a lot of money if you splash out on a set of guidebooks before you've settled on a definite route. Start off by borrowing a few guides from a library (even out-of-date editions are usually perfectly adequate for planning purposes), and then invest in a couple of new editions when your itinerary becomes more certain. If you're planning a long trip, there's no need to buy a guidebook for every country you're going to visit: you'll save money and luggage space by buying secondhand guides on the road, or swapping a guide you've finished with for a book on your next destination.

Choosing a guidebook

Personal recommendation is unbeatable, but you can also make your own judgement in bookshops by comparing the way Guidebook Series A describes a certain town and the way Series B does it. Look up a few things you're particularly interested in – wildlife, for example, or budget accommodation – and see how different books approach the topics. Do not be swayed by sumptuous photographs, and remember that you'll be lugging your chosen book around with you for quite a few weeks, so it shouldn't weigh too much. (Whatever the size of the book, you can save weight by ripping out and discarding the sections you know you'll definitely not need.)

Most guidebook series have a particular style of travel in mind. Guides published by Rough Guides (@www.roughguides .com), Lonely Planet (@www.lonelyplanet.com), Footprint (@www .footprintbooks.com) and Let's Go (@www.letsgo.com) are all written for independent travellers and so give detailed practical information for tourists across all budgets; Trailblazer (@www.trailblazer -guides.com) produces specialist guidebooks with an emphasis on overlanding and trekking; while Insight (@www.insightguides .com) guides are known for their inspirational photography but not their practical detail so much.

Whatever the focus of your guidebook, never expect it to be infallible: new editions are generally only published every two or three years, and in between things *do* change – prices rise, hotels shut down. Guidebook authors also have their own preferences (some series emphasize this, others play it down), so you may

Good guides and bad guides

"We're going to die."

"I know," I replied. We sat on the mountain ridge in silence. There was nothing more to say.

Dawn was approaching. The sun was rising leisurely over Lake Batur, northern Bali. I remember thinking it was the most beautiful sunrise I had ever seen. Oranges and purples filled the sky. Down below, specks of brown dotted the white sandy beach: men had risen early to prepare for the day's fishing. Life was going on as usual, unaware of our predicament. I laid back in the sun and closed my eyes.

We had begun to climb Mount Batur in the early hours of the morning, misled by a guidebook which had stated that the route was easy and a local guide unnecessary.

Two hours later, with a bruised back and a twisted ankle, we found ourselves stranded on a rock ledge. A sheer rock face loomed above us, and a steep drop onto boulders lay below. No one knew where we were. I really believed this could be the end.

Some time later, our knight in shining armour arrived in the form of an eight-year-old boy, wearing flip-flops and balancing a bucket of iced drinks on his head. We would have paid anything to have been led off the mountain but, crazily, in true Indonesian style, the bargaining began. We settled on $3; a bargain.

For the next nerve-racking three and a half hours, we scaled precipitous rock faces with no ropes or safety equipment. A couple of times we slipped, but somehow managed to hold on. To this day I cannot believe we made it.

At the summit we learnt that we'd taken the wrong path up the mountain. It was sheer luck that a local villager had spotted us and summoned our guide. I felt someone was watching out for us that day. Guidebooks contain lots of useful information, but local knowledge should always be consulted too.

Sasha Busbridge

not always agree with their choices. And it can be worth getting a second opinion on certain things – for example, the specific direction of a mountain trail – either from other travellers, or from local people.

Bear in mind, too, that there are many types of guidebook. Books that cover several countries in one volume are easier to carry than a set of individual books and include specific information on travelling between the countries contained in the book; on the down side, you may find that the smaller and less mainstream islands, towns, hotels and restaurants have been edited out because of space considerations. If, on the other hand, you know that you'll be sticking to just one city, region or route, do an Internet search to see if there's a detailed guide on that area. The *Rough Guide to Goa*, for example, contains a lot more local information than the general *India* guide, and also includes access and accommodation details for Mumbai, the gateway city to the region. There are also a useful number of activity guides, some of which, like *Trekking in Ladakh* (Trailblazer), are self-contained and include enough details on gateway cities and accommodation options for you to do without any other guidebooks; others, such as *Diving Indonesia* (Periplus), are best used in conjunction with general guides.

Maps

Most guidebooks include useful enough maps of major towns and resorts, but you might want to invest in a larger, more detailed map of the whole region or country you're intending to visit as well, particularly if you're going to be renting a car or a motorbike, or if you're planning to do some long-distance cycling. If possible, buy this before you leave home, as you can't rely on being able to find good maps when you're in Asia – check your guidebooks for specific advice on this.

Very large-scale maps for independent trekking should also be bought before you leave home (the best selection of trekking maps for Nepal and Tibet, however, is available in Kathmandu). Detailed town and city street maps, on the other hand, are often best bought on arrival, particularly big city maps that include bus routes.

Only a few maps cover the whole of Asia and the scale is so small on these (1:12,000,000) that they're only useful for a general overview. Better to invest in one or more of the major regional maps – Southeast Asia, China, the Indian subcontinent – published by Bartholomew, Nelles or Geocenter. The same publishers also do maps to a comprehensive range of individual Asian countries, as does Periplus. See p.421 of Directory for a list of recommended travel-book and map stores.

The backpacker trail

Guidebooks can have a huge influence on a town's tourist trade. If a hotel, restaurant or tour agent in a popular travellers' centre is given a favourable review in a Lonely Planet guide, for example, that business is almost guaranteed to receive a steady flow of backpackers. In a North Indian town, a tout runs through the normal routine: "Where you from? How long you been in India? Where you stay? I know cheap hotel." When we say that we've already decided to go to Dreamland Hotel, he smiles. "Ah, you must have the Rough Guide. All Rough Guide readers go to Dreamland; Lonely Planet readers go to Uphar Hotel, next door."

If a business does not appear in the guide, it will have to try harder to attract customers, possibly by resorting to touts or by making itself more competitive. On the door of a small restaurant in a tiny, but touristed, Indian village is pinned a sign that reads, "We're not mentioned in the Lonely Planet, but please give us a try anyway."

Lucy Ridout

Background reading

Other people's travel stories are often inspirational and will be full of good ideas on where to go and what to do; they will help prepare you for what lies in store, too. National newspapers, specialist travel magazines and travel websites are fruitful places to look for first-hand, up-to-date travel narratives, often accompanied by alluring photos, and below you'll find a roundup of recommended publications and websites that are well worth a browse. We've also included here a highly selective list of some pan-Asia books that couldn't be squeezed into our country-specific reading recommendations on pp.19–153.

Magazines

All the following magazines are aimed at independent travellers and, while none of them deals exclusively with Asia, you're guaranteed to find some sort of feature on Asia in every issue. Unless otherwise stated, they're all monthly publications, and all of them accept overseas subscriptions. Most have reasonably interesting websites, with a selection of news items and main features from current and back issues.

In the UK, *Wanderlust* (⊛www.wanderlust.co.uk; eight issues a year) focuses on fairly mainstream destinations for the independent traveller, with travel stories plus items on equipment, tour operators, travel-industry news and related TV and radio programmes; it also carries classified ads for people who are searching for travelling companions. *Global Adventure* (⊛www.globalmagazine.co.uk; seven issues a year) is fairly similar, while *Geographical* (⊛www.geographical.co.uk), the magazine of the Royal Geographic Society, includes more features on expeditions.

In North America, bi-monthlies *Outpost* (⊛www.outpostmagazine.com) and *blue* (⊛www.bluemagazine.com) are both great sources of information and inspiration on adventurous and unusual travel worldwide, while the quality monthly *Outside* (⊛outside.away.com) uses top writers to cover all aspects of independent travel, including plenty of features on gear and reviews of travel books.

The bimonthly adventure travel magazine *Action Asia* (⊛www.actionasia.com), published in Hong Kong, is widely available in Australia and looks at everything from trekking to white-water rafting.

For a more detailed take on the realities of daily life in the countries you're planning to visit, you could browse through some of the special-interest magazines that carry a more in-depth coverage of Asia than national newspapers at home. The *New Internationalist* (Ⓦwww.newint.org) focuses on areas such as environmental concerns, women's issues, education and poverty action; *Far Eastern Economic Review* (Ⓦwww.feer.com) does hard-hitting, readable reports on the political and economic stories in the region, and its website gives access to a mass of interesting background information. Many of Asia's main national newspapers, such as the *Times of India* and the *Bangkok Post*, also have online versions.

Online resources

There are millions of travel features out there on the web, from holidaymakers' blogs to tour operators' advertorials; below we've highlighted a few general sites to get you started. Useful country-specific websites are listed in country profiles; online accommodation booking services are listed on p.417; websites for travel agents and tour operators start on p.411; and travel-health websites are on p.419.

- **Boots'n'All** Ⓦ**www.bootsnall.com** Continent- and country-specific travel stories, forums, blogs and a constantly expanding list of expert "insiders" on individual countries who will respond to specific email queries.
- **Gap Year** Ⓦ**www.gapyear.com** Aimed at anyone considering making a longish trip this site features practical advice, inspirational articles, travel stories, live web chats plus forums on RTW travel, female travel and jobs and volunteer placements abroad.
- **Journeywoman** Ⓦ**www.journeywoman.com** Site aimed at women travellers, with unique sections, including "What Should I Wear?" featuring firsthand tips on acceptable dress in over one hundred countries and advice for solo travellers.
- **Lonely Planet Thorn Tree** Ⓦ**thorntree.lonelyplanet.com** Very popular travellers' bulletin boards, divided into regions.
- **Open Directory: Backpacking** Ⓦ**dmoz.org/Recreation /Travel/Specialty_Travel/Backpacking** Scores of backpacker-oriented links, including a lot of Asia-specific ones, plus travelogues, web rings and message boards.
- **Robert Young Pelton's Dangerous Places** Ⓦ**www .comebackalive.com** Online version of the book of the same name,

providing info on adventurous and "dangerous" places around the world, among them parts of Cambodia, India, North Korea, Pakistan, the Philippines and Sri Lanka. Includes statistics on the safety of local transport, a survival guide to "Gimmeyawalletland ", and the Black Flag Café forum.

- **Rough Guides** ⓦ**travel.roughguides.com** Interactive site for independent travellers, with Travel Talk forums, travel tips and features, plus online travel guides.
- **Utopia** ⓦ**www.utopia-asia.com** The top website by and for gay and lesbian travellers to Asia, with details on the gay scene in most Asian countries, plus links to gay meeting places and organizations.

Books

Recommended country-specific novels and non-fiction titles are highlighted in country profiles, pp.19–153, but below are some of the anthologies and more widely focused books that make good general introductions to travel in Asia:

- **ed. Miranda Davies and Natania Jansz** *Women Travel* If you're feeling a bit nervous about setting off, this edition of inspirational travel anecdotes from about eighty different women – tourists, long-term travellers, expats and volunteers – will give you heart. Despite the title, nearly all the travel experiences are as relevant to male readers as to female ones and there are plenty of pieces on trips around Asia.
- **ed. Kim Fay** *To Asia with Love: A Connoisseurs' Guide to Cambodia, Laos, Thailand and Vietnam* An eclectic group of Asia experts, expats and writers offer their insiders' tips on the food, shopping, sights, outdoor spaces and hangouts of Vietnam, Thailand, Laos and Cambodia. Also features a good reading list plus interesting leads for voluntary work and charity organizations.
- **Edward A Gargan** *The River's Tale.* A superbly written account of a year-long odyssey from the source of the Mekong River through China, Tibet, Burma, Laos, Thailand, Cambodia and Vietnam. The author's incisive observations of the people and countries along the way are placed in a broader context by descriptions of recent history and current economic and political regimes. He pulls no punches and his conclusions are sometimes pessimistic, but he's as willing to dissect himself as he is to examine others.
- **Jane Hope** *Introducing Buddha*; **Ziauddin Sardar** *Introducing Islam*; and **Vinay La** *Introducing Hinduism.* These three enjoyable cartoon-

and-caption guides to major Asian religions look light-hearted but are all seriously good primers. They're published by Icon Books.
- **ed. James O'Reilly & Larry Habegger** *Travelers' Tales Guides* (Ⓦ www.travelerstales.com). This outstanding series of travel-themed anthologies cherry-picks from travelogues, travel journalism and guidebooks to create lively, multi-faceted volumes on individual countries – including China, India, Nepal and Thailand – as well as on worldwide themes such as Food, Adventure and Self-Discovery.

Learning the lingo

English is the language of tourism throughout Asia, making it quite possible to do a six-month trip without ever consulting a phrase-book. Indeed, in India, one of the greatest pleasures is the number

△ Looking for signs at Jaipur railway station, India

of Indian English-speakers who are keen to debate local and international issues with English-speaking travellers.

That said, it's well worth learning at least a few phrases – and is essential if travelling off the beaten track – as, wherever you go, people will appreciate your efforts to speak their language. You'll probably be giggled at, but that's as good an icebreaker as any and, in the more remote spots, being able to string a basic sentence together can make the difference between having to cope with a plate of deep-fried locusts and enjoying a tasty bowl of noodles.

Though some languages are guaranteed to turn you into a tongue-tied fool (Mandarin Chinese with its four tones and everyday alphabet of 10,000 pictograms springs to mind, as the anecdote above underlines), others are relatively simple to learn. Bahasa Indonesia, for example, is generally considered to be the easiest language in the world. It's written in roman script, has a straightforward grammar, and is very similar to the Malay language that's understood throughout Malaysia and Singapore.

If you have the time, it's very satisfying to give yourself a proper grounding before you go. There's a huge range of teach-yourself language tapes and CDs available for most Asian languages now, including Hodder's *Teach Yourself* series, and other options from Routledge, Berlitz, Hugo and Lonely Planet. The Linguaphone tape courses are the most comprehensive, but are also expensive. Or go online and make use of the excellent free language courses offered by Word2Word (ⓦ www.word2word.com).

Alternatively, fix yourself up with some face-to-face language classes before setting off. Expatriate Asians quite often advertise lessons in local papers, or you might try setting up an informal language exchange via a community centre or even a neighbourhood Asian restaurant. Should you be planning a lengthy stay in Asia, the best way to learn the lingo is to attend a course on the ground – see Directory pp.412–414 for details of tour operators who offer language-course packages in China, Taiwan and Japan or, once you're there, check the local English-language press for ads and ask at tourist offices, embassies or universities.

Choosing a phrasebook

The easiest way to make yourself literate in an Asian tongue is to travel with a good phrasebook. Rough Guides, Lonely Planet, Berlitz and Hugo all publish a good range of handy pocket-sized phrasebooks and, as with guidebooks, you should compare several different ones before you buy. Think of a few situations – asking the price of a double room, for example, or saying that you're vegetarian – and look for them in the three or four rival phrasebooks. A user-friendly layout is also important and, where relevant, you'll probably want words and phrases to be written in local script – especially important for China, Japan, South Korea, Laos and Thailand.

6

What to take

You could quite happily set off for Asia with all your belongings stuffed into a plastic bag and stock up on clothes and extra bits as and when you need them. Most of Asia is brimming over with merchandise, so you don't need to pack a lifetime's supply of T-shirts or shampoo.

Of course a few things are best bought at home, as the quality of Asian goods is variable, and certain items will be difficult to find when you're away. But apart from these essentials, we'd advise you to take the very minimum you can and improvise on the rest. Buying on the road is nearly always cheaper, shopping for everyday stuff can enhance your travel experience and will almost certainly enhance the local economy a little bit, and, crucially, this approach means that you'll be able to travel light; a heavy load is a real hindrance and can spoil your trip by making you loath to stop off at places because you can't face dragging your huge pack along with you. Things really are bad when your pack begins dictating your itinerary, so start how you mean to go on and get your baggage under control right away. There are a few tips on how to lighten the load:

- Mail stuff to the place where you think you'll need it most. For example, if you're doing a three-month overland from Australia to Europe and you're planning to look for office work when you get to London, send your smart work clothes direct from home to a UK poste restante. Use surface mail, as poste restante/general delivery is usually only held for two months.

- Plan to send excess baggage back after you've finished with it (eg your thermal underwear and wool sweater after you leave Kathmandu) or, better still, buy your woollies when you get there and then sell them, junk them or send them home. Surface mail from Asia generally takes about three months and costs around $35/£20 for 5kg to the UK or the US; a bit less to Australia (see Chapter Thirteen).
- Rent or buy any special gear on the ground rather than taking it with you. For example, you can rent down jackets and sleeping bags in Kathmandu, sleeping bags (but no down jackets) in Lhasa and Chiang Mai (northern Thailand), diving and surfing gear in Bali and southern Thailand, and camping equipment in Malaysia's Taman Negara National Park; consult your guidebook for details. You may also be able to buy secondhand equipment from departing travellers – check guesthouse noticeboards.
- Avoid succumbing to gadget mania. Travel equipment suppliers and the gear pages in magazines and newspapers are filled with stuff you really will not need and should not buy, let alone take with you. There are lots more useful things you can spend your money on than, for example, a special banana-shaped pod that stops fruit from getting squashed in your daypack.

Backpacks

If you haven't already got a backpack, this is the one item that it's worth splashing out on. Choose a recognized-brand-name pack (such as Berghaus, Eagle Creek, Karrimor or Lowe-Alpine) as they are hard-wearing and ergonomically designed. A backpack can cost in the range £75–200 in the UK, $130–450 in the USA or A$200–600 in Australia, but think of it as an investment: a good pack could last you for many years and will certainly make your trip a more comfortable one. For details of recommended suppliers of backpacks and other travel equipment, see the Directory, p.422.

Backpack capacity is measured in litres or cubic inches – not that helpful really as it's hard to visualize your socks and T-shirts in liquid form. Our advice is to buy the smallest one that looks practical for you: a 40- to 55-litre one if possible, but certainly no bigger than 65 litres. Buying a smaller pack forces you to travel light, and there's no question you'll be grateful for that when you're battling with

△ Travelling light in Thailand

overflowing Bangkok buses or wandering up and down a roasting Colombo street.

Some travellers, on the other hand, claim you should buy as large a pack as you're ever likely to need, presuming that if you don't fill it to the brim on your way out, you'll certainly pick up enough trinkets on the trip to make it worth its massive size. In the end, though, it's not the capacity that matters so much as the weight of stuff that you cram into it. Many airlines specify a 20kg maximum for hold baggage, so that should definitely be your limit; a realistic optimum weight lies somewhere between 10kg and 15kg – it's definitely worth jettisoning stuff once the scales go over the 17kg mark.

Once you've decided on the size, check out the extra bits, particularly the pockets, compartments and additional strap attachments. Packs with more than one compartment are easier to use. And side- and lid-pockets are perfect for stashing bits and pieces you need to get at quickly – soap and a toothbrush for example, so that you don't have to root right through to the bottom of your pack in the sleeping compartment of an overnight train – as well as your map and guidebook, or your rain gear. Some backpacks have detachable front pockets which are actually daypacks, of which more on p.259. Bear in mind, though, that the more compact your pack, the easier it will be to lug on and off buses and trains, and to squeeze onto luggage racks and into left-luggage lockers. Fully stuffed side-pockets can add a good 30cm to the width of your pack, and attaching boots, sunhat and umbrella to external loops only makes your load more difficult to carry.

Choosing a backpack

You won't regret the time and care you take in choosing the right backpack. Always try them on before buying, don't order blind online, and think about the following:

- The best packs are made from heavy-duty synthetic fabrics; avoid the ones that feel flimsy and might tear easily. Zips should be sturdy, too.
- Most travellers' backpacks are constructed round a lightweight internal frame. This gives shape to the pack but, most importantly, it helps spread the load across your back. The smaller packs – under 40 litres – are often considered too small to warrant a frame, but they should come with thickly padded and contoured backs which also help distribute the weight and make the whole thing more comfortable. These days, uncomfortable, external frames are the province of serious, long-distance trekkers and backpacking travellers don't need them.
- A thickly padded hip belt is essential for carrying any load over 10kg. This transfers most of the weight off your shoulders onto your hips and legs – the strongest and sturdiest part of the body. By channelling the weight down to your lower body, you're also making yourself more stable: a full load resting solely on your shoulders will quickly tire you out.
- If you're not average size and build, check out the packs with adjustable back systems, where you can change the position of the shoulder straps in relation to the frame.
- Some packs are designed especially for women, with shorter back lengths and a differently contoured back shape and hip belt.

Is it a backpack? Is it a suitcase? . . .

. . . No, it's a travelpack. Some backpacks can also be turned into suitcases: a special flap zips over the straps and, with the aid of a handle, you can carry it like a suitcase or a shoulder bag – a useful feature for plane, bus and train journeys where dangling straps can get tangled up or ripped off. This also means that you can walk into a smart hotel without necessarily looking like a scruffy, impecunious backpacker. More handy still is the fact that most travelpacks can be unzipped all the way round to open like a suitcase, making them much more convenient than a conventional backpack, especially for overnight stopovers. They are also easier to lock.

Though all these features make travelpacks versatile, the cheapest versions rarely provide the long-distance support of a properly contoured backpack and most have a rectangular, suitcase-like shape which makes them much bulkier to carry on your back. If you choose this option, go for a travelpack with an internal frame, not just padding, and make sure there's a hip-belt as well as external compression straps to help secure the load. Some of the more expensive ones have really well designed harnesses that compare well with those on good backpacks.

Packing up and locking up

It's worth customizing your pack to make it as user-friendly, resilient and secure as possible. These ideas may be useful:

- Most backpacks are showerproof, but that doesn't make them monsoon- or tropical-storm-proof. To keep your stuff dry, either buy a special backpack liner, or make do with a large bin liner or two; alternatively, just wrap your most precious items in individual plastic bags.
- Pack your backpack so that you are not being pulled backwards all the time. This means distributing weight as evenly as possible from top to bottom, and keeping the heavier stuff as close to your body as possible. Be careful where you pack sharp or angular objects as you don't want them jabbing into your back.
- As well as tagging your pack on the outside, stick an address label to the inside of one of the side-pockets, so that there can be no dispute about whose it is. Tie a brightly coloured ribbon to one of the outside straps to make it easily identifiable in airports and bus stations.
- Though many backpacks are non-lockable as bought, a lot of them come with useful devices like double zips on the side- and lid-pockets so that you can use a small padlock on them. If not, think

about getting a couple of small holes punched into the fabric above the zip fasteners, so that you can use a mini-padlock to lock the zip to the hole; shoe-repairers and keycutters will do this for you, and will reinforce the hole with a metal ring. To lock the straps you can use specially designed little ladder locks or sacklocks (available from camping shops) and attach mini-padlocks to them. None of this prevents someone slashing your pack with a blade, but mini-padlocks are a deterrent to opportunist thieves. The bottom line, however, is never to leave your most valuable or important items in an unattended pack – that's what money belts are for (see below).

● Some travellers take a small chain and a spare padlock for securing their pack to luggage racks on overnight trains and buses (see pp.323 & 391).

Daypacks and shoulder bags

Unless your planning's gone seriously awry, you won't be carting your backpack around every day of your trip, so you'll probably need a much smaller bag for daily around-town necessities like your camera, guidebook, map, water bottle and sunblock. Many travellers like to use a daypack for this purpose, but there are advantages to using a shoulder bag instead: they are smaller and less unwieldy, and can easily be folded away into your main pack or worn comfortably at the same time as your main pack. They are also easier to access while you're walking along, and do not mark you out so obviously as a tourist, particularly in bars and clubs. Advice on what to carry in your daypack or shoulder bag on long-haul flights is given in Chapter Seven.

Choosing a daypack

You should be as fussy about choosing a daypack as you are with your main pack. This is what you're going to be carrying around all day every day, so it needs to be comfortable and well designed. For comfort, you'll need padded, adjustable shoulder straps, a padded back and an overall size and shape that's not too cumbersome.

For convenience, look at how the pack opens up and the number of pockets. Some daypacks zip open all the way round; although this is handy for digging out a wayward pen, it also makes the daypack easier to drop things out of when you're opening it up, and the pack can come unzipped if you don't keep it locked. The top-opening drawstring system is a more user-friendly alternative. External pockets can be useful – some are large enough to accommodate a one-litre water bottle on each side – but an internal pocket is more useful, ideal for documents, a wallet, a map or a bus ticket.

You will sometimes have to wear both your backpack and your daypack at the same time. This can be awkward, and a security hazard, so if possible empty your daypack and stuff it inside your main pack. Otherwise, you're probably best off wearing your daypack across your front; this helps your balance, too, and discourages pickpockets.

Some main packs are designed with built-in, detachable daypacks, which zip onto the outside of your main pack. If you go for this option, never carry valuables in the zipped-on mini-pack as you won't be able to tell if a pickpocket slashes it when you're on the move.

Money belts

Most travellers like to keep their valuables on their person at all times, and the safest and most convenient way of doing this is to wear a money belt. This is essentially a long flat pouch, made of fabric, plastic or leather, attached to a belt and designed to be worn around the waist. It should be worn *under* your clothes, and should be as discreet as possible – preferably invisible – so that it does not attract the attention of muggers and pickpockets. To keep it slimline, it should be used only to carry stuff that you don't need to access every twenty minutes. Keep your passport, your airline ticket, your credit card, travel insurance policy and the bulk of your cash in the money belt, but leave your petty cash, notebook and pocket torch for your daypack.

Don't confuse money belts with bum bags/fanny packs. A bum bag is a larger and an altogether more ostentatious item; it's worn over your clothes and can usually hold a small camera as well as sunscreen and sunglasses. As a security item the bum bag is useless and may as well be inscribed with flashing lights announcing "Valuable items inside, help yourself". It just takes one deft swipe of a knife for your bum bag to drop to the ground and into the hands of an opportunist thief.

Some people prefer neck wallets to money belts. These are similar pouches, designed to be worn either round the neck or over the shoulder. As with money belts, they should be kept under your clothes and out of sight. The main drawback with neck wallets is that they swing around more than money belts and therefore feel less safe and possibly more uncomfortable.

Choosing a money belt (or neck wallet)

These are a few points to bear in mind:

- It should be wide enough to accommodate your passport and long enough for your travellers' cheques. Take these along with you when making your purchase.
- Cotton is the most comfortable fabric: it absorbs the sweat and does not irritate the skin – and you can wash it when it gets dirty or smelly. Nylon and plastic are not recommended. When wearing a cotton money belt, it's a good idea to keep something waterproof – eg your free plastic-coated traveller's-cheque wallet – at the back of the money belt nearest your skin, so that any excess sweat will not obliterate vital documents such as airline tickets.
- If you're planning to spend a fair amount of time on the beach, consider buying – as a supplement to your money belt – a little waterproof canister that you can wear when swimming. These come in varying sizes (with names like "Surfsafe") and should be able to hold your room keys and/or security box key so that you don't have to worry about leaving your money belt with all its valuables unattended on the beach.

Clothes

Once you're on the road you'll almost certainly end up wearing the same two or three outfits week-in, week-out. Ideally you'll want to work that out before you leave home, but there's always parcel post to send back any excess. Nonetheless, try to be brutal with yourself at the packing stage. Ask yourself: do I *really* need five T-shirts and three pairs of jeans?

Your clothes will deteriorate faster than they do at home because of the heat, the extra sweat, and the pounding and mangling they'll go through at local laundries. To some this is a reason for taking new clothes: the newer the item, the better its chance of survival. On the other hand, why waste your money if things are only going to get ruined anyway? Whatever you decide, don't take your smartest gear, or anything that's of irreplaceable sentimental value.

The modesty factor

Most Asians do not enjoy seeing acres of exposed Western flesh displayed in public. They find revealing dress offensive and cheap, so you'll get a much better response from local people if you respect their views and adapt your attire accordingly. This is particularly important when visiting temples, mosques and shrines – if you're unsuitably dressed in these places you'll probably be refused entry.

Prudish (and sweaty) though it sounds, this means wearing long trousers or skirts for most day-to-day activities and keeping shorts for beach resorts. Singlets are also considered low-class, especially for women, who will get a lot of unwanted attention if they reveal their cleavages or are obviously not wearing a bra. The notice above the entrance gate to Bangkok's Grand Palace sums up the (usually unspoken) rules; it's illustrated with photos of unsuitably dressed men and women, and forbids "leggings, shorts, singlets, fishermen's trousers, torn and dirty clothing and flip-flops".

Lots of travellers ignore local clothing etiquette and may not even notice that it's an issue. This is quite easy to do if you're sticking to heavily touristy ghettos – Bangkok's Khao San Road, for example, or Sudder Street in Kolkata. But as soon as you deviate from the beaten track you'll start to feel more self-conscious. One young female traveller got stones thrown at her in Medan (a Muslim town in Sumatra) for walking around in shorts; another adopted local Indian dress (cotton pyjama-style tunic and trousers) for her six-month stay and found that this made villagers much less nervous of her – in fact, they would often start a conversation by complimenting her for wearing a *salwaar kameez*.

Stripping down for swimming and sunbathing is a Western practice that bemuses many Asians. When the Thais and Cambodians go swimming they walk straight into the water in their jeans and T-shirts; Indian women do the same in their saris or *salwaar kameez*. At established tourist-oriented beach resorts there'll always be foreigners wearing swimwear, but if you're going for a dip way off the tourist track it's always worth checking out local practices first.

For first-hand advice on acceptable clothing for women in about one hundred different countries, check out the "What Should I Wear?" section of the Journeywoman website (@www.journeywoman.com), which has sartorial tips and comments from dozens of women travellers.

And remember: Asia is full of clothes shops selling stuff that's ideal for the local climate. Note, however, that Asian sizes rarely go above men's UK/US trouser size 36 and women's UK size 16/ US size 14, though you can get Western sizes in touristed towns. Also bear in mind that tailoring in Asia is extremely inexpensive, and Asian fabrics are stunning, so you can always get new clothes made up, particularly in Bangkok, Hoi An in Vietnam, Hong Kong, Singapore and almost any big town in India (a tailored cotton shirt costs about $8/£5 in India). You may end up wanting to replace your entire wardrobe anyway: Asian men and women tend to dress far more colourfully than Westerners so you might feel rather drab in comparison if you wear nothing but sober blacks and khakis.

Packing for the heat

For tropical Asia you will need clothes that are long, loose and light:

- Long trousers and long sleeves are good because of the modesty factor (see box opposite), but also for sun protection and, curiously enough, for coolness as well. The more skin you expose to the sun, the faster your body moisture evaporates and the more dehydrated and, therefore, hotter you become. You only have to picture the flowing robes of an Arab sheikh to be reminded of this.
- Long sleeves and long trousers are also good protection against mosquitoes.
- Loose, baggy clothing improves ventilation and cuts down on sweat.
- Lightweight fabrics are faster to dry and smaller to pack.
- Cotton and linen are the most comfortable, as natural fibres are absorbent and let your skin breathe.
- Artificial fabrics such as lycra, nylon and rayon tend to encourage sweat and itchiness, and may even cause heat rash and fungus.
- T-shirts are quite heavy to wear and to carry, and take a long time to dry. Consider taking short-sleeved cotton shirts instead – or buy some on the road.
- Jeans are heavy to carry, hot to wear and take a long time to dry, though some travellers find they make them feel comfortably at home.
- Light-coloured clothing will help to keep you cooler (it reflects rather than absorbs the sunlight) and is less attractive to mosquitoes, but will also get dirtier faster.

Packing for a cold climate

The best way to pack for a trip that is to include a few weeks in a cold climate is to go for the layers technique. This means you can make the most of your tropical clothing by wearing several items at the same time (two short-sleeved T-shirts under a long-sleeved shirt for example), though you should also think about topping up with some of the following:

- A fleece jacket; these are warm and weigh surprisingly little. At the least take a micro-fleece top, which are very light and pack small.
- Thermal underwear is a good idea: ideally long johns and a long-sleeved undershirt, but woollen tights or thick leggings and a long-sleeved brushed cotton top will do instead. If you have money to spare, buy some silks (100-percent silk thermals), which feel incredibly light (and slinky) but are extremely warm.
- Warm socks are a must: go for the hard-wearing, double-thickness ones sold in camping shops. They're good for wearing with hiking boots in hot places as well.
- Woolly hat and scarf, or Balaclava, plus gloves are easily bought when you arrive; the yak-wool ones sold in Nepal are especially popular.

A clothing checklist

- Two pairs long trousers/skirts/dresses.
- Two T-shirts/short-sleeved shirts.
- One long-sleeved shirt.
- One micro-fleece top, lightweight fleece jacket, sweatshirt or similar item for moderate warmth.
- One pair shorts.
- A sarong.
- Swimwear.
- Underwear. Natural fibres are most comfortable. Easily replaced all over Asia, except for bras over size 38B. Don't bring too many, as you can wash and dry them in no time at all.
- Socks. To stop your feet getting ravaged by mosquitoes after sunset.
- Rain gear. A PVC poncho or cagoule might be useful and squashes into a small space.

Cracking the dress code

A friend of mine and I were in Amritsar and decided to walk from the hotel to the Golden Temple. We were both wearing ankle-length skirts and decently modest tops, but we may as well have been sporting sequined bikinis for all the anonymity that gave us. No sooner had we stepped out of the lobby than the stares began, levelled unashamedly and unmistakably at crotch height. It took us a while to realize that this was not the impolite lunacy of one or two individuals, but rather the local pastime for any male aged between 10 and 80. Our skirts were neither see-through nor hip-hugging, but maybe that was the attraction: what could be hiding behind those draped floral pleats? Which just goes to show that, however hard you try to be inconspicuous, as a foreign female you are always likely to be an object of curiosity.

Lucy Ridout

But in the tropical heat that comes with monsoons you'll feel more comfortable using an umbrella instead (PVC makes you sweat). Buy your umbrella when you need it; don't take one with you.

- Sunhat. Not many people wear them, but they do keep you cooler and prevent sunstroke. Broad-brimmed straw hats are a pain to carry when you're on the move, so either buy one there and then dump it, or opt instead for a baseball cap or squashy cotton number.
- A smarter option. You might find yourself invited to a festival, a wedding, or even a circumcision ceremony, so you'll want to at least look like you've made an effort. Smart gear is also useful when dealing with Asian bureaucracy. Something light that doesn't crumple is best.

Shoes

The footwear of choice for the perfect backpacker is the sports sandal or reef-walker, of which Teva are the best known: a go-any-where sandal with adjustable straps, and sturdy, contoured rubber soles. With a pair of sport sandals on your feet, you can negotiate rough terrain, go swimming, wade through rivers and wander the streets, without having to take them off. They are, of course, not as protective as walking boots, though not nearly as heavy either. Genuine Tevas are pretty expensive in the UK and Australia (from about £30/A$90 to £75/A$160), although in the States you should find them for $50–90. Ten-dollar clones are easy to find in places like Bangkok and Delhi, though don't expect them to last more than a couple of months.

Each extra pair of shoes adds a kilo or two to your load, so, sports sandals or not, you need to keep your shoe quotient down. Ideally this means you should take just one hardy pair for daily walking, plus a pair of thongs/flip-flops for beach and hotel. If you're planning to do any long-distance trekking, hiking boots will probably be useful enough to justify that extra space and weight, and you can always wear them rather than pack them whenever you're moving on, though some people find trainers an adequate substitute. These are a few pedi-points to bear in mind:

- You may be wearing these shoes every day for the next six months, so they must be comfortable and strong.
- Your shoes need to be airy, too, as not only do sweaty feet stink, but they can also fester and give you unpleasant flesh-rot in tropical climes.

- Leather sandals (Indian chappals) are the foot uniform of the East: do as most Asians do and wear sandals.
- In Asia, you will find yourself forever taking your shoes off to go into temples and mosques, and when visiting people's homes. Laces and other fiddly fastenings can become extremely annoying after a while.
- If you have big feet (that is, bigger than the Asian maximum size – men's 44/US 10½, UK 10; women's 40/US 9, UK 6½), be sure that your shoes will last you the whole trip, as you may not be able to buy any more off the peg. But you will be able to get some made for you – all the big cities have reputable shoemakers.

Essentials

An alphabetical list of things you will definitely need.

Batteries

Put new batteries in your watch, camera, alarm clock, flashlight and any other vital item before you leave home. Consider taking replacements as well: although you will be able to get most brands in major cities, you may not be near a major city when yours run out.

Contact lens stuff

You can get standard brand-name contact lens solutions at opticians and pharmacists in Asian capitals and major cities, so you don't have to take a huge supply with you. Take a pair of glasses as a backup, as your lenses may get damaged by dust and sand and it would be a shame to travel all that way and then not be able to see anything. Also, should you get an eye infection, you'll need to do without lenses until the infection clears up.

Contraceptives

Condoms are available over the counter in nearly every Asian nation, but try to buy them from air-conditioned shops or places where they keep them in the fridge so the latex doesn't perish; women may feel uncomfortable buying them because many Asian women don't. Do not rely on being able to buy other contraceptives in Asia: unless your guidebook advises otherwise, take enough to last you for the whole trip. See Chapter Twelve for more on this.

First-aid kit

Basic first-aid kit, medicines, antimalarials and insect repellents: see Chapter Twelve for details.

Flashlight (torch)

You may well be staying in places with sporadic electricity supplies, or even none at all; and a flashlight is always a help on overnight trains and when walking through dark, unfamiliar streets. The more compact your flashlight, the more likely you are to carry it with you. Head-torches, which are like mini miners' lamps on an elasticated headband, are pricey but have lots of advantages – leaving your hands free to wrestle with keys in the dark, say, or to hold up your skirt while peeing in the pitch black.

Glasses

Take your prescription with you. Any optician should be able to fit your frames with new lenses, or supply a new pair if required – and usually much more cheaply than at home.

Guidebooks, phrasebooks and maps

See Chapter Five for advice on choosing the most useful guide-books, phrasebooks and maps.

Padlocks and cable-locks

Small padlocks serve as a deterrent to anyone considering pilfering stuff from your backpack, and are also useful as extra security on hotel doors. Keep two sets of keys in different places, or take combination padlocks instead, so you don't have to worry about losing the key (just about forgetting the number). A cable-lock can come in handy for securing your pack to luggage racks on overnight trains, or to roof racks on long-distance buses.

Sarong

It's amazing what you can do with a 2m x 1m length of cloth: you can use it as a bath and beach towel, as a sleeping sheet or blanket, as a turban-style sunhat or a temple headscarf-cum-shawl. You can turn it into a shopping bag, an awning on a shadeless beach, or even a rope for hauling your friend up a mountainside. And, of course, like the women and men of Laos, Cambodia, Thailand, Indonesia and Bangladesh, you can also wear it! Sarongs are easy to buy in the West now, but you'll get a much bigger selection if you wait until your first port of call. You should be able to pick one up for around $8/£5 anywhere in Asia.

Sunglasses

Tropical light is intense, so you'll be glad to hide behind some dark glasses. The same goes for high-altitude glare in Pakistan, Nepal, Tibet, Bhutan and northern India. Buy them at home, as the quality is not as good everywhere in Asia.

Sunscreens

Take sun block and a bottle of high-factor suntan lotion (15 for average white skins) for the first few weeks, plus a lower-factor lotion for use once your skin's adjusted to the rays. Don't forget that you can get burnt just as easily in the mountains as by the sea: do not be deceived by the cooler air, as the UV rays are just as strong and the risk of getting skin cancer just as high.

Tampons

Available in most major cities across Asia, though check with your guidebook. Southern Sumatra, for example, is an exception, as is most of Laos outside Vientiane, much of Vietnam and all but the three big tourist centres in Cambodia.

Toilet paper

Toilet paper is only sometimes supplied in backpackers' accommodation in Asia. You can buy it in tourist centres and big cities, but take a small roll with you anyway (minus the cardboard centre to aid squashing and save space).

Toiletries

Unless you have very special requirements, you'll be able to restock your toiletry supply anywhere you go. And there'll be plenty of new lotions to experiment with, too – like the ochre-coloured face powder that some Thai women plaster on themselves to prevent sun damage, or the pure coconut oil used in India to ensure supple skin and lustrous hair. However, beware the large number of moisturizers, very popular with Asian women, that have a "whitening" effect on the skin, as they contain bleach.

Towel

Normal towels get disgustingly smelly very easily, take ages to dry and use up far too much valuable backpack space. Use a sarong instead. Or, if you must, take a tiny hand towel. Alternatively, there are a range of lightweight, quick-drying, high-absorbency travel towels on the market that do a reasonable job.

Optional odds and ends

An alphabetical list of bits and pieces that you may or may not need.

Adaptors

If you're taking a digital camera, iPod, mobile phone, hairdryer, laptop, or any other electrical appliance, you'll need a set of travel plugs/electrical adaptors so that you can plug in wherever you are. Guidebooks will tell you what the local voltage and usual socket formation is, or check out ⊛www.kropla.com, which has a very helpful list, complete with pictures, of the different sockets, voltage and phone plugs used around the world. You can buy sets of three or four travel adaptors from any of the travel equipment suppliers listed in the Directory, p.422.

Alarm clock or watch

For early departures.

Binoculars

Worth considering if you're going to be wildlife-spotting in national parks, or even trekking.

Books

New, English-language books are relatively expensive in Asia (India and Nepal are the exceptions), but secondhand bookstores and book exchanges are usually plentiful in travellers' centres, so there's no need to carry a whole library around with you. See pp.19–153 for country-specific titles that would make enjoyable travelling companions.

Cigarette lighter

Useful even for nonsmokers, for lighting mosquito coils, candles (during power cuts) and campfires; matches get soggy from the humidity and are more of a hazard.

Comfort food

Some travellers swear by Marmite, Vegemite, peanut butter or whatever – a little taste of home to soothe their stomach and their taste buds. Whatever you take, it should be small, non-perishable and hard to break or spill.

Compass

Only necessary if you're trekking without a guide.

Earplugs

To block out snoring partners, roaring all-night traffic, video music on overnight buses and other annoyances.

Games

For all those exhausting thirty-hour bus and train journeys. Pocket Scrabble, playing cards, Game Boy, Connect 4 – we've road-tested them all.

Gluestick

For recalcitrant Asian envelopes and stamps.

Handkerchief

Hopefully you won't be getting a cold, but you will be sweating a lot – and a hanky is useful for mopping your brow. Also practical for drying your hands after washing them in restaurants or public toilets (generally, only posh hotels and airports provide paper towels or dryers). A soaking wet handkerchief tied around your neck has a refreshingly cooling effect on your whole body.

iPod or personal stereo

An iPod, equivalent portable MP3 player or personal stereo is great for long bus journeys and for entertaining people in the more remote villages. Consider taking a pair of mini-speakers as well: you can get good-quality wallet-sized travel speakers for around US$50/£30. If your personal stereo has a record button, you can also make interesting audio-diaries – and audio letters to the folks back home. Don't forget to take an adaptor see p.269) for the battery charger.

Earplugs

Earplugs are essential for screening out the routine din of Asian hotels. Until you've been to Asia, you just can't imagine how noisy everyone is. We regularly had building work going on in the next-door room or in the one directly above us – and it always continued through the night because that's the coolest time to work! Then there's the morning throat-clearing chorus – at 5am – when the night's phlegm is hawked and spat out by every man in the locality. And in Indonesia, it's impossible to stay out of earshot of the early morning *muezzin* calls at the neighbourhood mosque; in Padang, our hotel had its very own mosque – in the room adjacent to ours!

Jo Mead

Laptop

Laptops can be useful if you're taking lots of digital photos or compiling a serious account of your trip, but they're heavy, something else to worry about, and hard to insure. See p.384 for a discussion of the pros and cons of taking yours travelling.

Mobile phone

Texting home is a very economical way of keeping in touch and most major phone networks have international agreements so you're likely to get a signal in cities across Asia; for details see p.379. Take a travel plug adaptor (see p.269) for the charger.

Mosquito coils

Buy them when you arrive, where they will be much cheaper. Some hotels provide them free. See p.360 for more on this form of mosquito repellent.

Mosquito net

Can be useful anywhere in Asia, though most tourist accommodation will provide nets or screened windows. Nets are much cheaper in Asia than in the West, but, if you do buy one from home, choose one which is impregnated with mosquito repellent. They're available from camping shops in the UK for £20–40, in the US for $12–40, and in Australia for A$65. Also pack a handful of hooks and a small roll of heavy-duty tape so that you can fix your net to beams, bedposts, window frames and ceilings.

Notebook or journal and pens

For all your profound observations and amusing anecdotes. (Don't forget to send in the best ones for the next edition of *First-Time Asia*.)

Penknife

If you take one, make it a Swiss Army knife (or a good cheap copy), as you might be glad of the blade and the bottle opener. Don't put your penknife in your hand luggage when flying, as it's considered a potential weapon and will get confiscated (see Chapter Seven).

Photos of home

A good icebreaker, and just as weird and interesting to the people you'll meet on buses and trains as a picture of a Dyak longhouse or a Vietnamese rickshaw would be to you.

Radio

If you're away for a long time, a short-wave radio can be a comforting link with home, especially if you're travelling alone. See p.385 for advice on tuning in overseas.

Sewing kit

Safety pins, needle and cotton, plus a couple of buttons for emergency repairs.

Sheet sleeping bag

More useful in tropical Asia than a down sleeping bag, but by no means essential: if you're worried about the cleanliness of the hotel sheets you can always use your sarong instead – or change your guesthouse. If you do want to take one, you don't need to buy one: either sew two sheets together or use a lightweight duvet cover instead.

Sink plug

Asian sinks tend not have plugs, so a universal sink plug (available from travel equipment stores and, more cheaply, from hardware stores) can be useful, especially for wet shaving.

Sleeping bag

Unless you're going to spend a long time camping or trekking in the colder and more remote parts of Asia, there's no point lugging a sleeping bag around with you. In popular trekking centres (like Kathmandu and Lhasa) you can rent four-season bags for as little as a dollar a day.

Stamps from your home country

No, not because we assume that everyone's a closet collector, but because Asian post is not always that speedy (see Chapter Thirteen), so you might want to give pre-stamped letters to travellers you meet who are heading home in the next week.

String

To use as a washing line and to suspend mosquito nets from. Some travellers swear by dental floss instead of string – it comes in a tiny box, and as well as helping to keep your gums healthy is strong enough to support your wet laundry and to tie up parcels.

Tent and other camping gear

Accommodation and food is so inexpensive in most parts of Asia that you won't need a tent, sleeping bag and camping stove to eke out your budget. Exceptions include Japan and Hong Kong, where hotel rooms will take a big slice out of your budget and campsites are plentiful (if a bit far from major tourist attractions). Camping gear is essential if you're heading into remote wilderness areas anywhere in Asia and are not planning to take a guide (guides usually provide food and bedding). In South Korea, for example, there are lots of mountain huts dotted over national park trails, but they provide nothing more than floor space and a roof. Before lugging your equipment halfway round the world, check relevant guidebooks for local places that rent out camping gear.

Wallet

Most Asian currencies are based on notes and, in countries where the denominations are very big, you'll find a wallet much handier than a purse because you'll have far more notes than coins. In Indonesia, for example, there's even a note for one hundred rupiah, currently equivalent to about one US cent. Inexpensive leather and fabric wallets are available all over Asia, so you might want to buy one when you get there.

Washing powder (laundry detergent)

Camping shops sell expensive travel-wash suds in tubes, but you're better off buying cheap individual portions of washing powder when you get there.

Water bottle and water purifier or tablets

If you stick to the beaten track, you shouldn't need your own water bottle, as bottled water is sold in all touristed areas. You should definitely take your own water bottle and purifying equipment if you're going trekking or venturing into remote areas. Buy a bottle that holds a litre and has a belt or shoulder-strap attachment. More information on water purification is given in Chapter Twelve.

Wet ones (baby wipes)

Not just for babies, but for sweaty travel-worn adults too. Good for cleaning yourself up on buses and trains, and for wiping hands before eating.

Cameras

Photos are a great way to jog your memory when you get home, and the best way to share your experiences both on the road and after your return. Weigh up the advantages of taking a bulky top-of-the range SLR (single lens reflex) with a variety of lenses against a point-and-shoot compact or the compromise zoom-compact option. Be realistic about what you intend to do with the pictures once you get home: if you're planning to sell them for publication or use them in slide shows and lectures, then an SLR is probably essential. But, if you just want them for your personal satisfaction, you may be happier with a smaller and less ostentatious camera (cameras draw a lot of attention wherever you are and can make you feel self-conscious – they also attract thieves).

Digital options

Opinions are still divided over whether digital SLRs are as good as they should be, but if you're going for a compact camera then a digital model is almost certainly the best option: they're small,

△ Capturing the moment, India

light and robust and have the great advantage that you can see your images straightaway and so re-shoot (or simply erase) any that you're not happy with – just the thing when you can't resist taking twelve shots of the same postcard–pretty ricefield or adorable orang-utan. There are various possibilities for storing your digital images while travelling, but whichever you choose you should take at least two decent-sized memory cards (capacity varies according to camera model and photo quality). When one card is full, the cheapest way to save its images is by burning them on to a CD either at an Internet café or, usually pricier but often more reliable, at a camera shop. The alternative is to travel with a portable storage device – some MP3 players, for example, have this facility. Don't forget to pack the battery charger and a travel plug adaptor (see p.269), and take your camera's USB cable as well, for downloading direct on to Internet café terminals where that service is available (though slow modem speeds generally mean that this is only viable for downloading a few photos at a time and not for transferring entire cards). Where downloading is feasible, you'll be able to email a few pictures to friends and family as well as adding them to a personal travel blog if you feel like it (see p.384 for more on that). For advice on buying a camera for your travels and practical tips on accessories, digital memory cards and image storage on the road, see ⓦadrianwarren.com.

Accessories

- Take a UV or skylight filter if you have an SLR camera, as the ultraviolet light in the tropics and at altitude can give an unnatural cast to pictures that makes them look washed out.
- Pack cleaning equipment, at the very least a little brush and air-cleaner, and use it daily: dust will quickly ruin both your camera and your pictures.
- Carry some silica gel with your camera lenses and film. This will absorb excess tropical moisture.
- Take spare batteries, as they're not always available in Asia.
- Consider taking a compact tripod.

Film

- Take a range of film speeds as the speed of the film determines its ability to cope with different light conditions. Much of Asia is very bright, so ASA100 film is generally fine. But for darker subjects, like a tropical rainforest, or the inside of certain temples, where you may be allowed to photograph but not use a flash, you'll need ASA400 or 800.
- You can buy print film all over Asia (though APS film is rare in remote regions), but slide film is less easy to find. Do not buy film

Picture etiquette

Remember that not everyone you see in Asia, no matter how photogenic, will want their photo recorded by you for posterity. Some tribal people in Indonesia and Thailand hate to be photographed as they believe that a tiny fragment of their soul dies with every snapshot taken; and for many orthodox Muslim women, to be photographed by strangers is almost tantamount to being indecently assaulted. You should therefore always ask before taking someone's picture – gestures can usually convey the idea.

Festivals and religious events may also be off limits, so check with local people first: masked festival dancers in Nepal believe they embody the deities during their performance, so taking photos of them is sacrilegious; and filming the sacred cremations in Varanasi, India, could easily get you lynched by mortified onlookers. Be equally sensitive when photographing temples, mosques and other shrines, and don't whip out your camera at an international border, airport or military checkpoint.

You'll even find that some people – like the Ifugao people in the Philippines, the Dani tribe of West Papua in Indonesia, and certain Nepalese sadhus – are now so used to having their pictures taken by tourists that they charge a per-picture fee.

that looks as if it's been stored in damp or humid conditions, and avoid film kept in a hot place or in direct sunlight.

● Many Asian baggage-check machines are film-safe. However, you should always pack your films (new as well as exposed) in carry-on baggage, as hold baggage gets a heavier dose of radiation, which can fog films. The higher the film speed, the more vulnerable it is to X-ray damage. X-rays are cumulative, so one X-ray incident isn't fatal, though if you are doing a lot of air travel consider keeping your films in a special lead bag (available from all decent camera shops), which will protect them from the rays.

Sharing digital images and developing film

A popular way of sharing your images with folks back home and with other travellers you've met along the way is to send them to an online photo company such as ⓦwww.kodakgallery.com or ⓦwww.snapfish.com. They upload your images on to a personal online album and will also print images and mail them to a home address. You can use these services for regular film via snail mail or by getting an Internet café to scan your developed prints and translate them into digital format. With digital images from cameras or phones you simply upload them, though you'll need to find a compliant Internet café first.

If you are using film, it should be processed as soon as possible after being exposed; a couple of months is fine, but you don't want films rolling about in the bottom of your pack for a year before getting them developed. Process-paid slide film can be sent air-mail to the processor for the pictures to be returned to a home address. If you decide to get film developed while on the road, you should definitely check the quality first, either by asking other travellers or by getting just one roll developed first. Sending either prints or negatives home is often a good idea, in case of loss, damage or theft.

Documents

Your most essential documents are your passport (with appropriate visas), airline tickets, travellers' cheques, credit card, and insurance policy. These should all live in your money belt (see p.260), which should be in permanent residence around your waist. Make two sets of photocopies of all your vital documents, including the relevant pages of your passport, your airline tickets, travellers' cheques receipt and serial numbers, credit card details and insurance policy. Keep one set of copies with you, but in a separate place from the originals (eg passport in your money belt; copies in your backpack), and leave the other set at home with friends or relatives in case of loss or theft. All the better if those friends or relatives have access to a fax machine, so they can get them faxed to you or the relevant issuing office straightaway. Some travellers recommend scanning all your important documents and then emailing them to your own web-based address, so that you can get hold of them almost anywhere on your travels, cybercafé availability permitting. If you want to do this, try it out before you leave home so you can make sure your documents convert into an attachment format that you can read online. For more on using email while you travel, see p.382. Alternatively, you could use an online system designed to do that for you, such as "intouch" (⊛www.roughguidesintouch.com).

Take an international drivers' licence if you're eligible, and a student card and international youth hostel card if you have them. Don't buy a hostel card just for the trip, though, as guesthouses tend to be cheaper and more convenient than hostels in most parts of Asia (Japan, Hong Kong and Singapore are the exceptions – see Chapter Eleven). In Bangkok you can buy fake student ID cards and press cards; no one will accept them in Thailand, but they may work elsewhere in Asia. Take eight passport-size photos with you to use for visa applications, visa extensions and any passes you might need to buy while you're travelling.

Your first night

There's nothing quite like a foreign airport for freaking you out and making you wonder why on earth you left home. Illegible signs, confusing instructions and crowds of unfamiliar people chatting incomprehensibly can be bewildering, even scary, especially when you've just spent a night without sleep. On top of all this, you'll perhaps be anticipating extortionate taxi fares, sleazy hotels and "friendly" helpers who turn out to be predatory touts or worse.

Rest assured, however, that even the most laid-back travellers find their first night in a new country a challenge, something that needs to be approached with a clear head and a sense of humour. After thirty hours on the move you'll probably be lacking both, so this chapter is designed to help you cope without them and ensure that your first experience of Asia is a positive one.

Planning your first night

If you follow only one piece of advice in this whole chapter, then it should be this: plan your first night before you leave home. The decisions and preparations you make in advance can go a long way to reducing the chances of trouble once you arrive.

Even if your aim for the trip is to wander where your fancy takes you, it isn't really advisable just to amble off the plane that first night in Shanghai, Singapore or Seoul trusting that something will turn up. It probably will, but the chances are you won't like it. So you should know where you are planning to stay and how you are going to get there.

As part of the planning, make sure you have all the right paperwork (tickets, passport and visas; see Chapter Two) and a rough idea of how long you intend to stay in the country – you may need to stipulate this on arrival.

Choosing where to spend your first night

Stage one is to work out in which area of the city you want to spend your first night or two. To have your destination clearly etched in your mind is absolutely essential, whether you decide to book ahead or just take potluck on the ground. Any reliable, up-to-date guidebook will help you decide (see Chapter Five), but here are a few extra tips:

- Choose an area that has a lot of budget hotels close together, so that if you don't like the first hotel it's easy to change to a different one.
- Pick an area that's close to the sights that interest you, and/or convenient for any

Down and out in Delhi

Three intrepid young men of my acquaintance set off for their year-long travels around the world, first stop Delhi, touching down at around midnight. In their enthusiasm to begin their adventure they abandoned their original plan to wait in the airport until daybreak and rushed outside to join the queue for taxis, which was a mile long. A driver and his friend approached from the side and offered them a cab. They accepted keenly: surely this would be better than hanging around waiting?

Once in the taxi they told the driver they had no idea where to go, but they needed a hotel. He knew just the place. Off they set through the dark Delhi streets. The first hotel was full. No matter, he knew another place. Yet more meanderings through the dark Delhi streets to learn that the second hotel too was full. They became concerned that he would charge them for all this useless ferrying around and pointed out they wouldn't pay for his mistakes. He replied it wasn't his fault and demanded the equivalent of $50 for the trip so far. Thinking this was too much they eventually, after a heated argument, handed over the equivalent of $30, suggested the cab driver and his chum called the police if they were unhappy, hoisted themselves and baggage into the dark Delhi streets and set off on foot. They flagged down a motorized rickshaw and, having learnt at least one lesson, asked how much it would cost to take them all to a hotel – forty cents! They loaded themselves and luggage aboard and were whisked away to an acceptable hotel where they got a bed for the night.

The next morning they were having breakfast and another foreigner approached them. He was leaving India; did they want to buy his guidebook? They definitely did. They read that the official fare from Delhi Airport to town was less than $8; they also found out about backpackers' places in the city. "Why didn't we buy one of these before?" they wondered.

Lesley Reader

onward transport connections you might be needing in the next few days.

- Check out how easy the area is to reach from the airport and, with the help of your guidebook, decide what method of transport you plan to use. Bear in mind that the cheapest options (eg some of the youth hostels in Hong Kong) may be significantly less accessible than pricier alternatives.

Once you've picked your area, draw up a list of three hotels you like the sound of, so that you have a ready-made contingency plan should one of them fall through. Consider booking in for two nights, which gives you your first day to sleep, clear your head and plan your next move. Plus, if the hotel's too expensive, or just not right, you've plenty of time to explore alternative options without having to repack your bags by midday and lug them round the neighbourhood.

Booking a room before you leave home

To be on the safe side, you can book your hotel before you leave home. Your guidebook should list phone, fax and/or website details of recommended hotels; alternatively, contact the relevant tourist office (see pp.19–153) to get some details of some places to stay. The only disadvantage of booking from home is the price. In Asia, the cheaper hotels and guesthouses rarely accept bookings without advance payment in cash (youth hostels are an exception; see p.417), so you will probably find yourself booking a more moderately priced room for your first night or two. But remember that prices are much lower in Asia than in Europe, the US and Australia, and that you can always move to a cheaper place later. Even though you may be planning to do your entire trip at subsistence level, your first night is not really the time to start – saving money takes time, local knowledge and quick thinking, and you'll lack all three when you first arrive.

Plenty of Asian hotels employ English-speaking staff, so you shouldn't have too much difficulty making yourself understood if you phone or email. Give them your flight number and the approximate time you expect to arrive at the hotel (allowing up to two hours to get through airport formalities, plus whatever time it takes to get into town) – and enquire about hotel courtesy buses as well. You might be asked for a credit card deposit. Once you've made your booking, confirm it in writing by mail, email or fax and take copies of all correspondence with you.

If you'd rather not contact the hotel yourself, you could either make your arrangements direct online, through Internet-based accommodation booking agents (see the Directory, p.417), or you could use a travel agent instead. Both these options could work out a little more expensive, as your choice will usually be limited to mid-range or expensive hotels.

The best budget option may well turn out to be the youth hostel, if there is one, in the city where you arrive. Some youth hostels can be booked from overseas using the Hostelling International websites (see the Directory, p.417). Women might also consider a homestay with a local woman for the first couple of nights: contact the Women Welcome Women World Wide organization (see the Directory, p.417) for details.

The plane journey

If you're coming from Europe or America, the flight into Asia is almost certain to be a long slog – NYC to Hanoi, for example, lasts a good thirty hours, while London to Mumbai takes at least eight. If you're doing things on a budget, chances are your journey will be convoluted, involving several touchdowns and possibly even a couple of long waits while changing planes. There's nothing you can do to speed the trip up, but here are a few suggestions on how to make it as bearable and comfortable as possible.

Hand baggage

Don't just throw all your backpack overflow into your hand baggage, but think about what you might need for the time you'll be in transit. If you pack too little into your hand luggage, you might freeze or go out of your mind with boredom; too much, and you might not be allowed to take it into the cabin (many airlines specify a 5kg maximum weight for hand baggage, while some others refuse anything that won't fit under your seat). Also, if you're wandering round transit lounges for several hours en route, you don't want to be dragging too much with you. Airlines also have stringent regulations about blades, knives and even nail clippers (and tweezers or lighters too, on occasion) – anything deemed a potential weapon in a hijack will be confiscated by airport security. A handful of airlines have a system of carrying such items for passengers and returning them at your destination but don't count on it; many simply confiscate the offending item at customs, and that'll be the last you see of your expensive Swiss Army penknife.

Handy items you might want to pack in your carry-on baggage include:

- Something to read (don't rely on the in-flight movies being riveting).
- A guidebook so you can plan your arrival strategy.
- Socks and a sweater. Even planes in tropical climates get cold when they're cruising at 36,000 feet; airline blankets are often in short supply.
- All valuables and fragile items, including your camera. Your checked-in baggage is not only more likely to go astray than your hand baggage, but is also treated much more roughly.
- Films. Checked-in baggage is subject to higher doses of security X-rays, which can fog film.
- Some basic toiletries, including a toothbrush: a quick wash and brush can improve how you feel very quickly and put that freshness back into your breath after a surfeit of airline food.
- Contact lens case and spare specs so you can sleep without waking to permanent haloes around your eyeballs.
- Moisturizer to combat the dry cabin atmosphere; cooling eye-gel, eye drops and a moisturizing face spray are stand-bys for many flyers for the same reasons.
- Chewing gum and/or sweets to help equalize pressure in your ears during takeoff and landing.
- A small bottle of water so you don't dehydrate either on the plane (you can fill it up from the water dispenser when you run out) or in transit lounges, where you might otherwise have to shell out for soft drinks in local currency. Even if transit lounge facilities accept hard currency, you will usually be given local currency as change, which is useless when you're heading somewhere else.
- Clothes appropriate for your point of arrival. In other words, it's a good idea to wear or take several layers of clothing so that you don't perish in your home country and boil when you arrive (or vice versa); also remember the modesty factor (see box on p.262).
- One set of clean underwear. You or your baggage may get delayed or separated and you don't want to be trying to buy new underwear on your first morning in Vientiane.
- Medicines. Include any medication you take regularly. A few

painkillers are a good idea, as flying is very dehydrating and headaches are common. Air sickness is not unusual: if you know you suffer, dose yourself with your favourite medication. If you don't know, but fear you might, put some in your hand baggage – they do take a while to work, but it's better to take them later than not at all.

- A pen, for filling in immigration forms.
- An inflatable neck pillow, eye shades and ear plugs if you're intending to sleep during the flight; these should effectively shut out the rest of the world and make sure you don't wake up with kinks like the Hunchback of Notre Dame.

You can of course fly with far more – a Game Boy and/or MP3 player or iPod, and snacks or more substantial food in case of delays, but also in case your appetite goes haywire on arrival (see p.295), causing you to venture out at 3am looking for munchies. If you know you're going to spend a few hours in transit at Singapore's Changi Airport, you might even consider including swimwear – the airport has its own swimming pool.

Checking in

At check-in you'll present your ticket and passport to the airline for inspection, and hand over your main baggage, which shouldn't weigh much if you take our advice in Chapter Six. If you haven't yet ordered your special meal, such as a vegetarian or diabetic option (see p.207), this is your very last chance, though don't bank on a positive outcome.

When you check in your bag, a baggage coupon will be clipped to your ticket or handed to you. Keep this safe. In the event that the worst happens, and you have lunch in London and dinner in Delhi but your baggage goes astray to Bangkok, you will need this counterfoil to complete the lost-luggage paperwork at your destination. You will also need the counterfoil if officials want to check that you are the owner of the bag. Some travellers slip a colour photograph of their case/rucksack into their hand baggage. If necessary you'll be able to show airport staff at the other end what is missing rather than struggle with descriptions in a foreign language at the end of a lengthy flight.

Due to increased airport security in recent years, many airlines specify that for intercontinental flights you should check in a minimum of three hours before departure. Some airlines may even require longer, so you should ask your travel agent, or call the airline in advance if you need to check. Whatever the minimum time given, it is advisable to check in as far ahead as possible.

Though it's a pain having to wait around for a couple of hours after you've checked in, the earlier you do so the more likely you are to get your preferred seat on the plane, which can make all the difference to your state of mind – and body – on arrival. If the plane isn't full, it is possible to change seats once you're on board, but it's much better to ask for what you want initially. If you have long legs, then go for the aisle seat, or make a special request for an exit-row seat where there are no seats immediately in front of you. Alternatively, the seats at the front of the cabin also have plenty of leg room, but you're likely to find yourself in among the babies as that's where the cots get put. Aisle seats have the advantage that you can get up and stretch your legs as often as you like without disturbing anyone, but you do get disturbed by everyone else in the row going in and out. A window seat, on the other hand, guarantees you extra in-flight entertainment: you get good views during takeoff and landing (some destinations are especially memorable – see box below), and the views can be extraordinary, particularly at sunrise or sunset, or during flights over mountain ranges (like those that dominate western Iran) or azure-fringed archipelagos (such as the islands of Indonesia) during daylight hours.

Memorable landings

Flights into parts of Asia offer some of the most spectacular scenery in the world:

- Planes arriving in Kathmandu of necessity make their descent within spitting distance of the soaring peaks of the Himalayas, including Everest.
- After flying across Sichuan's western mountain ranges, the landing at Lhasa seems like a miracle of faith over logic as the ground appears to rise up to meet the plane instead of the plane making a normal descent.
- The flight along the Himalayas towards Bhutan is spectacular enough, but the most remarkable part is the landing at Paro airport, as the plane twists and turns along the Paro valley, passing farms and temples on the cliffs on either side and finally the enormous medieval fortress, Paro Dzong, before crossing the river, apparently a hair's-breadth above the water, and eventually touching down.
- Flying in to the Philippines, you get a great view of the sparkling South China Sea and the seven thousand plus atolls that make up this island nation.

If you are a smoker, you might want to prepare yourself for managing without on the flight; it's increasingly difficult to find international carriers that allow smoking anywhere on the plane. And don't imagine you can creep off to the toilets for one – smoke alarms will alert the entire plane.

Coping with the flight

One way to ensure that the flight passes happily is to make full use of the in-flight bar service, offered free on most long-haul flights into Asia. Free drink can make the time go quickly, help you to sleep and calm your nerves if you're scared of flying. However, anyone who's ever got drunk on a plane will know just how magnified the usual side effects become. Your head aches violently, your heart pounds incessantly, and your body temperature soars to an unnatural high – not much fun. The other disadvantage of too much alcohol on the flight is that you'll arrive in Asia at your most befuddled, just when you need your wits about you. Whether or not you get drunk, alcohol exacerbates the dehydration which is a major cause of discomfort on long flights, so combat this by drinking lots of soft drinks and water. You'll be a regular visitor to the toilet on a long flight, but in any case it's a good idea to try and use the toilet before you get off at your destination. Tackling foreign public toilets with some or all of your baggage to worry about, and possibly having to pay for the facilities in local currency, is an avoidable extra hassle.

There is plenty of publicity about the health risks of flying, in particular DVT (deep-vein thrombosis), sometimes, erroneously, called "economy class syndrome". It seems to be related to long periods of immobility and dehydration, which make the blood flow in the legs slow to a level at which it pools and clots. This is painful but becomes life-threatening if a part of this clot then detaches and travels to the lungs where it can cause a lethal pulmonary embolism. A recent Australian study suggests that for healthy passengers with no other risk factors, the chance of DVT is about 1 in 40,000. Current advice suggests that to minimize the risks you should:

- Take exercise before and after flying, as well as during the flight. This speeds up circulation and cuts down the risk of blood pooling in the legs.

- Avoid sitting immobile for lengthy periods. Get up and walk around the cabin as often as possible – at least every two hours.
- Wear loose clothing – you don't want anything that will constrict blood flow to any part of your body, especially the legs.
- Even when sitting down on the flight do some calf-stretching exercises – these are detailed in many in-flight magazines or at ⓦwww.pharmweb .ie/dvt.htm.
- Avoid sitting with you legs crossed which can restrict the blood flow.
- Avoid sleeping pills – you'll be inert for hours.
- Do not get dehydrated – try to avoid caffeine and too much alcohol. and drink as much water or soft drinks as possible.
- Consider using "flight socks" which can help blood flow but need correct fitting.
- Discuss the flight with your doctor if you have any additional risk factors (previous DVT problems, or hereditary problems with blood coagulation, chronic illness, recent surgery, pregnancy, or if you are taking HRT or the oral contraceptive pill.
- Seek medical advice quickly if, after arrival, you develop pains in your legs, especially if your legs are swollen and especially if the pain is in one leg only. Breathing problems are a sign to seek urgent medical attention. In both cases be sure that doctors know you've been on a long flight.

Investigations are ongoing about the air quality in aircraft cabins and the extent to which air-conditioning systems can spread airborne diseases among passengers. However, there's no doubt that being in such close proximity to a few hundred people can put a strain on even the most robust immune system. Echinacea, available from most healthfood stores, is often recommended as a boost to the immune system to help ward off anything that comes flying your way.

Every now and again the media focuses on the phenomenon of "air rage" and we're treated to a flurry of stories of drunkenness, assaults and offenders dumped on foreign soil to find their own way home. Psychologists suggest that alcohol, stress, fear of flying, too little oxygen plus too much carbon dioxide in the cabin air and the fact that habitual smokers can't get their regular nicotine fix all lead to exaggerated human reactions which in some cases become extreme. Bear in mind that these types of incidents are rare though and if things do get out of control, the pilot has full power to land at the nearest airport and offload the offenders.

For a full description of the main health issues, take a look at ⓦwww.aviation-health.org, a campaigning organization which has an extremely thorough set of links to other sites of interest. One additional point, for divers – always leave at least twelve hours after a dive before flying, preferably 24 hours, especially if you've done multiple dives or a dive with decompression stops. The website listed above has more information.

The transit experience

Should you be turfed off the plane for a couple of hours' refuelling en route, or have to wait for a connecting flight, the transit experience doesn't have to be an unpleasant one, though sometimes you might just find yourself holed up in the transit lounge from hell: Moscow, for example, offers hard seats, dim lighting, no refreshments in the middle of the night, the most miserable cleaners in the Western hemisphere and, on occasion, resident refugees inhabiting cardboard boxes. On the other hand, some of Asia's airports are simply wonderful:

- Singapore's Changi Airport (ⓦwww.changiairport.com.sg) has a highly browsable English-language bookshop full of publications on Asia that you rarely see in the West. There's free Internet access throughout the terminal, a rooftop swimming pool and showers, and free two-hour city coach tours for transit passengers with sufficient time – there's a counter in the transit lounge and plenty of maps are available to help you locate things. The airport's transit hotel rents out rooms for short periods (with wake-up calls provided) so you can get some proper sleep.
- Kuala Lumpur International Airport (ⓦwww.klia.com.my) has the excellent *Airside Transit Hotel*, which rents out rooms for six-hour periods with toiletries, luxury towels and hairdryer provided. If you just need to freshen up, showers, a sauna and gym are also available.
- Jakarta's Soekarno-Hatta Airport is pleasingly laid out in pagoda-style buildings, connected by walkways that lead you through tropical gardens. There's a well-priced Asian food court and a *McDonald's,* too.
- Dubai's is a good airport – a huge white dome dominated by dramatic fountains, with shops selling reasonably priced duty-free electrical goods.
- Hong Kong's gleaming new Chek Lap Kok airport (ⓦwww .hongkongairport.com) has a relaxation lounge offering massage, hair-styling, manicure and hot showers.

- In the transit lounge at Osaka's Kansai International Airport (⊛www .kansai-airport.or.jp) you can rent therapeutic massage chairs that vibrate gently to ease away your in-flight stiffness. Lounges and showers are also available.

Many airports maintain their own websites (see ⊛www.azworld airports.com for links) which can provide useful information about the facilities. It's always worth asking your airline whether it is possible to pay to use the first- or business-class lounge – it's much quieter than the rest of the airport, the chairs are more comfortable and there'll be free coffee and newspapers.

At the other end of the scale, the website ⊛www.sleepingin airports.net provides pretty much all you'll need to know about the best (and worst) Asian airport floors and chairs on which to grab some sleep between flights.

Arriving

While some Asian international airports such as Tokyo have the look and the seamless efficiency to match anything in Europe, North America or Australasia, others, are more basic, although the days of grass landing strips and tin shacks operating as international airport terminals are largely extinct in Asia. Remember that airports the world over, even in your own country, can be soulless, confusing, intimidating places and certainly don't reflect the country as a whole. They are, literally, a rite of passage to be gone through by every traveller – ideally as painlessly as possible.

New arrivals are prime fodder for touts; you'll be amazed just how many services you can be offered in the short walk between customs and the taxi rank – hotels, hash, sex, diamonds, tour guides, you name it. The slightest flicker of interest, or even friendly eye contact, is encouragement enough to continue the

No harm in asking . . .

I was nervous about doing the big cross-Asia trip on my own, but as there was no one else to go with, off I went. Standing by the luggage carousel at Denpasar Airport in Bali (my first port of call), I got chatting to a couple of hip-looking American women, and asked if I could share a ride with them into town. It turned out we got on really well and we spent the next two weeks together, travelling as a threesome all round Bali. After that I was much more confident and happy to continue through Indonesia on my own.

Debbie King

encounter and if this is your first time in Asia, it will be written all over you, from your face to the way you walk. Not only do you feel vulnerable, but this is the time when you *are* most vulnerable. Much as you may hate to be unfriendly, in arrivals you should keep your eyes fixed unflinchingly forwards, your backpack strapped firmly to your back, and your plan of action bleeping loudly inside your head. It's a mad zone out there and right now you can't afford to be soft-centred.

Hopefully you're following our advice on p.206 and planning to arrive in daylight, so that you have plenty of time to sort out your ride into the city and your accommodation before it gets dark. A lot of the lowlife of any city emerges after sunset; with your senses and fears heightened by the shadows it is perfectly possible, and even sensible, to assume that absolutely harmless and helpful people are out to rip you off. If the worst comes to the worst and you do arrive in the middle of the night and don't know what to do, just wait in the airport until daybreak. The website ⊛www.sleepinginairports .net offers some useful advice on this.

Daylight or not, if you're on your own, think about linking up with other travellers who look as if they might be on the same budget as you and therefore heading to the same area of town – there's usually plenty of time to size people up in immigration and baggage collection queues. This will save money on taxi fares and will probably make you feel more confident about the whole arrivals procedure. Nonetheless, it makes sense to retain some healthy scepticism in encounters with fellow travellers, too.

Formalities

In general, the sequence of airport formalities is: immigration, baggage collection, customs, and then into the arrivals hall. If you follow the advice about paperwork given in Chapter Two, you shouldn't have too many problems, but the thing to bear in mind is to keep your cool, whatever happens: the queues may be a mile long, the officials may be obstructive and rude, the bags may take ages to arrive, but keep calm, be polite and don't get angry – showing your temper rarely works in Asia in any case. And, remember – you're on holiday!

It goes without saying, but we'll say it anyway. You shouldn't be trying to bring anything inappropriate into the country.

Most countries stipulate a duty-free allowance for alcohol or tobacco, some do not allow the import of certain food items and all prohibit the import of hard and soft drugs. In some Asian countries the penalty for smuggling drugs is death and lengthy jail terms are the norm in the remainder. It is up to you to find out what the regulations are in each country and obey them – guidebooks or the official government websites of individual countries are useful for finding this out.

Anarchists in the UK

The only time I've ever had trouble at immigration is when I went to Japan with my friend John. John is an archivist, which is what he told immigration officials when they asked. Unfortunately, they misheard, or at least misunderstood and, thinking he'd said "anarchist", hauled us both off for a thorough baggage check behind closed doors. Moral of that story: either give a simple version of your job title or make one up.

Bob Williams

Solo travellers should be especially vigilant when collecting baggage. Many a lone traveller has left their hand baggage on a trolley while lunging for their pack on the carousel only to turn around and find it gone. Keep at least one hand on your hand baggage at all times – even if it means sacrificing your trolley.

Changing money

Unless you managed to buy some local currency before you left home (see p.235), you'll need to change money before leaving the airport. Keep your eyes peeled for exchange facilities or ATMs as soon as you get off the plane, as some airports keep them hidden away on the air side of immigration, between the runway and passport control; you won't be able to re-enter this area once you've left, so change your money while you're passing through. Rates will probably be less favourable at the airport than in town, though, so you might want to change just enough for the first couple of days. These are a few other things to bear in mind:

● However hard it is to get your jet-lagged brain into gear, it is important to look at the exchange rate, work out how much local cash you should get, and check while you are still at the counter that you've been given precisely that – unscrupulous exchange counter clerks all over the world know that passengers just off long-haul flights aren't on the ball.
● Make sure you get plenty of small-denomination notes; you don't

want to start off arguing with a taxi or bus driver who has no change.

- Make sure you get and hold on to your exchange receipt. Because of the proliferation of black-market moneychangers across Asia, you will probably be asked to show at least one official exchange receipt when you want to change back leftover local currency at the end of your stay.
- Stash some of your cash in an easily accessible place so that you do not have to unzip your clothes and bare all to half the population of Kathmandu while trying to retrieve a taxi fare from your money belt.

Finding a place to stay on arrival

If you haven't pre-booked a place from home (see p.282), it's not too late. Many international airports have a counter for booking local hotel rooms, though these do charge a booking fee. The booking clerk rings the hotel and makes the reservation, then issues you with a voucher, which will either be the receipt for payment made at the counter or will specify the price you'll pay at the hotel. The clerk should also be able to advise you on the best way of getting there. The main drawback with this option is that only certain hotels – generally mid- to upper-range establishments – feature on these agents' booking lists and if they're not described in your guidebook, you won't have any idea of what the place is like until you get there.

△ Khao San Road guesthouse, Bangkok

If you're up to tackling the local telephone system and language, there is nothing to stop you ringing hotels yourself and finding a bed, although you should come armed with a list of options together with phone numbers – most public phones don't have directories. Remember to establish the price and make sure you get the hotel to hold the room for long enough for you to get there and claim it.

Probably the least desirable situation on your first night is to be tramping the streets with your pack on your back, looking for a place to stay. If, for whatever reason, this happens, then you should head for an area where there is plenty of accommodation so you'll have a few alternatives and short distances to tramp between places. This means that you need not be unduly concerned if the first place is full and your second closed down – particularly crucial if you arrive late in the day or if your visit coincides with the peak tourist season or a local holiday. For full details on accommodation, see Chapter Eleven. If there are two or more of you travelling together, it's easier if one of you sits in a café, bar or restaurant with the bags while the others do the trailing around to find a place.

Getting into town

The golden rule here is to put personal safety above everything, and that includes price. If you don't feel comfortable waiting an hour for a bus in a dark underground car park or sitting in an unlicensed cab on your own for forty minutes, then don't do it. You will have plenty of chances to save money later. On your first night, do what feels safe.

Airports always seem to be and often are a long way from where you want to go. Depending on where you are there may be a rail link (for example, Kuala Lumpur International Airport, Chek Lap Kok in Hong Kong and Narita in Tokyo), but more likely you'll be looking at road transport. The variety can be overwhelming: you might find motorbike taxis and three-wheeled sidecar taxis, air-conditioned limos and special luxury six-seaters, vans and family cars, and even cycle-rickshaws. Your most likely options for getting into town are:

- Official taxis. In some cases you join the taxi queue and get the next metered cab from the rank. In others there are prepaid taxi counters with fixed prices (often displayed on a noticeboard): you tell them where you're going, pay your money, collect a coupon that acts as a receipt (and may have your destination scrawled on it), and they find an official cab to take you. This is generally the most expensive but most reliable method: the cabs and drivers are licensed and, in theory at least, know the area well.

● Unofficial cabs. Touts for these hang about at most major airports and try to entice customers away from the official cabs. They may well be cheaper – providing you can haggle effectively over the price – but you'll end up at the mercy of a car and driver with no official recognition and uncertain local knowledge. *Always* agree the price before you get in.

● Courtesy buses. Many of the upmarket hotels operate courtesy bus services for their customers. If you are booked into a more expensive hotel, check whether this service is available.

● Airport buses. Many airports operate bus services, which are probably the most hassle-free and cost-effective means of getting into the city. Though slower than taxis, the buses usually have plenty of space for luggage, and often follow routes that are conveniently close to the main tourist and hotel areas. Sometimes you prepay your ticket inside the arrivals hall and sometimes you pay on board.

● Local buses. These are the slowest but the cheapest of the lot. You'll need to have small change to pay the fare and you should be prepared to be rather unpopular if you're hauling a mountain of luggage, even a small mountain, while commuters are trying to get to or from their workplaces. Some bus conductors might refuse entry if you've got piles of stuff; others may charge extra. Make sure you know where to get off! Our advice is to leave your first brush with Asian buses until the next day – at least then you'll have a better chance of seeing the funny side. For more on the delights of local buses see Chapter Ten.

Guidebooks are probably the best way to weigh up and check the price of your options but you might also like to take a look at the relevant airport website if there is one; see the links at ⓦwww .azworldairports.com. Getting this sort of information in advance is pretty vital: for example, it's useful to know that from Narita airport in Tokyo a ninety-minute, seventy-kilometre taxi ride into town will cost no less than $200/£115, whereas the sixty-minute train trip costs $11–28/£6–16 and the bus, which serves many of the downtown hotels, costs $25/£14.

Jet lag for beginners

You're wide awake and feeling peckish at 3am. Try as you might, your body just does not seem to understand that it's time for sleep right now. Though it's dark and most right-minded citizens of Manila are fast asleep, you're just not tired. Chances are you've got jet lag. It happens because we travel too far, too fast – in days of old when travellers went by land or sea, nobody suffered from the effects of zooming across lots of time zones and arriving at a strange time of day or night with their body clock still operating on home time.

Some of the possible effects of jet lag are disturbed sleep patterns, hunger pangs at weird times and severe fatigue and lethargy for several days. In general, the more time zones you go through, the worse the effects are likely to be. Received opinion says that for every hour of time change it takes a day to adjust (in other words, flying from London to Delhi should theoretically take you five and a half days to adjust). If you are exhausted before you leave home the effects are likely to be worse. The younger you are, and the less rigidly timetabled your life at home is, the more adaptable you're supposed to be.

Some people find that flights leaving home at night are better for minimizing jet lag, and that eastbound flights are worse than westbound (supposedly because your body clock adapts more easily to a longer rather than a shorter daily cycle). Also, being obliged to disembark during middle-of-the-night refuelling stops makes readjustment harder – try to find out if you'll be subject to this when booking your flight and perhaps try to find a different flight.

To combat jet lag you might want to try doing one, or all, of the following:

- Change your mealtimes to those of your arrival country a few days before you leave home. This is easier said than done if it means breakfast at 2am! The theory is based on the finding that the liver is the organ that takes the longest to adapt to the time change and by doing this you are getting the process under way before leaving home.
- Adopt the timetable of your new country as soon as you land there. In other words, go to bed at 11pm Manila time, not 11pm Eastern Standard Time. If you're dozy at 3pm, have an espresso or go for a run round the block, but whatever you do don't lie down and have a nap – doing so will only lead to your taking longer to adjust.
- Take a couple of strong sleeping pills an hour before local bedtime.
- Try melatonin tablets (not yet licensed for sale in the UK), an active herbal remedy treatment that dupes the body into believing it's night when taken at intervals.

- To avoid late-night hunger pangs, eat high-protein foods at breakfast and lunch, and high-carbohydrate, low-protein foods such as pasta at dinner.
- Do a short (five to ten minutes' worth), gentle exercise programme before bed. A few bends and stretches will get the kinks out of your body after the flight and help you wind down and relax ready for sleep.
- Try the aromatherapy method. A mix of geranium, lavender and lemongrass oils prior to travel should help you adapt, whereas geranium, camomile and lavender are useful after arrival. For further advice, consult Jude Brown's *Aromatherapy for Travellers* (Thorsons). Other complementary therapies, such as homeopathy, also offer remedies. It's worth consulting a practitioner for further advice.
- Switch on Star TV, the less-than-riveting Asian cable station.
- Soothe yourself with the thought that you'll be fully adapted in a couple of days, and meanwhile lie back and enjoy the coolness of the (very) early morning.

8

Culture shock

Do not be surprised if you don't enjoy your first few days in Asia. You might feel self-conscious, paranoid or just plain exhausted. You'll probably feel lonely and a bit frightened. You might even find yourself wishing you'd never come, hating the heat, sickened by the smells and appalled by the poverty. This reaction is quite normal and is called culture shock. Everyone experiences it in some form, and it's all part of the challenge of dropping yourself into an alien environment. The following are a few tips to help you acclimatize.

- Be kind to yourself for a few days after arrival. You may well be jet-lagged (see p.295), extremely tired, and overwhelmed by the unbearably hot and humid climate. Check out the tips on coping with tropical heat in Chapter Twelve.
- Venture out gradually. It takes time to find your bearings and get used to the ways of a new country. Start off by exploring the closer, more accessible places you want to see and save the more adventurous outings for later.
- Buy a decent map of your new city; you'll feel far more confident if you know where you are.
- However haltingly, try speaking a few words of the local language. It will make you feel much less alien and you might even make some friends. (See Chapter Five for some language-learning tips.)
- Do not feel obliged to have a completely "authentic" experience right from the start. If you feel like drinking milkshakes and eating

nothing but cheese sandwiches for the first few days, then why not? There'll be plenty more opportunities to experiment with local cuisine, so ease yourself in slowly.

And now for something completely different

Though your first brush with Beijing, Jakarta or Manila may be disappointingly banal – a Western-style cityscape of neon Coca-Cola ads, skyscrapers and middle-class office workers – it won't be long before you realize that the *McDonald's*-ization of Asia is only cosmetic.

Traditions run deep in Asia and, though urban fashions come and go, community life continues to revolve round religious practices and family units. From a Western point of view, traditional Asian values can seem stiflingly conservative, especially in relation to gender roles and social conformity. Many Asians find travellers' behaviour just as strange, not least because the whole idea of an unmarried youngster (or even a long-married oldster) sloping off around the world seems bizarre if not downright irresponsible.

Women in the traditional Muslim and Hindu communities of India, Nepal, Pakistan, Indonesia and Malaysia are encouraged to be economically dependent on fathers and husbands, and to keep a low profile in public, often hiding behind veils or scarves. This can be a shock to Western travellers, who will miss having contact with local women – and of course it has an effect on how local men see Western women, too. Asian men often address all conversation to a Western woman's male companion (if she has one), while solo women may be jeered at or worse. Advice on coping with sexual harassment is given in Chapter Fourteen.

Asia is the most populous continent in the world and your first bus ride in China or India will etch that fact indelibly in your mind. Crowds and queues are the norm and there's no point protesting when five more people try to cram onto an already overloaded share-taxi. Time to dust off your sense of humour and start a section on "quaint local customs" in your journal.

The same goes for the bureaucratic tangles involved in simple transactions like cashing a travellers' cheque, and for the haphazard timetables of most Asian buses. Indonesians have a great phrase for Asian timekeeping that translates as "rubber time" – sometimes it stretches, sometimes it doesn't.

Being an alien

As an obvious outsider (or "alien", as foreigners are known in Japan), you will arouse a lot of interest, for your novelty value as well as your commercial potential. What's considered nosy in the West is often acceptable in Asia, so try not to get offended by the unflinching stares, or by women stroking your oddly coloured skin and feeling your strangely fine hair. And, if you're blond-haired or black-skinned, get ready for movie-star treatment! Conversely, if you're of Asian stock yourself you might find you're treated with unusual suspicion, especially as a woman travelling with a white man – one of the many negative effects of the sex-tourism industry in Southeast Asia in particular.

Be prepared to answer endless questions about your marital status and also about your children: in most parts of Asia to be single is a calamitous state of affairs and to be childless a great misfortune. In fact, be prepared to answer questions about absolutely any private matter at all: how old you are, how much you earn and how much your air ticket cost are common conversational openers. People will read your letters over your shoulder, and eavesdrop quite blatantly, too, even if they can't understand what's being said.

Curiouser and curiouser

We've all been stared at and had our hair stroked and muscles squeezed before, but I do remember a rather more significant experience on a long-distance bus journey in Vietnam. We had a toilet stop after about two hours, and this "toilet" just so happened to be a very large open field. Naturally I was rather surprised to find a man standing only 10cm away from me in such a spacious latrine. As I was going about my business he certainly wasn't minding his, and he saw nothing wrong in leaning over and staring directly at my penis during my efforts to relieve myself. "That's OK," I thought and looked straight ahead as if I hadn't noticed. It was only when he bent over and started touching it and wiggling it that I really had trouble ignoring him. This unbridled curiosity and complete absence of the concept of privacy is one of the hardest things to adjust to.

Chris Humphrey

Sometimes it can be easier to lie about yourself – depending on who you're talking to, it may be less controversial to pretend that you're a Christian (or whatever), as agnosticism is incomprehensible to many Asian communities and atheism almost offensive. Lies can sometimes get you into more trouble of course, as the anecdote on p.302 illustrates only too well.

You may well be asked for your home address by complete strangers who like the kudos of collecting exotic Western pals, and you'll probably have your photo taken a few times, too – now there's a cultural somersault to make you think. In short, you're as fascinating to them as they are to you – and that must have some positive influence on global relations.

"Where are you going?"

It's amazing how quickly you tire of being in the public eye so much. One surprising irritation is being asked the same question

– in English – again and again. In India the line is nearly always "What is your mother country?", while in most parts of Southeast Asia it becomes "Where are you going?" The questions aren't meant to annoy, but are intended as friendly greetings: "Where are you going?" is simply the literal translation of "Hi!" or "How're you doing?" Just as in the West no one expects a full rundown on your state of health, no one in Asia really wants to know where you're heading; they just want to make contact.

Instead of getting irked by the constant chorus and more incensed still when they ignore your answer, try responding as local people do. In Indonesia, for example, you should reply "Jalan jalan", which means "Walking walking"; in Thailand "Bpai teeo" means "I'm out having fun"; and in Malaysia the even more cryptic retort, "Saya makan angin", literally translates as "I'm eating the wind".

On your best behaviour

However much you dislike the notion of being an ambassador for your country, that is how local people will see you. Similarly, your view of their country will almost certainly be coloured by how they treat you. So it pays for everyone to respect everyone else. No one expects you to traipse around Asia dressed in local fashions, but it is polite – and in some places expedient – to adapt your Western behaviour to suit the local culture. Because social rules tend to be more rigid in Asia, it's relatively easy for tourists to do the wrong thing – nine times out of ten, you'll be forgiven for being ignorant of the niceties, but there are a few behaviour codes you should definitely follow.

- In nearly all parts of Asia men and women dress modestly and find exposed flesh an embarrassment anywhere but the beach (and even when swimming they plunge in fully clothed in the more conservative countries). For more detail, see the box on p.262. Shoes are never worn indoors at home or inside temples and mosques, so remember to take them off in religious buildings and when entering people's homes – this includes some small guesthouses.
- Getting angry at anything is a very un-Asian thing to do. In fact, it's considered to be a loss of face and therefore an embarrassment for both the perpetrator and the recipient – a bit like being heard farting loudly in a posh restaurant. Always keep cool when expressing displeasure or making a complaint, trying to be as dispassionate as possible.
- Canoodling in public is frowned on in most parts of Asia (even Japan). It's quite common for friends of the same sex to wander about with their arms round each other, but passionate embraces with the opposite sex are considered rather gross, regardless of the couple's marital status.
- Throughout Asia, the head is considered the most sacred part of a person's body, and the feet are the most profane. Try not to touch anyone on the head (even kids) or to point at anyone, or anything, with your feet.
- Avoid making eye contact with members of the opposite sex – in some Asian cultures it's seen as an unabashed come-on.
- Take special care not to offend when visiting temples and mosques or attending religious festivals. Dress modestly, observe the behaviour of local devotees, and never come between people at prayer and their altar, or take photos without permission.
- Be sensitive when discussing religion and politics with local people. In most parts of Asia, a person's faith is inviolable and should not be questioned. Censorship is rife in some Asian countries and penalties can be severe for a resident who goes public with controversial views. This is very much the case in China at the moment, and in Tibet. Even in happy-go-lucky Thailand, anyone who makes disrespectful remarks about the king is liable to be put in jail. In India, on the other hand, opinionated political debate is standard fare on train journeys and in newspaper columns.
- For tips on avoiding embarrassing situations in Asian bathrooms, see Chapter Eleven.

Eating and food

Strange foods and bizarre eating habits are a major feature of the Asian experience, and can often be one of the highlights. After all, Asia is home to two of the world's greatest cuisines – Indian and Chinese – and you can be sure that tandoori chicken and Peking duck taste nothing like they do in the curry houses and takeaways of the West. Then there's the prospect of sampling real Thai food, regarded by nearly all travellers as one of Thailand's greatest assets. For some highlights of Asian cuisine so special that they're worth redesigning your itinerary for, see Chapter One. You will also probably encounter your fair share of unappetizing dishes and gut-wrenching cooking methods, but so long as you heed the advice on healthy eating and drinking given in Chapter Twelve you shouldn't go far wrong.

- Lots of Asian food is eaten with the hand (rather than a knife and fork). Sticky rice in Thailand is rolled up into tiny balls and then dunked in spicy sauces, and most meat and veg dishes in India, Nepal and Pakistan are scooped up with pieces of flat bread. Local people always use their right hand for eating because the left hand – which is used for washing after going to the toilet – is considered unclean (see Chapter Eleven). There's often a washbasin in the restaurant for

△ Street-food, Kathmandu style, Nepal

diners to use before and after eating, or at least a pail of water and a scoop.

- Chinese and Japanese food is eaten with chopsticks, as are noodles in all parts of Asia. But don't panic! Though it's a entertaining to watch a hapless tourist wrestling with the equivalent of two pencils and a slippery piece of spaghetti, most restaurant owners take pity on foreigners and offer spoons and forks as well.
- Asian dishes can be unbearably spicy – just one mouthful of a Lao chicken salad or a green Thai curry could be enough to send you hopping round the room in a blaze of oral agony. Water won't cool your palate down, but yoghurt is a great palliative, and so is beer, as both contain chemicals that dissolve the chilli oils. It is possible to retrain your taste buds to actually enjoy chilli-rich food (there really is such a thing as a "chilli high"), but if you can't face that, be sure to learn the local phrase for "not spicy, please".
- Despite the strong religious culture, vegetarians get a mixed reception across Asia. With nearly all its restaurants categorized as either "Veg" or "Non-Veg", India is by far the most veggie-friendly nation. Chinese chefs, on the other hand, regard meat-free meals as unbalanced and lacklustre. The best advice is to learn the phrase for "without meat or fish" (or, where relevant, the phrase for "I am a Buddhist") and to be prepared either to compromise when it comes to stocks and soups (which are nearly always made from fish or meat) or to eat mainly fresh market produce.

Some harsh realities

Poverty is a lot more visible in most parts of Asia than it is in the West, and in some places a lot more prevalent, too. Asia is home to some of the poorest people in the world, destitute people who live in slums or on street corners, who sometimes disable their own children so that they can be sure of earning something from street-begging. It is also home to some of the wealthiest people in the world, and the rich–poor divide is

The Mumbai Shuttle

The airport shuttle bus between Mumbai International and Mumbai Domestic drives through seemingly endless shantytown slums, a whole suburb constructed out of cardboard boxes, rice sacks and corrugated iron. As the bus slows down at traffic lights, the noses and outstretched arms of the people who live in these slums press against the bus window, chorusing "one rupee mister, one rupee". Travellers lock the windows shut and turn the other way. It's a distressing experience – and one that you'll have again and again in Asia.

Lucy Ridout

distressingly pronounced in many Asian cities – beggars congregate outside the most upmarket hotels, for example, and in places like Hong Kong it's hard not to be shocked by the sight of glossy banking headquarters built right next door to squalid tenement slums.

For Hindus, Buddhists and Muslims of all wage brackets, the giving of alms to the sick, the disabled and the very poor (as well as to monks and holy men) is almost an obligation, a way of adding credit to your karma. These donations serve as an informal welfare system, as in most parts of Asia there's no national health service or financial support for the unemployed.

Western tourists tend to be less used to dealing with beggars, and you would not be the first one to mask your discomfort with averted eyes and a purposeful stride. Giving is a personal decision, of course; you might prefer to donate to a charity instead, or to get actively involved with a local charity for a few days – see Chapter One for some suggestions. Supporting local small businesses is also a positive way of preventing the encroachment of poverty; see Chapter Nine for more about this. And it's always worth going out of your way to pay for small services – like giving kids in India a few rupees to stand in your bus queue for an hour, or agreeing to have your shoes shined by an elderly Malaysian man even though they don't really need a clean.

Bitter moon

Full moon over Hoi An, an ancient port town in Central Vietnam. I gazed off into the heavens from my café table; Hoi An had me feeling mystical. I smiled dreamily at nothing. Enter Don, all energy and intellect, clever not merely for his mastery of the English language, but for his sharp wit and precocious insights. He plopped into the empty chair across from me and I waited for the standard shoeshine pitch. Instead this beautiful 12-year-old boy asked me if I was in love. I pulled the picture of a new boyfriend (my "fiancé" for the trip) from my notebook. I kept the picture handy to ward off prospective suitors.

After twenty minutes of fluent chatter about Vietnam, America and tourism, it was clear that little Don had a crush. In the following days we shared discussions, lunches and laughs; he enjoyed practising his English and I enjoyed his energetic company. He took me to drink my first sugar cane and insistently paid for both drinks. It never occurred to me to ask Don where he got the money.

Later in my stay, I was out with a friend when we noticed Don. "Here comes my conscience," I laughed. My friend grimaced. "Don't look now, your conscience just disappeared with that German man." It was in that moment of rage and close-to-the-bone pain that I realized Don was a prostitute. He resurfaced a little while later with a fistful of money and disappeared into the night.

Andrea Szyper

Being a wealthy tourist

All over Asia, people will express amazement at the price of your air ticket – it will seem an absolute fortune to them. Regardless of how impecunious you are, or feel, to an Indian factory worker on less than a dollar a day or a Filipino waiter on the daily equivalent of $3, you are quite literally a millionaire. And your camera, watch and sunglasses will do little to change his or her opinion. Small wonder that Asians can't understand why travellers dress in torn and dirty clothing – surely if they can afford an air ticket they can stretch to a new outfit?

It's always worth trying to put money matters in context when people ask the price of your ticket, and to emphasize how hard you had to save to buy it. For example, your ticket probably cost you the equivalent of three months' rent, or about three weeks' wages. On the other hand, there's no question that you are comparatively rich – and that was probably one of the reasons why you chose to go to Asia (just as Arabs and Japanese choose to do their shopping in Europe).

Be aware that as a person with cash you can easily pump up local inflation just by paying over the odds for a taxi ride or even a mango. Traders then overcharge the next customer and so prices rise and rise. The worst-case scenario is when goods and services become so expensive that local people can no longer afford them and so traders start catering solely for foreigners. Ask locals about prices before buying, and do some bargaining – this is an age-old Asian practice and there's advice on how to do it in Chapter Four.

9

Responsible tourism

Culture shock works both ways and, with Asia playing host to tens of millions of tourists every year, it's impossible to overestimate the impact that the tourist industry is having on indigenous cultures. There is increasing awareness of this among travellers, and a number of global organizations are actively working to help minimize some of the negative cultural and environmental effects. The website of Tourism Concern (Ⓦwww .tourismconcern.org.uk), the main campaigning organization in the UK, features a short code of responsible practice for tourists, and the US-based Partners in Responsible Tourism (Ⓦwww.pirt .org) has produced similar guidelines. Both agree that the key to responsible travel is never to forget that the place we're holidaying in is someone else's home. Cultural sensitivity and environmental awareness are crucial.

In many cases much damage has already been done by multi-national corporations keen to profit from the lucrative tourist trade. One of the most alarming trends is the way in which big businesses squeeze out local enterprises and corner the market for their shareholders. It's not uncommon for villagers to be forced off their land because a major investor wants to build a hotel or a golf course there. Hotel complexes make a massive demand on

△ Porters in Nepal are particularly vulnerable to exploitation

local infrastructures and regularly wipe out village water supplies. In some cases, as in Burma, it is government officials who are forcing villagers to cooperate with their tourist projects. Many politically aware tourists are choosing to boycott Burma for this reason; see Chapter Fifteen for information on the Burma Campaign.

Individual travellers can do their bit to stop such exploitation by choosing to travel with socially aware tour operators; a good place to start is the *Good Alternative Travel Guide*, published by Tourism Concern, which lists and reviews a selection of locally run, community-based holidays in Asia and the rest of the world. For tourist businesses other than those listed in that book, however, be wary of confusing "ecotourism" with "responsible tourism". Many unscrupulous travel companies play on travellers' increasing desire to do the right thing and bandy around the term "ecotourism" to imply that they're a caring-sharing, environmentally responsible organization; what this often boils down to is that their trip features a walk to a waterfall or that their guesthouse is surrounded by trees. For details of general organizations concerned with encouraging responsible tourism in Asia, see the Directory, p.413.

Being culturally sensitive

- As a budget traveller, you're unlikely to be patronizing the *Hilton*s and *Sheraton*s of Asia – but you may be stopping off at *McDonald's* and *KFC*. Try to support local restaurants, shops and hotels instead. That way, profits stay within the community, local residents still have power in their own neighbourhoods and the place keeps its original character – which is, after all, what you've come all this way to experience.

- Try to eat local food, too, so that you're not promoting a two-tier culture: one for the tourists, another for the locals. It's in your interest, anyway, as local produce – including locally produced beer and soft drinks – is always much cheaper than imported brands.

- It's also important to support local initiatives when it comes to visiting ethnic villages, so that the people you go to see – such as the hill tribes of Laos, Vietnam and Thailand, the Dyaks of Kalimantan and Sarawak, or the Torajans of Sulawesi – profit from your curiosity. All too many tour companies advertise trips to see "the primitive people" without giving travellers any chance to communicate with them. The ethnic communities then become little more than human zoos and exotic photo opportunities (many Thai hill-tribe villages are a classic example of this). If possible, try to organize a tour with someone from within the community, or at least make a big effort to meet the people you've travelled so far to see. Tourism has a huge effect on these remote communities, thrusting them suddenly into a cash economy they have existed without for centuries.

- Some minority groups – like the Sakkudai of the Mentawai Islands off the coast of Sumatra – see tourist interest as a way of keeping traditions alive, of encouraging young people to learn the old ways. In Bali, too, young and old can now make a good living out of traditional performing arts. The difficult thing is for them to keep control of their own cultural heritage in an increasingly voracious tourist industry.

Just say no

One of the main tourist attractions in southern India is a six-hour boat trip along the narrow waterways of Kerala. Local kids are so used to the tourists that they now race, in relays, along the river banks yelling "One pen, one pen" at the boats. What began as a game on the boat that I took soon turned into a depressing case of bear-baiting as the tourists started to chuck pens into the water just so the little boys would dive in to grab them. The kids were just normal village boys, not destitute slum-dwellers, but they knew they could get some trinkets if they "performed" for the tourists – and that's how a demeaning relationship between locals and tourists begins. Though it's natural and generous to want to give little presents, the last thing you want to do is create a culture of beggars.

Lucy Ridout

- Think about ways in which you might be able to help local communities. The more rural and remote the more likely they are to benefit from your contribution. Buying local crafts in the places they are made, tipping the room boy a few cents, and engaging a local guide are just a few examples.

- However, it is vital not to exploit those who are so desperate to earn anything at all that they will agree to the job however meagre the pay offered and however demanding the conditions. This is especially applicable to porters in Nepal, where the International Porters Protection Group (⊛www.ippg.net) advises trekkers on how not to collude in this abuse. See p.101 for more details.

- Religious buildings and events are minefields for the culturally unwary. For example you should never climb on Buddha statues, allow yourself to sit or stand above a Hindu priest, or enter certain temples when menstruating. And you may need to dress in a particular way, too; see Chapter Six for advice on that. Any good guidebook will tell you about such taboos, so be sure to read that section before arriving.

- Be sensitive when taking photographs: not everybody wants to end up in your photo album. Ideally get to know people before you take pictures; at the very least ask permission. Some scenes are utterly taboo – cremations on the banks of the Ganges for example. See box on p.277 for more advice on picture etiquette.

Being environmentally aware

- As a responsible tourist, you should also try to minimize your impact on the environment. In practice, this can mean anything from being careful about rubbish disposal – in particular, don't dump non-biodegradable stuff like plastic bags and bottles and dead batteries in rural areas – to sticking to marked trails when you're hiking. Advice on getting involved in conservation projects in these areas is given in Chapter One, and there's a list of relevant organizations in the Directory on pp.415–417.

- The Himalayas have suffered a lot from inconsiderate trekkers, but there are several ways in which you can minimize your impact. The Kathmandu Environmental Education Project (⊛www.keepnepal .org; see p.101) publishes suggestions on how to trek without doing more harm than good.

- Coral reefs throughout Southeast Asia have also become degraded as a result of increased tourism. Reefs are extremely fragile and slow-growing ecosystems, so thoughtless snorkellers and divers have a huge impact when they tread on reefs and break bits off to take home. Souvenir-buyers have encouraged local fishermen to do the same on a larger scale, so don't fuel the trade by purchasing pretty shells and bits of coral.

- Keep your wits about you when shopping for other souvenirs, too. Many endangered species of animal and plant are (illegally) killed and harvested so that they, or bits of them, can be sold to tourists as mementos or medicines. Animal products on sale across Asia include ivory (from elephant tusks), tortoiseshell, and the body parts of bears and tigers. See p.405 for more on organizations that are seeking to safeguard animal populations across Asia.

- If you're very saintly you will also avoid buying bottled water – which creates tonnes of unrecyclable plastic waste every year – and filter your own from tap water instead (see Chapter Twelve). As a bonus, this more than covers the cost of a water filter after just a few weeks of travel. A compromise option is to make use of the drinking-water refill service offered in some tourist centres.

- Aeroplanes produce a huge amount of carbon dioxide when in flight – a major factor in global warming – so several organizations offer you the chance to make up for this environmental damage by donating to a green cause: see Ⓦ www.climatecare.org and Ⓦ www .futureforests.com.

- Behave as though you were paying the utility bills yourself wherever you are staying: don't waste resources.

10

Getting around

Travelling in Asia can be wonderful and frustrating, often at the same time. As the entire continent is teeming with people, so it is teeming with the means of getting them around. It's not so much a matter of discovering whether the journey you want to do is possible or not, but a question of deciding if it's better done by plane, train, high-speed ferry, slow boat, shared-taxi, tourist bus or local bus. The huge plains of India and China are perfectly suited to rail travel; the mountains of Nepal and northern India dictate road

△ Tsangpo river crossing in Tibet (see p.327)

and air travel; and the island states of the Philippines and the huge Indonesian archipelago, the mountainous jungle rivers of Borneo and the mighty Asian waterways of the Mekong and Yangzi are served by ferries and boats of all shapes and sizes. Within some cities you even have the option of rickshaws and bullock carts.

However, this exciting variety needs to be set against discomfort, lateness, some of the most terrifying driving on the planet, and unreliability, all enduring characteristics of Asian transport. Look on the travel itself as part of your adventure and you'll stand a better chance of keeping it in perspective. One way to do this is to allow plenty of time to get around. Delays are inevitable at some point, and you'll be far less stressed if you've allowed for them in your schedule. The golden rule is that distance is not an indication of the time needed for a journey.

Even within individual countries the variations can be huge and you shouldn't make too many assumptions. There may not always be a direct service between two points, for instance; instead your journey could involve two painfully slow local buses, a ferry and a rickshaw. On the other hand, trips that you assume will be unexciting can turn out to be extremely memorable. The Shimla Toy Train, for example, winds its way through the Himalayan foothills in northern India from Kalka up to the hill station of Shimla, while you sit on board in armchairs, reading the morning newspapers and sipping tea served by uniformed waiters.

Despite initial impressions in some cities, car ownership is not widespread; instead, bicycles, mopeds and scooters are common but the majority of Asians rely on public transport, and though systems may appear hideously complex and grotesquely overcrowded, they are cheap and often far more comprehensive than services at home. Be sure to check your guidebook for the journey you want to make and, if you are fascinated by the adventure of it all, take a look at the *Thomas Cook Overseas Timetable: America, Africa, Asia, Australasia* (Thomas Cook Publishing), available in good travel bookstores, which details some of the trains and ferries across the globe; the sheer enormity of the possibilities makes for exhilarating reading.

Planes

Most countries have an internal air network of some sort and many have several; budget airlines are springing up across the continent, increasing choice further. Air is the fastest, but also the most expensive, way of getting around, with the added disadvantage that you are flying over the country rather than exploring it. Still, when it's too much to contemplate the sixty to a hundred hours (it can take far longer) the bus takes to do the bone-rattling 1800-kilometre Trans-Sulawesi Highway in Indonesia, spending a few short hours doing the same route in the skies looks decidedly appealing (and excellent value at around $50/£29). If the thirty-hour train trip between Beijing and Guangzhou is more than you can bear, then the three-hour plane journey begins to look attractive at $130/£74. It's also worth remembering that in some countries a short plane ride can flip you into the wilderness, which might otherwise take days or weeks to reach. For example, the forty-minute flight between Kathmandu and Lukla in the Everest region can save you an extra five to seven days' walking, and access to many of the highland valleys of West Papua is virtually impossible without flying. Bear in mind that air fares are generally a lot lower than at home, so don't rule out buying plane tickets once you've arrived, especially if time is tight.

Several airlines offer internal air passes at good rates to tourists; these are definitely worthwhile if you are intending to cover a lot of ground quite quickly. Check the website ⊛www.airtimetable .com/airpass_asia.htm for a roundup of what is available. For example, Indian Airlines (⊛www.indian-airlines.nic.in) offers one-, two- and three-week Discover India passes for $400, $600 and $850. There are conditions attached to these passes but with one-way fares from Delhi to Varanasi at $135, Chennai to Kolkata $245, Mumbai to Varanasi $245 and Delhi to Chennai $285, it is easy to see that significant savings are possible. Even so, shop around; another Indian carrier, Jet Airways (⊛www.jetairways.com), offers a range of Visit India passes with one-week pass costing just $320. Other passes worth checking out include Discover Thailand with Thai Airlines (⊛www.thaiair.com) and the All Nippon Airways Pass (⊛www .anaskyweb.com).

Within Asia some airlines have formed alliances to offer more extensive passes, for example Bangkok Airways, Siem Reap Airways and Lao Airlines offer the Discovery Pass with coupons at $50 for internal sectors ie within one country, and $80 or $150 for international sectors. The ASEAN Pass is sold by national airlines in Brunei (Royal Brunei Airlines), Indonesia (Garuda), Malaysia (Malaysia Airlines), the Philippines (Philippine Airlines), Singapore

(Singapore Airlines), Thailand (Thai International Airlines) and Vietnam (Vietnam Airlines) and allows you to buy three to six flights within and between those countries for $130/£74 each.

Other airlines restrict their concessions to travellers who have travelled into the country with them, such as Malaysia Airlines' Discover Malaysia Air Pass, which currently costs $199 for five internal flights. Garuda offer the Visit Indonesia Pass with sectors varying between $70 and $175 depending on distance.

If you are thinking of buying an air pass, it pays to do your research in advance as many passes need to be bought before your arrival, or have conditions attached to their use; you'll also want to find out how much the flight would cost if you bought it locally. At certain times, national airlines may even offer a free internal flight or two to tourists travelling internationally with them; check what deals are available at the time of booking your international tickets.

When using Asian airlines, the following tips should make your trip easier:

- Some of the airlines flying internal routes are small setups with minimal backup both on and off the ground. Don't expect quite the organization or efficiency of airlines at home.
- It's worth avoiding certain domestic Asian airlines that have poor safety records; check with your embassy or ⓦwww.airsafe.com, which lists safety records of many Asian airlines, before you book.
- Make bookings in person and get confirmation in writing, especially if your ticket will be issued later. Take a note of the name of the person you dealt with, in case of problems later.
- Don't let the booking office keep your passport overnight – it can be useful to have photocopies of the key pages ready for them.
- Having booked a seat, you often need to reconfirm with the airline before travel. Check the rules when you book.
- If the airline seems to have lost your booking despite all the evidence you can produce, get them to look under your first or even your middle name, as misfiling is common.
- Some airline offices find it virtually impossible to issue confirmed tickets for flights from a city other than the one they are in. If you get a ticket under these circumstances, be sure to reconfirm with the airline when you get to the place you'll be flying from.
- Flights are often overbooked, cancelled or delayed at short notice due to monsoons, typhoons, heavy snowfall or lack of aircraft. The more flexibility you can build into your timetable, the better.

- Check in as early as possible; if flights are overbooked, boarding passes are often given out on a first-come, first-served basis.
- Follow the advice on hand baggage on p.283 – just because a flight is internal doesn't mean you can't get delayed and/or your baggage lost.
- Certain items are banned on Asian planes. Penknives and Swiss Army knives are often confiscated and some items are banned not because they could be dangerous but because they smell so bad – the durian fruit and fish sauce are the most notorious.

Long-distance buses

Bus travel in Asia is one of the most intense experiences the continent has to offer: all of human life is jammed together, often with a few animals as well, passing through the landscape slowly enough to appreciate it. Inside, many drivers personalize their vehicles with pictures of their favourite gods and goddesses, flashing fairy lights and an incense stick or two on the dashboard. For some drivers the bus is even their home and they eat and sleep on board when it's not in use.

The quality of buses, however, is very variable – the best ones feature air-conditioning, comfortable reclining seats and toilets on board; the worst have cracked or missing window glass, ripped seats and minimal suspension. Some "bus" services are even operated in trucks, rather than anything you would identify as a bus at home. Try to look at the bus before you book a seat, whatever the ticket-seller may tell you about his pristine speedmobile that will whisk you to your destination faster and more safely than any other operator's. The back seats are the bumpiest, the front seats give a grandstand view of the driver's technique and an earful of his choice of music and/or video. The most modern long distance buses have toilets on board but if not there are toilet stops, sometimes at restaurants with facilities, otherwise in the countryside en route (men go in one direction, women in another; pretend not to see anybody and bring your own toilet paper – which you'll need to burn or take away in a plastic bag afterwards). A long skirt can be useful for women travellers to keep their modesty intact in these situations. Regular food stops are usually scheduled at restaurants favoured by the driver but choices are often limited and you'll need to eat fast – it's a good idea to stock up on snacks before any long journey, plus plenty of drinking water.

Many cities have separate bus stations for local and long-distance destinations, and the larger the city the more likely it is to have several long-distance terminals, often on opposite sides of town, far from the city centre – Bangkok, Ho Chi Minh City, Jakarta and Beijing are among the most confusing. A good guidebook will provide you with enough information to orientate yourself and get into town, or vice versa.

Tickets are extremely economical when compared to travel at home – for example, a 32-hour trip between Jakarta and Lombok in Indonesia costs about $27/£16, the 989km 24-hour journey between Manila and Davao in the Philippines will set you back $24/£13, and in Cambodia the ten hours between Phnom Penh and Siem Reap costs $6/£3.50 or $2.50/£1.50, depending on whether you want to ride inside the cab or in the back of the pick-up truck. In many cases your ticket will includes a ferry crossing or two between neighbouring islands.

However, it can sometimes appear totally impossible to get a ticket or seat on a bus – there are just too many people and they are all far more adept at forcing their way through the crush than you. You could try booking through an agency for a small fee (often your accommodation will do this for you). As departure time gets close you could also consider paying a small boy to climb through a bus window and occupy a seat for you until you can get to it.

Asian buses are built for generally smaller Asian physiques, so don't underestimate the stamina needed to cope with several days and nights jammed on board. Consider booking two seats if you are quite large in any dimension and can afford it, although you'll have to be pretty assertive to keep both seats to yourself as the bus gets steadily more packed along the way. In countries with extensive train systems – India and China are prime examples – it's usually faster and more comfortable to do long-haul trips by train.

Tourist buses

In some countries where the tourist infrastructure is developing, private companies have started operating special tourist bus serv-ices exclusively for foreign visitors. On these buses, there's often plenty of space for luggage, including pushchairs and wheelchairs, though in other respects the vehicles themselves aren't particularly different from regular buses – many aren't even air-conditioned.

However, they do offer a direct, hassle-free, though generally more expensive, service between main tourist centres. To get from Kuta to Ubud on Bali by public transport, for example, you have to change at least three times in a part of the island where routes are especially confusing, but a tourist bus will get you there in one go for around three times the ordinary fare. In Nepal, tourist buses that ply between the main tourist destinations are generally safer than local services and have bigger seats. It pays to do some research, though – on the more straightforward routes you'll be paying a lot for very little benefit. In Thailand some of the tourist buses are actually cheaper than the government buses and have tourist-friendly pickup and drop-off points (in the main accommodation areas, for example). However, their safety record is poor, and many have a reputation for aggressive and even thieving staff; ask other travellers' advice before buying a ticket and check what your guidebook has to say.

Room on top

It is important to have the right attitude when travelling Asian-style, eg hanging from the side of a vehicle, teetering from the top like a flagpole in the wind or – if you are lucky enough to be inside – cramped in a fetal position with your knees in your face. These situations need meditation; releasing the mind from the perils of travel is an absolute necessity for psychological survival.

We'd stepped on a few hands on the climb to the last free spaces – on the roof – but the other passengers didn't seem to mind. It took a few minutes to get the overstuffed truck moving at a reasonable clip down a one-lane road with barely a shoulder on either side and a sheer drop into the marshlands. I hoped the luggage I was holding onto was firmly attached to the roof. Several times as we moved over to the side of the road we tipped until I could see my reflection in the water all too clearly. I figured if the truck rolled over I'd be fine in the water – until the truck and other passengers landed on top of me. Swaying like a willow tree in the wind, the vehicle recovered again and again from potentially disastrous situations and continued on its way in its charmed state of existence.

Shannon Brady

Is it safe?

There is no escaping the fact that much road travel in Asia is extremely hair-raising. Buses often travel far too fast for the conditions – overtaking on blind corners is a regular occurrence – and drivers frequently take some form of stimulant to stay awake as a lot of long-distance services travel at night. Not surprisingly, accidents are common – the English-language newspapers in

Karma armour

Most Asian people have a rather more fatalistic approach to accidents and misfortune than we do in the West. We are increasingly of the view that we can, and indeed have the right to, control anything nasty happening to us. In contrast, Buddhists and Hindus believe in karma, whereby a previous existence influences the events in their current life. Thus a traffic accident is more likely to be seen as preordained karmic retribution than a direct result of irresponsible driving. Muslims presage most plans with the word *Inshallah* ("if God wishes"), showing they accept that they do not have ultimate control over the future. This can be infuriating or even downright terrifying if you're on a bus with a maniac driver who seems intent on killing you all. It's unlikely that any of the other passengers will try to moderate any lunatic behaviour; you may want to try, or even get off and wait for the next bus.

Asian countries will report major smashes, especially if there is a tourist among the casualties. Remember that even once you've bought a ticket you can still decide whether or not to climb on board any particular bus. If you're seriously concerned about your own safety during the journey, you might be wise to get off at the earliest (safe) opportunity, regardless of how far you are from your intended destination.

Enjoying the journey

These suggestions may improve your journey:

- Baggage is often put on top of the bus where there may well be other passengers riding alongside it. As a security measure, you might consider chaining your pack to the roof rack (see p.258 for more) so you won't be anxiously craning your neck out of the window at every stop to see if your stuff's still there.
- Make sure you have plenty of water, food and toilet paper. Stops are often at weird times when you may not want to eat and at places with limited facilities.
- Consider packing earplugs, as Asian buses usually travel with music or videos turned up full volume for the entire length of the journey.
- A neck-pillow is an excellent idea on long bus journeys – much better than jolting up and down on the shoulder of the person next to you.
- A blanket, sarong or jacket is useful for warmth, especially on overnight trips.

- However uncomfortable, you should keep your money belt on and well hidden: you are vulnerable when sleeping, and theft isn't unknown.
- Never accept food or drink from strangers – this can be a means of drugging travellers before robbing them.

Trains

Trains offer a memorable and often safer means of travel across large tracts of Asia. Although often distressingly crowded and rather

△ New Delhi railway station, India

dirty, especially in the cheaper classes, train travel, like buses, thrusts you into the company of local people. You'll get brilliant views, too: the sun setting over rice paddies in central Thailand and southern India; soaring cliffs and white-sand beaches along the coast between Da Nang and Hué in Vietnam; and dizzying drops between the peaks en route from Peshawar to the summit of the Khyber Pass.

When booking a train ticket, make sure you know whether the

Hard seat hell

We boarded the train to Chengdu and our expectations for the coming journey were high. We were well stocked with fruit, chocolate and enough biscuits to see us through the coming twenty hours. We were also naively optimistic about the chances of upgrading our seats.

Tickets for hard seats were the only ones available. No amount of charm, joviality or bare-faced begging could persuade our stony-faced ticket vendor to part with the more comfortable hard sleeper or even the ludicrously overpriced soft sleeper options usually reserved for party cadres. "No," he informed us, "no have."

Later we discovered that a hefty hard-currency "present" would have secured a comfortable passage. Instead I waited in vain for a nonexistent legitimate bed to become available at the "next station . . . next station . . . next station". Sweat mingled freely with grime and smoke as the day turned into night and day again. My companions slept and my frustration and anger rose, aided by the neighbouring cherubic Chinese child clearing his sinuses, gulping and with an almighty hoik landing a dribble right on top of my big toe. His father looked on proudly.

Daniel Gooding

service is a stopping one or an express. Stopping services can stop at literally every sign of human habitation, even during the night. While these slow trains are a lively experience with plenty to keep you entertained, they can take twice as long as the express without a corresponding halving of the fare.

You don't necessarily have to wait until you are in the country to get train information. For example, Indian Railways, one of the most remarkable setups in the world, shifting over 11 million passengers daily, has a website (www.indianrailways.gov.in) supplying information on the entire network (in English or Hindi) in as much detail as anyone could need. Check out The Man in Seat Sixty-One (⊛www .seat61.com) for advice on train travel across the globe.

The security issues on trains are pretty similar to those on long-distance buses, except that you'll have all your stuff with you and your fellow passengers have more chance to move around. In addition to the tips on p.320, the following may help: lock your bags and padlock them to something immovable, like the berth or seat and keep small bags away from windows so they can't get rifled at stations. Solo women travellers in India and Pakistan may feel more comfortable in women-only compartments, especially on long trips.

Tickets

Ticket options vary from system to system – Indian Railways has seven different classes, and prices for those classes vary depending on what type of train you are on – but you'll usually have a choice between hard and soft seats or berths and between carriages with and without fan and air-conditioning. Generally, the longer the trip, the more advisable it is to go for a bit of comfort.

Fares are good value, with the very cheapest seats often the same price as the equivalent trip on a bus. For the twelve- to eighteen-hour journey between Beijing and Shanghai, expect to pay from $25/£14 to $62/£36 depending on the speed of the journey, while in Vietnam, the two-day haul from Hanoi to Ho Chi Minh City on the *Reunification Express* costs $36–59/£21–34 depending on the class you choose. On Indian Railways you have a choice of comfort and price, which is calculated on distance, class of travel and type of train. In unreserved second-class compartments it costs Rs103 ($2/£1) per thousand kilometres on the slowest type of train, rising through a huge number of intermediate classes to Rs3160

($73/£42) per thousand kilometres for air-conditioned first-class on the fastest expresses.

Getting hold of a ticket can be a major hurdle; long-distance, sleeper and first-class travel invariably need to be booked several days in advance (short-hop and third-class tickets can often be bought on the train). Although foreigners' ticket offices can cut down hassle in larger cities in China, Thailand and India, and women-only queues in India can help, you may spend hours fighting your way through a mass of people only to find the train you want is already fully booked. Many travel agents and hotel staff can buy tickets for you for a small fee – this is money well spent. You won't find many ticket barriers on Asian rail networks (Japan is an exception), but your ticket will be checked on board, often several times.

Train passes

Train passes are available for travel in India, Thailand, Malaysia and Japan. Check the details before you leave home as most rail passes are only available outside the country. Consider the individual passes carefully to work out whether they are good value or not. Thai and Malaysian passes may not be worthwhile unless you're travelling a great deal and you'd need to travel far to make India's Indrail Pass – available for periods of one to ninety days first- or second-class – financially worthwhile, the chief advantages being that it saves you queuing for tickets, gives priority for tourist quotas on busy trains and allows you to make and cancel reservations free of charge. On the other hand, the seven-day version of the Japan Rail Pass pays for itself in just one return trip from Tokyo to Kyoto and the fourteen-day pass with a Tokyo–Hiroshima return plus a couple of stopovers on the way.

Sleepers

Remember that if you book a sleeper service you'll be saving on accommodation costs, so it can be worth splashing out to get a good night's sleep. The sleeping areas usually consist of two or three tiers of bunks that may run the length of the railway carriage or be broken up into compartments by curtains or hard walls. Top bunks are marginally cheaper in some countries (China, for example), and are the safest for your luggage, but cigarette smoke tends to gather

Top train rides

- The Death Railway – so called because thousands of the World War II prisoners-of-war who built it died during its construction – from Kanchanaburi to Nam Tok in Thailand is a stunning feat of engineering. The track was blasted through mountains and rock faces and traverses numerous amazing bridges, passing along and over the River Kwai and stopping at flower-bedecked villages.

- The most scenic way of getting to Ooty, the former colonial outpost in India's Blue Mountains, is to take the Toy Train, a coal-fired, narrow-gauge, three-carriage antique that travels at around 11km per hour. You're treated to gorgeous views of the hills as you pass through forested slopes and tea plantations.

- The steam railway that links Peshawar and the Khyber Pass in Pakistan, passing through dramatic, barren tribal land, is pretty unmissable. The British-built railway has 34 tunnels and 92 bridges along its fifty-kilometre route, and is so steep in places that trains need another engine at the back to push them up.

- If money's no object, consider treating yourself to a ride on the *Eastern & Oriental Express*. This deluxe train is modelled on the original *Orient Express*, with wood panelling, cordon-bleu meals and first-class service throughout the 52 hours it takes to travel from Singapore via Kuala Lumpur and the River Kwai to Bangkok, at a cost of around $1725/£990 per berth. It also does a shorter, cheaper run between Bangkok and Chiang Mai for $1010/£580.

- With an average speed of 261.8km/hr, the *Nozomi-503* is the fastest train in the world, and also one of the smoothest. It's the star of the famous fleet of Japanese bullet trains or *shinkansen*, and races along the 895km coastal route from Tokyo to Hiroshima in just four hours.

- The railway from Golmud in China to Lhasa was started in June 2001 and its completion date remains uncertain. Eventually it will be 1142km long, with 960km of it over 4000m, reaching 5072m at its peak. The carriages are to be pressursied to cope with the altitude.

up there and you may be next to a blaring radio, a light that stays on permanently, or right under a fan, which can be chilly. On the bottom bunks you'll often get people sitting along the edge and talking, smoking, eating and playing cards while you try to sleep. Thai trains are a pleasant anomaly – staff fold sleepers down out of the seats at night and make them up with fresh linen for you. Sleeping compartments can get surprisingly chilly at night, so remember to keep your warmer clothing handy. In India you can rent extra bedding very cheaply on board.

Monsoon miracle

Thai ferries are always full and always run on time, or close to it. Broken gadgets are usually repaired with random pieces of wire, shoelaces or just held together manually. This is the miracle of Thai transportation. You're always going somehow – storms, rain and floods be damned. I hopped on the boat headed for Ko Tao. As we waited for passengers to board, I established myself on a wooden bench and watched a Thai official remove all the life jackets on board. I breathed deeply. My blind faith in Thai efficiency kicked in – we'd get there somehow, sometime. It began to rain and off we went. We dipped and trundled into the open sea, away from land, warm hotel beds and everything safe. After half an hour we encountered not waves anymore, but swells the size of two-storey buildings which rocked and crashed our little ferry from side to side, playing with us as a cat might bat a mouse around the room. We were reassured by the crew when the engines cut for a spell that it was only engine trouble, nothing more. I sat on my bench and attempted to read as water crashed through the doorways onto backpacks and eventually onto me.

The swells grew higher, meaner and quicker. Book forgotten, I looked at my white knuckles, straining to keep my body on board and in an upright position. Around me, the other passengers held on as I did to whatever they could to prevent themselves from being catapulted out of the boat. I thought of my mother. She'd be devastated to learn of my demise. No glory, no excitement. Another drowning in a raging sea. My story would end up in the obscure international section of newspapers.

Our prospects looked grim. So I began to pray and remembered, as words failed to flow, that I knew no prayers whatsoever. I wished I had been raised in some religious setting. Nonetheless, I continued: "Holy Mother of God," I chanted, "please save us." And after one hour she did. I watched the swells change from assaulting us head on, to broadside, to coming in from the stern as we slowly turned to Ko Pha-Ngan, an island between Ko Samui and Ko Tao. I was alive and thankful to walk on land.

Nicole Meyer

Boats

One of the highlights of travel in Asia is the opportunity to make some spectacular boat journeys. The island nations of Indonesia, with over thirteen thousand islands, and the Philippines, with seven thousand, offer countless long- and short-distance trips, but in most Asian countries you'll have the chance to cruise on rivers and across lakes and lagoons, as well as between islands. If you have the time, boat travel is a convenient and economical alternative to flying, with the bonus of great views and the chance to see marine and river wildlife at close hand.

In some areas of Kalimantan in Indonesia, Sarawak in Malaysia and Laos, for example, river transport is the only way to get around, whereas in many cities, such as Bangkok, river ferries and taxis are considerably faster than road transport, as well as being a cooler and more pleasant way to travel.

Bearing in mind that long-distance trips can last several days, it pays to make some advance preparations:

Best boat trips

- The Star Ferry across Hong Kong Harbour gives you the best views of the city's skyscraper skyline.
- Arriving at Puerto Galera on Mindanao in the Philippines. This is worth doing for the final part of an otherwise unremarkable journey from Batangas City. The approach to Puerto Galera itself is incredible – a tiny entrance through a narrow strait fringed with tropical palms before opening out into a huge and picturesque bay.
- Backwater trips in Kerala, South India. The two-hour public ferry service between Allappuzha and Kottayam takes you along waterlily-choked canals and across lagoons, slicing through farmland and coconut plantations, past temples, mosques and waterfront houses.
- Across the Brahmaputra (Tsangpo) River to Samye Monastery in Tibet. Amid stunningly cold, high-altitude scenery, a noisy, smoky flat-bottomed boat weaves between the sandbanks.
- The Bangkok *khlongs*. A ride on these inky-black, stinky canals gives an unsurpassed insight into Bangkok's watery suburbs as you swish by: teak houses where longboats are the family car, half-submerged temple grounds, kids playing in the water, men bathing and women doing the washing-up.
- The towering limestone outcrops in Ha Long Bay, Vietnam: 16,000 islands in 1500 square kilometres of water.
- The two-day journey by slow cargo boat down the Mekong River from Houayxai to Louang Phabang is one of the most popular things to do in Laos. It's not exactly a luxurious way to travel – there are no seats and no cabin accommodation – but the trip gives you plenty of time to appreciate the shifting panoramas of rice fields, limestone karst, temples and villages along the waterside.

- If you're travelling deck class, take a waterproof sheet to lie on as the floor gets very damp.
- Keep valuables, especially your camera and film, in waterproof bags. Particularly in smaller boats, ocean waves or wash from other river craft can sometimes drench you.
- Take your own food and water, as the quality of what's available on board – and there might be nothing – is variable. What's more, boats break down or get delayed or diverted due to bad weather conditions, and your journey may take longer than anticipated.
- It gets cold at sea – keep warm clothing near the top of your pack.
- Equally, the sun can be scorching, so keep sun protection, hats and lotion to hand.
- Put some sea–sickness tablets in your pack even if you don't normally suffer. The combination of big swells and deafening engines belching noxious fumes can affect even the most hardened stomach.

- Use your common sense and don't get on obviously vastly overcrowded boats. Ferries sink frequently in Bangladesh, the Philippines and Thailand.

City transport

It's in the cities that you'll see the full and glorious range of Asian transport, and here that you can witness the incredible juxtaposition of traditional and ultramodern. As well as buses, taxis and subway systems, be prepared for minibuses, motorcycle taxis, rickshaws, three-wheelers and even horse carts. You'll be flung into close, sometimes very close, proximity with your fellow passengers, who may be travelling together with their vegetables, goats and chickens for market, babies for the clinic and kids for school. A sense of humour is a prerequisite for travel this way.

Make it a point to find out how to get around a city, as this is a good way to increase your confidence in a place and helps you begin to feel less alien. You may adore Kolkata but be daunted by Delhi purely because you've worked out a couple of the central Kolkata bus routes, whereas the Delhi system remains a mystery, resulting in constant aggravation with taxi and rickshaw drivers.

Local buses

Most Asian cities have a mixture of large and small buses supplemented by a whole host of smaller minibuses, vans or motorized three-wheelers. The general rule seems to be that the smaller the vehicle, the less rigid the route and the greater the linguistic and geographical skills needed to find out where it is going; the smaller ones also stop wherever passengers want to get on and off. All these vehicles are incredibly cheap, but are very slow and packed solid with passengers, and, if the driver fancies a lunchtime break at the market en route, you'll have to wait the twenty minutes or so it takes him to buy and eat his noodle soup. You'll see all of Asian life on the buses, and depending on your mood they are either amazing or intensely frustrating.

In some places, such as Bangkok, it is possible – almost essential – to get a map of local bus services. Otherwise, get directions at the tourist information office, your hotel or from your guidebook. Ask again for your destination when you're on board, just to be sure the

Women, beware!

Monks in Thailand, Laos, Cambodia and Vietnam are allowed no physical contact at all with women. If they accidentally touch or are touched by a woman they must engage in a lengthy series of purification rituals. On public transport monks often congregate in particular places such as on the back seat of buses. No matter how crowded the vehicle, women travellers should not sit next to a monk and should be very careful if passing close to one. Local people will give up their seat for a monk and you should offer to do the same.

In Laos, it's taboo for women to sit on the roof of a bus or a boat. The Lao believe that a woman has the power to ruin the potency of the amulets carried by Lao men simply by placing herself physically above him. Furthermore, boats are thought to possess a guardian spirit, and a woman riding on the roof offends this spirit, which could invite dire consequences for passengers and crew.

bus is really going there. The following tips will help you negotiate the confusion more easily:

- Before you set off, find out the fare; check your guidebook, ask at your accommodation or check with other travellers or local people the correct fare and how best to pay.
- Take a pocketful of small-denomination coins or notes – getting change is a nightmare.
- You'll find that drivers, conductors and other passengers are generally helpful and concerned to get you where you want to go, although rush-hour commuters the world over aren't the most patient of folks and Asia is no exception.
- Give yourself as much time as you can and keep calm, and you'll soon be hopping around town like a local. Remember, it doesn't really matter if you get lost.
- Be very wary of pickpockets and slashers with razor-sharp knives who cut through material and the straps of shoulder bags.
- Women travelling on crowded city buses are, unfortunately, prime targets for sexual harassment ("Eve teasing" as it's called in India), and you may well experience groping hands, men squeezing past and "accidental" touches and brushes against you. It's your call whether to try to move away or make a loud public statement (though see the notes on staying calm on p.303).

Taxis

Most cities and built-up areas have official taxis, a convenient and usually very reasonably priced way to get from door to door. Find out what they look like and whether they should have meters or not, and you're ready to go.

There are, though, a few complications associated with using cabs. Most Asian taxis are supposed to have meters; however, these may or may not be a true indication of the full cost. Sometimes when prices go up the meters don't get adjusted until much later. In these cases, drivers carry official charts to convert from the meter price to the new fare. In other places there may be legitimate additional charges, such as entry to the central area of Singapore, tunnel toll charges in Hong Kong, expressway tolls in Bangkok, and surcharges after midnight. At many Asian airports the meter is officially suspended and taxis operate on a fixed price tariff to nearby destinations.

On occasions when the taxi meter is not working, drivers will negotiate a fare with the passenger. You may well experience taxi drivers claiming that the meter is not working or simply refusing to use it because they believe, usually correctly, that they can get a higher fare out of ignorant tourists than they can by using the meter. The situation varies from place to place: in some it is worth holding out and flagging down cab after cab until you get one to use the meter; in others you might as well start your negotiation with the first one that comes along.

If the driver says the meter isn't working, negotiate the price before you get in. The price is per cab, not per person, and this is a good chance to hone your bargaining skills (see p.233); the tactics are the same whether you're getting a ride or buying a mango. Generally speaking, cabs in Indonesia, Thailand and India are so cheap – well under $5/£3 to get across town – that if there are three or four of you with luggage, it's hardly worth bothering with a crowded bus. On the other hand, prices in Japan are sky high, up to $200/£115 for a sixty-minute ride from Central Tokyo to Narita International Airport; though taxis in Singapore and Hong Kong aren't so exorbitant, you'll still need to have plenty of spare cash to jump into them regularly.

Motorbike taxis

In many areas, motorbikes operate as taxis. They are a high-risk, big-thrill way to get around – a few minutes screeching through the rush-hour Bangkok traffic on the back of one and you'll understand the real meaning of fear. Bikes are especially useful in busy cities, though, as they can nip in and out of traffic jams and even zoom up one-way streets the wrong way.

Negotiate the fare before you get on and, no matter how derisory the helmet offered or the means of keeping it on your head, you should still wear it. The drivers may or may not be able to manage a backpack – you might have to wear it, which is very uncomfortable after a while, or get it balanced between the handlebars.

Cycle-rickshaws

Rickshaws are particularly useful for back roads where there is no other form of public transport, and for finding obscure addresses – many of the drivers know every inch of their territory. They are also a lovely, sedate way to travel, although you should be prepared to hop out at the foot of the most daunting hills, and if you're stuck in any traffic you'll be breathing in the exhaust fumes of every larger vehicle on the road.

A variety of different incarnations of rickshaw are found across Asia. The most ancient form, with a single man running on foot between two poles, pulling a seat perched above two wheels, has thankfully all but died out. Central Kolkata is the last outpost of such vehicles in Asia, and by the time you get there they may well have been replaced by cycle-rickshaws. It can feel morally uncomfortable sitting on the shaded, padded seat in a rickshaw while the wallah exhausts himself ferrying you around in the midday sun: are you shortening the poor chap's life, ensuring he suffers a chronically painful old age with wrecked joints, or are you making sure his children at least get a meal to eat that evening?

Cycle-rickshaws have different designs and names depending on the country: *cyclo* in Vietnam and Cambodia, *samlor* in Thailand and *becak* in Indonesia. With all rickshaws, negotiate the price before you

Better you take bus

I had always refused the Kolkata rickshaws despite their bell-ringing blandishments every time I set foot outside my hotel. However, one day after wandering all over the backstreets of the city I was foot-sore, worn out by the heat and flies, and found myself well off the beaten track. I approached the nearest rickshaw driver and named my hotel. He looked me up and down, took in my height and likely weight at a glance, and looked at the sun blazing down. Then he raised an arm towards the nearest main road: "Better you take bus," he decided.

Lesley Reader

get in and make sure it's clear whether it is for the vehicle or per person. The price will depend not only on the distance but also on the number of hills, amount of luggage and the effort the man thinks he'll have to put in. You can also negotiate an hourly rate if you plan to visit several places.

Motorized rickshaws

More sophisticated versions of rickshaws are motor-rickshaws, also known as auto-rickshaws (*auto* in India, *bajaj* in Indonesia, *cyclo mai* in Vietnam and *tuk tuk* in Thailand). They are noisy (*tuk tuk*s are so named because of the sound they make), smelly, unstable three-wheelers with the driver in front and enough space for a couple of passengers behind (but that doesn't stop four or five clambering aboard).

Driven by a grossly underpowered two-stroke engine, motor-rickshaws are extremely useful if you want wheels from A to B but balk at taxi fares. Like taxis they are usually supposed to have meters though it's often just as difficult to get the drivers to use them. Rides can be hair-raising, as these little vehicles are very nippy. Received wisdom in Bangkok is to find an elderly *tuk tuk* driver, the theory being that in this notoriously manic profession he has survived to drive again. There's only one problem – it seems virtually impossible to find a single driver of these machines who looks older than 16.

Vehicle rental

The laws on foreigners driving rental cars vary throughout Asia. In China, for example, visiting foreigners may only drive in certain areas: Beijing, Shanghai, Hong Kong and Sanya on Hainan Island. However, in most countries an International Driver's Licence (get this before you leave home) will give you full access to the roads. Expect to pay from \$30/£17 per day in Vietnam, \$20/£11 in Bali and \$40/£23 in the remainder of Indonesia (insurance and petrol not included) for a jeep or small saloon car. International rental companies such as Hertz, Budget, Avis and Europcar have offices in most capital cities, which means you can book your vehicle in advance, but these places are almost always more expensive than local firms.

If you want to travel by car, you should consider the additional cost of hiring a local driver as well; even though you'll have to pay the driver's food and, if you're touring overnight, lodging costs as well, it's not usually a significant additional expense. The advantage of a local driver is that you can spend all your time enjoying the scenery, won't have to worry about finding the way or adapting to the often terrifying local rules of the road, and you'll hopefully get good suggestions about side-trips, plus a useful insight into the local area and people. And, if anything goes wrong, it's far better that you aren't driving: killing a cow in Nepal carries roughly the same penalty as killing a person – up to twenty years in prison. An alternative is to rent a local taxi for a day, a week or whatever – a popular and economical idea in India. It's a good way to see a lot quite quickly, visit outlying districts and do it all in a bit of comfort. If you decide to drive yourself, the following tips may help:

- Carry all relevant documentation: in Indonesia you must carry the vehicle's registration papers as well as your own. Balinese police love to stop tourists and issue on-the-spot fines if they aren't carrying the right paperwork.
- Inspect the vehicle carefully before you accept it and make a note, also signed by the owner, of any scratches or dents, or you may get blamed for these.
- Check things you would take for granted in a rental vehicle at home: the lights, horn, windscreen wipers, door locks, petrol cap.
- Make sure you know how to get the bonnet up and check the spare tyre (is there one?), tool kit and jack.
- In some parts of Asia, insurance is not available for rental vehicles; if it is available, it's pricey. You should definitely buy insurance if you can, but make sure you know what's covered. In particular, check how much the excess is – the amount you will have to pay if there's a crash.
- Know the legal speed limits and find out the local rules of the road. The official version should be in any comprehensive guidebook, but spend some time observing what goes on around you – there's often a big gap between the legal and the habitual. In Beijing, nobody seems to obey red lights, while in Sumatra they are ignored if you are turning left.
- Be alert and considerate. Hardly a week goes by on the island of Phuket in Thailand without one foreign driver racing him or herself into a crumpled smash on the roadside.

Motorbikes

Motorbikes are available for rent in many places and are a great way to travel independently to out-of-the-way places at reasonable cost. All the above tips for car drivers apply to motorbikes, plus the following:

- Motorbike riding in Asia is not for learners or novices.
- Check the local licensing regulations to make sure you are legally allowed to drive.
- Check that the bike is insured for accidents and theft and be sure to see the documents. Make sure you know what the insurance deal is, ie will you have to pay an excess in the case of an accident?
- Examine the bike carefully – especially brakes, lights and tyres.
- Whatever the local laws dictate, driver and passenger should both wear helmets and always cover up. However tempting it is to feel the wind on bare limbs, it's madness not to have some sort of protection in case you come off. Consider taking your own helmet – those provided in Asia are often less than adequate.
- Be especially careful of exhaust pipes – many a pillion passenger ends up with a nasty burn on their calf, which can easily get infected in the tropical heat.
- Be aware that unpaved roads can be unpredictable, varying from sand to mud depending on the weather conditions; local driving styles are erratic and the rules of the road can be very alien.

Respect

When I walked through the bazaar of one town in Pakistan, even fully robed, I was stared at, catcalled by giggly young men and felt a little vulnerable – a shameless foreign woman unaccompanied in male territory. The next day I rode into the same market on my motorbike. No giggles. No lechery. Previously disapproving old men decided I was worthy of a nod. Young men approached to make intelligent conversation and ask about the bike. Suddenly I became a person; I had respect again. The bike takes the focus off you and your marital status, opens doors and is a great conversation starter.

Nicki McCormick

Bicycles

A bicycle is the only vehicle that millions of Asians will ever own, and bikes are available for rent pretty much everywhere. Levels of sophistication vary from mountain bikes to bone-shakers that barely hold together. If you want to rent a bike, ask at your guesthouse or at local shops; you'll get better rates for longer rents. Security can be a problem – the exception is in Chinese cities where there are official bike parks – and you should always use a chain or lock. A few words of warning:

- Try out the bike before parting with your money. Wonky front wheels, seats with springs sticking through and clunking chains get a bit wearing after an hour or so. Be especially careful to check the brakes. A working bell is essential all over Asia.
- Be aware that most bikes come without a helmet and without efficient lights, so you must be home by dark.
- Most other road users will behave as though you don't exist.
- Carry plenty of water – cycling is thirsty work.
- Protect yourself from the sun.
- Don't be overambitious and overdo it in tropical conditions. In Beijing, where distances are enormous, it doesn't cost much to get a taxi to take you and your bike back to your accommodation if you get too exhausted.

If you are intending to complete a lengthy part of your trip by bike, you'll most likely be bringing your own from home. Take a look at Bike Sutra (⊛www.bikesutra.com/asia_cycling.html) and Formosan Fat Tire Association (⊛www.formosanfattire.com), both of which have copious links to sites about cycling in Asia. See also Pakistan (p.107) and Mongolia (see p.95) for relevant websites and box on p.171 for some general hints on long-distance cycle routes. *Cycling Vietnam, Laos and Cambodia* (Lonely Planet) offers inspiration and plenty of practical advice on equipment, fitness for cyclists and useful routes. Many general Asian guidebooks also contain information for cyclists.

Hitchhiking

The cost of travel in Asia is so low that hitching isn't really necessary for tourists, though in out-of-the-way places, with the last bus gone, not a taxi in sight and still 40km to go to your hotel, it can sometimes become the only option. Most drivers will expect payment from their passengers. Hitchhiking carries the same risks wherever you are; just because you're on holiday, don't suspend the instincts that keep you safe at home. If you do decide to hitch a ride, bear in mind that in some areas (Tibet is one example) drivers of trucks and other private vehicles are not legally permitted to carry foreigners, and risk heavy penalties if they are caught doing so.

Walking

With the dizzying range of transport available, don't forget the pleasures of simply walking around – just get outside and wander where the fancy takes you. Asian life is lived on the streets – yes, there are beggars, hawkers and hustlers galore, but there are also millions of people going about their everyday lives, commuting to work, shopping at street markets, praying at tiny shrines, having a snack at food stalls, gambling or simply watching the world go by. Bear in mind that:

- Asian roads can be terrifying to cross. Walk with a local person between you and oncoming traffic. Move when they move; stop when they stop.
- Jaywalking is illegal in many places – Singapore is one; Indonesia another. Do obey pedestrian signs and use footbridges and underpasses if they exist.
- Pedestrian survival can depend on knowing the rules of the road: remember which way oncoming traffic is approaching from and be aware that drivers may interpret stop signs differently from you.

Tours

Just as tourist bus services can take the strain out of complicated connections, so there are plenty of travel agents and tour companies in Asia offering organized trips, which can make things a lot smoother. You may leave home vowing to see it all and do it all independently, but it's worth bearing a few things in mind:

- A day or half-day city tour can be an excellent way to orientate yourself. You'll see far more than you could on public transport and it'll help you decide what you do and don't want to spend more time exploring on your own. The Bangkok Tourist Bureau even offers tours of the more traditional neighbourhoods by bicycle.
- In some places, a tour is very often the only way to get to certain parts of the country – for example, some areas of Tibet, and Mustang in Nepal, are only accessible to trekkers on organized trips.
- Not all tours are super-luxury – there are plenty of less expensive trips aimed specifically at backpackers.
- Going on a tour with a group can be an economical way to see harder-to-reach regions.

- With longer trips, make sure you find out the full details of the itinerary and what is included, as well as departure and arrival times. A common complaint is that a "three-day trip" turns out to leave after lunch on Day One and arrives home in the early morning on Day Three.

11

Accommodation

ccommodation in most parts of Asia is astonishingly inexpensive. It's quite feasible to set aside $5/£3 a day or less for your accommodation budget in India, Nepal and many of the countries in Southeast Asia – though you'll get little more than a single bed and four walls for that money. You can scrape by on less if you share a double room, and less still if you sleep in dormitories with several others.

Although making the most of your money is important, you'll probably find that you're occasionally willing to pay a little more than rock-bottom rates in return for extra comforts like an attached bathroom, a quieter location, air-conditioning or more attractive surroundings. After a day-long bus ride in the sweltering heat or a marathon tour of every last Kathmandu temple, a comfortable room can restore your mental health faster than a bottle of Kingfisher beer. Good value for money is a factor right up the scale in Asia – for $40/£25 in Vietnam you'll get a double room with TV and minibar as well as shower and air-conditioning, while for $75/£45 you can stay in an Indian maharajah's palace.

Some hotels in China and Vietnam are not allowed to take foreign guests (simply because the manager hasn't submitted the requisite paperwork), so don't take offence if you're rejected on sight. Hoteliers in other countries, however, can be prejudiced – some mid-range and upmarket hotels in India won't take backpackers, regardless of how much cash you have. The suitcase-style travelpack is a useful disguise in such instances (see p.257); putting on your smartest gear helps too.

Accommodation in Asia is not confined to hotels. You may find yourself sleeping in a rafthouse on the infamous River Kwai, dossing down in pilgrims' *guruduaras* at the Golden Temple in Amritsar, or even sharing a tent with other trekkers at the foot of Mount Everest. More prosaically, major Indian train stations all offer "retiring rooms" for early-morning travellers, and there's always sleeper-car accommodation on the trains themselves.

In some countries, it's also possible to organize a homestay with a local family. You can do this officially and for a fee, through tourist offices (in India, Korea and Malaysia, for example) and specialist organizations (Japan, China, Korea, India, Nepal), or for free via the Women Welcome Women World Wide network (women only) and Internet groups such as Global Freeloaders; see the Directory, p.417 for contact details. Or you can do it on the spur of the moment, simply because you have no alternative, as in remote reaches of Tibet, Brunei and Sabah and Sarawak (East Malaysia). In India's New Age capital, Auroville, near Pondicherry, you can stay in one of thirty communes for a nominal fee so long as you help out on community projects. And South Korea operates a low-cost temple-stay programme (⊛english.tour2korea .com), where guests wear Buddhist robes, sleep in single-sex dormitories and join in the meditation and other temple activities.

Lowering the tone

The staff at the five-star Bombay hotel took one look at my scruffy T-shirt and well-travelled rucksack and said, "Sorry sir, the hotel is fully booked." I'd just finished a five-year contract in Bhutan – a country not noted for its designer clothes shops, or even its laundrettes – and was desperate for a few days of luxury. Though I waved wads of cash at the receptionist and flashed my credit card, he was just not willing to lower the tone of the establishment by admitting a backpacker: "Sorry sir, the hotel is fully booked." So I strolled down the street, found a public phone and called him up from round the corner. He didn't recognize my voice and answered, "Yes, sir, we have a room; how many nights?" Ten minutes later, I was back at the five-star, picking up the keys to my deluxe accommodation.

Gerry Jameson

Finding somewhere to stay

Any decent guidebook will list a range of accommodation, and these recommendations are useful starting points – bearing in mind that prices go up, hotels change managers, and guidebook writers have preferences that you may not share. For your first few nights in Asia we strongly recommend reserving a hotel room before you leave home (advice on how to do this is given in Chapter Seven, and there's a list of accommodation booking agents in the Directory, p.417). After that, you'll probably do what every other traveller does and trawl the streets yourself, especially if you're looking for budget places.

Because accommodation is so inexpensive, youth-hostel culture barely exists in most parts of Asia, and most backpackers head instead for traveller-oriented budget hotels known as guesthouses. There is usually quite an obvious distinction between places that call themselves guesthouses and those in the same price bracket that call themselves hotels. Inexpensive hotels are generally set up for local travellers (usually businesspeople and sales reps), rather than foreign ones, which can mean that rooms are too soulless for any more than a one-night stop.

If you're in a city, start your search in an area that has several hotels or guesthouses close together. That way you won't feel obliged to stay in the first fleapit you come across just because you've taken two buses to get there, nor will you be unduly upset if your first choice is fully booked or has closed down. Get there by mid-morning, if you can, as most guesthouses have a noon checkout time and, during peak season, will have an impromptu waiting list established by about 10am. If there are two of you, get one person to sit down and guard the packs while the other checks out two or three places to find the best deal.

Don't ignore a hotel just because it doesn't feature in your guidebook: it's not uncommon for some books' recommendations to be overflowing while the equally pleasant outfit next door is half empty.

If you don't have a guidebook, or want to get right off the beaten track, the most obvious places to look for inexpensive hotels are around bus and train stations. Though in some cities these hotels may well double as brothels, business is generally discreet and you may not even realize that most of your fellow guests are booking in and out within the hour. Having said that, if you get a bad feeling about a hotel or guesthouse, it's generally wise to trust your instincts and look for somewhere else instead: you may feel uneasy about the other "guests", you may get a bad vibe off the staff, or you may think the place looks too dirty or too much of a fire-hazard for comfort. Unfortunately you can't assume that tourist accommodation meets the health and safety regulations you may be used to at home; it's generally up to you to make that judgement for yourself.

Finding a room in high season or at festival time can be a real problem in some places, and prices always rocket when demand outstrips supply. In Pushkar, northwest India, the local authorities erect a special tent city to house the thousands of visitors who come for the annual camel fair.

Lots of guesthouses employ touts to bring in new customers and, though you might find their persistence incredibly irritating, they sometimes come up with useful leads, especially during peak season. Touts generally hang around bus terminals, train stations and ferry ports (though they sometimes ride the most popular routes

△ Beach huts, Ko Pha Ngan, Thailand

into town to get the choicest pickings) and will flash various cards, photos and brochures at you until you agree to go and see a place with them. In some cases the tout's commission is invisibly added onto your room rate. Before going off with a tout, always get an assurance of price, facilities and, crucially, its exact location on the map.

The guesthouse circuit

Most big towns on the tourist circuit in Cambodia, India, Indonesia, Malaysia, Nepal, Philippines, Thailand and the Vietnam, have a backpackers' enclave where you might find anything from ten to a hundred guesthouses packed cheek by jowl into a few hundred square metres. Such concentration ensures prices are kept low and gives you a range of options to check out without having to lug your rucksack too far. It's also a good place to meet new travel companions, especially if you're by yourself or in Asia for the first time. Travellers often say that the real highlight of their trip was the range of characters they met on the road and in the guesthouses: an interesting crowd can transform a dull guesthouse into a memorable experience.

On the downside, backpackers' centres do tend to take on a peculiar ghetto character of their own, a strange medley of watered-down Asian practices and cheapskate Western ones, which not only insulates travellers from the real Bangkok/Delhi/Kathmandu, but makes Bangkok, Delhi and Kathmandu seem indistinguishable. The same is true of popular backpackers' beach resorts, where travellers may hang out for weeks, if not months, without even venturing to the nearest town.

A typical no-frills guesthouse (like the ones on Bangkok's Khao San Road) has about thirty rooms packed into three or four storeys, most of them little more than white-walled cells with one or two beds and a ceiling fan – some don't even have a window; bathrooms are shared with other rooms on the floor. Though basic, rooms are generally clean and functional and, best of all, cheap – from $3/£2 a single (less if you share with several other people, dorm-style), so you can hardly complain about the decor. Some guesthouses also have more expensive rooms with en-suite bathrooms and air-conditioning.

In smaller towns, guesthouses can be far more appealing, with tropical gardens, cool central courtyards and more spacious rooms. They're often more welcoming than hotels, too, being family-run businesses offering just a handful of rooms. Beach accommodation is generally just as basic and cheap as city guesthouses, but looks a lot more idyllic. A standard beach bungalow (the usual term for guesthouses by the sea) on Malaysia's Pulau Perhentian islands, for example, is a rickety wooden A-frame hut built on stilts right on the beach, with a palm-frond roof and a verandah that looks out to sea.

Most people only use their rooms for sleeping and storing their packs, and spend their hanging-out time in the guesthouse café. These cafés serve Western food like cheese sandwiches and milkshakes, but are used mainly as a common room, a place to write journals and postcards and to swap anecdotes and recommendations with other backpackers. A genial café or roof terrace with good views can do a lot to compensate for a depressing room.

Some guesthouses also keep a noticeboard for travellers' messages and may offer Internet access and a poste restante service, too. The most efficient ones operate like small hotels and will sell bus and train tickets, do your laundry and store left luggage as well (though beware of leaving credit cards and other valuables in these; see Chapter Fourteen).

A few great guesthouses

Below is a very selective taster of some favourite places to stay, where you'll pay under $15/£10 a night for two people:

- With its charming courtyard garden and traditional wooden architecture, *Inn of the First Bend* is a pleasingly historic place to stay when visiting the old Naxi town of Lijiang in southwest **China**.
- In Dharamsala, northern **India**, the best rooms at the hillside *Kalsang Guest House* look down over the village, and from the roof terrace upstairs you get perfect views of the snowcapped Dhauladhar mountains.
- At the backpackers' resort of Cherating in **Malaysia**, the timber chalets at the catchily named guesthouse *The Shadow of the Moon at Half-Past Four* are thoughtfully designed and secluded in a wooded area just a few minutes' walk from the beach.
- In Chiang Mai, **Thailand's** laid-back northern city, *Yourhouse Guesthouse* offers large, simple rooms in a beautiful old teak house in the heart of the old city. They arrange treks and cookery courses as well.

- *Mount Davis Youth Hostel* boasts eye-popping views over **Hong Kong** harbour – a treat by day or night. It's set right on the top of a hill, so getting there's a trek, but you couldn't find a calmer or more panoramic spot on Hong Kong Island.
- Though the bungalows at the ridgetop *Londo 2* in Ubud, **Bali**, are sparsely furnished, each has two floors and its own kitchenette and the views over the surrounding palm-fringed ricefields are spectacular.
- Set plumb in the middle of a spectacular valley of sculpted rice terraces, *Hillside Inn* is one of just a few perfectly located guesthouses in the traditional **Philippines** village of Batad.
- Featuring fabulous views across the entire area, *Ambiente* in Ella, **Sri Lanka**, is a cool retreat in the hills just a short walk from the centre of the village.
- Boasting spotless rooms, a swimming pool, a beautiful garden and a stunning beach close by, *Bulan Baru (New Moon)* in Senggigi, on the Indonesian island of **Lombok**, is a brilliant spot to relax.

Room rates

Standards of budget accommodation vary quite a lot across Asia, so it might take you a while to work out whether or not you're getting good value for money. Rural guesthouses in Thailand, for example, are often characterful places with great views, a verandah or garden, and locally made furnishings – all for around $7/£4 a double. At the other end of the scale, Chinese hotels in all price brackets are generally a disappointment, being mainly faceless blocks lacking atmosphere or appeal; they're not that cheap either.

Expensive countries such as Singapore, Hong Kong, Japan and Brunei charge relatively large sums for even the most basic double room ($35/£20), so most budget travellers opt for dorm beds – although even these will set you back around $10/£6 a bed. Youth hostels can be a useful alternative in these countries and camping is cheaper still, though official city campsites tend to be inconveniently located in the suburbs; elsewhere in Asia, camping is only appropriate in national parks and on treks. See Chapter Six for advice on whether or not to take camping equipment. The following tips will help you make the most of your accommodation budget:

- A good way to save money if you're on your own is to use dorms, where a bed will be at least thirty percent cheaper than a single room. If no dorms are available you might want to split a double room with another traveller, again cheaper than a single room. Obviously you should only do this if you feel comfortable with the other person.

- Beds in many Asian hotels (as opposed to guesthouses) are very large, so it's quite acceptable for two people to book into a single room; a double room will have two double beds in it.

- In some places you can bargain over the price of a room (especially in low season); others might offer discounts for stays of a week or more.

- If travelling long distance, you can save a night's hotel costs by taking the overnight train or bus and making sure you get a reclining seat. Second-class berths on trains usually cost about the same as a single room in a guesthouse.

- Watch out for "luxury" service charges and taxes in mid- and upmarket places (up to 21 percent extra in Indonesia, for example), and for ridiculous room-service charges as well as overpriced food in the hotel restaurant.

- Using the phone in your room to make international calls is always costly, as most hotels add a huge surcharge to phone bills. Try to get your friends or relatives to call you back.

- Unless you pay by credit card in many upmarket hotels (in India, for example), you may have to put down a deposit against your possible phone bill and minibar tariff.

- An unorthodox way of finding cheap accommodation in Japan is to check in to a "love hotel" after all the lovers have departed for the night (usually around 10pm). These hotels are designed for secret and extramarital liaisons, but are definitely not brothels. They're completely legal and unsleazy, if a little kitsch – rooms tend to be plastered in mirrors, fake fur and romantic images – and are scrupulously clean. Because most clandestine liaisons take place during the day, overnighters get a huge discount.

Can I see the room please?

Always look at the room you're being offered before paying for it – this is normal practice throughout Asia and, though time-consuming, is definitely worth it. Once you've checked out a few places you'll be able to size up a room in five seconds, but for first-timers here's a checklist of essential points to look out for:

- If you like the hotel but aren't sure about the room, always ask to see another one: the view might be better, the neighbours quieter and, who knows, the fan might even be working in that one.

- Is the room clean? Check the sheets for blood spots (blood means fleas or bedbugs), the floor for cockroaches and the walls for squashed mosquitoes. Look under the bed for rat traps (squares of cardboard sprinkled with food and smeared with glue) and scour the window screens and mosquito nets for holes (which render them useless, unless you want to spend the whole night doing repair jobs with Band–Aids).

- Does everything work? Try out the lights, the fan/air-conditioning/heater, the flush toilet (if there is one) and the shower (ditto).
- Do the taps run fresh or salt water? Straight from the river? If you asked for hot water, check that it works.
- Is the room secure? Can you put your own padlock on the door? (Not applicable in China, where hotel rooms are locked and unlocked for you by the floor attendant.) Are the windows safe? Are there any peepholes in the door or walls?
- Is it quiet? Rooms on the main road will be noisy, but so will any place near a morning market, a night market, a disco, a hotel kitchen or an electricity generator – which you may not discover until the next morning. The same goes for rowdy neighbours (snorers, squabblers and noisy lovers), and 4am cockerels; even temples can be noisy if there's an all-night prayer session or festival.
- Is it comfortable? Check the bed for springs and the mattress for lumps. Are you certain it's worth saving a dollar a day by staying in a place with no window or somewhere with paper-thin walls and a creaking fan?

Checking in

In most parts of Asia, you'll be asked to register when checking in to any accommodation, however small. This usually entails writing your name, passport number and several other details in a ledger – a legal requirement in most countries which, in theory at least, enables the authorities to trace travellers in cases of emergency. For the most part, this should be quite straightforward, though registration forms in China are a notable exception, being painfully long-winded and sometimes written entirely in Chinese script.

Wherever you stay, avoid leaving your passport with hotel staff unless you absolutely have to do so. This is unavoidable in some parts of Vietnam, however, where hotel managers have to present their guests' passports at the police station. If you're asked to surrender your passport as security against your bill, offer to leave a monetary deposit instead. Your passport is your only official means of identity in a strange land and should be kept on your person at all times – besides which, you'll need it for changing money and other transactions.

Most people keep their passport, airline ticket and other valuables with them whenever they leave their hotel, not least because hotel security can be lax. However, you could also leave these items in your room and use your own padlock on the door (if you can), or put them in a hotel safety box, again secured by your own padlock, in a lockable small box or bag, or in an envelope that you've signed over the seal. Bear in mind, though, that sawing through a small padlock is not so difficult, and be aware that not all hotel staff are scrupulously honest.

Security should also be an issue when you're inside your hotel room with your valuables. Always lock the door from the inside, even when you're awake (people have a habit of drifting in for a chat at the most inopportune moments). And check on window access, too, in case a thief decides to climb in while you're asleep.

Bathrooms and how to use them

Though many guesthouses and hotels have Western-style showers, the traditional scoop-and-slosh method of bathing is also common right across Asia. Known in travellers' speak as a *mandi* (Indonesian for "to wash"), this basically involves dipping a scoop, jug or small bowl into a large bucket or basin of water and then chucking it over yourself – very refreshing in a chilly kind of way. The cardinal rule of the *mandi* is never to put your soap or shampoo into the basin of water and, though it often looks like a big stone bathtub, *never, ever* to get into it as this water might have to supply the next two weeks' worth of guests.

Washing in cold water is the norm throughout most of Asia, but in the high altitudes of Nepal, northern India, Tibet, Bhutan, Pakistan and north China, you'll definitely need a hot shower, so make sure it's operational before paying for your room. Some places only turn on the water heaters at certain times of day. You'll come across some intriguing bathing habits depending on where you are in Asia:

- In rural parts of Asia, the local river, lake or well doubles as the village bathroom and everyone congregates there at the end of the day for their evening wash. Men and women nearly always have separate bathing areas and, though they may be within sight of each other, there's absolutely no ogling or communication between the two groups. Both sexes wear sarongs in the water and no one strips off to wash. If you bathe in the local river, you should do as they do, or find a place much further upriver.
- Traditional Japanese hotels generally have old-fashioned bathtubs. These have no running hot water, but work instead by heating up the full tub with an element, like a kettle – enabling you to sit in the water and keep warm for hours on end. The same bath water is used by several hotel guests one after the other (not as unhygienic as it sounds if you think of it like a public Jacuzzi), so it's essential to wash yourself clean, using the scoop-and-slosh method, before hopping into the tub.
- In Bali, the most stylish guesthouses and hotels have beautifully designed "garden bathrooms" with roofs that are open to the sky, sculptured water flues and tropical plants growing round the *mandi* area.
- Most small towns in Korea have public bathhouses – a national institution that should definitely be experienced. In these you wash yourself on the side of the main pool and then climb in for a very hot soak and a chat with your neighbours. Most have separate pools for men and women.
- Traditional Bhutanese baths are heated with huge stones, which are first cooked to a high temperature in the embers of a fire and then thrown into the tub.

Toilet habits

Flush toilets and toilet paper are relatively new concepts in most parts of Asia and, apart from in tourist hotels, urban guesthouses and the wealthiest homes, it's usually a question of hunkering down over a squat toilet like everyone else does. Asians wash their bottoms rather than wipe them, using the bucket of water provided and their left hand. This explains why eating, shaking hands and giving things is always done with the right hand – see Chapter Eight for details.

Traveller-oriented guesthouses often provide sit-down toilets that are plumbed in but don't flush. In these you're expected to do the flushing manually by pouring a bucket of water down the bowl. These plumbing systems are very sensitive and get blocked up easily as, unlike Western ones, they're not designed to take paper or tampons. Many guesthouses have signs telling you to throw your waste in the bin instead and it's selfish not to obey the rules. Even if there's no sign and no bucket, you should chuck any paper waste into a plastic bag: a blocked drain in your en-suite bathroom will attract mosquitoes and all sorts of germs, and the stink will permeate your dreams.

The obvious way round all this is to adopt the Asian habit and wash instead of wipe. If that sounds too unpalatable, travel with your own roll of toilet paper as most places won't provide it. The one situation where it's hard to either wipe or wash is when you're out trekking in the wilderness. If you don't want to use leaves, either burn your paper with a lighter or dig a little hole and bury it – there's nothing like a ribbon of pink toilet paper for ruining a spectacular view.

Be prepared to come across a good percentage of gut-wrenchingly vile public toilets, particularly in bus and train stations, and on trains in China and India. Try and get into the habit of using hotel and restaurant facilities when you can, and don't be surprised by the following:

- Indoor bathrooms are considered unhygienic by many rural Asian communities, for whom the idea of having a toilet just a metre or so from the kitchen is quite disgusting. Indian villagers, for example, will set off for the fields every morning to do their ablutions away from the home or, if they live near the sea, they will do them on the shoreline so that the sea washes everything away. With that in mind, it pays to be careful where you swim and sunbathe on Indian beaches.
- Public toilets in China are often very public indeed – with only a low partition between squatters, and sometimes no partition at all.
- All Chinese and Japanese hotels provide special plastic slippers for wearing in the bathroom.
- Some public toilets in Japan play piped music to mask the sound of pissing, which is considered embarrassing for Japanese women. If you're lucky, you might even come across a singing toilet-roll holder, which plays *Für Elise* every time you yank the paper.

- In Thailand, toilet attendants in upmarket restaurants massage your neck and shoulders while you stand at a urinal.
- In the "fine city" of Singapore, there's a S$500 fine for failing to flush a public toilet and should you be caught urinating in a public space, you get your picture splashed over the front page of the national newspaper.

12

Staying healthy

There's no advice that we can give and nothing that you can do to absolutely guarantee you don't fall sick in Asia. You are subjecting your body to different food and water, extreme heat or cold, tropical sun and there are a whole host of new creepy-crawlies to contend with. Even the air you breathe will be carrying different cold and flu viruses from those you are used to. This chapter presents the facts that every visitor to Asia should know, gives advice on precautions and has suggestions to help you cope should you get ill. See p.287 for information about DVT (deep-vein thrombosis).

These points put things in perspective and help you to prepare:

● Millions of travellers go to Asia every year and millions return home safely, the vast majority having suffered nothing worse than a few days of travellers' diarrhoea.

● Almost everyone gets sick at some time during a lengthy Asian trip. However, the last thing you'll feel like doing if you're unwell is boarding a massively overcrowded bus for an overnight journey. Make sure you build enough leeway into your itinerary to allow you to rest up for a few days if you need to.

● Read up about diseases prevalent in Asia, as symptoms that probably just indicate flu at home may be something far more serious in the tropics. There are several good books on travellers' health – some people take them along, and they can make interesting if gory reading while you are squatting over the toilet for the twentieth time that day. Rough Guides' *Travel Health* and Lonely Planet's *Asia and India* (in

First-aid kit

Many of the items listed here are available in Asia, but it's better to have them to hand and replace them later if required. You'll save money and get a more individualized pack suited to your itinerary, likely activities and health issues if you put a kit together yourself rather than opt for a commercially packaged one. If you're trekking you should also consult a specialist guide/trekking book for additional items. Keep your first aid kit in your day sack – if you need it, you'll need it quickly and you won't feel like climbing on top of the bus to rummage around in your backpack.

Anti-diarrhoea tablets
Anti-fungal cream
Antiseptic cream
Asprin/paracetamol
Antihistamine tablets
Plasters, small and large (fabric ones work well for blisters)
Bite cream (Tiger Balm, available throughout Asia, is a good alternative; it is also useful for aching muscles and headaches)
Cold remedy

Gauze pads
Insect repellent
Lip salve/sun block for lips
Rehydration salts
Scissors
Sterile dressings
Sterile needles and syringes
Surgical tape
Thermometer
Throat lozenges
Tweezers

Prescription drugs

The following items are only available on prescription. Your doctor may be willing to give you a course of tablets to take with you if you explain where you are going. Make sure you know how and when to use them:

Antibiotics, for throat and bronchial infections, and for intestinal bacteria
Tinidazole, for giardia (see p.365)
Emergency treatment for malaria (see p.357)

their Healthy Travel series) are both packed full of vital information for before, during and after your trip. Dr Jane Wilson Howarth's *Bugs, Bites and Bowels* (Cadogan/Globe Pequot) outlines simply and clearly the illnesses you may get in the tropics, likely symptoms and what to do about them. If your priorities are intestinal then her book *Shitting Pretty* (Travellers' Tales) is the one to go for. Alternatively there are several excellent websites; see the Directory pp.419–420, for details.

● Things change fast; keep abreast of current developments by using the websites listed on p.419. Nasties such as SARS (Sudden Acute Respiratory Disease), bird flu and epidemics of dengue fever are prevalent in Asia.

- Go for a dental checkup before you leave home; toothache is unpleasant at the best of times, but finding dental treatment in Asia on a par with that at home can be even more difficult than finding other forms of medical care. However, private clinics in Bangkok have such an excellent reputation for quality treatment at good prices that it's becoming increasingly common to go there for dental work that would cost several times as much at home.
- Carry a first-aid kit (see box opposite). It may be bulkier and more extensive than you have at home, but it will be worth its weight in gold if you do actually need it. Don't forget to take any medication you use regularly with you.
- Make sure you have adequate medical insurance (see p.207). Some serious medical treatment and then a medical evacuation, for example, from Thailand back to the UK could set you back £30,000/ $53,000 or more.
- Some Asian illnesses don't show themselves straight away – if you get sick within a year of returning home from Asia, make sure you tell the doctor treating you where you've been.

Vaccinations

Get advice as early as possible about which vaccinations you require for your trip, as many are given as a course of two or three jabs in order to be effective. It's advisable to allow time gaps between certain vaccinations; in any case, you won't really want to subject your arm to four needles in one sitting. Similarly, you need to find out early about the type of malaria-preventive medication that is recommended for the areas you are visiting; you may need to start taking the tablets in advance of departure. Even if your itinerary is not finalized, compile a list of places you are planning to visit (as well as any others you may visit) and think about whether you are planning to stay in tourist resorts or off the beaten track, to travel during the monsoon, and whether you'll be camping. All of these will affect the advice you are given.

While your family doctor may offer some injections cheaply or free, you may want to contact a private travel clinic to make sure you get the most specialized information available. Many travel clinics have telephone information lines, are quick and convenient and, though they can be expensive, provide information that's up to date and extensive (see the Directory, pp.419–420 for contact details).

Complementary medicine

Complementary medicine offers a great many useful alternative or additional approaches to help combat the health risks of Asian travel. Probably one of the most useful aspects is in providing advice on building up your immune system before you travel. For example, echinacea provides a general boost to immunity and probiotics are a useful means of increasing the "good" bacteria in the gut that will help wipe out anything harmful that enters the digestive system. Homeopathy suggests arnica and cocculus as useful in combating jet lag; acupressure can offer relief for travel sickness; and herbal preparations can help with a variety of problems from fear of flying to stomach upsets. See Rough Guides' *Travel Health* for an idea of the extent to which homeopathy and herbal medicine can be useful. Contact a local practitioner, as specialist advice is needed on the correct preparations, quantities and the ways to use them.

Vaccinations don't offer lifelong immunity, so keep a record so you know when you need a booster. A very few jabs can cause reactions – unpleasant but much better than getting the disease.

Different countries vary in what inoculations they insist on for visitors, but the only time you are likely to be asked for documentation is if you have recently travelled to a country in South or Central America, where yellow fever is endemic. In this case, you must have had a yellow fever jab (and have the certificate to prove it). It's worth bringing your medical card, or a copy of it, showing which vaccinations you've had, as scams are not unknown: for example, border officials on the Thai–Cambodia border at Aranyaprathet–Poipet have been known to ask travellers who can't show what jabs they've had to swallow unidentified pills – and pay \$5/£3 for the "medication".

Diseases you should know about

Below is a rundown of diseases you might be exposed to and which vaccinations are available for them. Don't be unduly alarmed, however, as some of these are confined to limited regions or seasons (usually more prevalent during monsoon time):

- **Cholera** Vaccinations against this extremely severe diarrhoeal illness, transmitted via contaminated food and water, were previously recommended for travellers, but this is now thought to be too ineffectual and short-term. The best advice is to follow the guidelines given in this chapter regarding what you eat and drink, and steer well clear of any areas where you hear there's an epidemic. However, watch this space; a new vaccination taken as a fizzy drink, Dukoral, is proving to be highly effective and seems to confer some protection against travellers' diarrhoea too.

● **Dengue fever** This viral disease gives rise to severe fever and joint and muscle pain. It's spread by mosquitoes which, unusually, bite during the day. Dengue fever is painful and unpleasant, but the more serious, life-threatening dengue haemorrhagic fever can also occur, although the latter is most usually associated with a second or later bout of the illness. There is no vaccination and the disease is currently on the increase in Asia – see precautions for avoiding mosquito bites, p.359.

● **Hepatitis** There are several strains of this disease (Hepatitis A, B, C, D and E) in which viruses attack the liver, causing a whole raft of symptoms including yellow colouring of skin and eyes (jaundice), extreme exhaustion, fever, joint pains, weight loss and diarrhoea. It can also result in either cirrhosis of the liver or liver cancer in the long term. One of the most common of the serious illnesses that can afflict travellers, it can last for many months. Hepatitis A is transmitted via contaminated food, water or saliva; the long-term vaccine against it is a course of two injections, six to eighteen months apart, giving ten years' protection. The more serious Hepatitis B is transmitted through contaminated blood, needles and syringes and by sexual contact; the vaccine is given as a course of three injections over six months. For increased convenience, a combined vaccine for Hepatitis A and B is also available. There's no vaccine against the C, D or E strains.

● **Japanese encephalitis** This is a viral illness resulting in inflammation of the brain, found across Asia, although largely restricted to rural areas. It's transmitted via mosquitoes from infected animals and is very dangerous – the death rate is high, and so is the danger of brain damage if you survive. Inoculation provides only partial protection, and involves three injections spread over a month.

● **Malaria** There are several strains of malaria, most causing recurring bouts of fever, headache and shivering. All are serious, debilitating and difficult to treat successfully. The parasites that cause malaria are carried by night-biting mosquitoes. All travellers to Asia should consider taking a course of preventive tablets and do everything to prevent being bitten, as none of the drugs available is a hundred percent effective. See p.357–361 for more details.

Travelling with children

Health is the most serious concern for anyone thinking of taking children to Asia. As every parent knows, kids can get very sick very quickly, and although they often recover equally fast, it means that you need to think long and hard about taking them too far off the beaten track where medical treatment may be hard to find. You also need to brief yourself fully about all the potential health risks you might encounter and get advice from a specialist travel clinic as soon as you can, especially as vaccination and malaria prevention are more complicated for children. Once you are travelling, don't underestimate the stress and exhaustion that kids experience from too much hurtling around, which can make them run-down and more prone to illness. Be sure to include plenty of chilling-out time – you'll all have a better trip that way.

Most of the general publications on p.351 and websites listed in the Directory on pp.419–420 have sections devoted to travelling with children, and the malaria website listed on p.359 are also useful. A few publications offer sensible, down-to-earth advice about children's health. In the UK, the Nomad Medical Centre (@www.nomadtravel.co.uk) publishes a special information sheet on travelling with children, full of sensible tips. Other useful resources include the books *Your Child's Health Abroad* by Dr Jane Wilson-Howarth and Dr Matthew Ellis (Bradt Publications), Samantha Gore-Lyons *Are We Nearly There?* and Cathy Lanigan's *Travel With Children* (Lonely Planet) and the "Kids to Go" bulletin board at @thorntree.lonelyplanet.com.

- **Meningococcal meningitis** Caused by airborne bacteria, this disease attacks the lining of the brain and can be fatal; epidemics, though rare, do affect parts of the continent. The vaccine (different from the injection given to children) is given as a single injection and does not protect against all strains of meningitis. It takes two weeks to reach full immunity after having the injection.

- **Polio**, **diphtheria** and **TB** Most people will have been inoculated against these in childhood and, while they are rare in the West, they are still common in Asia. You should make sure you are still covered – you need a booster every ten years.

- **Rabies** Spread via the saliva of infected cats, dogs and monkeys, rabies is prevalent throughout Asia, with ninety percent of the world's deaths from the disease occurring in India. It's also estimated that two percent of the dogs in Bangkok are rabid, and the disease accounts for about five hundred deaths in the city every year. The vaccine, is a course of three injections before departure, then a booster is required – the first one after six to to twelve months and then every two to three years. Even then, you'll still need urgent medical help and further injections should you get bitten by an animal suspected of carrying the disease. Without previous vaccination at home, you'll need more injections if you do get bitten abroad.

- **Tetanus** Also known as lockjaw, the disease is contracted via open wounds (for example, a cut caused by stepping on a rusty nail). Make sure you are up to date before you leave home – you need a booster every ten years.
- **Typhoid** Spread by contaminated food and water, typhoid is characterized by extremely high fever, abdominal pains, headaches, diarrhoea and red spots on the body; patients need urgent medical help. Protection (which lasts one to three years) is either given by injection or a course of more expensive capsules. Be prepared for some pain, discomfort and possible fever after certain types of typhoid jab.

Mosquitoes

Given the number of diseases carried by mosquitoes (malaria, Japanese encephalitis, dengue fever), not to mention the unpleasantness of mosquito bites, you should do whatever you can to avoid getting bitten. This means wearing long sleeves and sloshing mosquito repellent on exposed skin during the dusk and darkness hours when the malarial mosquito operates, and sleeping under a mosquito net or with any open windows covered by a fine wire mesh. It's a good idea to have a shower and get changed (into light-coloured clothes) for the evening before it gets dark – mosquitoes adore sweaty skin, and also strong perfumes.

You might decide to take your own mosquito net with you – they are light and compact, and you can guarantee one brought from home won't be full of tears and cigarette burns. Ideally you want one that has been impregnated with Permethrin insecticide as an additional barrier against the bugs; you can also buy Permethrin separately to treat older nets.

Malaria

Malaria is one of the nastiest and most common tropical diseases worldwide – it affects between 300 and 500 million people each year and kills more than a million of them. Though most of these deaths occur among young children in sub-Saharan Africa, the disease is a serious risk for anyone travelling to Asia, where some of the most

Malaria in Asia

This is a broad overview of the malaria situation in the countries covered in this book. Be sure to check the current situation and appropriate preventive medication and emergency treatment with a medical specialist before you travel. Countries described as "malarial at lower altitudes" are mountainous in parts. Although they are not malarial at higher elevations, the cut-off line isn't totally clear and even transiting through lower altitudes can be risky.

Bangladesh	Malarial
Bhutan	Malarial at lower altitudes
Brunei	Not malarial
Cambodia	Malarial
China	Large areas are malarial. Seek detailed advice when you have an itinerary
East Timor	Malarial
India	Malarial
Indonesia	Malarial
Japan	Not malarial
Laos	Malarial
Malaysia	Malarial
Mongolia	Not malarial
Nepal	Malarial at lower altitudes
Pakistan	Malarial at lower altitudes
Philippines	Malarial
Singapore	Not malarial
South Korea	Malarial in parts. Seek detailed advice.
Sri Lanka	Malarial
Taiwan	Not malarial
Thailand	Malarial
Vietnam	Malarial

dangerous forms of malaria lurk, especially in the Thai-Cambodian and Thai–Burmese border areas, where the parasites that cause the disease have developed resistance to several drugs, most famously chloroquine, which was for many years the main drug used in prevention.

There is currently no vaccine against the disease, but there are a range of drugs that can prevent you contracting it, though none is a hundred percent effective. You must start taking them a specified amount of time before you arrive in a malarial area (the exact period depends on the drug) and, even more importantly, continue taking them for some time (again, determined by which drug you are taking) after you leave. It is possible to develop malaria back home if you ignore this regime – typically about two thousand British travellers contract malaria every year and ten of these die from the disease. Another consideration is that all drugs have potential side effects so you need to weigh up the risks.

For many decades the most commonly used malaria prophylaxis has been chloroquine (sold as Nivaquine and Avloclor in the UK, and Aralen in the US), taken weekly together with daily proguanil (sold as Paludrine). However, as strains of chloroquine-resistant malaria have evolved, other drugs have come into use. Mefloquine (sold as Larium) is probably the best known due to controversy that continues to rage over serious side effects in some users. However there are plenty of other options: the antibiotic doxycycline is the drug of choice in many areas where travellers are unsuited to or choose not to take Larium. A relatively new option, sold as Malarone, is a combination of atovaquone and proguanil and prescribed in areas where there is chloroquine resistance and other drugs may not be suitable. It's pricey but has reportedly fewer side effects. Before you travel, seek advice from your doctor or a specialist travel clinic about which drugs are recommended for malaria prevention in the areas you plan to visit. If you are heading a long way off the beaten track, it is also worth discussing with your medical adviser whether you should carry an emergency course of treatment – though this should be used until you can get to medical help rather than instead of it. If you develop any fever up to a year after you get home, be sure to get medical advice and make sure the doctor is aware that you've been to a malarial area.

The general books on p.351 and websites in the Directory on p.419 all carry information about malaria; in addition, check out Malaria Foundation International at ⓦwww.malaria.org for the latest information. Some of the most interesting news items relate to the Chinese preparation *qinghaosu* (known as artemisinin in the West), a derivative of the plant sweet wormwood (*Artemesia annua*), which has been used against malaria in China for over two thousand years; it's proving highly effective in areas where resistance has developed. You'll also spot items about attempts to genetically modify mosquitoes so they can no longer transmit the parasite that causes the disease.

Mosquito repellents

Hopefully all of the above has convinced you of the importance of avoiding mosquito bites. The most effective way to do this is by applying mosquito repellent to exposed skin; the most widely used is called DEET (Diethyl Tolumide). You can buy repellent containing up to 95 percent DEET, although strengths of over 35 percent can irritate skin and are not thought to be much more effective in any case. Wrist and ankle bands pre-soaked in the chemical are also available, or you can soak your own. Bear in mind that it's strong stuff and can cause skin reactions after extended use. You also need to be careful not to get it in contact with anything plastic (sunglasses, watch straps, shoes), as it tends to melt them. Locally bought repellents are often very good and much cheaper than ones bought at home. They may even be the same brand – Autan, for example, is widely available throughout Asia. Some equipment companies even produce travel clothing pre-treated with repellent – although the protection doesn't last much more than a few dozen washes.

There's also a range of natural products that work well. These substances aren't quite as repugnant to mosquitoes as DEET, but avoid its disadvantages. Most of these natural repellents are based around citronella or lemon eucalyptus, geranium and soya bean or coconut oil. Preparations containing neem oil are also useful. One advantage of using a mosquito repellent though is that it will ward off leeches, ticks and sandflies, too.

Some travellers believe that vitamin B1 tablets or garlic capsules, taken regularly, make the blood offensive to insects and so protect against bites, though there isn't much evidence for or against this yet.

At some point in your trip you'll encounter mosquito coils, which you can buy cheaply in boxes of eight or ten. Bright green and impregnated with chemicals, they are the main Asian way of deterring mosquitoes. To use a mosquito coil, you need to separate it from its pair (they always come entwined in twos and are really fiddly to separate), light it, let the flame burn for a second or two and then blow it out – to be effective coils should be smoking rather than burning. They also need to be suspended above the floor, and so come with a tin stand, the prong of which goes through the slit in the centre of the coil. Each coil smoulders for about eight hours. They're useful for protecting your ankles if you are sitting out on a verandah at night, or you can put coils beside the bed while you sleep; thoughtful restaurants put them under their tables. The coils are effective as long as you keep close to them, but you may find that after a few nights you end up feeling suffocated by the pungent smell.

Leeches

Any forays into the jungle, especially near the equator (or anywhere in the rainy season) mean potential encounters with leeches – tiny, thread-like blood-sucking creatures that attach themselves to your skin, zap you with an anaesthetic and anticoagulant, slurp away at the red stuff and, when they've had enough and expanded to many times their normal size, drop off and leave you dripping blood for a long time afterwards. The good news is they don't carry any nasty diseases; the bad news is that they can get through the tiniest holes, such as between the threads in most socks (and they love the eyeholes of boots). One glimpse of your ankle with a dozen or so of them attached is a short cut to hysteria.

To stop them attacking, silk socks, insect repellent and tobacco leaves in your socks are all useful, plus regular checks of your feet when you are walking. If you do fall victim, dab at the creatures with salt, a lighted cigarette or chewing tobacco (widely available across Asia) to get them to let go. Don't just pull them off in a panic – easier said than done – as this is likely to leave their sucking parts embedded in your skin, which can lead to infection.

Also available are several brands of electrically powered machines, that heat up tablets so that they release a repellent into the air. The disadvantages are that they rely on having a mains supply, need a fairly confined space and don't operate too well if there's a draught but the smell isn't as offensive.

The heat

The opportunity to experience a tropical climate is one of the big attractions of a trip to Asia, yet exposure to extreme heat is one of the major causes of illness for many travellers. To avoid problems, be sure to do the following when you arrive:

- Respect the heat. It isn't only mad dogs and Englishmen who go out in the midday sun, it's plenty of other travellers as well, but it's far better to stay in the shade during the extreme heat of the day, as most local people do.
- Dry yourself carefully after bathing – use medicated talcum powder or antifungal powder (both available throughout Asia) if you fall victim to heat rashes, prickly heat or fungal infections that thrive in the damp, humid conditions of the tropics.
- Dress sensibly – see p.263 for ideas on clothing that will help you keep cool in hot climates.

- Protect yourself from the extreme sun and be especially careful at high altitude, where you may feel cool but will still be exposed to huge amounts of ultraviolet light. Use plenty of high-factor sunscreen, even if you are just walking around (don't forget the tops of your feet, tops of your ears and backs of your hands). A hat or umbrella will stop your brains frying.
- Drink plenty of water. The heat will make you sweat, so you need to increase your fluid intake to compensate. If you stop peeing or your urine is becoming dark, then you're not drinking enough.
- Increase your intake of salt – you also lose this when you sweat. Many travellers add a pinch of salt to fruit juices and shakes (see rehydration advice on p.365). Muscle cramps are a sign that you are lacking enough salt in your diet.
- Be aware of the symptoms of heat exhaustion, which is common in hot, humid places and characterized by extreme fatigue, cramps, a rapid pulse, reddened skin and vomiting. Anyone with these symptoms needs a cool place to recover, plenty to drink and even wrapping in sheets or sarongs soaked in cold water. Hospital treatment is sometimes necessary. Heat stroke is a more serious, potentially life-threatening overheating of the body; if the patient continues to get hotter despite the treatments suggested or becomes confused, delirious or unconscious seek medical help fast.
- Get enough rest. It is very easy to get exhausted and run-down if you are racing round sightseeing in the heat all day and sampling the nightlife after dark. If you're tired, you're more vulnerable to illness.

Water

With a couple of exceptions – Singapore and Japan – tap water in Asia is not safe for tourists to drink, which means you should avoid ice in your drinks, too. However, bottled water is widely available in all but the most out-of-the-way places. Check the seals of the bottles before you buy, as some unscrupulous dealers collect empty bottles and refill them straight from the tap; such bottles might have the seal missing or have obviously been tampered with. Bottled water can make a surprising hole in your budget and you'll need to allow for it in your pre-trip calculations. In the cheapest countries, a few litres of bottled water will only set you back a dollar or so a day, but this is $90/£52 over a three-month trip, and you'll also have deposited a small mountain of non-biodegradable plastic bottles into the largely ineffectual Asian rubbish system.

One alternative is to boil drinking water to sterilize it – five minutes' boiling (ten minutes at high altitude) will kill off anything that is likely to harm you. While this is fine if you are camping or have access to cooking equipment, it is not convenient in most situations. Another option is to sterilize the water using chlorine or iodine tablets (available from outdoor-equipment shops or travel clinics). While these are cheap and easy, they are not effective against all the harmful organisms in the water (amoebic dysentery and giardia, to name a couple), and they leave the water with a definite chemical taste. Water filters also only do a partial job, and do not remove viruses (such as those that cause hepatitis). The most effective solution is to take a water purifier, which will both filter and sterilize the water. There are several on the market; before buying one, you should compare their sizes, weights, the speed at which they process water, and how often replacement cartridges are needed. Travel Equipment Suppliers (p.422) and Travel Clinics (p.419) stock water purifiers.

Food

The sights, smells and tastes of a bewildering array of Asian food are one of the greatest pleasures of any visit to the continent. A few minutes among the fruit and vegetables of even the smallest town market and you'll be dying to try out the unfamiliar bread-

△ Market food

fruit, rambutans and mangosteens, as well as variations on old favourites, such as red bananas. A walk through any Asian night market where cooks behind tiny stalls conjure up enticing, spicy meals of rice, noodles, seafood and soups will set your taste buds tingling. Head down any Asian street and the chances are you'll stumble across carts selling tea, soup or ice cream, women peeling pineapples or tiny neighbourhood restaurants wafting succulent odours into the air. Though not everyone will want to tackle the crunchy cooked fried grasshoppers of Thailand, the liberal chilli-fest of Sumatran Padang cuisine or the dog-meat delicacies of southwestern China, we guarantee you will make some unforget-table culinary discoveries.

While you should enjoy the new tastes and eating experiences to the full, it pays to exercise some control over what and where you eat:

- Avoid food that has been sitting out in the midday heat assaulted by flies, or anything that has be reheated. One of the reasons Indian food can have such a disastrous effect on foreign bowels is the common cooking style: slow-cooked casseroles and stews mean the temperature may never rise high enough to exterminate germs. Western food is often the most hazardous – ask yourself how long that cannelloni has been waiting around before its brief time in the microwave. In contrast, in a place like Thailand, stir-fries are whipped up on the spot and have no chance to languish all day in the tropical heat.
- Fruit that has been peeled for you by someone or doesn't get peeled at all, such as pineapples, papaya or grapes, can be a hazard, but fruit you peel yourself should be fine.
- Similarly, raw vegetables, including salad, are suspect, either because of the water they have been washed in or the human excrement that is used for fertilizer in some parts of Asia.
- Surrounded by so many unfamiliar foods, it can be difficult to get a balanced diet, especially as in some places, such as Nepal and parts of China, fresh fruit and vegetables are scarce. Consider taking vitamin tablets with you.
- Vegetarians and vegans are generally well catered for across Asia; many Asians are vegetarian on religious grounds and restaurants cater for them alongside carnivorous diners, often in imaginative and delicious ways. Indeed, sources of protein such as tofu are probably more widely available in Asia than they are in the West. However, be aware of the warning above.

Diarrhoea and dehydration

There are numerous causes for the diarrhoea and vomiting that strike travellers in Asia, from a straightforward reaction to a change of water and diet to more unpleasant bacteria and viruses. Whatever the cause, the main problem you'll face is dehydration, which will make you feel exhausted and dizzy, and give you a splitting headache. It's important to focus on rehydrating the moment any stomach problems start; worry about a diagnosis later.

You should be drinking two or three litres of water a day just to cope with being in the tropics, but if you get diarrhoea you'll need a lot more. In addition, your body will be losing important minerals and so you should always carry sachets of oral rehydration salts (ORS) with you. These just need dissolving in clean drinking water and are available under a variety of names (such as Dioralyte) in the West and throughout Asia. Even if you're vomiting, you should sip small amounts of the solution. If you can't get hold of commercial brands, dissolve approximately half a level teaspoon of salt and eight level teaspoons of sugar in a litre of clean water; it's important that the resulting mixture shouldn't contain too much salt – it mustn't be any saltier than the taste of tears. A small amount of fruit juice will improve the taste.

Diarrhoea and vomiting caused by changes to diet and water should run their course in two to three days, and as long as you keep drinking you'll be OK until you can start eating again; start with bland food, such as boiled rice. If the diarrhoea and vomiting are particularly severe, persist for more than three days without abating or are accompanied by blood or mucus in your faeces, or by fever, then you should seek medical help. There are several illnesses you should be aware of, including bacilliary or amoebic dysentery, typhoid and a particularly common one called giardiasis (or giardia), which produces rotten-egg belches and farts – not guaranteed to help you make friends.

Anti-diarrhoea tablets should be used extremely sparingly. Diarrhoea serves a purpose in ejecting toxins from your body. These tablets, which effectively halt the movements of your digestive system, stop the diarrhoea, but they block you up, don't attack the micro-organisms responsible for the problem and can actually make you feel worse. They are useful, however, if you absolutely *have* to travel.

As bizarre as it may sound, after a few months on the road you'll be gleefully swapping stories with fellow travellers of "the yellow frothy diarrhoea I had in Nepal" – probably while tucking into a pizza in Thailand.

Altitude

The problem of altitude is a serious one for anyone planning to trek in the Himalayas or visit Tibet or other high-altitude regions such as Ladakh in India, some parts of Xinjiang, Sichuan and Yunnan in China, the Karakoram region of Pakistan and Mount Fuji in Japan – anyone who usually lives at low altitude and goes over 10,000 feet (about 3000m) is at risk, whether trekking, flying in or arriving by bus or train.

The higher you go above sea level, the less oxygen there is in the air and the lower the air pressure that drives it from your lungs into your bloodstream. Your body needs time to adapt to this, and while this process is under way – probably for the first three days at altitude, especially if you have flown in – you are likely to experience headaches, shortness of breath, tiredness, loss of appetite, aches and pains, sleeping problems and nausea (collectively known as acute mountain sickness, or AMS). Relax totally and drink plenty of water (at least three litres daily) and the symptoms should pass, although having acclimatized you must still ascend slowly – no more than

△ Trekker, Nepal

300m per day with a rest day for every 900m climbed. If you go too fast the symptoms will return.

If your symptoms worsen, however, and especially if you start vomiting and experience loss of coordination, delirium, rapid heartbeat, breathlessness and blueness of tongue and lips, you must descend as soon as possible. Just a few hundred metres of vertical descent can be life-saving and usually brings about immediate recovery. Serious cases of AMS are very rare, but anyone planning to travel and especially trek over 3000m should inform themselves fully of the potential risks before setting off. The website ⓦwww .high-altitude-medicine.com/AMS.html contains everything you need to know.

HIV, AIDS and contraception

Unprotected sex is as unwise in Asia as it is at home. Reliable figures are not easy to find, but HIV and AIDS are prevalent across the region. As an indication, there are an estimated 4.5 to 5 million people in India with HIV/AIDS. In Cambodia 2.7 percent of the adult population has HIV/AIDS. The level of AIDS education is variable throughout Asia so travellers should assume they will be the one taking responsibility for the supply and use of condoms in any sexual encounter.

Condoms, often locally manufactured, are widely available in pharmacies and supermarkets, although local brands have a fairly mixed reputation – you'd be well advised to check use-by dates and buy from air-conditioned suppliers as far as possible, as extreme heat can rot the rubber. Expatriate residents in Asia usually keep theirs in the fridge – not a service most budget hotels offer – but it is worth trying to keep them in the coolest part of your pack along with your films. Women travellers may feel very conspicuous asking for condoms, especially in traditional Muslim areas such as Indonesia, so it's preferable to carry some from home, particularly bearing in mind the quality concerns.

Not sure of the word in the local language? It may not be as tough as you think. While condoms are the fairly tongue-knotting *bao cao su* in Vietnamese, they are *kondom* in Indonesian and Malay, *kandom* in Hindi and Urdu, and are informally known as *meechai* in Thailand after the charismatic former Minister for Health, Mr Meechai.

Approaching the small Thai island of Ko Tao, I was mesmerized. Across the water I could see a mass of trees, surrounded by white sands, coconut palms and rickety thatched huts. As we stepped off the boat, hordes of touts appeared advertising their beach resorts. Bewildered, we followed a young, stocky Thai man by the name of Chet, who drove us to a resort.

During many weeks on the island, poker playing with Chet developed into riskier games, and we started sleeping together. Armed with condoms, I didn't worry about health issues. I asked Chet if he had been tested for HIV and we discussed the chances of pregnancy. But the reality of the risks never truly set in; condoms were fast becoming an inconvenience and the belief that nothing could harm me grew. What can happen to you in paradise?

In the New Year I left for Australia but sometime in March, I began to feel ill. One morning looking in the mirror, I discovered the whites of my eyes were turning yellow. This was followed by my stomach and slowly the rest of my body. I was losing weight, my hair was falling out, and eventually I could barely stand. The doctor ordered an exhaustive series of blood tests. At last the results came: I had been diagnosed with Hepatitis B, the worst strain of the disease and one which you're destined to carry – and suffer from – for life. Hepatitis B attacks the liver – brutally; liver cirrhosis is a distinct possibility, as is liver cancer.

My world collapsed. I was treated with countless pharmaceuticals and, feeling partially recovered, I left for Britain three weeks later. Back home was worse: I faced hospital appointments, HIV tests and family hysteria. I contacted Chet, afraid that he too might be ill, or perhaps that he might pass on the condition to someone else, but he denied any knowledge of the disease and I felt angry, rejected, naive – and incredibly foolish.

I have now learned to live with the disease. But it dominates my life to an extent I could never have imagined. The cost of my trip feels enormous and will continue to do so, but at least I know now that you have to be on your guard – even in paradise.

Vicky Nicholas

Women travellers using the contraceptive pill should take a sufficient supply for the entire trip; your brand may not be available locally. However, the pills can be affected by the extreme heat and if you have diarrhoea or vomiting their effectiveness is reduced, so you'll need other protection.

Health care in Asia

Millions of people in Asia have only limited access to the good-quality, local, affordable health care that we sometimes take for granted. Of course, the situation varies from country to country, but don't be surprised if health facilities are few and far between, staff don't speak English, have only limited training and their equipment for diagnosis and treatment is woefully inadequate.

However, throughout much of Asia there are private hospitals that exist alongside the underfunded and overstretched public system. In some cities with a large expatriate population or plenty of tourists, such as Kathmandu, you'll even find specialist travellers' clinics. Check locations in your guidebook, or with the embassy, if you get sick, but private places are often the best option.

You should make it clear on arrival that you can pay (many hospitals accept credit cards) and set about contacting your insurance company (see p.207 for more on medical insurance). In most cases, you'll end up paying the bill and reclaiming the costs later.

Throughout Asia there are plenty of pharmacies and even local corner shops selling drugs that in your home country would be available on prescription, or from trained personnel. This means that on the surface it is apparently easy to self-medicate, although you'll need to know how to take the drugs, as the person selling it may not. One potential hazard is that many of the drugs distributed in Asia are fakes, possibly below strength, useless or even potentially poisonous. If you do need to buy medicine in Asia, it pays to buy from large, efficient-looking operations, whether hospitals, pharmacies or doctor's surgeries and always check that the packaging and labelling looks correct and intact, and look at the expiry date.

Traditional medicine

Many Asian countries have their own traditional health systems, and clinics are invariably willing to treat foreigners, although you may need to take an interpreter with you, unless you're fairly fluent in the local language. While opinions in the West vary about the efficacy of such treatments, a considerable body of anecdotal evidence suggests Eastern medicine can help in many situations where Western medicine offers little.

Ayurvedic medicine, which has flourished in India for five thousand years, is a holistic medical system that looks at the whole body and detects imbalances in the system. The body is believed to be controlled by three forces – *pitta*, the sun; *kapha*, the moon; and *vata*, the wind. An imbalance in these is regarded as leading to disease; treatment, often with herbal remedies, concentrates on restoring the balance.

In Tibetan medicine, which derives from ayurvedic medicine, health depends on the balance of the three humours – *beken* (phlegm), *tiba* (bile) and *lung* (wind). A diagnosis is made by examining tongue, pulse and urine and by diagnostic questioning; treatment may be with herbal remedies and/or changes of diet and activity.

China has another ancient holistic medical system with largely herbal remedies, though the often bizarre ingredients in traditional Chinese medicine – such as snake gall bladder and scorpion oil, not to mention the notorious rhinoceros horn – have served to give it a somewhat besmirched reputation outside the country. Acupuncture, where needles are inserted at various vital points on the body, is available in clinics across China and Japan – make sure that sterile needles are used. There are also non-invasive forms of treatment, such as massage in Thailand and shiatsu in Japan, where finger pressure is used to work on much the same parts of the body as acupuncture.

Finally, bridging the gap between health care and beauty treatments are traditional spa treatments, available throughout Asia, especially in the more upmarket hotels of Bali, Malaysia and Thailand, where everything from mud wraps to aromatherapy massage and reflexology is on offer to soothe and detox both body and mind. Bear in mind that racing around to fit in all the sights and experience everything that a country has to offer can be a high stress experience. A few days or even hours out to recharge the batteries can have positive effects on short- and long-term health.

13

Staying in touch

Not only is it fair and reasonable that your friends and family at home will want to keep in touch while you're away, but you may be surprised at the extent to which you are delighted by contact with them. Travelling abroad is huge fun and wildly exciting, but it can also be stressful, disorienting and at times depressing and lonely, and communication with familiar people at these times can be very comforting.

You'll find the quality of most mail, Internet and telephone services in Asia very high. However, there are big price differences between communication methods – not a problem if money is no object, but worth thinking about if, like most travellers, you are on a budget.

How will we know where you are?

Family and friends are naturally concerned that there will be periods when they have literally no idea where you are. If you do some of the following before you go, it can help to reassure them that you have at least a tentative schedule and aren't as inaccessible as they may fear:

● Provide them with a copy of your flight schedule (include carriers and flight numbers), and notify them of any changes as you go. If there is an Asian plane crash while you are away, they will naturally fear you are on board unless they know otherwise.

- Give them your email address but impress on them that although you will be checking mail regularly there will be times when you aren't near an Internet café.
- Consider a software package that lets you set up a website; you can update it with an SMS from your mobile and arrange that they get an SMS alert when you make an entry. Check out *intouch* by Rough Guides (⊛www.roughguidesintouch.com), which has security advantages as well for keeping copies of important documents.
- If they are totally unable to cope with technology then give them a list of post restante addresses, the dates when you'll be checking the mail and the approximate amount of time (usually two to three weeks) that they'll need to allow for a letter to get there.
- Establish a phoning-in schedule – for example, every four weeks. Don't promise to phone at an exact time or even on a specific day, though, as if you can't get to a phone for a genuine reason, you could cause a great deal of worry.
- Consider taking your mobile (see p.379) but be sure to tell them if your number changes.
- Think about joining a voicemail scheme, which gives you access to a private answerphone. You leave your message for callers; they call in and leave their own messages, which you can call in and listen to (and you can change your own message at the same time). When you enquire about a scheme, make sure you check whether it is easily accessible from public phones in the countries you are visiting; most schemes rely on touch tone phones for access. Check out ⊛www .lonelyplanetekit.com for one such scheme.
- Decide to communicate with the wider world along with your nearest and dearest and set up a blog (see p.384).

Mail

To see Asian society in microcosm, get yourself to the post office. In Indonesia you'll see the hi-tech types heading for the public Internet access, while old men struggle to address letters to relatives a couple of islands away, parents queue to send cash to needy children studying away from home, and large businesses register piles of parcels to their overseas customers – Asian post offices perform pretty much the same functions as their Western counterparts and come in all sizes. In the larger ones, you'll find different services available from different counters, usually with a jostling crowd around them rather than a queue. Even the tiniest villages have some system of postal collection and delivery, albeit sometimes bizarre.

Mail is quicker and more reliable from towns and cities, although variability in delivery time is a common complaint among travellers. Generally, mail does seem to reach its destination (although avoid posting anything other than letters from Nepal, where the service is notoriously unreliable). However, it pays to be vigilant – stick the stamps on yourself and ask for them to be franked while you wait, as there

Bhutan postal runners

I lived for some time in a remote village in Bhutan. There was no road to the village and mail was delivered every two or three weeks by a "runner" whose job was literally to run between the nearest post office and all the outlying villages, delivering and collecting mail. He operated on a two-week circuit, travelling across mountain passes, over rivers, through sparsely populated forest, and sleeping wherever he was given hospitality at night. In the past, runners carried spears to fend off bears (still a considerable hazard in the area), but these days they are more likely to carry transistor radios for company. These also have a bear-scaring purpose, as it is widely believed that if a bear hears voices approaching it will run away.

Lesley Reader

Correspondence tips

- If there has been a big disaster in your area, then, as well as a letter, a quick phone call home will set minds at rest.
- Don't make rash promises to write to people that you are then going to break. If you tell your parents you'll write daily/weekly or whatever, then you really should stick to it or they'll panic about your safety, especially if this is your only means of communication. If you're an irregular and unenthusiastic letter writer, then don't forget that a signed postcard is enough to stop people worrying. Faxes can be useful – cheaper than phoning but more immediate than letters.
- Don't write to close friends and family in the midst of a bout of dysentery or the day before a bungy-jump and then not contact them again for a few weeks.
- If you send a huge number of postcards the cost can add up, so include it in your budget. The postage rate for cards is often equivalent to that for an aerogramme, which can carry much more news, so check out rates when you arrive. From Singapore it costs the equivalent of US$0.30 (17p) to send a postcard anywhere in the world by airmail or around US$0.60 (34p) for a letter to Europe or the US.
- Take some stamps from your home country with you – you may well meet other travellers from home at the end of their trip who'll be happy to drop a few letters in the post for you when they land.

is a danger they might be steamed off and reused. It also helps to know what the word for "stamp" looks like in the local language – check your phrasebook, as few counters are labelled in English and staff generally speak little English.

Poste restante

You've got a few options for receiving mail. Most convenient is to use the poste restante service available at post offices in most Asian cities: you just turn up with your passport for ID and collect your mail.

The actual system varies enormously across the continent. In some places you get to look through the entire batch of mail that has arrived for any foreigner over the last two years; in others you ask for a particular letter of the alphabet to trawl through. Sometimes you give your name to the clerk who hunts through the mail for you, and some post offices even keep a record of all poste restante mail logged in a book or on a computer. In most countries the service is free, although there is sometimes a small charge (in China, for example). Generally the post offices in the more popular tourist destinations are more reliable and organized – Bangkok, Singapore, Kathmandu and Kuta (Bali), for example; on the other hand, poste restante services are currently most limited in Cambodia (Phnom Penh, Siem Reap and Sihanoukville only) and Laos (Vientiane and Louang Phabang only).

You should be able to get the precise address of the post office you want to use from a good guidebook; otherwise mail bearing your name followed by "Poste Restante, General Post Office" and the name of the city should get to them. Anyone who writes to you should print your surname in capital letters and underline it. Most places file mail alphabetically by surname, but it pays to check through under your first name as well, or any other name or title that your nearest and dearest may have used.

Generally post offices only keep mail for a month or so before either returning it or junking it. This means you have to tread a fairly careful line between getting there too early or too late for your letters. The best plan is to get mail sent to a few key places on your itinerary for which you have reasonably fixed dates. Some post offices operate a forwarding system for mail that arrives after you've left. You must go and register in person for this service, but it's generally not very reliable.

Getting mail addressed to you at hotels is usually the last resort. It'll be coming through the post office in any case, so it's just as easy and probably safer to collect it from there. You can't rely on hotels to have an efficient system and your letters could easily end up in someone's desk drawer, the wastepaper basket or winging their way back home to the sender.

Receiving parcels

It'll save grief if you remember that parcels and packages are generally less reliably received by travellers than letters. So many parcels go missing en route that it's better to tell people at home not to send them.

If you really must get something sent out to you, it's safer to use a courier company. These specialize in getting stuff moved around the world reliably and quickly, but at a price; they charge by both the weight and size of the package. Because they operate door to door, they will not deliver to a poste restante address – your best bet is to arrange to collect the package at their local office. Packages should take between four and seven working days to arrive from the US, UK or Australia.

Sending letters

Sending letters and postcards from Asia isn't difficult. Address them clearly, writing the destination country in the local language and script, if possible, to speed up processing. Label as airmail, get them weighed at the counter, stick on the stamps or franked label (some post offices use a franking machine) and drop them in the appropriate box. Usually an express service and a registered service are available at extra cost. Here are two correspondence tips:

- Warn those at home that mail can take three weeks or so in each direction. Airmail to the West from Vietnam varies between four days and four weeks. Post from Singapore, on the other hand, is among the fastest in Asia, a couple of days to Europe is standard.
- Number the letters to people you are writing to regularly so they know if any have gone missing and get them to do the same if they are writing to you. Don't forget to ask whoever is your most regular correspondent to keep your letters – they make vivid reading when you're back. Some travellers don't write a diary but keep copies of

the letters they write as a record of the trip instead (take carbon paper with you or buy it en route).

Shipping stuff home

Sending parcels home is rather more time-consuming than sending letters. You should probably set aside at least half a day to get the formalities completed, but this is definitely preferable to carrying a Sri Lankan mask, Balinese chest or Indian rug with you on the rest of your six-month trip.

Basically, your choices are to send them by airmail (the most expensive option), surface mail or via cargo agents. Charges for parcels sent through the postal system, whether airmail or surface, are calculated by weight. Many post offices in tourist areas sell boxes and tape for packing your goods; others, such as Hong Kong, even have a packing service. In Vietnam it is obligatory that the parcel is wrapped for you.

The Indian system involves a lengthy process whereby the customs desk at the post office first needs to examine the goods you are sending. You are then required to have them stitched into white linen parcels (the stitchers operate outside all post offices) before they are accepted for mailing. For some idea of prices, access the websites of the Hong Kong (ⓦwww.hongkongpost.com) or Singapore (ⓦwww.singpost.com) postal services.

Most cargo agents, on the other hand, ship by volume, with one cubic metre the minimum amount they'll handle. This is the best option if you have something heavy to send. Precise costs depend on the destination, but, as an example, from Lombok

> ### Suits you, sir
>
> The tailors in Khao San Road, Bangkok, said they could make me a suit in two days for the equivalent of £30. Despite my ten-month backpacking itinerary still stretching ahead of me, I decided that a made-to-measure silk suit was something I must have. In fact, I ordered two.
>
> The process itself was fascinating: after just two fitting sessions the assortment of pieces of fabric that had been tacked inside out, draped around my body and marked up deftly with chalk lines were transformed into two superb suits – a pale cream one and a rich, deep brown one.
>
> I packaged them up at the main post office, labelling them merely as clothes being returned home – two pairs of trousers and two jackets. In hindsight, parcels like this containing clothes from Bangkok are probably viewed fairly suspiciously, or else I was just unlucky. The box was opened when it arrived several months later at Liverpool docks, and duty of £60 was imposed on these imported items. Despite costing me twice as much as I had expected, my suits were still bargains.
>
> Jonathan Tucker

prices to Australia start at $158/A$210, to Canada $196/C$240, to New Zealand $170/NZ$250, the UK $175/£100 and to the USA $220, all per cubic metre. Delivery times will be faster if you're sending from port cities than from inland towns where the goods will have to be transported to the coast first.

Whichever method you opt for, it makes sense to send fewer larger packages rather than numerous small ones. Always make sure that, *including* the packaging, what you're sending is just under the maximum of the weight/volume band rather than just over into the next band, which might be considerably more expensive – it's worth checking prices and weights/volumes with the post office or shipping agent before you start parcelling stuff up.

Bear in mind that whatever you send home is subject to examination by customs in your own country. They are not only looking for illegal substances, but are entitled to charge import duty/taxes on new goods that you are bringing into the country. Check the appropriate government websites before you embark on a major shopping spree or it may all end up costing more than you expect. In the UK check ⊛www.hmrc.gov.uk and in the US ⊛www.customs.gov.

Finally, classier souvenir stores the world over will always offer to arrange shipping for you. You'll be paying them extra for the service, and there are always some rip-off merchants who take your money and send nothing, so try to go by personal recommendation if you can.

Photographs

Sending pictures home is a good way of keeping friends and family informed; they'll really believe you are at the Taj Mahal when they see the usual cheesy shot of you posing in front of it. The old issues of slides versus prints and what to do with films and negatives for months on the road in the tropical heat is now largely obsolete as most travellers use digital technology (see p.275).

The best option is to download pictures from the camera onto CDs, or your blog or website, or into emails and blast them into cyberspace – many Asian Internet cafés now have the technology. It is worth keeping a careful list of pictures, though – it sounds silly, but after another six months' travelling you won't be able to remember which Thai temple, Malaysian island or Tokyo skyscraper is which.

Phoning home

You'll be able to call home from pretty much any city or large town in Asia and direct dialling means you won't have to deal with an operator in a foreign language. Don't forget the time difference when you phone, though. You'll probably get a better reception from your loved ones if you don't wake them at 3am.

△ Buddhist monk, Thailand

Shall I take the mobile?

Taking your mobile/cell phone on your Asian travels is definitely worth thinking about. Mobile telephone systems across Asia are highly sophisticated – when you land and switch on your phone, your network searches for the local partner, you confirm that you want to use them and off you go. The advantages of not needing to mess with local phone systems are obvious and it may well put your family's minds at rest to know that you are reasonably accessible – although whether you want that is another matter entirely, and it may simply make everyone frantic if you switch off and don't let them know, or enter one of the many signal-free black holes across the continent (best to warn them about this before you go). There are a few other things to think about:

- Check with your phone provider in advance whether it will work in the countries you are visiting (see also ⓦwww.gsmworld.com /roaming/gsminfo/cou_id.shtml). Most UK, Australian and New Zealand mobiles use GSM technology, which works fine in most parts of Asia but unless a US or Canadian phone is a special triband handset it probably won't work; check with your provider.
- You'll have to speak to your phone provider before leaving home in order to get international access, or "roaming", switched on. Most pay-as-you-go systems don't operate from oveerseas so you will probably have to change contracts, which may take some time to set up.
- Before you leave home, you must investigate carefully the precise costs involved in calls that you'll make, or that are made to you, while you are overseas – or you could easily end up bankrupting yourself.
- Texting is usually far cheaper than phoning from overseas. Check with your provider how much it costs to send and receive SMS.
- It can also be very expensive to pick up your voicemail overseas – you may want to switch this facility off altogether before you head off.
- Don't forget you'll need to recharge your phone as usual, which means bringing an adaptor for the local electricity supply.
- Programme useful numbers into the phone before you leave home: your embassy or consulate in the countries you'll be visiting, any hotels you have booked, etc.
- Change the numbers you have in your phone so they'll work from overseas – you'll need to add the international country code. Check your guidebook for this.
- Make a note of the mobile's serial number, your own phone number and your network's customer service and emergency numbers and

keep this separate from the phone. If your phone gets lost or stolen you'll be able to prevent it being used.

A cheaper alternative, especially if you are staying in one country for significant periods and using your phone mostly to communicate within that country – to arrange hotels, keep in touch with travelling companions and so on – is to buy a local SIM card, though you will have to check that your phone accepts other SIM cards and perhaps get it unblocked first. The disadvantage is that your number will change with the card. Mobile-phone shop staff across Asia will advise on the best card for your needs, bearing in mind where you are travelling; travellers' forums are also a good source of advice (see p.249). For an idea of price, expect to pay around Rs50,000 ($5/£3) for a SIM card in Indonesia, which should include around Rs20,000 ($2/£1) credit. Top-up cards are widely available. If you do change the SIM card on your own phone you may need to re-enter all your saved numbers; some phones allow you to store them in on the hardware of the phone, in other phones they are on the SIM card itself – check before you leave home.

One advantage of taking your mobile is that you could use it for the Safety Text scheme (see p.392), which aims to encourage travellers' safety.

Public telephones

You'll find public telephones throughout the continent, both coin- and phonecard-operated, and some countries (Thailand and Singapore, for example) have phones that also accept credit cards. Don't count on them having instructions in English. In most cases, if you're calling home, it's easier to phone from post offices or telephone offices rather than phones on the street, if only to get away from the noise. Avoid making international calls from hotels as they not only charge higher rates for the call, but often slap a service charge on top, too; just speak long enough to leave your number and get them to call you back.

When making a call at a post office or telephone office, you'll be directed to a booth, in some cases having paid a deposit, and you can then dial your call direct. The length of the call is logged and the price calculated automatically; you pay the balance or get change from your deposit when it's all over. It's worth checking whether there is a cheaper discounted time to call (typically at weekends and in the middle of the night – which may well be more convenient for the folks at home); if calls are charged by the second or by the minute (in which case you'll be charged for the full minute even if you just use ten seconds of it) and whether there is a minimum call time (typically 3min).

Reverse-charge (collect) calls, charge cards and phone cards

Many telephone offices allow you to make reverse-charge calls or have a Home Country Direct facility, but you may pay a nominal charge for these. With a reverse-charge call, the person you are calling is contacted and asked to accept the charges for that call before you are put through. Home Country Direct is a system that allows you to reach the operator in your home country and then use a credit card to pay for the call or arrange a reverse-charge call through them.

In theory you can use BT, AT&T, MCI, Telstra and other phone charge cards (purchased at home) to make international calls through card phones in many Asian countries. These cards enable you to bill the cost of the call to your home number or put the cost onto a previously authorized credit card account. The advantage of these telephone charge cards is that they save you using up your cash when you're travelling. Before applying for any of these cards you need to check they are usable in the countries you intend to visit. As it can be difficult to get hold of the right local number to access the system when you're on the road, get a list of them beforehand from your issuing company for every country you intend to visit.

There are also an increasing number of companies issuing prepaid telephone cards that you can use across Asia. Typically calls are cheaper when compared with the cost of paying for a call at a phone office. However, be sure to do your research as they are not always as cheap as they first appear, many cards have an expiry limit even if you haven't used up the credit, some levy a daily service charge, others charge for every connection.

Internet phone

Although it's relatively new, the technology to use the Internet to make phone calls either to another computer (with compatible software) or to any ordinary telephone (landline or mobile) certainly exists. However, it isn't widespread across Asia yet – you'll have most opportunities in the major traveller centres; look out for signs advertising "Net 2 Phone". This is certainly the cheapest way to speak to somebody at home but be warned that the sound quality isn't fabulous.

Using your own laptop with a sound card and the appropriate software does, of course, make the whole thing more accessible but you really need headphones as well to bump up quality and if you aren't careful you'll be carrying a pack full of electronic gizmos across the world. Check out ⓦwww.net2phone.com if this doesn't put you off completely.

Fax

Facilities for faxing are widely available across Asia, but take a bit more hunting out than phones. Try post offices, telephone offices and the business centres of international–class hotels (the most expensive option). You'll be charged by the page or minute (find out which, before you send the message) and you will also pay a charge if you receive faxes. Charges for faxes are usually in line with the telephone charges of the country.

Email

Access to the Internet is ubiquitous these days and public facilities are widely available. You'll find Internet cafés in backpacker centres, the departure lounges of many international airports, and public email services in major post offices and telephone offices. However, don't expect too much outside the major population conurbations and tourist centres. The way Internet cafés charge varies enormously: some do it by the minute, others in 10-, 15- or 25-minute units, but generally costs do work out a lot cheaper than sending a fax or making a phone call. There are three ways of using email abroad (see below).

Using your existing account

One option is to use your existing, home-based email account accessed via the website of your Internet service provider; check before you leave home whether it offers this service and make sure you know your username and password. Even if you have an existing account, consider subscribing to a free email account for the duration of your trip and getting all your friends to copy their mail to the new account in case your home account is difficult to access. It is often possible to arrange to forward mail from your home account to another address while you are on the road, keeping a copy in your home account if you want. This gives you the best of both worlds.

Setting up a free email account

Even if you don't already have Internet access at home, you can set up a free web-based account either before you leave home or in Asia. Several companies offer free accounts, such as ⓦwww.yahoo .com and, by far the most popular, Hotmail (ⓦwww.hotmail.com) – any Internet café will have Hotmail bookmarked for easy access. All you need to do to set up an account is access the website and follow the instructions; staff in any Internet café can help you with this if necessary.

Give friends and family your email address and they can send you messages any time – they will stack up in a nice pile in your inbox, ready for you to access whenever you can. You can of course use your new account to send email as well. Bear in mind these hints:

- Access your account regularly as it will be shut down if it isn't accessed within a certain period (typically forty days or so).
- Make full use of folders to keep your inbox as small as possible and decrease downloading time.
- Send an email to your account with important telephone numbers or scans of your vital documents – you can print them out in an emergency.
- One advantage of setting up the account at home is that you can do some experiments to see how the account copes with receiving attachments before you leave – this is something that can be problematic.

Using Internet cafés as poste restantes

The third, and least desirable, option is to use local Internet café addresses as email poste restantes. This involves getting a particular cybercafé's email address and giving it to the people who'll be emailing you, so it's only really viable if you're staying in one place for a while. It isn't an ideal option, particularly as places vary considerably in efficiency. Many Internet cafés print out the day's emails and keep them in a file for a few weeks, much as a post office would with letters; others just let you scroll through their inbox, which means anybody could open your stuff and it could easily get deleted by accident. The important thing to remember when using an Internet café address is that your correspondent should write your name in the subject box.

Set up a weblog?

A weblog (or blog, for short), is an online journal/diary where you can post your adventures and pictures. Anybody surfing the web has access and can see what you are up to – which includes complete strangers as well as your friends and family. Check out the websites ⓦwww.travelpod.com and ⓦwww.travelblog.org to see how it's done – and to sign up for your own.

Shall I take the laptop?

Given the heat, humidity, dust, rough travel, unreliable electricity supplies and potential for loss or theft of a laptop across Asia, it's probably advisable to leave yours at home and stick to public Internet facilities. But on the other hand spending hours each day in stuffy, smokey cafés, staring at a screen is hardly the stuff of an Asian idyll. People do travel with their own laptops or PDAs, especially if they want to maintain a blog or download a lot of photographs. There's an excellent forum at ⓦwww.travelpod.com for discussions about and practical advice on taking this sort of kit with you. Also see ⓦwww.kropla.com for details of which phone plugs are used across Asia, how to set up your modem before you go, and how to hardwire phone plugs where necessary. However, be warned that most budget accommodation doesn't run to phone sockets in the room. Also, the chances are you won't be able to use your usual ISP – in any case it's exorbitant if you need to phone internationally from hotel rooms for access. You'll need to do some web research on local Internet access for the countries you are visiting and may need to set up as a temporary subscriber to a local ISP. One final point, if you do decide to go ahead and bring the laptop, make sure your insurance provides cover against loss or theft.

The media

You won't have to rely solely on contact with your friends and family for news from home. Newspapers from Europe, Australia and North America are often available surprisingly quickly in Asian capital cities and tourist centres. However, the supply is sometimes unreliable and the price high – check the Internet versions for up-to-the-minute news. Most Asian countries also publish good-quality English-language newspapers of their own for English-speaking local people, tourists and expatriates. Several of the magazines mentioned in Chapter Five, such as the *Far Eastern Economic Review*, as well as the Asian editions of *Time* and *Newsweek*, are published locally – airports and the bookshops in luxury hotels are usually a good source if you have any difficulty finding them or, alternatively, check out the online versions.

Television

Satellite and cable television have reached some very remote corners of Asia, and you'll find league soccer from England and Italy is televised throughout the region. Most mid- to top-range hotels offer CNN or BBC World, and Asian satellite networks such as Star or MTV, while some restaurants use them to lure in customers.

Radio

Worldwide radio networks, including the BBC, Voice of America and the Australian Broadcasting Corporation, broadcast across the globe 24 hours a day, while many countries have an indigenous English-language radio station or schedule. A radio is a great way of getting up-to-the-minute news in the more remote areas and it's well worth considering taking one. A pair of earphones will mean you can listen when people around you – on buses, in dorms, etc – are sleeping.

Buy a radio with the greatest number of short-wave bands you can afford, as most stations change their frequency during the day and you'll want to be able to keep up with them. Get hold of a copy of the programming schedule for your country's international network before you leave home – it'll tell you which frequencies to pick them up on at which times across Asia.

Major international broadcasters, such as the BBC World Service (ⓦwww.bbc.co.uk/worldservice), the Voice of America (ⓦwww.voa .gov), Radio Australia (ⓦwww.abc.net.au/ra/), Radio Canada International (ⓦwww.rcinet.ca) and Radio New Zealand International (ⓦwww.rnzi.com), publish schedules and frequencies on their websites.

14

Crime, safety and sleaze

While news of tragic accidents, violent weather conditions, kidnappings and fatalities in the region dominates the world's media, most people who run into trouble in Asia are the victims of far more ordinary petty theft, robbery and con tricks. However, having your stuff stolen is no joke, getting taken for a ride leaves a nasty taste in the mouth, and losing your passport, travellers' cheques and credit cards can be a major inconvenience and possibly even ruin your trip. The information in this chapter should help to steer you away from the potential pitfalls, and help you to cope if disaster strikes.

The underlying rule is to employ the same instincts you use to keep you safe at home. If it's your first time in Asia it's easy to overreact and be spooked without real reason. However, this is better than blithely wandering into danger with your eyes fixed on the blue horizon, white-sand beach and glittering sunshine. Just because you're on holiday, doesn't mean the crooks are.

We've said it before, but nobody should set foot in Asia without adequate insurance; see p.207 for more information.

Read up, find out, calm down

Supplement your guidebook reading with up-to-the-minute information from newspapers and magazines. Even the most dramatic civil war isn't going to find its way into a guidebook for several months at the least, but it'll be splashed across the world's media in a couple of hours. Travellers' newsgroups and bulletin boards on the Internet are also an excellent resource (see p.249 for a list of some of the best).

Concerned about keeping their citizens safe abroad, Western governments generally have a department at home to advise on safety issues overseas (see p.420) – log on to their websites to find out the current situation in the places you are intending to visit. In the event of an emergency while you're travelling, contact your embassy or consulate abroad (see p.402 for advice on how they can help you).

The Suzy Lamplugh Trust (®www.suzylamplugh.org) publishes a great little pocket-sized book *Passport to Safer Travel* by Mark Hodson (available via the website or from good bookshops) and also has vast amounts of individual country information on its website.

Get it into perspective

Asia has its own specific hazards, aside from the ones that travellers will find anywhere in the world. Most recently the Asian Tsunami of December 2004 devastated parts of the region, but there are other ongoing hazards including landmines in a surprising number of countries (see p.395), terrorist groups in the southern Philippines; civil unrest in parts of Indonesia and in Nepal; the ever-volatile relations between India and Pakistan; violence that often precedes elections in India and Bangladesh; active volcanoes right across the continent; riptides on many Indian Ocean beaches; and drug-resistant malaria on the Thai–Cambodian and Thai–Burmese borders.

You should always put any information you receive into perspective. If you read about rioting in Xinjiang province in China and you're heading for Shanghai, it's a good idea to stay alert, but with the distance between the two at almost 4000km, chances are you'll be out of the line of fire. If, on the other hand, one of the larger Indonesian volcanoes erupts fairly exuberantly on a small island just 20km across a stretch of ocean from where you were planning a

△ Cambodian warning sign

fortnight by the sea, it may be an idea to think again. You might also want to take a look at Robert Young Pelton's *Fielding's the World's Most Dangerous Places* and its associated website (see p.249), which, despite its decidedly gung-ho title and being somewhat out of date regarding some areas, is a detailed and fascinating account of wars, political upheaval and crime across the world, putting some of the dangers to travellers into the global political context.

Another fascinating read, especially if you're the sort of person who likes to plan for every eventuality, is *The Worst-Case Scenario Survival Handbook: Travel*, by Joshua Piven and David Borgenicht, which details a mixture of fascinating and outlandish skills such as how to crash-land a plane on water, or how to climb out of a well.

You might find *Travel Survival* (Rough Guides) of more practical use: an illustrated manual for adventure travellers, it includes advice on how to survive in extreme environments along with guidance on coping with natural disasters.

Take the course? Watch the video?

As more and more travellers head off into the great unknown, increasing numbers of resources are available to help them prepare for every eventuality. Several companies run courses aimed at first time travellers ranging from a day to three days and with plenty of experiential learning mixed in with lectures. Contact Objective Travel Safety (☎01788/899029, ⊛www.objectivegapyear .com); PlanetWise (☎0870 200 0220, ⊛www.planetwise.net) or The Knowledge Gap (☎01884/258724, ⊛www.kgap.co.uk). Caroline's Rainbow Foundation (⊛www.carolinesrainbowfoundation .com) produces a short safety awareness video "Time of Your Life" which is intended to be used as a springboard for further research by first-time travellers.

Theft

Most crime against tourists is opportunistic theft of one sort or other. A few guidelines will help minimize the chances of it happening to you:

- Stay alert. When you are out in public places never "zone out" with your MP3 player, iPod or whatever – you need to be aware of what's happening around you at all times – that way you'll be more likely to anticipate problems and be able to get out of untoward situations.
- Carry travellers' cheques, credit cards, most of your cash and vital documents in a concealed money belt kept on you at all times, unless they're in short-term storage in security boxes or safes at a hotel.
- Even in short-term storage it's a good idea to keep them in a bag that you can lock with your own small padlock or a stiff envelope with your signature across the seal so you'll know if it has been tampered with.
- Only carry with you the cash you need for the day.
- Don't leave your valuables on the beach while you swim – keep them locked away in a safety deposit box and keep the key with you in one

of the waterproof canisters that are available for just this purpose (see p.261).

● Never leave your passport, travellers' cheques and credit cards in a guesthouse safe while you go off trekking. Many a visitor has returned a week or so later to find everything intact, only to realize, when their credit card bill comes in, that the card has been used right up to its limit while they've been slogging through the jungle.

● Keep photocopies of important documents and emergency numbers (eg passport, travellers' cheque numbers, airline tickets, insurance policy, emergency telephone number in case of credit-card theft) in a separate place, plus a small stash of cash in case of robbery. It's possible to email vital information to yourself, including scans of documents, or to store them securely on a site such as *intouch* (see p.372).

● Don't flaunt what you've got. Avoid wearing a lot of jewellery, use a cheap watch and carry your camera in your daypack.

● Use padlocks to lock your pack and attach it to immovable fittings on long-distance journeys. This also prevents anyone putting anything (such as drugs) in your pack.

● Use your own padlock to supplement or replace the one on your guesthouse door.

● Never carry important stuff in backpack pockets on your back; they are especially vulnerable to theft. You can always carry a small pack on your front where you can keep an eye on it.

● Beware of accepting food or drink from anyone. On public transport, some rogues ply the unwary with drugged food and drink and, while they are sleeping off the effects, steal everything they own. Others spike drinks in bars and clubs and then rob their victims – only go out drinking with friends and always keep a very close eye on your drink.

● Don't automatically trust other Westerners, and be just as careful in dormitories as you are in other situations – a small percentage of travellers fund their own journeys by thieving from others.

● Never disclose your bank details to anybody you meet on the road – no matter how much you think you love them.

The natural world

Asia is full of volcanoes that erupt, winds that become typhoons, snakes that bite, rivers that flood, land that slips, and earth that moves and cracks asunder at regular intervals. Or so it can appear, if you have a disaster mentality and don't manage to temper what you read with reality.

Your safety in your hands

You need to be aware that in Asia you'll bear a greater responsibility for your own safety than you would at home. In the West official bodies oversee transport, hotels and outdoor activity companies, for example, carrying out official inspections and taking action against violators. In Asia it's probably best to assume that none of this happens, which means you need to be alert in ways that you've perhaps never thought about before. A few things to bear in mind:

- If you are with a group of people, watch out for each other and make sure everyone gets home safely.
- If you are diving be sure to check the certification of your guide/instructor. Is the equipment well maintained and working correctly? Use the buddy system, check the provision of oxygen and first-aid kit on the boat and find out the location of the nearest recompression chamber.
- If you are trekking or rafting what are the credentials of the guides? Where is the first-aid kit and the nearest hospital? How would an injured person get there?
- If a local travel agent is keen to sell you a tour, are you certain the area is safe? Check official websites for up to date information – things can change very fast (see p.420)
- Do you know the quickest way out of your hotel in case of fire?
- If the driver of your vehicle appears to be hell-bent on suicide, get out as soon as it is safe to do so – buying a new ticket is a small price to pay (see p.319).
- Consider signing up for the Safety Text scheme (ⓦ www.safetytext .com), which is a delayed texting system that sends a text to a number you choose if you haven't cancelled the alert by the time you specify. If you get back safely, no one knows what you've been up to, but if you don't then they can come looking.
- If you are travelling alone, consider leaving a note in your hotel room detailing your plans for the day.

Volcanoes, earthquakes and tsunamis

Being at the confluence of several of the world's largest tectonic plate which are constantly shifting, Asia has a much higher level of volcanic and earthquake activity than many travellers are used to. Seismologists are notoriously unable to predict when and where the next big event will take place, but realistically the chances of being caught in a severe earthquake or a volcanic eruption are extremely slim.

If you are unfortunate enough to be involved in a strong quake, you should stay indoors if possible (corrugated-iron sheets flying off roofs are a common cause of fatalities). Stay away from windows to avoid splintering glass and shelter in a doorway if the building looks in danger of collapse (the lintel supporting a wall above a door is the strongest part of the structure).

Tsunamis and tidal waves happen when earthquakes disturb the ocean bed causing vast walls of water to race across the globe. The tsunami of 2004 has made countries much more aware of the possible effects of such events and early warning systems are being set up across Asia. The best advice is to take local warnings and alerts seriously and do what you are told, even if it turns out to be a false alarm – if you are advised to move inland then do so, no matter how appealing your beach bungalow beside the waves.

Although phone lines will be damaged after any major event, try to get in touch with friends and relatives at home as soon as possible, to let them know you're safe.

Typhoons

If you know that a typhoon is expected in your town, the best advice is to get yourself established in a guesthouse or hotel that feels safely and solidly built (don't be stingy about paying up and moving to a better place for the night), and stay indoors. Ideally you should sleep in a room that is not on the ground floor which could get submerged. Keep all windows closed and move your bed away from them if possible – flying debris might smash the glass. Expect to be stranded in your room for up to 24 hours after the typhoon hits, while you wait for the flood waters to subside, so get yourself enough drinking water, some food and a good book before you tuck yourself away.

Dangerous animals

The chances of coming face to face with poisonous snakes and savage animals are obviously higher in the jungles of

Kalimantan than most places back home, but you should be fine if you listen to local advice and take sensible precautions:

- Be careful not to antagonize snakes. They usually avoid human contact, but will strike if threatened.
- Trek with local guides who know the terrain and the hazards.
- Keep fires or lanterns burning at night if you are camping in the jungle.
- Never walk without shoes – you're giving snakes and biting insects easy access to bare skin.
- Shake out your shoes each morning; scorpions love to sleep inside.
- If you do get bitten by a snake, immobilize the limb and avoid all movement. The aim is to reduce your heart rate and the speed with which any toxin spreads through your body. If possible remember what the snake looks like to help with identification. Send someone for medical help. Under no circumstances contemplate anything surgical with a Swiss Army knife.

Typhoon Linda

I arrived in Chumphon, South Thailand, to find preparations in full swing. Typhoon Linda was on her way, due in around 1am, and was expected to cause more damage than her predecessor who'd hit the town two months earlier. What happened then, I asked. "The water came up to here," said the guy in the restaurant, indicating a tidemark on his wall that was 1.5m above the floor, "and we all had to stay indoors for 48 hours because you couldn't get down the street without swimming." At the house next door, a lady was dragging her best teak furniture up to the first floor – she didn't want a repeat performance of the last time, she explained, showing off her own tidemarks, also 1.5m high. Her husband, meanwhile, was storing his motorbike in a neighbour's upstairs loft.

Every downstairs room in the town seemed to have a tidemark. And Linda was set to be even more vicious. A crowd stood outside the TV shop, where all the sets were tuned to the weather station, and a loudspeaker van was circulating through the town, issuing official-sounding instructions.

Faced with the prospect of spending two soggy days confined to my hardboard cell of a guesthouse, I decided to relocate, choosing a hotel room on the third floor, where the outside walls didn't seem likely to crumble in a Force 10. I stocked up on 48 hours' worth of food and water, battened down the window shutters, got my torch out in case the power lines went down, and fell asleep wondering how things would look in the morning.

Not very different, as it turned out. A few puddles, but no obvious devastation. The guesthouse manager looked happy: Linda had diverted at the last minute, and had struck Prachuap instead, 170km up the coast. And so it was that the newspaper pictures of razed houses and submerged town centres, and the scenes of distraught families that filled the TV screens that evening, were of a town that I'd left the day before, and not of Chumphon after all.

Lucy Ridout

Transport

Anyone who has spent even a few minutes on a bus hurtling along the Trans-Sumatran or West Bengal highways (or, in fact, almost any main road in Asia) has a very clear idea of the dangers of road travel on the continent. Driving is fast, furious and often heedless, with overtaking on blind corners the norm and horns rather than brakes the response to any surprise event or potential hazard. Vehicles are poorly maintained, road conditions horrendous and driving schedules very pressurized, so drivers are often exhausted.

The trouble is that the other options are often no better. Ferries in Asia are regularly overloaded and lack even the most basic safety equipment, and many of the small domestic aircraft companies have dubious safety standards. For this reason, many travellers feel much safer on trains and, in countries where there is a rail network, it is often the safest way to travel. Make safety rather than economy your main consideration, and if it means surrendering your ticket rather than boarding what seems like a certain death trap, or even getting off a bus halfway to your destination, then do it.

War, unrest and bandits

Armed conflicts are more frequent around the world than we'd like to think in our snug little armchairs at home. The big ones, new ones and ones that are particularly relevant to our economy hit the media but others smoulder away, largely ignored by the rest of the world. Gruesome as it seems, there are those who will book a plane ticket and head off into danger zones at the first mention of trouble (a growing phenomenon known as "terror tourism") but for the rest of us, this type of news is always an indicator to reroute ourselves, and fast.

Below we list some of the most significant for travellers to Asia. But things do change fast – check with all the sources listed in the Directory on p.420; plenty of these may have sorted themselves out by the time you travel, although new ones may well have taken their place:

- **West Papua, Aceh, Maluku, Central Sulawesi and West Timor in Indonesia**. Independence movements are in opposition to the Indonesian government in both West Papua and Aceh. Problems also persist in Maluku and Central Sulawesi, where there has been religious violence between Christians and Muslims. Though East Timor has now won independence from Indonesia, the province of West Timor remains host to thousands of East Timorese refugees, and pro-Indonesian militias are still on the rampage here – the border areas especially are unsafe.

- **Cambodia, Sri Lanka, Nepal, India, Pakistan, the Philippines, Bangladesh, Laos and Vietnam**. Unexploded landmines are a real danger – take local advice and never wander off paths.

- **Kashmir** has been a longstanding no-go area for tourists as militant separatist groups fight it out with government forces and Western hostages have been taken, who are sometimes never seen again. In June 2002, India and Pakistan massed more than a million soldiers along their border and came to the brink of nuclear war over the sovereignty of Kashmir. The situation is now much more stable but this is an indication of the volatility of the area, so seek up-to-date advice when planning your trip.

- **Sri Lanka**. The Tamil Tiger guerrillas fought with government forces for almost two decades for an independent state, with a death toll of more than sixty thousand. A formal ceasefire was signed in February 2002 and although regarded as holding, there have been violent incidents since then. Tourists are more likely to be unwittingly caught up in violence than to be targeted but it is still important to get up-to-date information. Despite the devastation of the island by the 2004 tsunami violent factional in-fighting among the Tamil Tigers has increased and added to the danger.

- **The Philippines and eastern Sabah (Malaysia)**. Kidnapping has increased alarmingly in the Philippines in recent years but has also affected islands nearby. It is vital to check out the situation in the Philippines and in neighbouring Malaysia and Indonesia.

- **Bangladesh**. In the Chittagong Hill Tracts, the United People's Democratic Front is engaged in terrorist activity which has included the kidnap of Westerners. Local tribal feuding has complicated the situation further.

- **Nepal**. Since February 1996 the Communist Party of Nepal (Maoist) has been engaged in a guerrilla war attempting to topple the government of the country. Figures aren't easy to come by but more than twenty thousand people may well have died in the conflict. Starting in the remote west of the country, the attacks have now spread and in August 2004, Kathmandu was surrounded and put under siege. Trekking groups have been targeted for cash and equipment. It remains to be seen whether a three-month ceasefire declared by the rebels in late 2005 turns into a more lasting peace.

However, bear in mind the earlier comments about getting things into perspective: Indonesia, Malaysia, the Philippines and Sri Lanka continue to attract thousands of visitors who have trouble-free visits and return home safely. Just be sure to keep abreast of Asian news, check the websites on p.420 at regular intervals while you're on the road and, most important of all, seek local advice if you are uncertain about any potential destination.

It's also worth remembering that democracy in many parts of Asia is often a very different creature to the familiar form in the West, and in the run-

Dangerous sports

Halfway through a week-long visit to North Korea I was desperate to escape the watchful eyes of our minders, the other guests I was being kept in close confinement with, and to stretch my legs after hours cooped up in a minivan. Foreign visitors are not allowed to walk in Pyongyang unaccompanied, but as the hotel was on an island in the river, and the bridge was guarded to prevent unauthorized escape, it seemed permissible to at least run around the island. Midway through my first lap an old woman brandishing a rake leapt out of a bush and shouted "Get back to hotel!" I was accompanied back by a security official in a black suit riding a pink bicycle, who continued to ride close behind me as I ran round the small hotel car park.

Nicholas Reader

up to and even following elections there can be a high level of tension and violence. Every election in India and Bangladesh brings several deaths and hundreds of injuries through fighting between the supporters of different parties. In some cases, violence follows elections – particularly in the case of disputed results. It is best to give Asian elections a wide berth – in fact political gatherings of all kinds are undoubtedly best avoided. If you do get caught up in trouble, obey any curfews imposed by the authorities. Strikes in Asia can also be a different type of event from those at home and often involve a high degree of local tension and disruption. Keep your ear to the ground for any that are planned and then just sit tight until it's over.

Common scams

Many of the common scams perpetrated on hapless tourists in Asia are legendary. These scams change, evolve and become more sophisticated, but never really go away. The best source for up-to-date versions is other travellers – they've been there, seen it, and probably been caught by it as well. Talk to people on the road, check travel forums on the Web and learn from their mistakes. You also need to be aware that some of the police in parts of Asia are less upstanding than you might expect; if you have reason to visit the police take a companion and if possible a local person to translate for you.

Watch out for:

- Various miscalculation tricks when you're changing money, especially when dealing with hundreds of thousands of Indonesian rupiahs. There are even rigged calculators in some places. Work out what you should have and count it carefully before you leave the counter.

Indian shoeshine

At 6am on my first day in India, I arrived by airport bus in the centre of New Delhi. Not wishing to appear more vulnerable than my bloodshot eyes and untanned skin made me look, I shouldered my pack and began to walk as confidently as I could.

After a few minutes my worst fears were realized when I felt a tap on my shoulder and turned round to face a very dark, scrawny man with a glint in his eye. He was frantically pointing at my feet. I looked down to discover a neat pile of dung – about the size of a molehill and as perfectly formed – resting on the top of my right shoe. My immediate reaction was amazement: how on earth had this pile of shit managed to tread on me?

As I stood awestruck, my Indian friend knelt down, produced a rag from the cloth bag slung over his shoulder, and started to wipe my shoe clean. He performed this task with a full-bodied, jerking action, which caused the bag to slip from his shoulder. When I saw its contents, the penny dropped and the mystery was solved.

This man had crept up behind me, scooped a portion of dung from his bag and skilfully dolloped it on top of my shoe as I walked. Now, of course, he demanded his fee for cleaning my shoes, holding up his soiled rag as evidence of his hard work.

Ross Velton

- Sleights of hand over the denomination of note you have given in payment in a shop or post office. Tricksters hide the note and produce one of a much lower denomination, telling you that you haven't paid enough. Keep your wits about you and know what you are handing over.
- Hotel touts and some taxi drivers, who will be desperate to get you to hotels where they either have an interest or will get a chunk of commission (it'll go on your bill, never fear). So beware if they tell you the hotel you want is full or perhaps even that it has burned down. If they claim that the place has no beds, it is worth going to ask at reception yourself, especially as they sometimes have official-looking stooges on the steps outside, repeating the misinformation.
- Certain taxi drivers who tell you major sights are closed and that you're much better taking a tour with them as your driver for the day

– or going to visit their brother's shop instead of the Taj Mahal. Insist they take you where you want to go.

- The classic scam in Thailand and India – persuading gullible tourists that they are being offered an amazing deal on cut diamonds or other gems. Travellers are attracted by the prospect of hundreds, if not thousands, of dollars' profit to be made in their own country by selling the diamonds at home. So, despite knowing nothing about precious stones, they spend $100 on a handful of sparklers and ten times out of ten arrive home to learn their hands are full of pretty, but totally worthless, cut glass.

- Rogue policemen at Delhi railway station, who insist that to remain in Delhi you have to register with them and, needless to say, pay to do so. The best way to tackle this is to offer to go to the police station and fill in the forms there – but on foot; never get into an "unmarked" police car.

- In India there have been increased reports of foreigners held against their will and only being released when they have produced large sums of money by cashing travellers' cheques or using ATMs. These incidents often appear to be set up by local people apparently "befriending" the tourists. Unfortunately the best advice is to be suspicious of the motives of anyone appearing to be overly friendly.

- In the Kulu/Manali areas of India worrying numbers of travellers have been attacked and gone missing. It's probably best to avoid travelling here; check the current situation on travel forums on the Web.

Room service

In a hotel in Danang, Vietnam, a woman walked straight into my room while I was lying there naked under my mosquito net. She didn't mess around: "Would you like sex, mouth, love, touch or massage with no clothes?" When I said a polite "No, thank you", she looked at me rather despondently and added, "Do you have any washing, then?"

Chris Humphrey

The only guest at the only hotel in town, I spent the evening on the verandah listening to tales of the days of the Raj. Charming and well educated, the manager was the perfect host, until he casually slipped into the conversation, "Do you need your own room tonight or would you prefer to share mine?" I acted suitably horrified and haughty, demanded my own room and barricaded the door, just in case.

Nicki McCormick

Sexual harassment

Much of the Asian continent is awash with Western films, and magazines that portray the West as sexually uninhibited, with Western women taking a proactive role. Add to that a population of Western female travellers who relate to men in ways unheard of among the Asian population, dress in ways local people might consider highly provocative, and – perhaps the greatest difference of all – actually have the freedom to travel around the world unchaperoned, it isn't surprising that misunderstandings and misconceptions are rife. Generally, the local perception of Western female travellers is of sexual availability and promiscuity, which means that harassment, both verbal and physical, is unfortunately alive and flourishing across the continent. As one example, there have been an increased number of reports of sexual assault on female travellers in Goa. The following tips may help:

- Always carry enough cash so that you can take a taxi back to your hotel if you need to.
- Make sure your hotel room is secure. Be especially careful to check door and window locks. You may want to use your own padlock and/or wooden door wedge.
- Never open the door of your hotel room to anyone unless you know and are confident about the person outside.
- Be especially careful if you are out drinking – spiked drinks are often a prelude to sexual assault.
- Observe how local women dress – if you cover up similar bits of flesh you may feel more comfortable and attract less unwelcome attention. Wearing a bra and not wearing anything too clingy can help avert some stares.
- Be aware of the different interpretations placed on some behaviour in other cultures. For example, smiling and making eye contact with a man in India, Pakistan and Indonesia is interpreted as a distinct come-on, as is a casual touch.
- Talk about the sister of the man hassling you; equate yourself with her and ask how he would want her treated in similar situations.
- Adopt a mythical husband: some women travellers wear a ring, or carry pictures of a mythical husband and kids with which to bore potential pests.
- Try not to let any hassle get you down to the extent where you close yourself off to all local contact and friendliness – it isn't personal.
- Join up with other solo women travellers for some of your trip if it suits you.
- Don't stay alone out of mistaken pride; there's no right or wrong way to travel.
- Above all, don't automatically trust other Westerners because of familiarity or distrust local people because of their apparent strangeness.

Don't forget it can work both ways: some men feel extremely uncomfortable with the upfront approaches of many Asian prostitutes. While many women cope with sexual harassment as a part of everyday life, for many men this experience comes as a rude, and often distressing, awakening. The best advice is to stay polite, remain calm and walk away from any encounter that makes you feel uncomfortable.

Drugs

Many Asian governments seem to have double standards when it comes to drugs: they openly condemn them yet seem to turn a blind eye to the fact that they are routinely sold to tourists in certain places. The penalties for trafficking or possession are nontheless serious: Malaysia enforces the death penalty for drug smuggling, and in Thailand long prison sentences (49 or 99 years aren't unusual) plus hefty fines that you or your family will need to pay before you are released are the punishment for attempting to take drugs out of the country.

Even buying drugs for your own immediate use just isn't worth the risk; set-ups by dealers and the police are common. Added to that, using any drugs will make you less alert, less aware of your surroundings and far more likely to be the victim of other crimes such as robbery or sexual assault. The situation is made more complicated by the fact that in some areas, drugs – typically marijuana and opium – seem to be sold openly, for example in *bhang* shops in parts of India (principally to help religious meditation), and are smoked in public without any retribution. However, the best advice is still to steer clear.

There are around 1200 Britons in prison overseas for drugs offences at any one time – it really isn't worth the risk of joining them, however tempting it seems. A look at the Prisoners Abroad website (Ⓦ www.prisonersabroad.org.uk) should be warning enough.

Some precautions:

- Pack your own bag and check it in at the airport.
- Never check anybody else's bag in for them.
- Never carry anything across a border for anybody else – and that includes a baby, baby buggy or anything as apparently innocuous.
- Never drive anybody else's vehicle across a border for them.
- Don't sit in vehicles to cross a border – get out and walk.

If disaster strikes

Your embassy or consulate abroad can:

- Issue emergency passports.
- Contact friends and family and ask them to help with money or tickets.
- Advise on getting money transferred.
- Help you get in touch with local doctors, lawyers and interpreters.
- Contact and visit you in local prison.
- Visit you in hospital and pass messages to your family if you wish.
- Advise on local organizations that help trace missing persons.
- Offer advice and support if you are with somebody who dies.

Your embassy or consulate cannot:

- Give you money (though they may be able to cash a cheque or give you a loan under very strict criteria).
- Pay your bills or pay to get you home, except in very exceptional circumstances.
- Intervene in legal proceedings or give legal advice.
- Get better treatment for you than for other prisoners or hospital patients.
- Get you out of prison.
- Arrange employment, accommodation or work permits.

You may also need to:

- Contact the police. If you are the victim of a crime they'll need to take a statement from you. See the note on p.399 about going to police stations.
- Contact your insurance company. Carry your policy number and their emergency number with you and leave copies at home. There are claims procedures that you must take care to follow in the event of theft or your claim will be invalid. You will need receipts for recently bought goods and for expenses you have incurred, and you'll need a police report to support your claim. The correct procedures must also be followed; if you need hospitalization you will have to inform your insurers within certain time limits. Check your policy details.
- Cancel your credit cards if they're stolen; if travellers' cheques have been stolen, contact the issuing company to order your replacements (see p.235).

15

Coming home

Everyone expects to suffer from culture shock when they go away to distant places, but it can be an even greater shock when you arrive back home. People's lives have moved on, the dog has had puppies and Uncle Toby really doesn't want to hear in graphic detail about Delhi Belly or cosmic enlightenment on Mount Kinabalu. You may feel that your experiences have totally changed your life and the direction you see yourself moving in, while those closest to you hope you've "got it out of your system" and are now ready to settle down. The following tips may help you cope:

- Before you go away, put some money aside as an arriving-home fund, and vow not to touch it while you are on your travels – coming home can be bad enough, never mind returning without a cent.
- Make sure you keep in touch with people at home and try to paint a realistic picture about your experiences and thoughts. You can then discuss things more easily and honestly when you get home, and people won't be so surprised by the way you may have changed.
- Stay in touch with other travellers you meet on the road, who may now be going through a similar experience.
- Keep in touch with local people you meet on your travels rather than cutting yourself off from the experience – if you haven't yet sent them any photographs you may have promised, for example, then do it as soon as you get home.
- While you're still travelling, make some plans, however rudimentary, for the immediate future after you return. The worst possible

△ Backpackers reunited

homecoming is to come back to nothing. Even if it's only a plan to save up and travel some more, at least it's a plan of action.

● Compile an album, CD or file or two of your best photos, with labels to remind you of place names, people and dates. They will give you pleasure for years to come and are a great way of sharing your experiences. They might even inspire you to return one day.

Getting involved

Whatever the delights of Asia, there is no doubt that some of the poorest people on the planet live there, their lives often made harsher by autocratic political regimes, big-business interests, exploitation, ignorance and appalling health and educational opportunities. You may want to find out about these aspects of Asia before you set off or to get involved with these issues when you return; this is a positive way of using your experiences for the benefit of others and beginning to make sense of everything that you saw and did while you were away. Below we list some major organizations campaigning about issues in Asia. Though these are all big organizations, if you digest the information and follow the links on their websites, you'll end up learning about a lot of very important, smaller-scale or less well-known campaigns. Here are a few worth investigating:

- **Amnesty International** campaigns for human rights worldwide, publishing reports on the situation in countries across the globe. It is best known for its campaigns for individual prisoners of conscience, involving flooding various governments with letters and postcards on behalf of individuals unfairly imprisoned. However, it also campaigns against the death penalty, torture and the use of child soldiers. Amnesty's website has a huge amount of information (much of it detailing things that governments would rather keep deeply buried), plenty of suggestions for ways to help and a superb range of links to other human-rights-related sites; Ⓦwww.amnesty.org.
- **The International Campaign to Ban Landmines** brings together over 1400 groups in ninety countries, all campaigning to ban landmines and increase the amount of resources devoted to de-mining, the rehabilitation of victims, and increasing awareness of the use of mines worldwide. This is highly relevant for Asian travellers as so many countries are affected (see p.396). There's a long way to go – landmines are still being planted and hundreds of people are killed each week by them; Ⓦwww.icbl.org.
- **One World** is a community of more than 1600 organizations fighting poverty worldwide. The site has huge amounts of information on trade, education, climate change and debt and some excellent links; Ⓦwww.oneworld.net.
- Probably most famous for its well-publicized direct action protests, **Greenpeace** is a worldwide campaigning group concerned with all manner of environmental issues, including toxic-waste disposal, nuclear issues, climate change, genetic engineering and forest conservation, indeed any issue that relates to the state of the environment; Ⓦwww.greenpeace.org.
- The **World Society for the Protection of Animals** campaigns against animal cruelty and to relieve animal suffering throughout the world. Its campaigns include improving the lives of dogs in Asia, opposing bear-baiting in rural Pakistan, bear-farming in China, bear

parks in Japan and the trade in marine turtles in Japan and Indonesia; ⓦwww.wspa.org.uk.

- Another campaigning organization concerned with animals, the **Environmental Investigation Agency**, exposes and campaigns against the illegal trade in wildlife and the destruction of the natural environment. Current concerns include the illegal export of tigers from India so their body parts can be used in traditional medicine, the trade in bear parts, the state of the world's forests, the destruction of the ozone layer and the threat to elephants, to orang-utans and to whales, dolphins and porpoises in the oceans; ⓦwww.eia -international.org.

- The **Free Tibet Campaign** is working towards ending the occupation of Tibet by China and allowing the Tibetan people to decide their own future. It works through public campaigns (including letter-writing), direct action and raising awareness; their website has excellent links for anyone interested in Tibet and plenty of suggestions for action by individuals; ⓦwww.freetibet.org.

- We haven't included Burma in this book because of ongoing concern about the human rights situation there and the suppression of democracy within the country; the pro-democracy leader Aung San Suu Kyi has called for outsiders to boycott the country because of this. The **Burma Campaign** is involved in lobbying for sanctions against Burma and the site has excellent briefing materials on the situation in Burma, a good set of links to other sites of interest and suggestions for ways that individuals can help; ⓦwww .burmacampaign.org.uk.

- The **End Child Prostitution, Child Pornography and Trafficking of Children for Sexual Purposes Campaign (ECPAT)** is a global network of organizations and individuals working together in these fields. This is a particularly relevant issue for anyone interested in Asia as the Philippines and Cambodia are notorious for sex tourism. However, these are just two examples: the site makes it clear just how depressingly widespread these practices are; ⓦwww.ecpat.net.

- Supporting tribal people throughout the world, **Survival International** campaigns against governments, companies, extremist missionaries, guerrilla armies and anyone who violates tribal people's rights, and works closely with tribal people themselves to do this. In Asia it is currently campaigning on behalf of the Jummas, who live in Bangladesh's Chittagong Hill Tracts; the Wanniyala-Aeto in Sri Lanka; the Penan in Sarawak, Borneo; the Jarawa people of the Andaman Islands in India; and the 300 tribes of West Papua in Indonesia; ⓦwww.survival-international.org.

- **Jaisalmer in Jeopardy** Saving the architectural heritage of this neglected Rajasthan town; Ⓦwww.jaisalmer-in-jeopardy.org.
- **The Esther Benjamin Trust** The trust works for Nepalese children, some of whom have been imprisoned, are living as street children or working in Indian circuses; Ⓦwww.ebtrust.org.uk.
- **Labour Behind the Label** This is the UK arm of a worldwide network aiming to improve conditions for garment workers worldwide – especially relevant to Asia where so many appalling conditions persist. There are plenty of links to US-based organisations; Ⓦwww.labourbehindthelabel.org.
- **The Citizen's Foundation** has established 180 schools in seventeen cities in Pakistan, focusing especially on slum areas, and emphasizing the importance of the education of girls; Ⓦwww .thecitizensfoundation.org.

Making your trip work for you

Sooner or later you'll return from wandering the globe and need to consider what to do next. You will be in a better position to sell yourself to future employers, either at home or overseas, if you can not only describe your trip as an immensely enjoyable experience but can also point to skills that you have developed while travelling.

Don't forget that resolution to learn Hindi, Thai, Japanese, Mandarin or whatever language fascinated or defeated you while you were away. Local evening classes are the most sociable way of doing this or, if you live near a university with foreign students, you may be able to arrange one-to-one tuition or exchange English lessons for the language you want to learn.

Putting up a website about your travels, if you haven't done it on the road, can be a satisfying way of crystallizing your experiences and feelings, as well as a great way of developing computer/web-design skills. True, the net is already full of boringly self-important websites, but there are also plenty of quality personal sites too. The best travellers' sites are both entertaining and useful – see the online sections of Where To Go, p.19–153, for some inspiration.

Working in the travel industry

In the longer term, your experiences in Asia can help prepare you for work in the travel industry. See *Working in Tourism* by Verity

Collins (Vacation Work Publications) for an overview of the type of work that is available. While you're on the road, keep your eyes and ears open, as you may have the chance to quiz people already working in the industry; back home, travel fairs are a good place to meet potential employers and people already working in the field.

Jobs as tour guides with adventure travel companies are highly sought after and a great way to keep travelling. However, you'll have to qualify in first aid and convince the tour operator of your background knowledge, sense of responsibility and cool head in an emergency before they'll entrust a group of paying customers into your care. Look in the travel press for job advertisements before you go (in the UK, *Wanderlust* magazine carries these), so you have some idea of what they are after. Many of the adventure travel companies listed in the Directory (p.412) advertise for staff on their websites.

Travel writing and photography

It may be possible to sell the story of your journey and/or photos when you get back, perhaps to student magazines or local newspapers. To sell your pictures, you'll need slides or top quality digital images rather than prints, and you should have a good look at the type of travel articles favoured by different newspapers and magazines, both regional and national. Unless you have a track record or good contacts, you're unlikely to elicit much interest before you go, but it's worth writing articles on your return and submitting them "on spec" to the publications you have selected.

If you are interested in becoming a guidebook researcher/writer, look on the websites of the publishers of the major guidebook series – they all include guidelines on how to write for them. See ⊛www .roughguides.com/about/workforus.html if you are interested in writing for Rough Guides.

Travel writing and photography aren't easy areas to break into and your work will need to be really top-notch. For some tips have a look at Michael Busselle's *Guide to Travel and Vacation Photography*; Lonely Planet's *Travel Photography: A Guide to Taking Better Pictures* by Richard l'Anson; Guy Marks' *Travel Writing and Photography*; or Purwin Zobel's *The Travel Writer's Handbook*.

First-Time Asia

Directory

Discount flight and courier agents

Australia and New Zealand

Best Flights ☎1300/767757, Ⓦwww.bestflights.com.au.

Destinations Unlimited New Zealand ☎09/414 1680, Ⓦwww.travel-nz.com.

Flight Centre Australia ☎131600, Ⓦwww.flightcentre.com.au; New Zealand ☎0800/243544, Ⓦwww.flightcentre.co.nz.

Harvey World Travel Australia ☎132757, Ⓦwww.harveyworld.com.au; New Zealand ☎09/478 7118, Ⓦwww.harveyworld.co.nz.

STA Travel Australia ☎1300/360960, Ⓦwww.statravel.com.au; New Zealand ☎0508/782 872, Ⓦwww.statravel.co.nz.

Trailfinders Australia ☎02/9247 7666, Ⓦwww.trailfinders.com.au.

Travel.com Australia ☎02/9249 5444 or 1300/120482, Ⓦwww.travel.com.au; New Zealand ☎0800/468332, Ⓦwww.travel.co.nz.

Travel Online New Zealand Ⓦwww.travelonline.co.nz.

Travelshop Australia ☎1300/767908, Ⓦwww.travelshop.com.au.

UK and Ireland

Apex Travel ☎01/241 8000, Ⓦwww.apextravel.ie.

Austravel ☎0870/166 2020, Ⓦwww.austravel.com.

Bridge the World ☎0870/814 4400, Ⓦwww.bridgetheworld.com.

cheapflights.com Ⓦwww.cheapflights.com.

ebookers ☎0800/082 3000, Ⓦwww.ebookers.com.

expedia.co.uk Ⓦwww.expedia.co.uk.

Lee Travel ☎021/427 7111, Ⓦwww.leetravel.ie.

North South Travel ☎01245/608291, Ⓦwww.northsouthtravel.co.uk.

Quest Worldwide ☎0870/442 3542, Ⓦwww.questtravel.com.

STA Travel ☎0870/160 0599, Ⓦwww.statravel.co.uk.

Trailfinders UK ☎0845/058 5858, Ⓦwww.trailfinders.com; Republic of Ireland ☎01/677 7888, Ⓦwww.trailfinders.ie.

Travel Bag ☎0870/890 1456, Ⓦwww.travelbag.co.uk.

USIT Northern Ireland ☎028/9032 7111, Ⓦwww.usitnow.com; Republic of Ireland ☎01/602 1904, Ⓦwww.usit.ie.

US and Canada

Air Brokers International ☎1-800/883-3273, Ⓦwww.airbrokers.com.

Airtreks ☎1-877/AIRTREKS, Ⓦwww.airtreks.com.

cheapflights.com US Ⓦwww.cheapflights.com; Canada Ⓦwww.cheapflights.ca.

Educational Travel Center ☎1-800/747-5551 or 608/256-5551, Ⓦwww.edtrav.com.

expedia.com US ⓦ www.expedia
.com; Canada ⓦ www.expedia.ca.

Long Haul Travel ⓣ 1-866/548-4548
or 416/360-7711, ⓦ www.longhaul
travel.ca.

STA Travel US ⓣ 1-800/329-9537,
Canada ⓣ 1-888/427-5639, ⓦ www
.statravel.com.

TFI Tours ⓣ 1-800/745-8000 or
212/736-1140, ⓦ www.lowestair
price.com.

Travel Cuts ⓦ www.travelcuts.com.
US ⓣ 1-800/592-CUTS; Canada
ⓣ 1-888/246-9762.

travelocity.com US ⓦ www.travelo
city.com; Canada ⓦ www.travelocity
.ca.

Worldtek Travel ⓣ 1-800/243-1723,
ⓦ www.worldtek.com.

Specialist tour operators

Australia and New Zealand

Adventure Travel Company
Australia ⓣ 03/9696 8400, ⓦ www
.adventuretravel.com.au. New
Zealand ⓣ 09/379 9755, ⓦ www
.adventuretravel.com.au. Agent
for all the big adventure-tour and
overland operators, with trips
including climbing Mount Kinabalu,
Ho-Chi Minh City to Hanoi by
bicycle and a cooking course in
Chiang Mai.

Allways Dive Expeditions Australia
ⓣ 1800/338239, ⓦ www.allwaysdive
.com.au. Dive and accommodation
packages to Indonesia, Malaysia,
Thailand and the Philippines.

Intrepid Adventure Travel Australia
ⓣ 1300/360887, ⓦ www.intrepid
travel.com.au. Well-priced small-
group tours that use local transport
and travellers' style accommodation.
Aimed at backpackers and adventurous tourists.

Kumuka Expeditions ⓦ www
.kumuka.com.au. Australia

ⓣ 1300/667277; New Zealand
ⓣ 0800 440499. Specializes in
adventure tours and overland expeditions to Nepal, India, Sri Lanka,
China and Southeast Asia.

San Michele Travel Australia
ⓣ 1800/222 244, ⓦ www.asiatravel
.com.au. Long-running Asia specialists with an emphasis on Indonesia.

Sundowners Australia ⓣ 03/9672
5300, ⓦ www.sundownerstravel
.com. Overland rail travel, including Trans-Siberian Express, the Silk
Route and Mongolia.

Surf Travel Company Australia
ⓣ 1800/687873, New Zealand
ⓣ 09/473 8388, ⓦ www.surftravel
.com.au. Flights and accommodation packages to the best surfspots
throughout Indonesia and beyond.

Travel Indochina Australia
ⓣ 1300/138755, ⓦ www.travel
indochina.com.au. Goes beyond
the more obvious sights in
Thailand, Laos, Vietnam, China and
Cambodia and offers cross-border
trips too.

Vodka Train ☏ 03/9672 5353, ⓦ www.vodkatrain.com Budget two-to three-week Trans-Siberian rail packages, for 18–35-year-olds. Part of Sundowners.

UK and Ireland

Cactus Language ☏ 0845/130 4775, ⓦ www.cactuslanguage.com. Good value language courses and packages in Japan, China and Taiwan for all levels and durations, from one week.

Dragoman ☏ 0870/499 4475, ⓦ www.dragoman.co.uk. Extended overland journeys in purpose-built expedition vehicles.

Exodus ☏ 0870/240 5550, ⓦ www .exodus.co.uk. Adventure tour operators and overland expedition specialist.

Explore ☏ 0870/333 40001, ⓦ www .exploreworldwide.com. Small-group tours, treks, expeditions and wildlife safaris. Also covers North Korea.

Footprint Adventures ☏ 01522/804929, ⓦ www.footprint -adventures.com. Trekking, wildlife and birding trips to many Asian destinations.

Gecko Travel ☏ 023/9225 8859, ⓦ www.geckotravel.com. Small-group adventure holidays to less-travelled destinations in Southeast Asia and Sri Lanka.

Imaginative Traveller ☏ 0800/316 2717, ⓦ www.imaginative-traveller .com. Adventurous tours to over-looked parts of Asia, including walking, cycling, camping, cooking and snorkelling.

Intrepid Travel ☏ 0800/917 6456, ⓦ www.intrepidtravel.com.

Well-priced small-group tours that use local transport and travellers' style accommodation. Aimed at backpackers and adventurous tourists.

Off the Map Tours ☏ 0116/240 2625, ⓦ www.mongolia.co.uk. Mongolia specialist, featuring trek-king, mountain-biking, horse-riding and Trans-Siberian trips.

Red Spokes Cycle Adventure Tours ☏ 020/7502 7252, ⓦ www .redspokes.co.uk. Challenging small-group cycle trips along the classic routes – Karakoram Highway, Lhasa–Kathmandu, Manali–Leh – and in Laos, Vietnam and Thailand.

Responsible Travel ⓦ www .responsibletravel.com. Online agent for over a hundred tour operators that have been hand-picked and screened for their positive envi-ronmental and socially responsible policies.

The Russia Experience ☏ 020/8566 8846, ⓦ www.trans-siberian.co.uk. The experts on Trans-Siberian and Mongolian travel.

Vodka Train ☏ 020/8877 7650, ⓦ www.vodkatrain.com. Budget two-to three-week Trans-Siberian rail packages, for 18–35-year-olds.

US and Canada

Above the Clouds Trekking ☏ 802/482-4848, ⓦ www.above clouds.com. Treks in Nepal, Bhutan and India.

Adventure Center ☏ 1-800/228-8747 or 510/654-1879, ⓦ www .adventure-center.com. Hiking and soft-adventure specialists whose trips include a Rajasthan desert safari and a Mongolian wilderness adventure.

Amerispan ☎1-800/879-6640, ⓦwww.amerispan.com. Language courses and packages in China, Japan, Taiwan and Thailand.

Backroads ☎1-800/462-2848 or 510/527-1555, ⓦwww.backroads .com. Cycling, hiking and multi-sport tours in Bali, Bhutan, Cambodia, China, Japan, Nepal, Thailand and Vietnam.

Cactus Language ☎1-888/270-3949, ⓦwww.cactuslanguage.com. Good-value language courses and packages in Japan, China and Taiwan for all levels and durations, from one week.

Mir Corps ☎1-800/424-7289; ⓦwww.mircorp.com. Trans-Siberian-Express trips, plus tours to China, Tibet and Mongolia.

REI Adventures ☎1-800/622-2236, ⓦwww.rei.com/travel. Climbing, cycling, hiking and multisport tours in Bhutan, China, Nepal, Thailand, Tibet and Vietnam.

Wheels Up! ☎1-888/389-4335, ⓦwww.wheelsup.com. Provides

discounted air fare, tour and cruise prices for disabled travellers.

Worldwide Quest Adventures ☎1-800/387-1483, ⓦwww.world widequest.com. Small-group trekking, rafting, wildlife and cycling adventures in Cambodia, China, India, Mongolia, Nepal, Pakistan, Thailand and Vietnam.

Voluntary work, conservation projects and placements

Australia and New Zealand

Australian Volunteers International ☎1800/331-292, Ⓦwww.ozvol.org.au. Runs various volunteer programmes including short-term youth placements (for 18–28-year-olds) of six to ten weeks in India and the Philippines; student partnerships for four to ten months in India and Nepal; plus postings for up to two years for skilled professionals.

Earthwatch Australia ☎03/9682 6828, Ⓦwww.earthwatch.org /australia. Large, long-established, organizer of volunteer placements on scientific projects, such as assessing the hydrological history of Mongolia's Gobi desert, exploring the roots of the Angkor civilization in Cambodia, and documenting macaque behaviour in Sri Lanka.

Go MAD: Go Make A Difference Ⓦwww.go-mad.org. Designed by and for travellers who want to volunteer at small, local organizations. No fees or forms. Links to volunteer organizations, mostly orphanages and schools, in Cambodia, India, Indonesia, Laos, Nepal, Thailand and Vietnam.

i to i International Projects ☎03/9775 2086, Ⓦwww.i-to-i.com. Short-term voluntary placements teaching English or doing care, construction, media or health work in China, India, Mongolia, Nepal, Sri Lanka, Thailand and Vietnam.

UK and Ireland

British Trust for Conservation Volunteers (BTCV) ☎01302/572244, Ⓦwww.btcv.org.uk. One of the largest environmental charities in Britain, with a programme of international working holidays in Japan and Nepal.

Coral Cay Conservation ☎0870/750 0668, Ⓦwww.coralcay .org. Reef and rainforest conservation projects, including coral reef surveying in the Philippines and rainforest conservation in the Philippines and Malaysia. Volunteers are accepted from two weeks upwards; mandatory dive training is included where relevant.

Earthwatch Europe ☎01865/318838, Ⓦwww.earthwatch .org/europe. Large, long-established organizer of volunteer placements on scientific projects, such as assessing the hydrological history of Mongolia's Gobi desert, exploring the roots of the Angkor civilization in Cambodia, and documenting macaque behaviour in Sri Lanka.

Go MAD: Go Make A Difference Ⓦwww.go-mad.org. Designed by and for travellers who want to volunteer at small, local organizations. No fees or forms, just links to volunteer organizations, mostly orphanages and schools, in Cambodia, India, Indonesia, Laos, Nepal, Thailand and Vietnam.

Greenforce ☎0870/770 2646, Ⓦwww.greenforce.org.

Environmental charity that runs scientific surveys with the help of volunteers on ten-week placements, eg surveying the reefs off Sabah in East Malaysia and conservation work in Nepal.

Indian Volunteers for Community Service (IVCS) ☎020/8864 4740, Ⓦwww.ivcs.org.uk. Inexpensive, three-week to six-month visitors' programme at a rural development project in India.

i to i International Projects ☎0800/011 1156, Ⓦwww.i-to-i.com. Vast range of short-term voluntary placements teaching English or doing care, construction, media or health work in China, India, Mongolia, Nepal, Sri Lanka, Thailand and Vietnam.

Link Overseas Exchange ☎01382/203192, Ⓦwww.link overseas.org.uk. Six-month placements for 17–25-year-olds teaching, working in Tibetan communities or working in orphanages or with the disabled in China, India, Nepal or Sri Lanka.

Teaching and Projects Abroad ☎01903/708300, Ⓦwww.teaching -abroad.co.uk. Two week work-experience placements for students in business, medicine journalism, veterinary medicine, or photography plus one- to six-month volunteer teaching, conservation and other short-term placements in Cambodia, China, India, Mongolia, Nepal, Sri Lanka and Thailand.

Travellers Worldwide ☎01903/502595, Ⓦwww.travellers worldwide.com. Placements from two weeks to a year teaching, sports coaching or in conservation, or work placements in law, medicine, tourism or journalism in Brunei, China, India, Malaysia and Sri Lanka.

Year Out Group ☎07980/395789, Ⓦwww.yearoutgroup.org. Umbrella organization representing around thirty different gap-year and year-out placement finders, both paid and unpaid.

US and Canada

CIEE International Study Programs ☎1-800/40-STUDY, Ⓦwww.ciee.org. Two- to four-week volunteer projects and longer-term English-teaching placements for students in China, India, South Korea, Thailand and Vietnam.

Earthwatch ☎1-800/776-0188, Ⓦwww.earthwatch.org. Large, long-established organizer of volunteer placements on scientific projects, such as assessing the hydrological history of Mongolia's Gobi desert, exploring the roots of the Angkor civilization in Cambodia, and documenting macaque behaviour in Sri Lanka.

Global Volunteers ☎1-800/398-8787, Ⓦwww.globalvolunteers .org. One- to three-week projects at orphanages and schools in China and India.

Go MAD: Go Make A Difference Ⓦwww.go-mad.org. Designed by and for travellers who want to volunteer at small, local organizations. No fees or forms. Links to volunteer organizations, mostly orphanages and schools, in Cambodia, India, Indonesia, Laos, Nepal, Thailand and Vietnam.

i to i International Projects ☎1-800/985-4864, Ⓦwww.i-to-i.com.

Short-term voluntary placements teaching English or doing care, construction, media or health work in China, India, Mongolia, Nepal, Sri Lanka, Thailand and Vietnam.

One! International ℡780/467-6254, Ⓦwww.one-international.com. Canadian-based organisation needing volunteers for placements working with street children in Mumbai.

Projects Abroad ℡1-888/839-3535, Ⓦwww.projects-abroad.org. Two-week work-experience placements for students in business, medicine, journalism, veterinary medicine, or photography, plus one- to six-month volunteer teaching, conservation and other short-term placements in Cambodia, China, India, Mongolia, Nepal, Sri Lanka and Thailand.

Accommodation booking agents

Hostelling International

Ⓦwww.hihostels.com

Australia ℡02/9565 1699, Ⓦwww.yha.org.au

Canada ℡613/237-7884, Ⓦwww.hihostels.ca

Ireland ℡01/830 4555, Ⓦwww.anoige.ie

New Zealand ℡0800/278299, Ⓦwww.yha.co.nz

UK ℡0870/770 8868, Ⓦwww.yha.org.uk

US ℡301/495-1240, Ⓦwww.hiayh.org

Homestays

Experiment in International Living (EIL) Ⓦwww.experiment.org. Stays of one to four weeks with a family in Japan, Nepal or Thailand.

Global Freeloaders Ⓦwww.globalfreeloaders.com. If you have a couch or spare room and are willing to host other travellers at your own convenience, you can stay for free in people's homes around the world, with hundreds of registered hosts across Asia from Karachi to Dili. Free online registration, feedback, testimonials etc.

Servas Ⓦwww.servas.org. International organization with a global network of hundreds of volunteer hosts who accommodate registered travellers at their homes around the world.

Women Welcome Women World Wide UK ℡01494/465441, Ⓦwww.womenwelcomewomen.org.uk. "5W" is an organization of women living in all parts of the world who are happy to meet, show round and usually accommodate women travellers. There are members in nearly all parts of Asia. Minimal fee to join.

Online hotel finders

Asia Hotels Ⓦwww.asia-hotels.com. One of the best Asia-specific accommodation booking sites, with thousands of hotels on their books, in 24 countries. Prices are

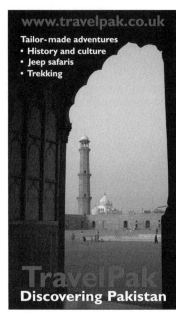
discounted by up to fifty percent, with a few coming in at under $30/£20 a night, but most from $40/£30 upwards.

Asia Hotels Network Ⓦ www.asia hotels.net. Reasonable selection of hotels in the major tourist destinations.

Bookings Asia Ⓦ www.bookings -asia.com. Some discounts and a

good spread of hotels with rooms for as little as $10/£7 in cheaper Asian destinations, but mainly $25/£17 and above.

Hostel World Ⓦ www.hostelworld .com. Budget accommodation (not hostels) across the world, from dorms in Dhaka to guesthouse rooms in Kathmandu. From US$5.

Health: travel clinics, information lines and online resources

Online resources

Ⓦ health.yahoo.com Information on specific diseases and conditions, drugs and herbal remedies, as well as advice from health experts.

Ⓦ www.cdc.gov The US government's official site for travel health.

Ⓦ www.fitfortravel.scot.nhs.uk Scottish NHS website carrying information about travel-related diseases and how to avoid them.

Ⓦ www.istm.org The website of the International Society for Travel Medicine, with a full list of clinics specializing in international travel health. Publishes outbreak warnings, suggested inoculations, precautions and other background information for travellers.

Ⓦ www.tmvc.com.au Contains a list of all Travellers' Medical and Vaccination Centres throughout Australia, New Zealand and Southeast Asia, plus general information on travel health.

Ⓦ www.tripprep.com Travel Health Online provides comprehensive database of necessary vaccinations for most countries, as well as destination specific medical-service-provider info.

Ⓦ www.who.int The World Health Organization website includes travel and health advice, disease outbreak news and detailed info on diseases.

Ⓦ www.wtgonline.com Excellent country by country information.

Australia and New Zealand

Travellers' Medical and Vaccination Centres Ⓦ www.tmvc.com.au. Twenty-two travel clinics throughout Australia and New Zealand.

UK and Ireland

British Airways Travel Clinics 213 Piccadilly, London W1 (Mon–Fri 9.30am–5.30pm, Sat 10am–4pm, no appointment required), ☏ 0845/600 2236; 101 Cheapside, London EC2V 6DT (Mon–Fri 9am–4.30pm, by appointment only), ☏ 0845/600 2236, Ⓦ www.ba.com /travelclinics.

Dun Laoghaire Medical Centre 5 Northumberland Ave, Dun Laoghaire, County Dublin ☏ 01/280 4996, ℻ 01/280 5603. Advice on medical matters abroad.

Hospital for Tropical Diseases Travel Clinic 2nd floor, Mortimer Market Centre, off Tottenham Ct Rd, London WC1E 6AU (Mon–Fri 9am–5pm, by appointment only; ☏ 020/7388 9600, Ⓦ www.thehtd.org. A recorded Health Line (☏ 0906/133 7733; 50p per min) gives written information tailored to your journey by post.

Liverpool School of Tropical Medicine Pembroke Place, Liverpool L3 5QA ☏ 0151/708 9393, Ⓦ www.liv.ac.uk/lstm.

MASTA (Medical Advisory Service for Travellers Abroad) Twenty-five regional clinics; call ☎0870/606 2782 for the nearest, or see Ⓦwww.masta.org. Also operates a prerecorded 24-hr Travellers' Health Line (UK ☎0906/550 1402, £1 per min), giving written information tailored to your journey, which is also available online.

Nomad Pharmacy Ⓦwww .nomadtravel.co.uk. Operates travel clinics in its five UK stores, plus a telephone helpline ☎0906/863 3414 (60p per min).

Travel Medicine Services PO Box 254, 16 College St, Belfast BT1 6BT ☎028/9031 5220. Offers medical advice before a trip and help afterwards in the event of a tropical disease.

Tropical Medical Bureau Ⓦwww .tmb.ie. Information on eleven clinic locations across Ireland.

US and Canada

Centers for Disease Control 1600 Clifton Rd NE, Atlanta, GA 30333 ☎1-800/311-3435 or 404/639-3435, Ⓦwww.cdc.gov. Publishes a vast amount of information for travellers. Travelers' Health Hotline on ☎1-877/394-8747.

International Association for Medical Assistance to Travellers (IAMAT) Ⓦwww.iamat.org. Offices in Canada and the US. A non-profit organization supported by donations. Publishes a variety of information and a list of English-speaking doctors overseas.

MEDJET Assistance ☎1-800/963-3538 or 205/595-6626, Ⓦwww.medjet assistance.com. Annual membership programme for travellers that, in the event of illness or injury, will fly members home or to the hospital of their choice in a medically equipped jet.

Official advice on international trouble spots

Australia Department of Foreign Affairs Ⓦwww.dfat.gov.au

Canada Foreign Affairs Department Ⓦwww.dfait-maeci.gc.ca

Ireland Department of Foreign Affairs Ⓦwww.irlgov.ie/iveagh

New Zealand Ministry of Foreign Affairs Ⓦwww.mft.govt.nz

UK Foreign and Commonwealth Office Ⓦwww.fco.gov.uk

US State Department Ⓦtravel.state .gov

Travel book and map stores

Australia and New Zealand

Mapland 372 Little Bourke St, Melbourne, Vic 3000 ℡03/9670 4383, Ⓦwww.mapland.com.au.

Map Shop 6–10 Peel St, Adelaide, SA 5000 ℡08/8231 2033, Ⓦwww.mapshop.net.au.

Map World 280 Pitt St, Sydney, NSW 2000 ℡02/9261 3601; 136 Willoughby Road, Crow's Nest, Sydney, NSW 2065 ℡02/9966 5770; 65 Northbourne Ave, Canberra, ACT 2601 ℡02/6230 4097; 900 Hay Street, Perth WA 6000 ℡08/9322 5733. Ⓦwww.mapworld.net.au.

Map World 173 Gloucester St, Christchurch ℡0800/627 967, Ⓦwww.mapworld.co.nz.

UK and Ireland

Blackwell's Map Centre 50 Broad St, Oxford OX1 3BQ ℡01865/793550, Ⓦmaps.blackwell.co.uk. Branches in Bristol, Cambridge, Cardiff, Leeds, Liverpool, Newcastle, Reading and Sheffield.

The Map Shop 30a Belvoir St, Leicester LE1 6QH ℡0116/247 1400, Ⓦwww.mapshopleicester.co.uk.

National Map Centre 22–24 Caxton St, London SW1H 0QU ℡020/7222 2466, Ⓦwww.mapstore.co.uk.

National Map Centre Ireland 34 Aungier St, Dublin 2 ℡01/476 0471, Ⓦwww.mapcentre.ie.

Stanfords 12–14 Long Acre, London WC2E 9LP ℡020/7836 1321, Ⓦwww.stanfords.co.uk. Also at 39 Spring Gardens, Manchester M2 2BG

℡0161/831 0250, and 29 Corn St, Bristol BS1 1HT ℡0117/929 9966.

The Travel Bookshop 13–15 Blenheim Crescent, London W11 2EE ℡020/7229 5260, Ⓦwww.thetravelbookshop.co.uk.

Traveller 55 Grey St, Newcastle-upon-Tyne NE1 6EF ℡0191/261 5622, Ⓦwww.newtraveller.com.

US and Canada

110 North Latitude US ℡336/369-4171, Ⓦwww.110nlatitude.com.

Book Passage 51 Tamal Vista Blvd, Corte Madera, CA 94925 ℡415/835-1020, and at 1 Ferry Plaza #46, San Francisco, CA 94111 ℡1-800/999-7909 or 415/927-0960, Ⓦwww.bookpassage.com.

Distant Lands 56 S Raymond Ave, Pasadena, CA 91105 ℡1-800/310-3220, Ⓦwww.distantlands.com.

Globe Corner Bookstore 28 Church St, Cambridge, MA 02138 ℡1-800/358-6013, Ⓦwww.globecorner.com.

Longitude Books 115 W 30th St, #1206, New York, NY 10001 ℡1-800/342-2164, Ⓦwww.longitudebooks.com.

Map Town 400 5 Ave SW #100, Calgary, AB T2P 0L6 ℡1-877/921-6277 or ℡403/266-2241, Ⓦwww.maptown.com.

Travel Bug Bookstore 3065 W Broadway, Vancouver, BC V6K 2G9 ℡604/737-1122, Ⓦwww.travelbugbooks.ca.

World of Maps 1235 Wellington St, Ottawa, ON K1Y 3A3 ℡1-800/214, Ⓦwww.worldofmaps.com.

Travel equipment suppliers

Australia and New Zealand

Kathmandu Shop 35, Town Hall Arcade, cnr Kent and Bathurst Streets ☏ 1800/333 484, ⓦ www .kathmandu.com.au. A mail-order company with outlets in all major Australian and New Zealand cities, offering an extensive range of quality outdoor and climbing gear.

Mont 491 Kent St, Sydney, NSW 2000 ☏ 02/9264 5888, ⓦ www.mont .com.au. Manufacturers of outdoor equipment with shops in Sydney and Chatswood plus products in many other outlets across Australia and New Zealand.

Mountain Designs ☏ 07/3856 2344, ⓦ www.mountaindesigns.com. Over thirty shops across Australia plus four in New Zealand, all selling light-weight mountaineering and adventure equipment, specializing in sleeping bags, Gore-Tex and fleeces.

Paddy Pallin 507 Kent St, Sydney, NSW 2000 ☏ 1800/805398, ⓦ www .paddypallin.com.au. Specializes in hiking and camping gear for outback conditions, but also caters for backpacker travel worldwide. The website carries useful advice on choosing gear. Fourteen branches across Australia.

UK

Cotswold Outdoor 23–26 Piccadilly, London W1J 0DJ ☏ 020/7437 7399, ⓦ www.cotswold-outdoor .co.uk; also in Betws-y-Coed, Bournemouth, Cirencester, Glasgow, Grasmere, Harrogate, Keswick, Kingston-upon-Thames, Manchester, Nottingham, Reading, St Albans and Southampton. Sells a huge range of outdoor and adventure gear for most activities and climates. Mail order available.

Field and Trek ☏ 0870/777 1071, ⓦ www.fieldandtrek.com. Online and mail-order shopping available, in addition to stores at Ambleside, Birmingham, Brentwood, Brighton, Bristol, Cambridge, Canterbury, Chelmsford, Chester, Gloucester, Guildford, Liverpool, London, Manchester, Oxford, Slough and Southampton. Stocks a massive choice of gear by a variety of manufacturers including their own-brand items.

Itchy Feet 162 Wardour St, London W1F 8ZX ☏ 020/7292 9750; also 4 Bartlett Street, Bath BA1 2QZ ☏ 01225/337987, ⓦ www.itchyfeet .com. Travel equipment and clothing in-store and via their online mail-order service.

Nomad Pharmacy and Travellers' Store 3 Wellington Terrace, London N8 0PX ☏ 020/8889 7014, ⓦ www .nomadtravel.co.uk; also in WC1, SW1, Bristol and Southampton. Specialist in travellers' medical supplies and first-aid equipment, but also stocks general-purpose travel accessories and equipment.

US and Canada

Campmor 810 Route 17, North Paramus, New Jersey 07652 ☏ 1-800/525-4784, ⓦ www.campmor .com. Online and mail-order specialist for outdoor clothing, footwear and camping gear, plus specialist outdoor sports equipment. The New Jersey store also has a gear repair department.

Mountain equipment Co-op (MEC) ☎1-888/847-0770, ⓦwww .mec.ca. Outdoor gear at ten stores across Canada plus online ordering.

The North Face ☎1-800/362-4963, ⓦwww.thenorthface.com. Internationally renowned maker of backpacks and other outdoor and camping equipment. Has eight stores in the US and more than 2000 dealers worldwide.

Recreational Equipment Inc (REI) ☎1-800/426-4840, ⓦwww.rei.com. More than eighty stores selling outdoor gear and clothing, plus online shopping available. The website has useful advice on choosing gear.

Sierra Trading Post ☎1-800/713-4534, ⓦwww.sierratradingpost.com. Clothes, shoes and travel equipment. Mail order and online shopping available.

Travel Smith ☎1-800/950-1600, ⓦwww.travelsmith.com. Mail order and online sales of travel clothing, footwear, luggage and accessories. Also has outlets in Reno NV, Cheyenne WY and Cody WY.

Final checklist

Documents

Full details on all the following items are given in Chapter Six.

❏ airline tickets

❏ credit card

❏ guidebooks

❏ insurance policy

❏ international driver's licence

❏ International Student Card (ISIC)

❏ International Youth Hostel Card

❏ maps

❏ passport

❏ passport photos

❏ phrasebook

❏ phone card/phone-home card

❏ photocopies of all your vital documents

❏ travellers' cheques

The bare essentials

❏ alarm clock/watch

❏ backpack/travelpack

❏ clothes

❏ daypack/shoulder bag

❏ fleece jacket or sweatshirt

❏ moneybelt and/or neck pouch

❏ padlocks or cable-locks

❏ sarong

❏ shoes

❏ sun hat

❏ waterproof money-holder ("Surfsafe")

Basic odds and ends

❏ camera equipment and film/ memory cards

❏ contact lens solution/glasses

- ❏ contraceptives and/or condoms
- ❏ first-aid kit
- ❏ flashlight (torch)
- ❏ mini-padlocks and a chain
- ❏ mosquito repellent
- ❏ sunglasses
- ❏ sunscreen
- ❏ tampons
- ❏ toilet paper
- ❏ toiletries
- ❏ towel

Optional

- ❏ batteries
- ❏ books
- ❏ cigarette lighter
- ❏ compass
- ❏ earplugs
- ❏ games
- ❏ gluestick
- ❏ handkerchief
- ❏ iPod/personal stereo
- ❏ mobile phone
- ❏ mosquito net
- ❏ notebook/journal and pens
- ❏ penknife
- ❏ photos of home
- ❏ rain gear/umbrella
- ❏ sewing kit
- ❏ sheet sleeping bag
- ❏ shortwave radio
- ❏ sink plug
- ❏ stamps from your home country
- ❏ string
- ❏ travel plug adaptor
- ❏ wallet
- ❏ water bottle, water purifier or purification tablets

Travel store

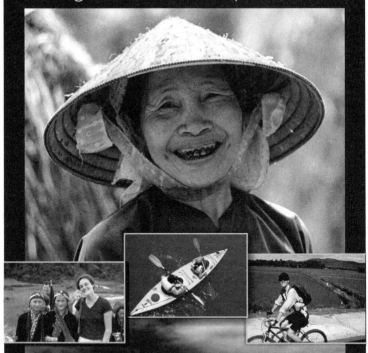

NOTES

NOTES

TRAVEL

& MORE

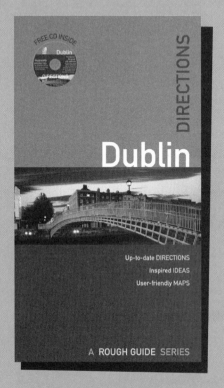

Visit us online

www.roughguides.co[m]

Information on over 25,000 destinations around the wo[rld]

- **Read** Rough Guides' trusted travel info

- **Share** journals, photos and travel advice with other readers

- Get exclusive Rough Guide **discounts** and travel deals

- Earn membership points every time you contribute to the

  Rough Guide community and get free books, flights and trips

- Browse thousands of **CD reviews** and artists in our music area

ONLINE

stay in touch!

Rough Guides' FREE full-colour newsletter

News, travel issues, music reviews, readers' letters and the latest dispatches from authors on the road

If you would like to receive roughnews, please send us your name and address:

Rough Guides, 80 Strand
London, WC2R 0RL, UK

Rough Guides, 4th Floor, 345 Hudson St
New York NY10014, USA

newslettersubs@roughguides.co.uk

ROUGHNEWS

Small print and

Index

A Rough Guide to Rough Guides

Published in 1982, the first Rough Guide – to Greece – was a student scheme that became a publishing phenomenon. Mark Ellingham, a recent graduate of English from Bristol University, had been travelling in Greece the previous summer and couldn't find the right guidebook. With a small group of friends he wrote his own guide, combining a highly contemporary, journalistic style with a thoroughly practical approach to travellers' needs.

The immediate success of the book spawned a series that rapidly covered dozens of destinations. And, in addition to impecunious backpackers, Rough Guides soon acquired a much broader and older readership that relished the guides' wit and inquisitiveness as much as their enthusiastic, critical approach and value-for-money ethos.

These days, Rough Guides include recommendations from shoestring to luxury and cover more than 200 destinations around the globe, including almost every country in the Americas and Europe, more than half of Africa and most of Asia and Australasia. Our ever-growing team of authors and photographers is spread all over the world, particularly in Europe, the USA and Australia.

In the early 1990s, Rough Guides branched out of travel, with the publication of Rough Guides to World Music, Classical Music, and the Internet. All three have become benchmark titles in their fields, spearheading the publication of a wide range of books under the Rough Guide name.

Including the travel series, Rough Guides now number more than 350 titles, covering: phrasebooks, waterproof maps, music guides from Opera to Heavy Metal, reference works as diverse as Conspiracy Theories and Shakespeare, and popular culture books from iPods to Poker. Rough Guides also produces a series of more than 120 World Music CDs in partnership with World Music Network.

Visit www.roughguides.com to see our latest publications.

Many Rough Guide travel images are available for commercial licensing at www.roughguidespictures.com

Rough Guide credits

Text editors: Ella O'Donnell, Claire Saunders, Clifton Wilkinson
Layout: Amit Verma
Cartography: Maxine Repath
Picture editor: Kate Noble
Production: Aimee Hampson
Proofreader: Susannah Wight
Cover design: Chlöe Roberts
Editorial: London Kate Berens, Geoff Howard, Ruth Blackmore, Polly Thomas, Richard Lim, Alison Murchie, Karoline Densley, Andy Turner, Keith Drew, Edward Aves, Nikki Birrell, Helen Marsden, Alice Park, Sarah Eno, Joe Staines, Duncan Clark, Peter Buckley, Matthew Milton, Tracy Hopkins; New York Andrew Rosenberg, Richard Koss, Steven Horak, AnneLise Sorensen, Amy Hegarty, Hunter Slaton, April Isaacs
Design & Pictures: **London** Simon Bracken, Dan May, Diana Jarvis, Mark Thomas, Jj Luck, Harriet Mills; **Delhi** Madhulita Mohapatra, Umesh Aggarwal, Jessica Subramanian, Ajay Verma, Ankur Guha

Production: Julia Bovis, Sophie Hewat, Katherine Owers
Cartography: London Ed Wright, Katie Lloyd-Jones; Delhi Manish Chandra, Rajesh Chhibber, Jai Prakash Mishra, Rajesh Mishra, Ashutosh Bharti, Animesh Pathak, Jasbir Sandhu, Karobi Gogoi
Online: New York Jennifer Gold, Kristin Mingrone; **Delhi** Manik Chauhan, Narender Kumar, Shekhar Jha, Rakesh Kumar, Lalit K. Sharma, Chhandita Chakravarty
Marketing and publicity: London Richard Trillo, Niki Hanmer, David Wearn, Demelza Dallow, Louise Maher; **New York** Geoff Colquitt, Megan Kennedy, Katy Ball; **Delhi** Reem Khokhar
Custom publishing and foreign rights: Philippa Hopkins
Manager India: Punita Singh
Series editor: Mark Ellingham
Reference director: Andrew Lockett
PA to Managing and Publishing directors: Megan McIntyre
Publishing director: Martin Dunford
Managing director: Kevin Fitzgerald

Publishing information

This fourth edition published March 2006 by
Rough Guides Ltd,
80 Strand, London WC2R 0RL
345 Hudson St, 4th Floor,
New York, NY 10014, USA
14 Local Shopping Centre, Panchsheel Park,
New Delhi 110017, India
Distributed by the Penguin Group
Penguin Books Ltd,
80 Strand, London WC2R 0RL
Penguin Putnam, Inc.
375 Hudson Street, NY 10014, USA
Penguin Group (Australia)
250 Camberwell Road, Camberwell
Victoria 3124, Australia
Penguin Books Canada Ltd,
10 Alcorn Avenue, Toronto, Ontario,
Canada M4V 1E4
Penguin Group (New Zealand)
Cnr Rosedale and Airborne Roads
Albany, Auckland, New Zealand

Typeset in Bembo and Helvetica to an original design by Henry Iles.
Printed at LegoPrint S.p.A.
© Lesley Reader and Lucy Ridout 2006

448pp includes index
A catalogue record for this book is available from the British Library
ISBN-13: 978-1-84353-609-3
ISBN-10: 1-84353-609-9

The publishers and authors have done their best to ensure the accuracy and currency of all the information in **The Rough Guide to First-Time Asia**, however, they can accept no responsibility for any loss, injury, or inconvenience sustained by any traveller as a result of information or advice contained in the guide.

1   3   5   7   9   8   6   4   2

Help us update

We've gone to a lot of effort to ensure that the fourth edition of **The Rough Guide to First-Time Asia** is accurate and up to date. However, things change – places get "discovered", opening hours are notoriously fickle, restaurants and rooms raise prices or lower standards. If you feel we've got it wrong or left something out, we'd like to know, and if you can remember the address, the price, the time, the phone number, so much the better.

We'll credit all contributions, and send a copy of the next edition (or any other Rough Guide if you prefer) for the best letters. Everyone who writes to us and isn't already a subscriber will receive a copy of our full-colour thrice-yearly newsletter. Please mark letters: "**Rough Guide First-Time Asia Update**" and send to: Rough Guides, 80 Strand, London WC2R 0RL, or Rough Guides, 4th Floor, 345 Hudson St, New York, NY 10014. Or send an email to **mail@roughguides.com**

Have your questions answered and tell others about your trip at **www.roughguides.atinfopop.com**

Acknowledgements

Special thanks to Catherine Darjaa for significant contributions to the section on Mongolia and David Leffman for help with the section on China.

Thanks to all the following people for their anecdotes about travelling in Asia:

Juliet Acock, Shannon Brady, Locky Brennan, Sasha Busbridge, Daniel Gooding, Chris Humphrey, Gerry Jameson, Debbie King, Karen Lefere, Mark Lewis, Laura Littwin, Nicki McCormick, John McManus, Jo Mead, Neil Poulter, Nicholas Reader, Laura Stone, Andrea Szyper, Chris Taylor, Jonathan Tucker, Ross Velton and Bob Williams.

Photo credits

Cover
Main front cover image: Havelock Island, Andaman Islands, India © Neil McAllister, ALAMY
Bottom front cover image: Buddhist Temple, Sri Pushparama, Sri Lanka © Panoramic Images, GETTY
Back cover image: Taj Mahaj, Agra, India © Frans Lemmens, The Image Bank, GETTY

Title Page
Woman panning for gold, Mekong River, Laos © R McLeod, ALAMY

Full page
Swayambunath stupa, Kathmandu, Nepal © A1 PIX

Colour introduction
Incense sticks, Hoi An, Vietnam © Lesley Reader
Akihabara district, Tokyo © Bill Heinsohn, ALAMY
Reclining Buddha at Wat Pho Temple, Bangkok © Glen Allison, ALAMY
Woodcarving Lesson, Bali, Indonesia © Lesley Reader
Vietnamese water puppets © Christian Kober, ALAMY
Beijing street scene © A1 PIX

Couple on elephant © Adrian Weinbrecht, GETTY
Varanasi, India © Gavin Hellier, ALAMY

Things not to miss
01 Gili Islands, Indonesia © Sang Man
02 Starfish grasshoppers and other insects on a skewer for sale at a night market © Kevin Foy, ALAMY
03 Cargo boats on the Mekong River, Luang Prabang, Laos © Jim Holmes, AXIOM
04 Reclining Buddha, Galvihara © I. Corse, TRIP
05 Masked dancer, Bhutan © Lesley Reader
06 Jaislamer, Rajasthan, India © David Knoble, ALAMY
07 Gunung Bromo © C.Gray, TRIP
08 Great Wall of China © Steve J. Benbow, AXIOM
09 Rice terraces, Banaue, Northern Luzon, Philippines © Leslie Garland, ALAMY
10 Ao Prao beach, Ko Lanta, Thailand © Nicholas Pitt, ALAMY
11 Orang-utan © D. Saunders, TRIP
12 Karakoram Highway, Pakistan © C. Bradley, AXIOM
13 Female guard, Reunification Express, Vietnam © Peter Raynor, AXIOM
14 Terracotta Army © B. Turner/TRIP
15 Diving with a whale shark
16 Kyoto © Jamie Marshall

Index

Map entries are in colour.